AMERICAN
CONSTITUTIONAL
LAW

AMERICAN
CONSTITUTIONAL
LAW

BY

BERNARD SCHWARTZ

Professor of Law and Director of the
Institute of Comparative Law
New York University

WITH A FOREWORD BY

A. L. GOODHART, K.B.E., Q.C.

Master of University College, Oxford

GREENWOOD PRESS, PUBLISHERS
NEW YORK

342.73
539a

d

Originally published in 1955
by the Cambridge University Press

First Greenwood Reprinting 1969

Library of Congress Catalogue Card Number 79-90158

SBN 8371-2518-9

PRINTED IN UNITED STATES OF AMERICA

For
BRIAN MICHAEL

CONTENTS

FOREWORD

When an American begins his study of the British constitution he may find some difficulty in understanding it. He is told that the Sovereign is divorced from all politics, but when he reads the Queen's Speech at the opening of Parliament it seems to him that she is advocating legislation which is to be enacted in the coming session. Again, he finds that the House of Lords still has great powers of obstruction, but that these are not exercised even when there is a Labour government in power. Finally, although he is told that the Rule of Law, protection against arbitrary arrest, freedom of speech and of the press, are essential elements in the English polity, he is also informed that they receive no constitutional protection and that they can be abolished by Parliament at any time. It is only after further study that he begins to realize that law in the books and law in action may be two entirely different things.

An Englishman who seeks to understand the American system of government is in even greater danger of committing a similar error, for he is inclined to think that all that he needs to do is to read the Constitution of 1789 and its twenty-two amendments, but, unfortunately for him, he will soon find out that this will land him in a morass of misunderstanding and error. It ought to be obvious that a document which contains less than 8000 words can hardly be more than an outline. This is not to decry the Constitution, for if its authors had attempted to create a detailed governmental structure it would not have survived the stresses of the century and a half during which the thirteen States along the Atlantic coast stretched across the continent, and the population increased fifty-fold. To understand this Constitution it is, therefore, necessary to study its history, and, in particular, its development in the decisions of the Supreme Court, because, as the late Mr Justice Jackson has said, the American system is, in large part, 'government by lawsuit'.

It is not an easy task to explain to an Englishman, who must always think unconsciously in terms of Parliamentary supremacy, a system which is so legalistic in character, but Dr Schwartz has, I believe, accomplished this with outstanding success in the present book. He has been helped by two circumstances. In the first place, he has a thorough and practical knowledge of the British form of government, so that he is able to draw illuminating contrasts between the two systems, and to emphasize important points of difference which might otherwise escape notice. Secondly, his training as a lawyer has enabled him to explain technical legal points without confusing either himself or the reader.

The book is divided into two parts. The first deals with the basic principles of the Constitution, while the second is concerned with certain modern developments which are of peculiar interest today. This division is a convenient one, because a foreign reader can hardly understand any of the problems now at issue unless he has an accurate picture of the Constitution as a whole.

Perhaps the most important part of this picture is the devotion which is accorded to the Constitution by the people whom it governs. The well-meaning foreigner, who frequently suggests that sympathy should be shown to the Americans because they are forced to live under an out-moded system of government, may well be surprised to find that the overwhelming majority of them are convinced that it requires little or no amendment. It is not only in Fourth of July orations that the Constitution is described as 'God-given'. It is true, of course, that a system of government based on a division of powers, and on a series of checks and balances, may be less rapid in its actions than is a unitary system in which supreme power is placed in the hands of a small number of men, but this has never been regarded by Americans as a valid criticism. They think that the speed of governmental action can be bought at too high a price, and that it is safer, on some occasions, to be able to rely on efficient brakes.

Dr Schwartz does not accept the view that the Constitution is above criticism, and in a number of instances he suggests possible amendments, although he recognizes that they stand little chance of adoption. But he does make it clear that many of the strictures which have been directed against the Constitution are unfounded, and that where there have been failures of government these have usually been due to the men who work the machine rather than to the machine itself.

The English reader will be interested to find that some of the problems which are now being considered in the United States are also of immediate importance in Great Britain. The first is concerned with the maintenance of our civil liberties at a time of 'cold war'. To what extent, for example, should freedom of speech be accorded to those who advocate the forcible overthrow of the existing system of government? The second is concerned with the modern development of the administrative process. In this field

Dr Schwartz is especially expert, for he has written books on the British, French, and American systems: it is not surprising, therefore, to find that his chapter on 'Administrative Law', with its analysis of the American Administrative Procedure Act, 1946, contains much that will be of value to English students.

It is an honour to have been asked to write a foreword to a book which will undoubtedly take a permanent place in the literature of political science.

A. L. GOODHART

OXFORD
November 1954

PREFACE

The American who spends some time outside of the United States is struck immediately by the widespread interest displayed in the institutions of his country. Such interest appears, indeed, to be at an all-time high, now that the United States has come to play such a significant role in world affairs. Throughout the world, there is the keenest desire to learn more about the country which, for good or ill, has emerged from its isolationist state to a position of international leadership.

Essential to an understanding of the United States is some knowledge of the American system of constitutional law. For it is no exaggeration to say that the Federal Constitution is the fulcrum upon which American institutions turn. The interpretation of that instrument by the courts has, without a doubt, played a significant part in American history—and this is true not only of legal history in the narrow sense. It may be going too far to say that the history of the United States could be written in terms of leading Supreme Court decisions. But it is certainly true that a study of American history that did not consider them would be a distorted one.

It is the purpose of this book to present the workings of the American system of constitutional law to a British audience, with emphasis upon the significant changes that have occurred therein in recent years. There are, in the author's experience, few fields where comparative analysis can be more fruitful than in that of public law. This is especially true when the law compared is based upon common-law traditions and techniques similar to that upon which the law of Britain is grounded. Nor should the use of the comparative method lead to the feeling that the author's primary purpose is to place the British system in an unfavourable light in comparison with its American counterpart. It is not intended to set up the American law as a yardstick to which the British practice must conform nor to judge the House of Lords and other English courts by appealing to the superior moral jurisdiction of the United States Supreme Court.

The author cannot let this opportunity go by without expressing his gratitude, as an alumnus of the University, at having this volume published by the Cambridge University Press. Publication of his work under the University seal is for him a fitting expression of the respect and affection engendered in him by two years' residence in what is, without a doubt, the most beautiful university he has encountered.

The Master of University College should be paid public thanks for his kindness in consenting to write a foreword, which so greatly increases the value of the book for the British reader. Thanks are also due to the *Canadian Bar Review* and the *Modern Law Review* for permission to use material that originally appeared in their pages.

BERNARD SCHWARTZ

INSTITUTE OF COMPARATIVE LAW
NEW YORK UNIVERSITY
May 1955

PART ONE

THE STRUCTURE

Chapter I

THE BASES OF THE AMERICAN SYSTEM

English writers on constitutional law, reads a well-known passage by A. V. Dicey, have 'good reason to envy professors who belong to countries, such as...the United States, endowed with constitutions of which the terms are to be found in printed documents, known to all citizens and accessible to every man who is able to read. Whatever may be the advantages of a so-called "unwritten" constitution, its existence imposes special difficulties on teachers bound to expound its provisions. Anyone will see that this is so who compares for a moment the position of writers, such as Kent or Story, who commented on the constitution of America, with the situation of any person who undertakes to give instruction in the constitutional law of England.'[1] American jurists, asserts Dicey, who have written upon constitutional law, have known precisely what was the subject of their work. 'Their task as commentators of the constitution was in kind exactly similar to the task of commenting on any other branch of American jurisprudence. The American lawyer has to ascertain the meaning of the articles of the constitution in the same way in which he tries to elicit the meaning of any other enactment.... The task, in short, which lay before the great American commentators was the explanation of a definite legal document in accordance with the received canons of legal interpretation.'[2]

It is, however, a mistake to assume that constitutional law in a country governed by a written organic instrument, such as the American Constitution, involves solely an application of the legal canons of construction. It may be, as the United States Supreme Court stated almost a generation ago, that 'When an act of Congress is appropriately challenged in the courts as not conforming to the constitutional mandate the judicial branch of the Government has only one duty,—to lay the article of the Constitution which is invoked beside the statute which is challenged and to decide whether the latter squares with the former.'[3]

But this picture of American constitutional law as only a mechanical process akin to the judicial construction of a contract or a will, though true in some cases, is at variance with reality in the majority of instances. The American Constitution does not purport to prescribe its provisions in minute detail. And, perhaps even more important, it is not a self-executing

1 Dicey, *Law of the Constitution* (9th ed. 1939), 4.   2 *Ibid.* 5.
3 *United States* v. *Butler*, 297 U.S. 1, 62 (1936).

document. The *ought* laid down by the Constituent Assembly of 1787 must run the gauntlet of judicial interpretation before it attains the practical status of an *is*. This is, in a sense, true of all legislation; but it is especially true of a constitution whose terms must, of necessity, be less specific and detailed than those of an ordinary law. A constitution is, in practice, what the courts say it is. The American Constitution, like other organic instruments, would lose much of its practical efficacy if its terms were to be read by the courts in a destructive spirit.

American constitutional law is more than mere exegesis of a fundamental text. The organic instrument lays down only the framework of the governmental system in vigour in the United States. That is, indeed, its great virtue, which has enabled it to serve successfully as a charter of government for over a century and a half. 'The Constitution is a written instrument. As such its meaning does not alter', an American judge has declared. Yet, 'Being a grant of powers to a government, its language is general, and as changes come in social and political life it embraces in its grasp all new conditions which are within the scope of the powers conferred'.[1]

The text of the American Constitution may, as Dicey insisted, furnish a convenient basis for a commentator upon American constitutional law, which is lacking to his English counterpart. Yet one who looks only to the language of the organic instrument will obtain a partial and distorted picture of the working of the American constitutional system. The words of the fundamental law have remained essentially what they were in 1787. But the American governmental structure has changed so drastically in the past century and a half, especially so far as the extent and manner of exercise of State authority are concerned, that it would scarcely be recognizable to the Founding Fathers.[2] Having just engaged in a revolution against what they conceived to be excessive governmental authority, their primary concern was to ensure against the possibility of similar excesses in the constitutional structure they were establishing. Above all, they tried to prevent a concentration of political power such as that which they felt, rightly or wrongly, existed in the person of George III. 'The example of such unlimited authority that must have most impressed the forefathers', eloquently asserted Mr Justice Jackson in 1952, 'was the prerogative exercised by George III, and the description of its evils in the Declaration of Independence leads me to doubt that they were creating their new Executive in his image.'[3]

---

1 Brewer, J., in *South Carolina* v. *United States*, 199 U.S. 437, 448 (1905).
2 As the members of the Convention that drew up the Constitution in 1787 are usually called in America.
3 *Youngstown Sheet & Tube Co.* v. *Sawyer*, 343 U.S. 579, 641 (1952).

It was their fear of inordinate governmental authority that led the draftsmen of the American Constitution to emphasize the division of political power as its dominant characteristic. Power was, first of all, parcelled out between the nation and the individual States. The central Government could exercise only the authority expressly delegated to it in the Constitution. All powers not conferred upon it were explicitly reserved to the Governments of the respective States. And, within the Federal Government itself, distribution of authority was also the order of the day. The doctrine of the separation of powers became the corner-stone of the political structure created in 1787. The three departments of government were to be separate and distinct. They were to be independent of one another and each could exercise only the type of authority—legislative, executive, or judicial—delegated to it by the Constitution. 'In the government of this commonwealth', reads a State constitution which served as a model to the men of 1787, 'the legislative department shall never exercise the executive and judicial powers, or either of them; the executive shall never exercise the legislative and judicial powers, or either of them; the judicial shall never exercise the legislative and executive powers, or either of them; to the end it may be a government of laws, and not of men.'[1]

By such consistent division of authority, the framers of the American Constitution sought to ensure against the type of government which they felt had induced the Revolution of 1776. The power reserved to the States was to check the over-aggrandizement of that vested in the nation. And the separation of powers within the Federal Government was to curb a concentration of authority in the executive such as that which, in their view, had taken place under George III.

The structure of limited government created in conformity to the text of the Constitution adopted at the end of the eighteenth century is, however, wholly unlike that which exists in the United States of the middle of the twentieth century. The balance between State and nation, upon which the proper working of a federal system depends, has become basically altered. The authority of the central Government has been constantly increasing at the expense of that retained by the Governments of the States. Intervention by Washington in matters that were formerly deemed to be purely within local competence has, indeed, become so frequent that one wonders whether the States are not doomed to become mere vestigial survivals of a formerly flourishing federal system.

Within the national Government, also, the equilibrium between the three departments has become disturbed. The power of the American executive has been growing incessantly at the expense of the legislative

[1] Constitution of Massachusetts, 1780, Part I, Art. xxx.

and judicial branches. This shift in the constitutional centre of gravity[1] in the United States has drastically altered the separation of powers upon which the American Constitution was, as we have seen, grounded. It has made the presidential office the most powerful elective position in the world. In actual fact, indeed, the President of the United States today possesses far more authority than would have appeared possible to most Anglo-American contemporaries of King George III.

Important though the above development has been, it is, of course, not reflected in the text of the American Constitution. It remains basically what it was when it was originally framed in 1787. An analysis of American constitutional law limited to the language of the organic instrument would thus scarcely serve to give an accurate account. It is in this sense that Dicey's assertion of the difference between the English constitutional lawyer and his counterpart in the United States is not a precise one. The latter may, it is true, be furnished with a convenient framework for his inquiries by the terms of his written Constitution. It must, however, be emphasized that that document today furnishes only the essential framework of the American governmental structure.

The term 'constitutional law', states a leading English treatise on the subject, 'means the rules which regulate the structure of the principal organs of government and their relationship to each other, and determine their principal functions'.[2] And, it should be stated parenthetically, the constitutional lawyer is concerned primarily with those rules which are legal in nature, i.e. those which are recognized and enforced by the courts, rather than with what, since Dicey, have been termed 'conventions of the constitution'. In seeking out the rules of his constitutional law, the task of the American jurist is not as different from that of his English confrère as is commonly supposed. 'The true law of the Constitution', states Dicey, 'is in short to be gathered from the sources whence we collect the law of England in respect to any other topic',[3] with emphasis upon the reported decisions of the law courts. But these are also the sources to which the American constitutional lawyer looks. Developments since the drafting of his Constitution have been so great that most questions of constitutional law can no more be solved today by reference to its text alone than can questions of real property law solely by reliance upon the first chapter of the Statute of Westminster II. American constitutional law, like that in Britain, is essentially derived from the decisions of the courts. Those decisions, of course, are based upon the provisions of the American organic

1 The term used in Allen, *Law and Orders* (1945), 274.
2 Wade and Phillips, *Constitutional Law* (4th ed. 1950), 2.
3 Dicey, *op. cit.* 34.

law. Yet, as is so often the case with a legal text which has been in effect for some period of time, its interpretation by the courts has become in many ways even more important than the bare text itself. And it is with such interpretation, as exemplified in the case law, that the American jurist is primarily concerned.

WRITTEN CONSTITUTION

It is erroneous to assume, as so many people do, that the difference between American and English constitutional institutions stems only from the fact that the fundamental law in the United States is a written instrument. Gladstone's famous contrast of the British Constitution as 'the most subtle organism which has proceeded from progressive history' with the Constitution of the United States as 'the most wonderful work ever struck off at a given time by the brain and purpose of man' is based upon just such a supposition. It suggests that the American Constitution is a product of manufacture rather than growth.[1]

Even with regard to the document drafted in 1787, this assumption is incorrect. 'It would be erroneous...to describe the frame of government, signed by Washington and his fellow-delegates at Philadelphia, as their invention. It is not so much a creation of political theorists as a codification by practical statesmen of doctrines which experience showed had worked well, or were needed for the well-working of government in their country.'[2] The misconception upon which Gladstone's contrast is based is even clearer so far as contemporary constitutional conditions in the United States are concerned. As has already been indicated, the American political picture has changed so drastically since the founding of the Republic that it would be almost unrecognizable to the men of 1787. The American Constitution of today is primarily a product of progressive history, just as is that which governs the political institutions of Great Britain.

It is not the fact that it is a written document that makes the American Constitution so different from that which prevails in Britain. The experience with written constitutions in most Continental countries serves to show this. The constitutional situation in a country like France, for example, is certainly more similar to that which exists in Britain than to that in the United States, even though the French organic law has been a written one ever since the overthrow of the *ancien régime*. So far as the basic difference between the American and English systems is concerned, which, as we shall see, arises from the American rejection of the doctrine of parliamentary supremacy, the position in France is, indeed, exactly like that in Britain, despite the written character of the French Constitution.

1 Burdick, *The Law of the American Constitution* (1922), 3.   2 *Ibid.*

8 *The Structure*

Constitutional lawyers in France, it should be noted, are accustomed to deny that there is any such resemblance between their constitutional system and that on the English side of the Channel. Thus, to take the question of delegation of legislative power to the executive, with which students of constitutional law have been much concerned in recent years, as an example, that question, asserts a recent French text, involves a special legal problem in countries, like France, which have a written constitution. 'In effect, in systems such as the English one, the absolute supremacy of Parliament, unlimited by any formal Constitution, allows Parliament to delegate to the Government all the powers which it deems necessary. In countries which have a written and rigid Constitution, on the contrary, Parliament possesses legislative authority only from the Constitution and cannot, without violating it, charge the executive with legislating in its place.'[1]

From a practical point of view, the situation in France with regard to limitations upon the authority which may be delegated to the executive is basically like that in Britain, because of the lack in the French system of any judicial control of the validity of the laws enacted by the legislature. 'The restrictions placed on the action of the legislature under the French constitution are not in reality laws, since they are not rules which in the last resort will be enforced by the courts. Their true character is that of maxims of political morality, which derive whatever strength they possess from being formally inscribed in the constitution and from the resulting support of public opinion.'[2]

The situation in a Continental country like France is of particular significance to the English constitutional lawyer who seeks to understand the fundamental difference between his system and that which prevails in the United States. That difference does not stem solely from the written character of the American Constitution. The French experience shows that a constitution which cannot be enforced by the courts contains but empty words. It is judicial review which ensures that the American Constitution is not violated and gives that instrument its practical meaning. The failure of the French judiciary to assert a power of review over the constitutionality of acts of the legislature has made the various constitutions in France mere paper instruments and has, in effect, placed the French legislature in a position of practical supremacy not unlike that enjoyed by the Parliament in Britain.

1 Vedel, *Manuel élémentaire de droit constitutionnel* (1949), 498.
2 Dicey, *op. cit.* 135.

JUDICIAL REVIEW

The doctrine of judicial review of the constitutionality of laws, rather than the mere fact that its Constitution is a written one, sharply differentiates the American system from that in Britain. The foundation stone of the constitutional structure in Britain is the doctrine of parliamentary supremacy. This means, as Sir Ivor Jennings has pointed out, that 'Parliament has the right to make or unmake any law whatever, and that no person or body is recognised by the law of England as having a right to override or set aside the legislation of Parliament.'[1] The English courts can only interpret and may not question the validity of Acts of Parliament.[2]

The rejection of the doctrine of legislative supremacy in the United States did not result merely from its possession of a written constitution. Written organic laws in Continental countries, such as France, have not, by themselves, interfered with the practical supremacy of their legislatures. Nor should it be assumed, with Dicey,[3] that the failure of the French courts to challenge the supremacy of Parliament is due to the fact that France, like England, is governed under a unitarian system, while that which exists in the United States is federal. It may be that judicial enforcement of constitutional provisions is more desirable in a federal government, but the experience of the Swiss Confederation shows that it is far from absolutely necessary for its survival.

'There is a story told', states Lord Bryce, 'of an intelligent Englishman who, having heard that the Supreme Federal Court was created to protect the Constitution, and had authority given it to annul bad laws, spent two days in hunting up and down the Federal Constitution for the provisions he had been told to admire. No wonder he did not find them, for there is not a word in the Constitution on the subject.'[4] The authority of the American courts to review the constitutionality of laws does not find its source in any express delegation to them in the Constitution. It is a power which has been assumed by the Supreme Court itself in one of the most daring decisions ever rendered by a judicial tribunal.

The assumption by the American Supreme Court of the authority to review is one which has often been condemned by outside observers as a usurpation. 'The inference is the unmistakable one', writes Harold J. Laski, 'that, in the last analysis, the Supreme Court, by exercising this power of judicial review, is, in fact, a third chamber in the United States.'[5] And, in

---

1 Jennings, *The Law and the Constitution* (4th ed. 1952), 139.
2 Wade and Phillips, *op. cit.* 38.   3 Dicey, *op. cit.* 157–8.
4 Bryce, *The American Commonwealth* (1917 ed.), vol. I, 252.
5 Laski, *The American Democracy* (1948), 111.

a similar vein, the leading French study of judicial review of the constitutionality of laws by the American Supreme Court is entitled *Government by Judiciary*.[1]

To American jurists, on the contrary, the decision by their courts on questions of constitutionality is of the very essence of the judicial power delegated to them by the Constitution. 'The power of interpreting the laws', reads a famous passage from Story's *Commentaries on the Constitution of the United States*,[2] 'involves necessarily the function to ascertain, whether they are conformable to the constitution, or not; and if not so conformable, to declare them void and inoperative. As the constitution is the supreme law of the land, in a conflict between that and the laws, either of congress, or of the states, it becomes the duty of the judiciary to follow that only, which is of paramount obligation. This results from the very theory of a republican constitution of government; for otherwise the acts of the legislature and executive would in effect become supreme and uncontrollable, notwithstanding any prohibitions or limitations contained in the constitution; and usurpations of the most unequivocal and dangerous character might be assumed, without any remedy within the reach of the citizens.... The universal sense of America has decided, that in the last resort the judiciary must decide upon the constitutionality of the acts and laws of the general and state governments, so far as they are capable of being made the subject of judicial controversy.'

Under the theory which has been adopted by the American courts, the authority to declare constitutionality flows naturally from the judicial duty to determine the law. 'It is emphatically the province and duty of the judicial department', declared Chief Justice John Marshall in the very first case in which the doctrine of judicial review was asserted by the American Supreme Court, 'to say what the law is. Those who apply the rule to particular cases must of necessity expound and interpret that rule. If two laws conflict with each other, the courts must decide on the operation of each. So if a law be in opposition to the constitution; if both the law and the constitution apply to a particular case, so that the court must either decide that case conformably to the law, disregarding the constitution; or conformably to the constitution, disregarding the law; the court must determine which of these conflicting rules governs the case. This is of the very essence of judicial duty.'[3]

The American theory assumes a veritable hierarchy of law-makers

1 Lambert, *Le Gouvernement des juges* (1921).

2 (1833), §1570.

3 *Marbury* v. *Madison*, 1 Cranch 137, 177 (U.S. 1803). For a discussion of judicial review in operation during the 150 years since this case was decided, see *Supreme Court and Supreme Law* (Cahn ed., 1954).

within the State. At the apex is the Constituent Assembly, to whom alone the people have delegated the authority to create the organic instrument under which the State is governed. The provisions of the Constitution enacted by it constitute the supreme law of the land. The law made by any other organ of the State is valid only in so far as it does not conflict with the Constitution. Next in the law-making hierarchy come the elected representatives of the people, who are given the authority to enact statutes, whose provisions are legally binding upon all, provided only that they are not inconsistent with the Constitution. At the base of the law-making hierarchy is the administration. Its exercises of law-making power are valid only if they do not conflict with the Constitution and the statutes enacted by the legislature.

It is the subordinate position of the legislature and administration in the hierarchy of law-makers that has made the assertion by the American courts of their review power a necessity. If the supreme position of the Constitution is to be maintained in practice, the courts must refuse to enforce legislative or administrative acts which conflict with its provisions. To hold otherwise would be, in effect, to nullify the efficacy of the restrictions contained in the organic law. 'To what purpose are powers limited, and to what purpose is that limitation committed to writing, if these limits may, at any time, be passed by those intended to be restrained?'[1]

It is judicial enforcement alone that makes the provisions of the American Constitution more than mere maxims of political morality. Unless the courts can intervene in cases where they are violated, the principle of supremacy of the fundamental law becomes but as 'sounding brass or a tinkling cymbal'.[2] A constitution is only a paper instrument if the restrictions contained in it cannot be given effect by the courts. 'How vain is a paper restriction if it confers neither power nor right', eloquently exclaimed an American congressman a century and a half ago, 'Of what importance is it to say, Congress are prohibited from doing certain acts, if no legitimate authority exists in the country to decide whether an act done *is* a prohibited act? Do gentlemen perceive the consequences which would follow from establishing the principle that Congress have the exclusive right to decide on their own powers? This principle admitted, does any Constitution remain? Does not the power of the Legislature become absolute and omnipotent? Can you talk to them of transgressing their powers, when no one has a right to judge of those powers but themselves?'[3]

1 *Marbury* v. *Madison*, 1 Cranch at 176.
2 The phrase used in *National Labor Relations Board* v. *Robbins Tire & Rubber Co.*, 161 F. 2d 798, 804 (5th Cir. 1947).
3 James A. Bayard in the House of Representatives, 20 February 1802, quoted in Warren, *Congress, the Constitution, and the Supreme Court* (1925), 42.

SEPARATION OF POWERS

To the student of comparative law, the outstanding characteristic of the American system of constitutional law is the doctrine of judicial review of the constitutionality of Acts of the legislature. Although, as we shall see,[1] the American Supreme Court has been tending of late to exercise much more self-restraint in its exercise of the power to declare laws invalid than was its wont a generation ago, its authority in this field is certainly still far greater than that claimed for English courts. It is the successful assertion by the judiciary in the United States of the review power that has prevented the development in that country of the doctrine of parliamentary supremacy and has made its constitutional system so different from that which prevails in Britain.

The doctrine of parliamentary supremacy upon which English constitutional law is based is inconsistent also with the separation of powers which is provided for in the American Constitution. It has already been indicated that the growth of executive power in the United States has drastically disturbed the balance between the three branches of government. But this does not mean that there has been anything in the American system like the fusion of power which has characterized the governmental system in Britain. By English standards, the structure of the Federal Government in the United States is still dominated by the doctrine of the separation of powers. The separation of powers, states a leading text on English constitutional law, is practised in the United States rather than in England. 'It is in the United States that there is a real division of powers between the three organs and strict adherence to the doctrine of separation of powers.'[2]

The doctrine of the separation of powers, according to a famous decision of the United States Supreme Court, though not expressly provided for in most American constitutions, is implicit in all, as a conclusion logically following from the separation of the three departments. 'It may be stated then, as a general rule inherent in the American constitutional system, that, unless otherwise expressly provided or incidental to the powers conferred, the legislature cannot exercise either executive or judicial power; the executive cannot exercise either legislative or judicial power; the judiciary cannot exercise either executive or legislative power.'[3]

The English doctrine of parliamentary supremacy is, as has been pointed out, one which is wholly foreign to American public law. The authority

1 *Infra*, ch. VIII.
2 Wade and Phillips, *op. cit.* 20.
3 *Springer* v. *Government of the Philippine Islands*, 277 U.S. 189, 201 (1928).

of legislatures in the United States is restricted by the limitations contained in the various American constitutions. And, in addition, American legislatures are limited by the doctrine of the separation of powers. Even though a specific power is not precluded by the Constitution, it cannot be exercised by the legislature if it is non-legislative in nature. Nor can the legislature delegate to another department authority which is not deemed germane to the generic powers conferred upon it.

To assume that the separation of powers provided for in the American Constitution, though undoubtedly strict by English criteria, is a 'doctrinaire concept to be made use of with pedantic rigor',[1] is, however, completely to misapply the constitutional doctrine. It is a mistake to think of that doctrine as dividing the American Government into three watertight compartments. 'If we look into the constitutions of the several states', wrote James Madison in *The Federalist*,[2] 'we find that notwithstanding the emphatical and, in some instances, the unqualified terms in which this axiom has been laid down, there is not a single instance in which the several departments of power have been kept absolutely separate and distinct.'

The proper approach in cases involving an alleged violation of the separation of powers is that contained in one of Mr Justice Holmes's most famous dissents. 'It does not seem to need argument', he asserted, 'to show that however we may disguise it by veiling words we do not and cannot carry out the distinction between legislative and executive action with mathematical precision and divide the branches into watertight compartments, were it ever so desirable to do so, which I am far from believing that it is, or that the Constitution requires.'[3]

It is, of course, recognized that there are lines beyond which one cannot go in the American system. Certain powers belong clearly to one of the branches of government. Thus, the executive cannot exercise law-making authority, in the absence of a valid legislative delegation, for the power to make the laws is a function vested exclusively in the legislature.[4] But, if the power at issue does not so obviously fall within the exclusive orbit of one of the three branches, a more difficult problem is presented. One can, it is true, carry the doctrine of separation of powers to an analytical, logical extreme, as did the American Supreme Court in a well-known case.[5] The

1 Cardozo, J., in *Panama Refining Co.* v. *Ryan*, 293 U.S. 388, 440 (1935).
2 No. 47.
3 *Springer* v. *Government of the Philippine Islands*, 277 U.S. at 211.
4 *Youngstown Sheet & Tube Co.* v. *Sawyer*, 343 U.S. 579 (1952), the now famous steel seizure case, discussed *infra*, ch. VII, contains a recent striking application of this principle.
5 *Springer* v. *Government of the Philippine Islands*, 277 U.S. 189 (1928).

power in question there was the voting upon government-owned stock in certain corporations. The court examined the power to vote such stock, decided that it was clearly not legislative or judicial in nature, and hence concluded that it must be executive. 'It is clear that they are not legislative in character and still more clear that they are not judicial. The fact that they do not fall within the authority of either of these two constitutes logical ground for concluding that they do fall within that of the remaining one of the three among which the powers of government are divided.'[1]

The court's approach in the particular case is like that followed in the familiar parlour game—'It is not animal. It is not vegetable. Therefore, it must be mineral.' One wonders whether it is the way to deal with difficult cases of separation of power. The better approach would appear to be that of Justice Holmes, in his dissent, which has already been cited. In his view, if the authority at issue does not manifestly belong to one of the three branches, it falls 'into the indiscriminate residue of matters within legislative control'.[2] In such a case, it is for the legislature to determine which branch shall exercise the particular power. The Holmesian approach, recognizing that there are powers of a doubtful nature which need not be arbitrarily fitted into Montesquieu's trichotomy, holds that it is within the legislative competence to assign their exercise how it will.

It is the abandonment of its 'parlour game' approach that has enabled the American Supreme Court in recent years to uphold as valid grants of authority to the executive which would formerly have been considered to be violative of the separation of powers. This has permitted the American administration, like that in Britain, to be vested with substantial legislative and judicial authority, of the type which has been found necessary on both sides of the Atlantic for the effective completion of modern statutory schemes.

SEPARATION BETWEEN LEGISLATURE AND EXECUTIVE

According to an outstanding English treatise on constitutional law,[3] three questions may be asked in ascertaining whether there is in a constitution a separation of powers in relation to the legislature and the executive:

(a) Do the same persons or bodies form part of both the legislature and the executive?

In Britain, the answer must clearly be in the affirmative. The working of the English cabinet system of government is, indeed, dependent upon the convention which requires that the Queen's Ministers shall be members of one of the Houses of Parliament. 'Their presence in Parliament makes

---

1 277 U.S. at 202. 2 *Ibid.* at 212.
3 Wade and Phillips, *op. cit.* 22.

a reality of their responsibility to Parliament and facilitates co-operation between them and the Legislature, both features which are vital to parliamentary government.'[1]

In the United States, on the other hand, the question referred to must be replied to with an unqualified negative. Just as the working of the English system depends upon the status of the Queen's Ministers as members of Parliament, so does that of the American Cabinet depend upon the converse proposition. Under the American Constitution, the executive is set up as a separate branch, wholly independent from the legislature. There is, as Lord Bryce aptly pointed out,[2] in the government of the United States, really no such thing as a cabinet in the English sense of the term. At the head of the American executive is the President, who is elected directly by the people for a fixed term. The members of what is called the 'Cabinet' in the United States are the heads of the ten executive departments. Neither the President nor the members of his Cabinet are members of the Congress; they need not even be members of the party in power in the Congress. Nor, under the American practice, can members of the legislature become connected with the executive branch. If an individual congressman chooses to accept a position in the Cabinet or other executive office, he must first resign his membership in the legislature, which is, of course, the very opposite of what the individual seeking cabinet office in Britain must do.

(b) Does the legislature control the executive or the executive control the legislature?

The English constitutional system is characterized by the principle of ministerial responsibility. 'The House of Commons ultimately controls the Executive. Strong government has been combined with responsible government by ensuring that Parliament, while leaving the task of governing to the Government, can insist on the dismissal of a Government which does not obtain parliamentary support for its general policy.'[3] The practical effectiveness of parliamentary control under contemporary conditions should not, however, be overemphasized. 'In the last resort the House can compel the Government either to resign or to dissolve Parliament. The last resort is, however, far, far away if the Government possesses a party majority. The British Government is one of the strongest, if not the strongest, in the world. It normally has at its command a stable parliamentary majority whose support is based on loyalty to the personnel and acceptance of the principles of the party from which the Government is drawn, upon dislike of the alternative which would be drawn from the

1 *Ibid.* 2 Bryce, *op. cit.* 85.
3 Wade and Phillips, *op. cit.* 23.

Opposition, and upon the big stick of dissolution which the Government can, if need be, wield. . . . Though in one sense, it is true that the House controls the Government, in another and more practical sense the Government controls the House of Commons.'[1]

The constitutional picture in the United States is a wholly different one. The principle of ministerial responsibility is unknown in America. 'Under the Presidential system', as Lord Balfour has pointed out, 'the effective head of the national administration is elected for a fixed term. He is practically irremovable. Even if he is proved to be inefficient, even if he becomes unpopular, even if his policy is unacceptable to his countrymen, he and his methods must be endured until the moment comes for a new election.'[2] The sole responsibility of the President is to the electorate, not to the legislature. Nor is the position any different with regard to the members of the American Cabinet. They are accountable not to Congress, but to the President alone, who can appoint and dismiss them at will. It is true that their appointment must be confirmed by a majority vote of the Senate. But the convention has developed for Senate approval to be accorded almost as a matter of course in most cases, on the theory that the President is entitled to execute the laws through a Cabinet of his own choosing.

It is, of course, not accurate to think of the American executive as entirely irresponsible to the legislature. Executive authority itself is dependent upon delegations from the legislature, and the President will normally not be unresponsive to the desires of the Congress, in order to secure enactment of the legislation which he deems essential for the effective carrying-out of his policies. Of particular significance in this respect is the complete dependence of the executive upon Congress for appropriation of the funds needed for the carrying-on of its activities. Yet these are all only indirect pressures. There is no direct machinery of legislative control in the American system akin to the vote of censure. An adverse vote of Congress does not affect the position of the President or the members of his Cabinet. 'If they propose to take a step which requires money, and Congress refuses the requisite appropriation, the step cannot be taken. But a dozen votes of censure will neither compel them to resign nor oblige the President to pause in any line of conduct which is within his constitutional rights.'[3]

The absence of legislative control over the executive in the United States is accompanied by a corresponding lack of control by the executive

1 Jennings, *Parliament* (1940), 8.
2 Quoted in Wade and Phillips, *op. cit.* 22.
3 Bryce, *op. cit.* 93.

over the Congress. To the American observer, perhaps the most striking aspect of the control which the English Government has over the House of Commons is to be found in its direction of the business of the House. Most legislation is introduced by the Government, and it is it which determines how the time of the House shall be spent. There is no analogous authority in the American executive. The President does, it is true, possess the power to veto bills passed by the Congress, and such bills cannot become law unless they are subsequently passed again by each House, with a two-thirds majority. Yet, aside from the veto power, the President does not participate directly in the legislative process. Neither he nor his Cabinet has any responsibility for initiating bills, nor is there machinery available to them for securing their passage analogous to that at the disposal of English Governments.

The conduct of congressional business is regulated solely by the American legislature itself. If the President's party possesses a clear majority in both Houses, the executive does, as a practical matter, play a substantial part in legislation. He can then normally secure enactment of bills introduced for him by his party's leaders and disapproval of those which are opposed to his policies. Even at such times, however, the Congress may not vote in all cases in accordance with the executive's desire. Party discipline is not nearly as strict in America as it is in Britain, and the predominance of his party in the Congress does not necessarily result in complete approval of the President's legislative programme. And, it should be noted, the American executive never has any control over the way in which the time of the legislature is spent. Consideration of a bill upon the floor is mostly dependent upon the committee to which it is sent in the first instance. And the extent of discussion upon the floor is solely within the direction of the particular House. In the Senate, indeed, the well-nigh universal rule is that of unlimited debate, for the majority necessary for a closure of discussion is almost never obtained in that chamber.[1]

(c) Do the legislature and the executive exercise each other's functions? Here we are on more debatable ground.[2] In the United States, as in Britain, the necessities of modern administration have compelled the legislature to delegate to the executive the authority to promulgate rules and regulations which have the force of law. Delegated legislation, if valid, has the same legal effect as a statute enacted by the legislature, and it is consequently difficult to reach any conclusion but that the promulgation

---

1 A two-thirds majority is necessary for closure to be moved successfully in the Senate. As has been indicated, the tradition in that chamber in favour of unrestricted debate has made it most difficult to secure that majority.

2 Wade and Phillips, *op. cit.* 24.

of rules and regulations by the executive involves an exercise of legislative authority. To this extent, then, in America, as in Britain, there is an exercise by the executive of a function which, by its nature, belongs to the legislature. It should, however, be pointed out that, in the American system, the courts have imposed limits upon the authority which can be delegated. Unless the enabling Act contains a standard—a limit upon or a guide to the exercise of the power conferred—it is invalid.[1] This has precluded wholesale delegations, of the type which has given rise to strong criticism in Britain; but it has not prevented necessary grants of legislative authority to the executive.

The above should clearly indicate that there is a separation of powers between the legislature and the executive in the United States to an extent which is wholly foreign to the British governmental structure. In Britain, the dominant characteristic is the fusion, rather than the division, of authority between Parliament and Government. In America, the Congress and the President are largely independent of one another. The absence of the principle of ministerial responsibility renders the executive free of direct legislative control. And the lack of strict party discipline permits the Congress to remain comparatively free from executive direction. The autonomy of the two branches in America makes the constant co-operation between legislature and executive, upon which the working of the British system depends, almost impossible to attain. It is true that, in recent years, the American executive has been given substantial powers of delegated legislation. The consequent growth in executive authority has led many American jurists to deplore what they have considered to be undue disintegration of the doctrine of separation of powers. It cannot be denied, in fact, that the growth of executive power has upset the equilibrium between the departments which the framers of the American Constitution intended. Still, as the above analysis demonstrates, the separation of powers between the legislature and the executive in the United States remains a relatively rigid one by English standards.

SEPARATION OF JUDICIARY

The three questions asked above with regard to the separation of powers between the legislature and the executive may also be asked, as the English text already referred to points out,[2] in dealing with the relationship between the judiciary and the other two organs of government:

(a) Do the same persons form part of the judiciary and the executive or the judiciary and the legislature?

1 See *infra*, p. 286.   2 Wade and Phillips, *op. cit.* 25, 27.

So far as the United States is concerned, a negative answer is even clearer than it is with regard to the situation in Britain. In the British system there is, at least in form, some blending of the judiciary and the executive. Thus, the Lord Chancellor, who is a Cabinet Minister, presides over the highest appellate court, and the final court of appeal from the Colonies is in form a committee of the Privy Council, an executive organ. Yet these are only formal exceptions to the separation of powers. 'In substance the personnel of the Executive and the Judiciary is separate.'[1] There is a similar formal violation of the separation doctrine in Britain in the position of the House of Lords, which is both a chamber of the legislature and the highest court of appeal. Yet, here again, as English jurists have little difficulty in realizing, the violation is only one of form. 'The House of Lords sitting as a court is in substance a court of law with only a historic and formal connection with the House of Lords sitting as a second chamber.'[2]

In the American system, the separation of personnel between the judiciary and the other two branches is complete in form as well as substance. No member of an American court is connected with the executive or the legislature. There is no relationship between the Supreme Court, the highest appellate court, and the Congress analogous to that which exists with regard to the House of Lords in Britain. The Chief Justice of the American court is solely the head of that tribunal, and neither he nor its other members can take any part in legislative business, as is the case with the Lords of Appeal in Ordinary who occasionally participate in the work of the upper House of the Parliament. If the holder of executive or legislative office in the United States is appointed to the Bench, he must relinquish his office. Thus, of the 1954 Supreme Court, two justices had to resign from the President's Cabinet and two from membership in the Senate in order to accept their judicial appointments.

(*b*) Does the executive or legislature control or influence the judiciary or the judiciary control or influence the executive or legislature?

With regard to the second part of this question, the answer is clear on both sides of the Atlantic. The courts are hardly in a position to exert any direct dominion over the other two branches. They do, it is true, serve to check illegal executive action. And they are the ultimate enforcers of the laws enacted by the legislature. In the American system, indeed, their role in this respect is considered to compel them to refuse to enforce any legislative act which they find to be contrary to the provisions of the Constitution. Yet the position of the courts in this respect, in both countries, is considered to involve only an exercise of the judicial function and not any

1 *Ibid.* 26.   2 *Ibid.* 28.

attempts at interference with the work of the other two branches. The English judge who declares executive action to be *ultra vires* of the enabling statute is only performing his duty of interpreting and applying the law to the facts of the case before him. And the same is true of his American colleague when he declares a law unconstitutional. 'The American judge must in giving judgment obey the terms of the constitution, just as his English brother must in giving judgment obey every Act of Parliament bearing on the case.'[1]

The question of executive and legislative control of the judiciary has been a more crucial one in the common-law countries. For, without judicial independence in this respect, there is, as Anglo-American history demonstrates, no effective safeguard against governmental abuse of power available to the ordinary citizen. The independence of the judiciary has been settled in Britain since the Act of Settlement, which established the principle of judicial security of tenure. Though judges of the superior courts may be removed by an address from both Houses of Parliament, it is almost beyond the realm of possibility that such an address would be moved today to interfere with judicial independence.[2] A more difficult point arises out of the power of the House of Commons to reduce the judges' salaries. The American rule, which prohibits diminution of the compensation received by the judiciary during their continuance in office, seems a preferable one.

The American Constitution expressly states that 'The Judges, both of the supreme and inferior Courts, shall hold their Offices during good Behaviour, and shall, at stated Times, receive for their Services, a Compensation, which shall not be diminished during their Continuance in Office.'[3] Executive or legislative attempts to reduce the judges' salaries, such as was done in Britain under the National Economy Act, 1931,[4] would be declared invalid by the American courts as contravening this express provision of the Constitution.[5] American judges may be removed from office only by impeachment proceedings instituted before the Congress, which, in effect, is not very far from the English removal procedure. Though there have been cases in which American judges have been impeached, yet, since the failure of an attempt at the beginning of the last century to impeach a Supreme Court justice because his views were opposed to those of the dominant party in Congress, there has been little likelihood of impeachment of American judges on political grounds.

It should, of course, be pointed out that the American judiciary is

---

1 Dicey, *op. cit.* 159.   2 Wade and Phillips, *op. cit.* 28.
3 Article III, section 1.   4 See Wade and Phillips, *op. cit.* 236.
5 *O'Donoghue* v. *United States*, 289 U.S. 516 (1933).

dependent upon the legislature for its appropriations. As a practical matter, however, the judicial estimates are passed by the Congress with as little partisan controversy as there is in Britain. Federal judges are appointed by the President and confirmed by the Senate. It cannot be denied that political factors often enter into such appointments. Yet, once appointed, the American judge enjoys full independence, because of the constitutional provision quoted above. He may, it is true, not be wholly uninfluenced by political considerations if he hopes to be considered for higher judicial office. And the power of the President to appoint to higher judicial office does, it must be admitted, constitute a weakness in the American system, for American lower court judges are often not as little concerned with promotion as are their English brethren.[1]

(*c*) Do the executive and judiciary or the legislature and judiciary exercise each other's functions?

Here, again, the answer is not difficult so far as the exercise of non-judicial functions by the judiciary is concerned. On both sides of the Atlantic it is felt that this might compromise judicial independence. It is for this reason that the American courts have refused, almost from the beginning of their existence, to render advisory opinions at the request of either the executive or the legislature. Such giving of advice, it has been feared, might involve a too direct participation in legislation and administration.[2] As it was expressed by *The Times* with regard to a proposal to have the right to give advisory opinions conferred upon the English courts,[3] such a procedure reintroduces 'the practice of the Stuarts, under which the Executive—then the King in person—took the opinion of the Judges upon questions which they might afterwards have to determine....It would compel the Judges to act in certain cases at the bidding of the Executive as its official advisers.'[4]

Not so clear is the situation concerning the exercise of judicial functions by the legislature and the executive. With regard to the legislature, the development in the common-law countries has been consistently away from allowing it judicial authority. In its origins, Parliament may well have been primarily a judicial body. But that has not been true for

1 It should be emphasized that what is said above applies only to the federal courts. In the vast majority of the American States, judges are elected for a term of years. It is difficult to imagine a more unsatisfactory method of choosing members of the judiciary, and, as might be expected, in practice, political factors predominate in the choice of State judges under the elective system.

2 The example of the French Conseil d'État, which directly participates in legislation and administration in this way, has not commended itself to most Anglo-American observers.

3 For a discussion of this proposal, see Schwartz, *Law and the Executive in Britain* (1949), 202–4.

4 *The Times*, 27 April 1928, p. 17, col. 2.

many years. And the judicial powers of the Parliament are now almost wholly conferred upon the House of Lords, sitting as a separate court from which lay peers are barred. In the United States, too, there has been a similar trend, though its progress has been a slower one. What has been termed 'legislative justice'[1] has, indeed, persisted in the American system until relatively recently. Thus, even today in most American States, tort claims against the State are adjudicated upon by committees of the legislature.[2] Such jurisdiction on the part of the legislature is, however, merely a vestigial survival, and one may hope for its speedy disappearance from the American system.

The trend with regard to executive justice has, on the contrary, been the opposite one in both countries. The conferment of the authority to decide disputes upon non-judicial bodies is, in fact, one of the distinctive developments of our time. 'A host of controversies as to private rights', as a former Chief Justice of the American Supreme Court expressed it 'are no longer decided in courts.'[3] The delegation of judicial power to the executive has definite implications upon the position of the courts as guardians of the rights of the citizen. 'It is idle to boast of an independent Judiciary if major justiciable issues are excluded from the jurisdiction of the courts and entrusted to administrative authorities.'[4] Few will deny that executive justice has great advantages. But the trend toward it must not be carried too far if the courts are to retain their constitutional position as one of the co-ordinate branches of government. In the United States, it should be pointed out, the dangers arising from the grant of judicial authority to the executive do not appear to be as great as they are in Britain. The constitutional grant to the American courts of 'the judicial power' enables them to assert an inherent authority to review the legality of the decisions of executive officers.

RULE OF LAW

In Britain, the doctrine of the separation of powers today means little more than an independent judiciary.[5] In the United States, as we have seen, the doctrine means much more, for it has prevented the fusion of functions between the legislature and the executive which has taken place in Britain. To the political scientist, concerned mainly with the actual working of the government in Washington, the division between the President and the

---

1 See Pound, 'Justice according to law', 14 *Columbia L. Rev.* (1914), 1.
2 This has not been true of the Congress since the passage of the Federal Tort Claims Act, 1946, which, in a manner similar to that provided for under the English Crown Proceedings Act, 1947, establishes the tort liability of the Federal Government.
3 Hughes, C.J., *N.Y. Times*, 13 February 1931, p. 18, col. 1.
4 Wade and Phillips, *op. cit.* 26.   5 *Ibid.* 21.

Congress will be of primary significance. It will explain how Governments are chosen and how their programmes are enacted into law. To the constitutional lawyer, whose interest is focussed on the law enforced by the courts, the status of the latter is of even greater moment. It is the position of the judiciary in the United States that has enabled the American Constitution to be enforced as the true supreme law of the land. It is the separation between the judiciary and the other departments of government that is the basis of the independence of the courts in the Anglo-American world. And, as the common lawyer well knows, it is the independence of his judiciary above all which gives practical meaning to the rule of law which he asserts with pride to be the most fundamental characteristic[1] of his constitutional system.

It is today almost a truism to Anglo-American constitutional lawyers that the famous definition of the rule of law enunciated by A. V. Dicey in 1885 is no longer an accurate one. According to Dicey, the rule of law means, in the first place, 'that no man is punishable or can be lawfully made to suffer in body or goods except for a distinct breach of law established in the ordinary legal manner before the ordinary courts of law'.[2] This implies that every citizen is entitled to have his rights adjudicated in a common-law court and is clearly at variance with fact, in the light of the development of the modern administrative process. Under contemporary conditions, the citizen's rights and obligations are as likely to be determined by executive decision as by the decision of a law court. And executive agencies possessing adjudicatory authority 'are not ordinary courts in Dicey's sense. "Judicial" as their functions clearly seem to be, they are not "courts" in the common-law meaning of the term. And they differ from common-law courts in precisely the particulars which furnish the reasons for the common law's insistence that every individual shall be entitled to have his rights tried in a law court.'[3] Nor is it correct to say today with Dicey[4] that the rule of law excludes the existence of wide discretionary authority on the part of the Government. The vesting of discretionary power in the executive is, on the contrary, the essential characteristic of present-day enabling statutes. Few of the regulatory and social-service schemes undertaken by the modern State would be feasible if their details were not, to some extent, left to administrative discretion.

To one nurtured upon Anglo-American constitutional traditions, justice according to law is the outstanding characteristic of the State where the

1 Lord Hewart, Introduction, in Amos, *The English Constitution* (1934), vi.
2 Dicey, *op. cit.* 188.
3 Dickinson, *Administrative Justice and the Supremacy of Law* (1927), 35.
4 Dicey, *op. cit.* 202.

rule of law prevails. This does not militate against the possession of wide powers of decision by the executive. The rule of law does not necessarily demand judicial justice in the settling of all disputes. What that concept does require is justice according to law either as the determining or the controlling factor. In so far as decision-making authority is committed to agencies other than courts, judicial control of their determinations is essential. It is only to the extent that judicial justice serves to keep these other agencies within the bounds of legality that the rule of law can be said to be maintained. 'For just in so far as administrative determinations are subject to court review, a means exists for maintaining the supremacy of law, though at one remove and as a sort of secondary line of defence.'[1]

The common lawyer would thus reply in the negative to the question of whether the growth of executive authority has been inconsistent with the rule of law. The constitutional principle is preserved by the assertion by our law courts of the authority to hold governmental action to the standard of legality. Executive action that does not meet that standard will be set aside, upon the bringing of the appropriate action in the competent court. Judicial control, in the Anglo-American view, still ensures the subordination of government to law, as it is administered by the ordinary courts of the land.

The rule of law rejects the conception of the dual State, in which the administration of justice is characterized by its dual character. In such a State, law plays a controlling part only in the ordering of the relations between private citizens. Legal concepts are not applicable to the political sphere, which is regulated by arbitrary measures, in which the dominant officials exercise unfettered discretionary prerogatives. A system of law and a system of force exist side by side in a State of this type. 'There are certain areas into which law penetrates only slightly. For example, a person who is suspected of antagonism to the regime may be picked up by the secret police, held incommunicado for a long period of time, tried secretly by an administrative board, and sentenced to hard labor—without benefit of defense counsel and without any possibility of appeal. On the other hand, there are other areas which are on the whole governed by well-defined legal standards.'[2]

It is a dualized legal order, in which governmental acts are placed in a privileged position of immunity from control by law, that is opposed to the constitutional concept of the rule of law. A State in which government is not vested with any such immunity, in which governmental acts are subject to as strict legal scrutiny as are the acts of ordinary citizens—such a State is not one whose institutions are inconsistent with the rule of law.

1 Dickinson, *op. cit.* 37.   2 Berman, *Justice in Russia* (1950), vii.

Looked at from this point of view, the constitutional law of both the United States and Britain has been dominated by the concept of the rule of law. The keystone of the Anglo-American constitutional structure has been the principle of legality enforced by the courts of law. That principle presupposes that governmental action is valid only if it does not conflict with the prescriptions laid down by the constitution and statute law. Or, to put it another way, governmental action is valid only if it is *legal*. It is illegal if it is inconsistent with the directions of an organ superior to the particular governmental actor in the hierarchy of law-makers within the State. It is, as a noted French constitutional lawyer has eloquently expressed it, 'this principle essentially which protects the individual, and one can assert that there are not, there cannot be, and there ought not to be, any exceptions to it. A State which does not recognize it or which recognizes it only with reservations and exceptions does not truly live under a rule of law.'[1]

To the American observer, effective fulfilment of the principle of legality requires judicial enforcement of constitutional as well as statutory law. From his point of view, the doctrine of parliamentary supremacy constitutes a lacuna in such fulfilment in Britain, for legality in the British system is synonymous with the expressed will of those who for the time being make up the majority of the legislature. 'It is not enough', as Sir Ivor Jennings has aptly pointed out, 'to say with Dicey that "Englishmen are ruled by the law and by the law alone" or, in other words, that the powers of the Crown and its servants are derived from the law; for that is true even of the most despotic State. The powers of Louis XIV, of Napoleon I, of Herr Hitler, and of Signor Mussolini are derived from the law, even if that law be only "The Leader may do and order what he pleases".'[2]

Basic in the American conception of the principle of legality is the notion of principles above the State, which are enforced by the courts. Such principles are, in the American system, those laid down in the Federal Constitution. Legislative acts which conflict with them will be declared invalid by the American courts. 'It must be conceded', the United States Supreme Court has asserted, 'that there are such rights in every free government beyond the control of the State. A government which recognized no such rights, which held the lives, the liberty, and the property of its citizens subject at all times to the absolute disposition and unlimited control of even the most democratic depository of power,

1 Duguit, *Traité de droit constitutionnel* (3rd ed.), vol. III, 732.
2 Jennings, *op. cit.* 46.

is after all but a despotism. It is true it is a despotism of the many, of the majority, if you choose to call it so, but it is none the less a despotism.'[1]

It will doubtless be objected that emphasis upon the distinction between the American and English systems in this respect does not present a fair picture of the constitutional situation in England. The essential principles of a modern democratic society are as much a part of the higher law of England as they are of that of the United States. It may well be that they can, in theory, be abrogated by Parliament, whose actions inconsistent with them will in no way be interfered with by the English courts. In practice, however, a legislature responsible to an informed electorate will respect the basic principles of the English constitutional system.

This is not to deny that there is an important difference between American and English constitutional law upon this point. In the United States, the principles of constitutional law are declared, at least in their essentials, in a written instrument, whose provisions are enforced by the courts. In England, the fundamentals of the constitution are, it is true, respected by the legislature; but they are, in the last resort, only self-limitations by Parliament of its own sovereignty. And recent experience in other countries should show how ineffective mere self-limitations may prove to be when put to the test.

1 *Citizens' Savings & Loan Ass.* v. *Topeka*, 20 Wall. 655, 662 (U.S. 1874).

Chapter II

THE FEDERAL SYSTEM

To the English observer, the American constitutional system is sharply differentiated from the one with which he is familiar, not only because of the separation of powers between the three departments of government, but, even more so, because of the division of authority between the national and State Governments. The doctrine of parliamentary supremacy is wholly inconsistent with a federal form of government, such as that which exists in the United States. In a federal system, the authority of the central legislature is limited by that possessed by the legislative organs of the governmental units which make up the federation. Such circumscription of power is essential to the functioning of federalism. It is entirely incompatible with the unrestricted sovereignty of Parliament, upon which the working of the constitutional system in Britain turns. 'The principle, in short,' states an outstanding English text, 'which gives its form to our system of government is (to use a foreign but convenient expression) "unitarianism", or the habitual exercise of supreme legislative authority by one central power, which in the particular case is the British Parliament. The principle which, on the other hand, shapes every part of the American polity, is that distribution of that limited...authority among bodies each co-ordinate with and independent of the other which...is essential to the federal form of government.'[1]

The recognition of this basic difference between the American and English constitutional systems does not, however, of itself enable the outside observer to obtain an accurate picture of the functioning of federalism in the United States. For, as Viscount Haldane, L.C., pointed out in an important case, not all federal governmental systems are alike. 'In a loose sense the word "federal" may be used...to describe any arrangement under which self-contained States agree to delegate their powers to a common Government with a view to entirely new Constitutions even of the States themselves. But the natural and literal interpretation of the word confines its application to cases in which these States, while agreeing on a measure of delegation, yet in the main continue to preserve their original Constitutions.'[2]

Within the British Commonwealth itself there are examples of both

1 Dicey, *Law of the Constitution* (9th ed. 1939), 139.
2 *Attorney-General* v. *Colonial Sugar Refining Co. Ltd.*, [1914] A.C. 237, 253.

types. The system which prevails in Canada is a good illustration of the first kind of federation. 'Now, as regards Canada, the second of the resolutions, passed at Quebec in October, 1864, on which the British North America Act was founded, shows that what was in the minds of those who agreed on the resolutions was a general Government charged with matters of common interest, and new and merely local Governments for the Provinces. The Provinces were to have fresh and much restricted Constitutions, their Governments being entirely remodelled. This plan was carried out by the Imperial statute of 1867.'[1] The Commonwealth of Australia, on the other hand, exemplifies the second type of federation referred to by Lord Haldane. The principle of the Australian Constitution is federal in the strict sense of that term, namely, in that the federalizing States, while agreeing to a delegation of a part of their powers to a common government, preserved in other respects their individual constitutions unaltered.[2]

The continuance in force of the State constitutions under the Australian organic law is of fundamental importance. In the Canadian system, both the national and State Governments derive all of their authority from the Constitution. By that instrument, 'a general power was given to the new Parliament of Canada to make laws for the peace, order, and good government of Canada without restriction to specific subjects, and excepting only the subjects specifically and exclusively assigned to the Provincial Legislatures by s. 92. There followed an enumeration of subjects which were to be dealt with by the Dominion Parliament, but this enumeration was not to restrict the generality of the power conferred on it.'[3] In other words the Federal Government in Canada possesses all legislative authority not expressly granted to the Provinces. The latter have no 'powers of legislation either inherent in them or dating from a time anterior to the Federation Act.... Whatever is not thereby given to the provincial legislatures rests with the [Dominion] parliament.'[4]

The situation in Australia is an entirely different one. The inherent legislative power there is vested in the States, whose Constitutions continued in force, rather than in the newly created Commonwealth Parliament. The authority possessed by the latter is solely that transferred to it under the Constitution by the federating Colonies. 'It is plain that excepting in so far as such powers were so transferred they remained exclusively vested in the States.'[5] The authority which is delegated to the Commonwealth Parliament 'is not conferred in general terms. It is, unlike the

1 [1914] A.C. at 253.   2 *Ibid.* at 238.   3 *Ibid.* at 253.
4 *Bank of Toronto* v. *Lambe* (1887), 12 App. Cas. 575, 587.
5 *Attorney-General* v. *Colonial Sugar Refining Co. Ltd.*, [1914] A.C. at 254

corresponding power conferred by s. 91 of the Canadian Constitution Act of 1867, restricted by the words which immediately follow it. These words are "with respect to", and then follows a specific list of enumerated subjects.[1] The powers not listed remain in the exclusive possession of the States. The Federal Government of Australia is thus one of enumerated powers, while the State Governments retain all authority not surrendered.

The same is true of the Federal Government of the United States. The framers of the Australian Constitution did, in fact, consciously follow the American example, in preference to that furnished by the Canadian system. In the American, as in the Australian, system, the States which made up the federation retained the sovereignty which they did not surrender to the national Government by their adoption of the Constitution. It cannot be denied, in the words of an acute English student, that 'when the fifty-five men who met at Philadelphia in 1787 drafted the Federal Constitution they were, in fact, giving birth to a single commonwealth'.[2] Yet 'none of the members of the Federal Convention would have dreamed of denying the character of sovereignty to any of the thirteen states which were forming a more perfect union'.[3] The result was that, as was later to be the case in Australia, the framers of the American Constitution vested the central Government only with those powers expressly enumerated in that instrument. All authority not conferred upon the Federal Government was retained by the individual States.

In the case already referred to, Lord Haldane described the governmental system provided for under the American Constitution as 'the true federal mode'.[4] And certainly the desire to establish a proper balance between the national and State Governments was one of the fundamental factors influencing the draftsmen of the American organic law. They sought to achieve such balance by ensuring that the central Government would not be so strong that the States would soon develop into mere dependencies of it. And they did this by limiting the Federal Government to those powers expressly granted to it, while the States could exercise all powers except those denied to them by the Constitution. It is the equilibrium which was thus established that called forth Lord Haldane's characterization quoted above.

This concept of federalism, which pervaded the governmental philosophy of the framers of the American Constitution, is one which is almost entirely foreign to the English constitutional system. To the American observer, indeed, English government is characterized by its completely unitary cast. It is true that even the English system is not dominated solely

1 *Ibid.* at 255.   2 Laski, *The American Democracy* (1948), 138.   3 *Ibid.*
4 *Attorney-General* v. *Colonial Sugar Refining Co. Ltd.*, [1914] A.C. 237, 253.

by a centralizing tendency. Such a system—i.e. one which is absolutely centralized—is, in fact, one which can exist only in theory; a State without any local government at all is inconceivable in practice. Yet, though local government may be of more importance in England than the outside observer, especially one trained in a federal system, at first realizes, it can hardly be denied that its sphere is still, by American standards, a most limited one. Central control over local activities exists in England to an extent that is still unheard of in the United States, even in an age that has witnessed a heretofore unprecedented expansion of authority in Washington. It may well be that centralization in England has never yet meant what it has meant in Continental countries—the building-up of a complete hierarchical order, with the central Government at the apex and the local authorities at the base in a position of complete subordination. But the difference is mainly one of method. Though the English system is characterized by methods of central control which are not as blunt as the definite subordination which prevails in a country like France, the extent of central supervision in it is, as a discerning commentator has pointed out, 'probably in fact as great as that assigned to a French Minister of the Interior'.[1]

MAIN FEATURES

Federalism in the United States, according to a leading authority on American constitutional law, embraces the following elements: (i) as in all federations, the union of a number of autonomous political entities (the States) for common purposes; (ii) the division of legislative powers between the national Government and the constituent States, a division which is governed by the rule that the former is a 'government of enumerated powers', while the latter are governments of 'residual powers'; (iii) the direct operation, for the most part, of each of these centres of government, within its assigned sphere, upon all persons and property within its territorial limits; (iv) the provision of each centre with the complete apparatus of law enforcement, both executive and judicial; and (v) the supremacy of the national Government within its assigned sphere over any conflicting assertion of State power.[2]

For the British reader to obtain a clearer picture of the main features of the federal system established by the American Constitution, a word will have to be said about each of these elements.

1 Sieghart, *Government by Decree* (1950), 95.
2 Corwin, *The Constitution of the United States of America: Analysis and Interpretation* (1952), xi. Professor Corwin also lists dual citizenship as a sixth element of American federalism. It does not, however, seem important enough to warrant separate treatment in the present work.

(1) *Union of autonomous States*

'We the People of the United States,' reads the Preamble of the American organic instrument, 'in Order to form a more perfect Union... do ordain and establish this Constitution.' Though this language may be evidence for the view that the Constitution emanated from the people, and was not the act of sovereign and independent States,[1] there appears to be little doubt but that, as a matter of practical reality, it was the States themselves, rather than the whole people of the United States, that formed the American union. The delegates to the Convention of 1787 that drew up the Constitution were appointed directly by the legislatures of the different States and ratification was by vote of conventions elected in each of the individual States. In many ways, indeed, the American nation was formed by the voluntary union of thirteen autonomous sovereigns, previously tied together only by the loose bonds of the confederation which had been formed after the Revolution. 'The Constitution', as Mr Justice Douglas has declared, 'is a compact between sovereigns.'[2]

It is true that the American States have not possessed many of the important attributes of sovereignty since the adoption of the Constitution. And the indissoluble character of the American Union was established beyond doubt after four bloody years of civil war by the defeat of the Southern States that had attempted to secede. But, as the United States Supreme Court stated in 1868, 'the perpetuity and indissolubility of the Union, by no means implies the loss of distinct and individual existence, or of the right of self-government by the States.... Under the Constitution, though the powers of the States were much restricted, still, all powers not delegated to the United States, nor prohibited to the States, are reserved to the States respectively, or to the people. And we have already had occasion to remark at this term, that "the people of each State compose a State, having its own government, and endowed with all the functions necessary to separate existence", and "that without the States in union, there could be no such political body as the United States". Not only therefore, can there be no loss of separate and independent autonomy to the States, through their union under the Constitution, but it may not unreasonably be said that the preservation of the States, and the maintenance of their governments are as much within the design and care of the Constitution, as the preservation of the Union and the Maintenance of the

---

1 *Ibid.* 59.
2 Dissenting, in *New York* v. *United States*, 326 U.S. 572, 595 (1946). But see the famous assertion to the contrary by Marshall, C.J., in *McCulloch* v. *Maryland*, 4 Wheat. 316, 403–4 (U.S. 1819).

National government. The Constitution, in all its provisions, looks to an indestructible Union, composed of indestructible States.'[1]

(2) *Division of powers between nation and States*

Legend has it that, at a critical moment in the proceedings of the Philadelphia Convention that drew up the American organic instrument, Alexander Hamilton, irked by obstacles to the national centralization which he so ardently desired, petulantly exclaimed that the States ought to be abolished.[2] Hamilton's exclamation was, however, uttered in the heat of anger at State obstructionism, and neither he nor anyone else at the Convention actually urged such a bold step. 'No political dreamer' of that time, as the highest American court put it almost a century and a half ago, 'was ever wild enough to think of breaking down the lines which separate the states and of compounding the American people into one common mass.'[3] On the contrary, if there was one thing that the framers of the American Constitution sought to do, it was to keep a significant place in the system they were creating for the States, whose delegates they were. All of the existing States were carried over into the new constitutional régime, with their names, boundaries and governments unaltered, and with functions that were still extensive. Furthermore, the Constitution authorized the Congress to admit new States to the union; and, from 1791 onwards, this power was exercised, as the different portions of the country became sufficiently developed, until the admission in 1912 of New Mexico and Arizona brought the number to the present forty-eight.[4]

It is clear, as the above demonstrates, that it was not at all the intention of the draftsmen of the Federal Constitution to do away with the separate States and out of their elements to form a single national State. 'The people of the country are not thrown into a single mass, under simply one government endowed with full powers wielded from one center.'[5] Nor was it the intent of the men of 1787 to reduce the States to mere administrative units. While acting to form the 'more perfect Union' which they felt necessary, they were clearly determined that it should be a Union not only of 'indestructible States',[6] but of States which should retain as much of their sovereignty as would not conflict with the functions of the national Government. 'No reasonable doubt as to this purpose can exist in the mind of one who reads the Federal Constitution. He finds certain defined powers granted to the national government. On the other hand, he finds the

1 *Texas* v. *White*, 7 Wall. 700, 725 (U.S. 1868).
2 Ogg and Ray, *Introduction to American Government* (9th ed. 1948), 62.
3 *McCulloch* v. *Maryland*, 4 Wheat. 316, 403 (U.S. 1819).
4 Ogg and Ray, *op. cit.* 62.   5 *Ibid.* 61.
6 *Texas* v. *White*, 7 Wall. 700, 725 (U.S. 1868).

existence of the States recognized, and certain express limitations put upon their powers.'[1]

The American constitutional system is thus based upon a division of power between the national Government and the States. As has already been pointed out, such division is grounded upon the principle that the Federal Government is a government of enumerated powers, limited to the authority delegated to it in the Constitution, while the States are governments of residual powers, retaining all of the authority not granted to the Government in Washington. This principle appears to be implicit even in the terms of the Constitution as it was originally drafted. Some doubts, however, having arisen on the point, the Tenth Amendment, ratified in 1791, expressly incorporated the principle into the organic law.[2] 'The Tenth Amendment', as the federal Supreme Court has told us, 'was intended to confirm the understanding of the people at the time the Constitution was adopted, that powers not granted to the United States were reserved to the States.'[3]

The principle given legal force in the Tenth Amendment to the Federal Constitution flows naturally from the origin of the American system in a union of autonomous States which surrendered only certain portions of their sovereignty to the central Government. The latter could, it was true, clearly exercise the powers which the States had relinquished. But the authority not thus renounced, the States retained for themselves.

If there has been one accepted constitutional rule in the American federal system, it has been that prescribing that the national Government is a 'government of enumerated powers'.[4] Indeed, as early as 1819, the Supreme Court of the United States asserted that 'The principle, that it [i.e. the Federal Government] can exercise only the powers granted to it, would seem too apparent, to have required to be enforced by all those arguments, which its enlightened friends, while it was depending before the people, found it necessary to urge; that principle is now universally admitted.'[5] It is, of course, true that the powers wielded by the Government in Washington today are immeasurably greater than they were at the time this assertion was made. And, to many people, they even appear, at some points, to have been carried much beyond the grants contained in the Constitution. In the eye of the law, however, as one treatise expresses

1 Burdick, *The Law of the American Constitution* (1922), 435.
2 The Tenth Amendment reads: 'The powers not delegated to the United States by the Constitution, nor prohibited by it to the States, are reserved to the States respectively, or to the people.'
3 *United States* v. *Sprague*, 282 U.S. 716, 733 (1931).
4 *Kansas* v. *Colorado*, 206 U.S. 46, 81 (1907).
5 *McCulloch* v. *Maryland*, 4 Wheat. 316, 405 (U.S. 1819).

it, whatever expansion in national authority has taken place 'has resulted solely from progressively wider and more penetrating applications of powers already possessed. President, Congress, and courts have no proper authority except such as can be found somewhere...within the four corners of the constitution.'[1]

Implied powers. What has just been said shows that the American system has been based upon what Professor Wheare terms 'the federal principle', i.e. the method of dividing powers so that the general and regional Governments are each co-ordinate and independent.[2] Under the Federal Constitution, State and nation has each had its respective domains marked out for it. And, to ensure against over-aggrandizement of the central Government, its powers were, we have seen, limited to those enumerated in the Constitution. All others were expressly declared in the Tenth Amendment to be reserved to the States, unless specifically prohibited to them. 'From the accepted doctrine that the United States is a government of delegated powers, it follows that those not expressly granted, or reasonably to be implied from such as are conferred, are reserved to the states or to the people. To forestall any suggestion to the contrary, the Tenth Amendment was adopted. The same proposition, otherwise stated, is that powers not granted are prohibited.'[3]

However, it should not be thought from the above that federal authority in the American Constitution is limited to that expressly granted in that instrument. Though the Federal Government is one of enumerated powers, its authority is not described in minute detail, and it has been held to possess, not simply those powers that are specifically or expressly given it, but also those necessary and proper for the effective exercise of such express powers.[4] This has been true ever since the landmark case of *McCulloch* v. *Maryland*,[5] decided by the United States Supreme Court in 1819.

That case involved the constitutionality of the incorporation by the Federal Congress of the second Bank of the United States in 1816, which served as a depository for Government funds and which was authorized to print bank-notes which would serve as a convenient medium of exchange. Nowhere in the American Constitution is the Federal Government given the express authority to establish such a national bank. 'This government is acknowledged by all, to be one of enumerated powers', conceded the opinion of John Marshall, the great Chief Justice, who, more than anyone

1 Ogg and Ray, *op. cit.* 65.

2 Wheare, *Federal Government* (3rd ed. 1953), 11.

3 *United States* v. *Butler*, 297 U.S. 1, 68 (1936).

4 Willoughby, *Principles of the Constitutional Law of the United States* (2nd ed. 1935), 54.   5 4 Wheat. 316 (U.S. 1819).

else, has left his imprint upon the development of American constitutional law. 'Among the enumerated powers we do not find that of establishing a bank or creating a corporation. But there is no phrase in the instrument which...excludes incidental or implied powers; and which requires that everything granted shall be expressly and minutely described.'[1]

Looking to the express language of the Constitution, the Chief Justice found delegated there the powers to impose and collect taxes; to borrow money; to regulate commerce; to declare and conduct a war; and to raise and support armies and navies. 'The sword and the purse, all the external relations, and no inconsiderable portion of the industry of the nation, are entrusted to its government.'[2] If the establishment of a national bank would aid the Government in its exercise of these granted powers, the authority to set one up would be implied. 'We admit, as all must admit,' declared Chief Justice Marshall in an oft quoted portion of his opinion, 'that the powers of the government are limited, and that its limits are not to be transcended. But we think the sound construction of the constitution must allow to the national legislature that discretion, with respect to the means by which the powers it confers are to be carried into execution, which will enable that body to perform the high duties assigned to it, in the manner most beneficial to the people. Let the end be legitimate, let it be within the scope of the constitution, and all means which are appropriate, which are plainly adapted to that end, which are not prohibited, but consist with the letter and spirit of the constitution, are constitutional.'[3]

The doctrine of implied powers thus enunciated by John Marshall was of the utmost importance for the effective operation of the fledgling Federal Government. Under delegations of authority as undetailed as those contained in the American Constitution, the effective functioning of the Government in Washington would be rendered most difficult if its powers were limited to the bare language of the constitutional grants. The doctrine of implied powers has permitted the central Government to deal with matters not specifically mentioned in the Constitution, by enabling it to exercise, not only the authority expressly conferred, but also all powers necessary and proper for the exercise of such express authority.

(3) *Direct operation of States and nation upon all within their territorial limits*

According to the eminent authority on American constitutional law already referred to, one of the salient features of the federal system provided for in 1787, which at the outset marked it off most sharply from all preceding federations, was the direct operation of both the State and national Governments, within their assigned spheres, upon all persons and

1 *Ibid.* at 405–6.   2 *Ibid.* at 407.   3 *Ibid.* at 421.

property within their respective territorial limits.[1] This feature was of cardinal significance, for it enabled the national Government to attain a position far superior to that of its counterpart in all prior federations. In them, the member States generally agreed to obey the mandates of a common government for certain stipulated purposes, but retained to themselves the right of ordaining and enforcing the laws of the union. This was, indeed, the system provided for in the Confederation of the American States which was set up after the Revolution. It was the fundamental weakness of the central Government set up under the Articles of Confederation that led the men of 1787 to make the basic change under discussion.

In the American system, the Federal Government has been vested with authority, not only over the member States, as was true of previous federations, but also over their citizens. This means that the Government in Washington need not depend upon the concurrence of the individual States for compliance with its commands to be secured. Its mandates operate directly upon all persons and property within the territory of the union. And those subject thereto must comply, just as they must obey the laws of the State in which they reside. The result, of course, is that each individual in the United States is subject to the decrees of two Governments, those which emanate from Washington and those which issue from the capital of his State. 'While all are directly under one national government for certain purposes, they are also under one or another of forty-eight state governments which are not mere arms of the national government, but instrumentalities of original, separate, and to a considerable extent independent, political units.'[2]

(4) *Possession by States and nation of the complete apparatus of law enforcement*

What makes the feature of the American system just discussed—i.e. the power of both State and national Governments, in their proper spheres, to operate directly on all within their territorial jurisdiction—of such great practical significance is the provision of each centre of government with its own complete apparatus of law enforcement, both executive and judicial. Each centre is consequently able by itself to ensure that its laws and decrees will be executed. This gives to both States and nation a degree of independence of each other which neither could attain to if it were dependent upon the other for the execution of its mandates.

It is often difficult for the English observer, accustomed to the functioning of his own unitary system of government, to realize that American federalism involves what amounts to an almost complete duplication

1 Corwin, *op. cit.* xi.   2 Ogg and Ray, *op. cit.* 61.

of governmental services. Instead of the single national Government which characterizes the English system, there are in the United States really forty-nine individual Governments—that in Washington and those in the forty-eight States. And each of these Governments is provided with the complete accoutrements of government; each is composed of fully developed legislative, executive and judicial branches. Each State 'has a written constitution providing for three departments of government, with a legislature of two houses[1] elected by popular vote, and a popularly elected governor as head of its executive department. Each state has a judicial system not essentially dissimilar in external organization from that of the other states.'[2]

It is easy for the English observer to comprehend the importance of the Federal Government in the American system. And it is not difficult for him to obtain an essentially accurate picture of its functioning. What is harder is for him to secure a similar comprehension of the workings of government at the State level. For it is difficult for him to understand a system in which governmental power, instead of being concentrated in the unitary source with which he is familiar, is dichotomized. Not unnaturally, he tends to liken the Federal Government to the central Government with which he is familiar, and he consequently tends to think of it as the only Government of real significance in the American system. Such undue magnification of the Federal Government at the expense of the States is, however, inconsistent with the true working of American federalism. The impact of government upon the average American even now occurs more frequently upon the State than upon the federal level. And, though it is well known that the powers of Washington have increased prodigiously during the present century, what is not so generally realized is that there has also been an important augmentation of State authority during the same period. 'To confirm this fact of the enormous growth of state powers', declares a recent treatise, 'one has only to compare the list of things that his own state is now doing—in the fields of taxation and finance, education, public health and safety, social insurance, conservation of resources, regulation of transportation and trade, control of elections, and what not—with the activities of any one of the states a hundred, or even fifty, years ago.'[3]

Even with the constant expansion of federal authority that has occurred in the past few decades, it is still the States which perform many of the most essential governmental functions in the American system. Thus, to

1 It should be noted that the State of Nebraska now has a unicameral legislature.
2 Dodd, *State Government* (2nd ed. 1928), 3.
3 Ogg and Ray, *op. cit.* 66.

cite a few significant examples, public education is provided for almost entirely by the States and their political subdivisions, and the same is true of most health and welfare activities thus far undertaken by Government in the United States. Poor relief, unemployment insurance, workmen's compensation, a wide variety of public health activities, services for the benefit of agriculture and the conservation of natural resources—all of these are provided for by the American States, though, it may be true, subject, in recent years, to an ever-increasing degree of federal supervision in some of these fields. In addition, since, in the American system, as we shall see, it is the States that are vested with authority over commerce that is not interstate in character, they are able to regulate their own local economic systems. Most States have laws regulating banking, insurance, public utilities, local transportation, as well as various occupations and professions. And, finally, law enforcement through police officers is almost entirely left to the States and localities within them. It may be the Federal Bureau of Investigation that receives the larger newspaper headlines; but the vast majority of the police work in the American system is actually performed at the local rather than at the national level.

The co-ordinate functioning of State government, endowed with fully developed legislative, executive and judicial branches is a feature of American federalism that must constantly be borne in mind, even though, for practical reasons, the attention of the observer comparing constitutions is focussed primarily upon the Government in Washington. 'The power and prestige of the national government must not be permitted to blind us to the immense importance of the states in our constitutional and political system. After all, our nation is the *United States* of America; and while the activities of the national government attract more attention and get more headlines in the newspapers, the states, on their part, now perform more tasks, spend more money, and provide more services than at any time in the past. Operations of the national government come close to the average citizen a good deal more frequently than they once did—for example, when he pays his federal income tax, makes his social security contribution, is drafted for military service, or even mails a letter. But the governments which chiefly guard and control him from the cradle to the grave are rather those of his state and its subdivisions. . . . Vast as is the machinery of government centering in Washington, it would be vaster still, and its operations more cumbersome and congested, if the states did not, in their respective spheres, take care of by far the larger proportion of the work to be done.'[1]

1 Ogg and Ray, *op. cit.* 77.

(5) *Supremacy of national power*

A system like the American one—in which there coexist both Federal and State Governments, each capable of exercising most important governmental functions—must, if it is to work in practice, make provision for settling conflicts between States and nation. The mere existence of two sets of governments, operating in the same territorial area, makes conflicts between the two almost inevitable. Even if each order of government is wholly unmotivated by a desire to extend its own authority, there will always be cases where the action of one may impinge upon the competence of the other. Unless some means is provided for resolving conflicts of competence, the federal system itself may break down.

The American constitutional system has dealt with this problem of conflicts between States and nation by the doctrine of the supremacy of the Federal Government within the sphere assigned to it. Such supremacy is expressly provided for by Article VI of the Federal Constitution, which provides: 'This Constitution, and the Laws of the United States which shall be made in Pursuance thereof; and all Treaties made, or which shall be made, under the Authority of the United States, shall be the supreme Law of the Land; and the Judges in every State shall be bound thereby, any Thing in the Constitution or Laws of any State to the Contrary notwithstanding.'

It is the principle of national supremacy thus enunciated in the American organic instrument which has, in the long run, ensured the effective working of the federal system set up by it. It prevents the national Government from becoming subordinate to the States in the manner that had destroyed the effectiveness of the Confederation of the thirteen States that had originally been formed after the Revolution.

The effect of the national supremacy clause of the Constitution is to make it impossible for the States to interfere with the functioning of the Federal Government. On the contrary, the mandates of Washington are to prevail in all cases unless they themselves are unconstitutional. 'The states', declared Chief Justice John Marshall, 'have no power...to retard, impede, burden, or in any manner control, the operations of the constitutional laws enacted by congress to carry into execution the powers vested in the general government. This is, we think, the unavoidable consequence of that supremacy which the constitution has declared.'[1]

The outstanding feature of the American federal system, states the leading English study of federalism, is the footing of equality upon which the general authority and regional authorities stand. 'The principle of

1 *McCulloch* v. *Maryland*, 4 Wheat. 316, 436 (U.S. 1819).

organization upon which the American association is based is that of the division of powers between distinct and co-ordinate governments.'[1] This is, in many respects, an accurate description of the system set in operation by the Federal Constitution. We have already seen how the framers of that document clearly intended the States to continue to be important theatres of governmental action. And, under the doctrine of so-called 'dual federalism', soon to be discussed, the co-ordinate nature of States and nation was strongly emphasized.

At the same time, it is important to bear in mind that the national supremacy clause of the Constitution prevents the principle of equality between the two centres of government from being carried to its ultimate extreme. The States are co-ordinate and independent only when they act in fields outside those in which the Federal Government can act. But, while the States may be able freely to act in such fields, their spheres of action are circumscribed by the basic rule that whatever the central Government ordains—within the broad and constantly expanding area of its authority—is *supreme law*, enforceable as such and binding no less upon State executives, legislatures and judiciary than upon officers of the nation itself. If State action is shown to be incompatible with any legitimate exercise of power by the national Government, it loses all claim to validity.[2] And this is true even though the State action in question is taken within a sphere in which the States could otherwise act.

The effect of the Constitution upon State action of this type is shown by the leading case of *Gibbons* v. *Ogden*,[3] where the American Supreme Court held that certain statutes of New York granting an exclusive right to use steam navigation on the waters of the State were null and void so far as they applied to vessels licensed by the Federal Government to engage in coastwise trade. 'It has been contended', said Chief Justice Marshall, 'that if a law, passed by a state, in the exercise of its acknowledged sovereignty, comes into conflict with a law passed by Congress in pursuance of the constitution, they affect the subject, and each other, like equal opposing powers. But the framers of our constitution foresaw this state of things, and provided for it, by declaring the supremacy not only of itself, but of the laws made in pursuance of it. The nullity of any act, inconsistent with the constitution, is produced by the declaration that the constitution is the supreme law. The appropriate application of that part of the clause which confers the same supremacy on laws and treaties, is to such acts of the state legislatures as do not transcend their powers, but though enacted in the execution of acknowledged state powers, interfere with, or are

---

1 Wheare, *op. cit.* 2.   2 Ogg and Ray, *op. cit.* 71.
3 9 Wheat. 1 (U.S. 1824).

contrary to, the laws of Congress, made in pursuance of the constitution, or some treaty made under the authority of the United States. In every such case, the act of Congress, or the treaty, is supreme; and the law of the state, though enacted in the exercise of powers not controverted, must yield to it.'[1]

JUDICIAL ENFORCEMENT

According to the authority already referred to,[2] the elements just discussed constitute the main features of American federalism. It would seem, however, that there has been left out from his enumeration that feature which is, in many ways, the most characteristic trait of the American system— namely, the enforcement of the principles of federalism by the judiciary.

A federal State is, of necessity, a law State *par excellence*. 'That a federal system...can flourish only among communities imbued with a legal spirit and trained to reverence the law is as certain as can be any conclusion of political speculation.'[3] For a federal system properly to operate, there must be some machinery set up to ensure that the division of authority laid down in the organic instrument is adhered to. As it was expressed during the Convention of 1787, which drew up the American Constitution, if the weaknesses which had rendered ineffective the Confederation of States established after the Revolution were to be avoided in the new system, the latter must incorporate 'a coercive principle'—the real question was whether it should be 'a coercion of law, or a coercion of arms'.[4]

In the early history of the American Republic, the answer to this question was not entirely certain. During the past century, however, it has become firmly established that the line between national and State powers was to be drawn by the federal Supreme Court. And the role of the court, in this respect, is essentially that of giving effect to the national supremacy clause of the Constitution. 'This clause may be called the central clause of the constitution, because without it the whole system would be unwieldy, if not impracticable. Draw out this particular bolt, and the machinery falls to pieces. In these words the constitution is plainly made not merely a declaration, a manifesto, dependent for its life and usefulness on the passing will of statesmen or of people, but a fundamental law, enforceable like any other law in courts.'[5]

It is the United States Supreme Court, implementing the supremacy clause through the exercise of its power of judicial review, that is thus the ultimate arbiter of the federal system. And few, if any, functions of that tribunal are of greater practical importance. It is the highest court which

1 *Ibid.* at 210–11. 2 Corwin, *op. cit.* xi.
3 Dicey, *op. cit.* 179. 4 Quoted in Corwin, *op. cit.* xi.
5 McLaughlin, *The Confederation and the Constitution* (1905), 247.

ensures that national authority is not frustrated by a 'crazy-quilt'[1] of conflicting local laws. And, at the same time, it is that body which guarantees that the States will not ultimately be swallowed up by the Government in Washington. It is, indeed, difficult to conceive how a federal system like the American one could work in practice if the power now exercised by the Supreme Court were not vested in some tribunal like it. 'What is essential for federal government is that some impartial body, independent of general and regional governments, should decide upon the meaning of the division of powers.... No alternative scheme with less inconveniences seems possible, consistently with maintaining the federal principle.'[2]

DUAL FEDERALISM DOCTRINE

The division of power between Washington and the State Governments provided for in the Federal Constitution has, in practice, been dominated by what has been termed the doctrine of *dual federalism*. That doctrine was based upon the notion of two mutually exclusive, reciprocally limiting, fields of power, the governmental occupants of which confronted each other as absolute equals.[3] Under it, both Federal and State Governments have marked out for them a rigidly defined area of power. So long as they remain within their respective boundaries, their acts are valid and will not be questioned by the courts. But if they overstep those bounds, then their acts are *ultra vires* and void. This conception of federalism is based upon the principle of competition between States and nation. Each is the occupant of a particular field of power, within which, subject to certain exceptions where there is concurrent authority, it alone has the exclusive power to act. In this view, the proper equilibrium necessary for the functioning of a federal system is secured and maintained by the strict demarcation of federal and State authority. States and nation are conceived of as equal rivals, and unless there is rigid delimitation of their respective competences, it is feared that the union itself may be disrupted by their rivalry. Especially is this true so far as the expansion of federal authority is concerned. The reserved powers of the States must be jealously guarded, lest they be swallowed up by the Government in Washington.

The complete cleavage of State and federal power required by this conception of federalism has, of course, been most difficult to obtain in practice. The line between State and national authority in the American Constitution is not drawn with anything like mathematical precision. The

1 The term used by Frankfurter, J., concurring, in *Morgan* v. *Virginia*, 328 U.S. 373, 388 (1946).　　　　2 Wheare, *op. cit.* 66-7.
3 Corwin, *The Commerce Power versus States' Rights* (1936), 135.

central Government is vested with certain express powers, and all other authority is, as we have seen, reserved to the States. In some cases, the specific grant is clearly intended to confer exclusive authority over the subject in the Federal Government. Such is the case, for example, with the power to declare war. In other cases, the grant to the nation is held not to exclude some concurrent exercise of authority over the particular field by the States. This is true, for example, with regard to the power vested in the Congress to regulate commerce. 'The constitution', stated a member of the United States Supreme Court over a century ago, 'containing a grant of powers, in many instances, similar to those already existing in the state governments, and some of those being of vital importance also to state authority and state legislation, it is not to be admitted, that a mere grant of such powers, in affirmative terms, to congress, does, *per se*, transfer an exclusive sovereignty on such subjects to the latter. On the contrary, a reasonable interpretation of that instrument necessarily leads to the conclusion, that the powers so granted are never exclusive of similar powers existing in the states, unless where the constitution has expressly, in terms, given an exclusive power to congress, or the exercise of a like power is prohibited to the states, or there is a direct repugnancy or incompatibility in the exercise of it by the states.'[1]

In those cases where a particular field is subject to the regulatory authority of both States and nation, the concept of dual federalism has required a line to be drawn dividing the area in which the Federal Government could operate from that over which the States had exclusive jurisdiction. In the American constitutional system, the drawing of this line, as is well known, has been considered a judicial function, to be exercised ultimately by the Supreme Court in Washington. 'It is unquestionably no easy task', declared the Chief Justice of that tribunal in 1847, 'to mark by a certain and definite line the division between foreign and domestic commerce, and to fix the precise point, in relation to every important article, where the paramount power of Congress terminates, and that of the State begins. The constitution itself does not attempt to define these limits. They cannot be determined by the laws of Congress or the States, as neither can by its own legislation enlarge its own powers, or restrict those of the other. And as the constitution itself does not draw the line, the question is necessarily one for judicial decision.'[2]

The resolution of conflicts between federal and State authority is thus, like the determination of most constitutional issues in the American system, ultimately a judicial question. In deciding it, the federal Supreme

1 *Houston* v. *Moore*, 5 Wheat. 1, 48 (U.S. 1820).
2 *License Cases*, 5 How. 504, 574 (U.S. 1847).

Court has, in the past, appeared to be most concerned with the need to maintain the concept of dual federalism, under which an equal balance is kept between nation and State, with each having marked out for it its own exclusive area of jurisdiction. This has led the court to deal strictly with federal exercises of power which were seen to infringe upon the domain reserved to the States. For the great fear of those anxious to preserve dual federalism has, since the Civil War put an end to the extreme pretensions of the advocates of States' rights, been the danger of expansion of federal authority to an extent which would destroy the even equilibrium between States and nation.

REGULATION OF COMMERCE

The working of dual federalism in practice can be seen most clearly in the decisions of the American Supreme Court dealing with the regulation of commerce by the Federal Government. Article I, section 8, of the American Constitution confers upon the Congress the power 'to regulate Commerce with foreign Nations, and among the several States, and with the Indian Tribes'. It is clear from this provision that the control of inter-state and foreign commerce is vested in the Federal Government. But not all commerce is interstate or foreign in character. And the States are not prohibited from exercising regulatory authority over all other commerce. 'The grant of commercial power to Congress', declared the Supreme Court in an important case, 'does not contain any terms which expressly exclude the States from exercising an authority over its subject-matter. If they are excluded it must be because the nature of the power, thus granted to Congress, requires that a similar authority should not exist in the States.'[1]

The power to regulate commerce, in the American system, depends upon the distinction between interstate and intrastate commerce. It is only the former that falls within the competence of the Federal Government under the commerce clause of the Constitution. It is, as one of the greatest of American Chief Justices has pointed out, 'clear, that the power of Congress over this subject does not extend further than the regulation of commerce with foreign nations and among the several States; and that beyond these limits the States have never surrendered their power over trade and commerce, and may still exercise it, free from any controlling power on the part of the general government. Every State, therefore, may regulate its own internal traffic, according to its own judgment and upon its own views of the interest and well-being of its citizens.'[2]

1 *Cooley* v. *Board of Port Wardens*, 12 How. 299, 318 (U.S. 1851).
2 *License Cases*, 5 How. 504, 574 (U.S. 1847), *per* Taney, C.J.

Under the concept of dual federalism, as has been indicated, State and nation each has its own exclusive area of authority. 'The general government, and the States, although both exist within the same territorial limits, are separate and distinct sovereignties, acting separately and independently of each other, within their respective spheres. The former in its appropriate sphere is supreme; but the States within the limits of their powers not granted, or, in the language of the tenth amendment, "reserved," are as independent of the general government as that government within its sphere is independent of the States.'[1] It follows, therefore, that, so far as the regulation of commerce is concerned, the Federal Government cannot infringe upon the field of local commerce reserved to the States.

But the distinction between interstate and intrastate commerce is nowhere defined in the American Constitution. Nor, in the American system, is the line one which has been drawn by the Federal Government itself. The position of the American judiciary, under the doctrine of judicial review of the constitutionality of laws, has made them the ultimate arbiters of disputes between federal and State power. And it cannot be denied, as has already been pointed out, that the American courts, concerned primarily with preserving dual federalism against undue encroachments by the Government in Washington, have, until recently, drawn the line in the field of commerce, as in other fields, strictly against the exercise of federal regulatory authority.

As good a case as any to illustrate this is *Hammer* v. *Dagenhart*,[2] usually known as the *Child Labor Case*, one of the *causes célèbres* of American constitutional law. It involved the constitutionality of an Act of Congress which forbade the transportation in interstate commerce of goods made in a factory which employed children under a specified age. The purpose of the Congress in passing this law was to aid in the suppression of child labour by denying the markets of interstate commerce to those who sought to profit from it. This, however, the Supreme Court held, was beyond the power of the federal legislature. By its enactment of this statute, Congress was seeking primarily to regulate the manner in which manufacturing establishments were carried on. This was essentially a matter of local concern whose regulation was reserved to the States. 'In interpreting the Constitution', reads the opinion of the court, 'it must never be forgotten that the Nation is made up of States to which are entrusted the powers of local government. And to them and to the people the powers not expressly delegated to the National Government are reserved.... The power of the States to regulate their purely internal affairs

1 *The Collector* v. *Day*, 11 Wall. 113, 124 (U.S. 1870).
2 247 U.S. 251 (1918).

by such laws as seem wise to the local authority is inherent and has never been surrendered to the general government.... To sustain this statute would not be in our judgment a recognition of the lawful exertion of congressional authority over interstate commerce, but would sanction an invasion by the federal power of the control of a matter purely local in its character, and over which no authority has been delegated to Congress in conferring the power to regulate commerce among the States.'[1]

In *Hammer* v. *Dagenhart*, it should be noted, the Act at issue clearly purported to be limited to the confines of the express power of the Congress to regulate interstate commerce. It did not in terms seek to interfere with the authority of the States over local production. 'The act', declared Mr Justice Holmes, in one of his most celebrated dissenting opinions, 'does not meddle with anything belonging to the States. They may regulate their internal affairs and their domestic commerce as they like. But when they seek to send their products across the State line they are no longer within their rights.'[2] With this opinion, the majority of the court refused to agree. 'In our view the necessary effect of this act is, by means of a prohibition against the movement in interstate commerce of ordinary commercial commodities, to regulate the hours of labor of children in factories and mines within the States, a purely state authority.'[3]

INFLUENCE OF 'LAISSEZ-FAIRE'

What was the practical consequence of the American Supreme Court's decision in the *Child Labor Case*? 'If there is any matter', asserted Justice Holmes in his dissent, 'upon which civilized countries have agreed—far more unanimously than they have with regard to intoxicants and some other matters over which this country is now aroused—it is the evil of premature and excessive child labor.'[4] Yet it seems clear that the virtual result of the decision in *Hammer* v. *Dagenhart* was to render ineffective attempts at the governmental regulation of child labour in the United States.

It is true that the court's decision did not affect the authority of the individual States to control production and commerce within their own boundaries. But State authority must necessarily end at the State limits and is hardly competent to cope with economic activity which, for the most part, extends over more than one State. In addition, regulation limited to that exerted by the States must, of necessity, vary from State to State. State control is most unlikely to have the uniform character necessary for effective economic regulation. 'Hammer v. Dagenhart creates

1 247 U.S. at 275.   2 *Ibid.* at 281.   3 *Ibid.* at 276.   4 *Ibid.* at 280.

therefore a defect of power of great significance. It means that so long as any state chooses to permit the use of child labor in the manufacture of goods within its borders it may send those goods into every other state to enter into competition with their own goods made under higher standards, and neither the states thus adversely affected nor Congress has any power to remedy the situation.'[1]

If a practice like child labour is effectively to be proscribed, it must be by regulation that is national in character. Under the *Child Labor Case*, however, such national regulation was practically precluded. In effect, then, the result of that case was to prevent effectual regulation of child labour in the United States.

The result reached by the American Supreme Court in cases like *Hammer* v. *Dagenhart* fitted in perfectly with the *laissez-faire* theory of governmental function which dominated political and economic thinking in the United States before the great depression of the early 1930's. To bar federal intervention in a case like the *Child Labor Case* was to exclude the possibility of any effective regulation in such a case. This was, of course, exactly what was demanded by the advocates of *laissez-faire*. To them, the economic system could function efficiently only if it was permitted to operate free from governmental interference. The concept of dual federalism, as it was applied by the Supreme Court, was a necessary complement of *laissez-faire* in the United States. By rigidly excluding the Federal Government from exercising regulatory authority over a subject such as that involved in the *Child Labor Case*, on the ground that it was within the sphere exclusively reserved to the States, the American Supreme Court virtually decreed that the subject of child labour should be left only to whatever controls were afforded by the workings of an unrestrained system of *laissez-faire*.

By the court's decision in the *Child Labor Case*, there was, in reality, created what one commentator has aptly termed a 'realm of no-power... —the very Utopia of *Laissez-Faireism*! And all these results sprang from a conception of the federal relationship which regards the National Government and the states as rival governments bent on mutual frustration, and on a conception of the judicial role which makes it the supreme duty of the Court to maintain the two centers of government in theoretical possession of their accustomed powers, however incapable either might be in fact of exercising them.'[2]

The desire to maintain dual federalism as a necessary complement of

1 Dickinson, '"Defect of Power" in Constitutional Law', in *Selected Essays on Constitutional Law* (1938), vol. III, 9.

2 Corwin, *Constitutional Revolution, Ltd.* (1941), 99.

laissez-faire was the primary motive behind Supreme Court decisions like *Hammer* v. *Dagenhart* which appeared unduly to limit the authority of the national Government. 'Indeed, maintenance of the Federal Equilibrium became... the be-all and end-all of judicial review.'[1] Such desire is, however, much weaker today than it was half a century ago. Contemporary public opinion has required Government in the United States, as in most other parts of the world, to take an ever-growing direct interest in matters that were formerly thought to be beyond its scope. Active intervention by the State in social and economic affairs, such as is felt to be necessary at the present time, can, as a practical matter, normally best be carried on upon a national, rather than a purely local, scale. Business in America is today nation-wide in scope, and regulation limited to State boundaries would prove futile to cope with most economic abuses. In addition, the uniformity needed for effective regulation could hardly be secured by individual regulatory laws on the part of each of the forty-eight American States.

Until the need for national intervention became acute, it is not surprising that the American Supreme Court adhered to the concept of equilibrium between States and nation that had dominated the thinking of the framers of the Constitution. And when expansion of federal authority became essential, if the social and economic problems of the present century were to be dealt with adequately, the Supreme Court, as we shall see, like the rest of the country, abandoned, albeit somewhat tardily, the concept of dual federalism and upheld the growth of national power. That is, however, a matter which is fully dealt with later on in this book,[2] for it is one of the modern developments in American constitutional law to which Part II is devoted.

1 Corwin, *op. cit.* 99.   2 *Infra*, ch. VI.

Chapter III

THE CONGRESS

'The power and jurisdiction of Parliament, says Sir Edward Coke, is so transcendent and absolute, that it cannot be confined, either for causes or persons within any bounds.'[1] This doctrine of parliamentary supremacy is the dominant characteristic of British political institutions. Under it, according to the almost proverbial English aphorism, 'Parliament can do everything but make a woman a man, and a man a woman'.[2] It is its sovereign position in this respect that sharply differentiates the legislature in Britain from its counterpart in the United States. The existence of a written constitution in that country, whose provisions are enforced by the courts, has prevented the American Congress from asserting for itself anything like the supreme status assumed by its counterpart in Britain. Like the other organs of the Federal Government, the Congress possesses only the powers expressly or impliedly granted to it by the Constitution. And, if it acts beyond the terms of the grant in the fundamental law, its acts will be set aside by the American courts as *ultra vires* and unconstitutional.

Yet, though the American legislature is not sovereign in the British sense, its position in the federal governmental structure should not be minimized. To the Congress is delegated all of the legislative power conferred by the American Constitution. The very first section of Article I of that instrument provides that 'All legislative Powers herein granted shall be vested in a Congress of the United States, which shall consist of a Senate and House of Representatives'. Because of the doctrine of the separation of powers, which, as we have seen,[3] has been of such significance in the American system, this means that the Congress alone is the source of all federal legislation. Although, under modern constitutional theory, the executive, too, may exercise authority which is legislative in character, its powers in this respect are entirely subordinate ones. They must find their source in delegations from the Congress, or else they cannot validly be exercised.

It is hardly necessary to impress upon the modern jurist the importance of a governmental organ, like the American Congress, which is the source of all legislative authority. 'Formerly', as Dean Pound informs us, 'it was

[1] Blackstone, *Commentaries*, vol. 1, 160.
[2] And, legally speaking, of course, Parliament can even do these things.
[3] *Supra*, p. 12.

argued that common law was superior to legislation because it was customary and rested upon the consent of the governed. Today we recognize...
that legislation is the more truly democratic form of law-making. We see
in legislation the more direct and accurate expression of the general will.'[1]
Living, as he does, in an age of ever-increasing exercises of legislative
authority, it is not difficult for the contemporary constitutional lawyer to
appreciate the crucial significance of the law-making organ in the governmental structure. A study of American constitutional law which did not
seek to give some description of the organization and functioning of the
American Congress would, indeed, contain a gap which would destroy its
usefulness as a descriptive account. As it was aptly expressed by Woodrow
Wilson in his now classic work, *Congressional Government*, 'As the House
of Commons is the central object of examination in every study of the
English Constitution, so should Congress be in every study of our own.
Any one who is unfamiliar with what Congress actually does and how it
does it, with all its duties and all its occupations, with all its devices of
management and resources of power, is very far from a knowledge of the
constitutional system under which we live; and to every one who knows
these things that knowledge is near.'[2]

FUNCTIONS

'We are all familiar with the observation', declared a high executive
official in 1945 to a committee of the American Congress charged with
inquiring into the problem of legislative reorganization, 'that this is a
different sort of world from that which existed when the Constitutional
Convention devised the framework of our Government. Yet we still lack
a penetrating and practical restatement of the role of representative assemblies in the light of the changed problems with which they deal and
the altered conditions under which they operate. We are up against the
fact that legislative bodies have not changed very much but the kinds of
problems with which they must cope have changed radically. Your own
talents and the keenest minds you can command could very well be
devoted to rethinking the functions of the Congress under present conditions. A sound reformulation of the role of the representative body is basic
to all the work of your committee. Only on such a basis can one develop
standards by which to judge and develop proposals for changes in organization, procedure, staffing, and other matters.'[3]

1 Pound, 'Common law and legislation', 21 *Harvard L. Rev.* (1908), 383, 406.
2 Wilson, *Congressional Government* (10th ed. 1894), 57.
3 H. D. Smith, Director of the Bureau of the Budget, in *Hearings before the Joint
Committee on the Organization of Congress* (1946), 670.

As that organ of the Federal Government which alone is vested with the power to enact laws, the primary province of the Congress is, of course, to legislate. It would, however, be erroneous to think of the functions of a modern legislative assembly solely in terms of law-making. 'The political philosopher of these days of self-government', wrote Woodrow Wilson in 1884, in criticizing the extent to which the work of the Congress was then devoted almost exclusively to legislation, 'has...something more than a doubt with which to gainsay the usefulness of a sovereign representative body which confines itself to legislation to the exclusion of all other functions.... Quite as important as legislation is vigilant oversight of administration; and even more important than legislation is the instruction and guidance in political affairs which the people might receive from a body which kept all national concerns suffused in a broad daylight of discussion. There is no similar legislature in existence which is so shut up to the one business of law-making as is our Congress.'[1]

It cannot be denied that there is a great deal of truth in this criticism of a representative assembly whose time is spent solely in passing laws. Important though the legislative function itself may be, a legislative body is hardly worthy of the title of Congress or Parliament if it merely grinds out legislation as a sausage-maker grinds out sausages.

Under contemporary conditions, the national legislature is the one great forum of expression which can be reached by the individual citizen. His congressman or his member of Parliament is the one national official who is in contact with, and responsible to, a relatively small local area. It is through its representative in the national assembly alone that the locality is normally able to make its views heard on the national level. But the legislative body is more than a 'committee of grievances' where those represented can ventilate their opinions and complaints. It is even more important as a moulder than as a receptacle of public opinion. Its job in this respect is to enlighten and educate by ensuring adequate discussion of the important issues before the nation. The debate in the legislature should clarify those issues and enable the nation intelligently to support or oppose the position finally taken in the two chambers.

As consequential as its position as the forum of the nation is the modern legislature's role as overseer of the administration. It is almost a truism that the critical point of present-day governmental developments is the consistent growth of executive authority. The type of regulatory activity which contemporary public opinion requires the State to engage in can, as a practical matter, be carried on only by the executive branch of the government. For its officers to operate effectively in the administration of

1 Wilson, *op. cit.* 295, 297.

the vast regulatory and social service schemes undertaken by the State, they must be vested with large areas of discretionary authority. The delegation of powers to the executive in a particular field does not, however, relieve the legislature of responsibility over that field. 'The Congress does not really get rid of a subject by delegating powers to the Executive.'[1] The consistent transfer of authority to the administration only increases the difficulty, from the point of view of the effective working of representative democracy. 'Initially', states the Director of the Legislative Reference Service of the American legislature, 'the pressure may have been on Congress for legislation (or upon the President as party leader); ultimately, the highly intricate task of continuously intervening in the economic order has by virtue of legislative authorization and delegation of power become the task of a bureau or commission. Here is a transfer in the equilibrium of power and effectiveness, and the transfer is away from the operative significance of representative government and toward the bureaucratic ascendancy of the technically competent.'[2] If the trend toward bureaucratic predominance is successfully to be resisted, the legislature must not surrender control as it has delegated power. Unless the exercise of the authority delegated to him is closely supervised by the elected representatives of the people, the administrator is, in effect, placed in a position of almost complete irresponsibility. It is this which makes oversight of the executive so important a part of the work of a modern legislature. 'Since the English Revolution of 1688, it has been a part of the Anglo-American tradition that elected representative assemblies control the policies and acts of the executive branch of the government. This doctrine was firmly embedded in the American state and federal constitutions.'[3]

It may thus be seen that the exercise of its authority to enact laws is but part of the work of a legislature like the American Congress. 'The primary tasks of modern legislative assemblies', stated an acute student of government over a decade ago, in terms which sum up what has been said above with regard to the functions of the American Congress, 'may be arranged in four classes. First, but not necessarily foremost, is the function of law making. At least equally important is the responsibility of supervising the executive; the legislature in this role may be compared to a board of directors of a business corporation which, at least theoretically, endeavors to hold "administrative officers to a due accountability for the manner in which they perform their duties". A third legislative office, broad in its implications, involves activities as an organ of public opinion; a law-

1 Wallace, in *Hearings before the Joint Committee on the Organization of Congress*, 905.
2 Griffith, *Congress: its Contemporary Role* (1951), 2.
3 White, quoted in Galloway, *Congress at the Crossroads* (1946), 231.

making body may serve as a national forum for the expression, formulation, or moulding of opinion. The remaining function, which may be termed membership, concerns internal matters especially the judging of the qualifications and conduct of the delegates to the legislative assembly.'[1]

COMPOSITION

The proper exercise of these basic legislative functions presupposes the organization of the legislature in a manner which will enable it to perform them efficiently. The primary source of the rules of organization of the American Congress is, of course, to be found in the Federal Constitution itself. Thus, it is that instrument which provides that the Congress shall consist of a Senate and a House of Representatives. The House of Representatives, it goes on to say, shall be composed of members chosen every second year by the people of the various States. No person may be a representative who has not attained to the age of twenty-five years, and been seven years a citizen of the United States, and who is not, when elected, an inhabitant of the State in which he is chosen. It should, perhaps, be added parenthetically that, in practice, the residence requirement has been an even stricter one. By custom and usage it has become the well-nigh universally accepted, though unwritten, rule that members of the House of Representatives must be residents of the districts which they are elected to represent.

The Senate of the United States is composed of two senators from each State. Under the Constitution as it was originally adopted, the members of the Senate were to be chosen by the legislatures of the various States. To the framers of the American organic instrument, the composition of the Congress represented a necessary compromise, if the federal system contemplated by them was to be acceptable to the country. The lower House of that body was to be chosen directly by the people of the States, with representation upon the basis of population. The upper House, on the contrary, was to represent the States, rather than the people. Each State, no matter how large or how small, was allotted the same number of senators, and they were to be selected, not through election by the people, but by the choice of the State legislatures.

This concept of the members of the Senate as, more or less, ambassadors to Washington from the State Governments, rather than representatives of their people, became increasingly anachronistic with the growth of representative democracy during the nineteenth century. It remained, however, unchanged until the adoption of the Seventeenth Amendment

1 McGeary, *The Developments of Congressional Investigative Power* (1940), 23.

to the Constitution in 1913. Since that time, the members of the Senate have been chosen by the popular vote of the people of their States. The amendment referred to did not, it should be noted, completely do away with the original conception of the Senate, for it did not effect any change in the equal representation of each State in that body. Each State is still entitled to two senators, regardless of its size. This leads to inequalities of representation which appear quite shocking. Thus, the people of the State of New York, who consist of more than 13,000,000 persons, are represented in the Senate by the same number of senators as are the people of the State of Nevada, whose population is little more than 100,000 persons.

Members of the American Senate must, according to the Constitution, be at least thirty years of age, citizens of the United States for at least nine years, and inhabitants of the State from which they are chosen. They are elected for terms of six years, as compared with the two-year terms which, as we have seen, the Constitution provides for members of the House of Representatives. The fact that its members are elected for longer terms plus its relative smallness in size—96 as compared with 435 members— has enabled the Senate to function more efficiently than the House. Neophyte congressmen require much the better part of their two-year term to acquire an understanding of the workings of the House. Unless they are re-elected, they can hardly hope to play an effective part in the legislative process. It is for this reason that suggestions have frequently been made for increasing the terms of House members to four years. Since a constitutional amendment would be required for such a change, it is, however, extremely unlikely that it can be accomplished in the immediate future.

It has already been indicated that, at the present time, the members of both Houses of the American legislature are elected directly by the people whom they represent. The times, places and manner of holding such elections are prescribed by the various State legislatures. In addition, the qualifications of individual voters are, under the Constitution, left to the States to determine, for Article I, section 2, provides that, for the election of members of Congress, 'the Electors in each State shall have the Qualifications requisite for Electors of the most numerous Branch of the State Legislature'. The authority of the States in this respect is, it is true, drastically restricted by the Fifteenth and Nineteenth Amendments to the Constitution, which bar limitations of suffrage based upon race, colour, previous condition of servitude, or sex.[1] But, these restrictions aside, the regulation of the suffrage in the United States is almost wholly within the control of the individual States.

The same is not true with regard to election disputes. Here the American

1 See *infra.* p. 225.

system follows the rule which prevailed in Britain before the Parliamentary Elections Act, 1868—namely, that the national legislature itself is conclusively to determine such disputes. 'Each House', reads the relevant constitutional provision, 'shall be the Judge of the Elections, Returns and Qualifications of its own Members',[1] and this has been construed to bar judicial proceedings in election dispute cases. Since the legislative determination of the qualification of its members is vested with finality, it may happen that, though neither House may formally impose qualifications in addition to those specified in the Constitution, or waive those that are mentioned, each may in practice do either of these things.[2] Thus, to take a notorious example, in 1900, the House excluded a duly elected representative from the State of Utah because he was a Mormon with several wives, although there was no constitutional disqualification alleged. The system provided for under the Parliamentary Elections Act, 1868, in Britain certainly seems superior to that which prevails in the United States, where all too often contests over seats in the Congress have been awarded to the candidates of the dominant party. 'Congress', concludes one of the foremost American students of the legislative process, 'should vest in the courts jurisdiction to hear and decide in the first instance contested election cases in order both to obviate the evils of the traditional method of settling such contests and to save the time, money, and labor involved. The present system causes injustice to individuals, sometimes defeats the will of the people, and tends to multiply contests. It also imposes a heavy burden upon the committees concerned, takes the time of the House, and costs about $4000 per contest.'[3]

PRIVILEGES

'Parliamentary privilege', states the leading treatise upon legislative procedure in Britain, 'is the sum of the peculiar rights enjoyed by each House as a constituent part of the High Court of Parliament, and by members of each House individually, without which they could not discharge their functions, and which exceed those possessed by other bodies or individuals.'[4] The privileges of the legislature in Britain, according to the learned author, include the freedom from arrest and the freedom of speech of its members, and the power of each House to inflict punishment for contempt and to provide for its own proper constitution. The first two belong primarily to the individual members of each House and only secondarily and indirectly

---

1 Article I, section 5.
2 Willoughby, *Principles of the Constitutional Law of the United States* (2nd ed. 1935), 255.   3 Galloway, *Congress at the Crossroads* (1946), 23.
4 May, *A Treatise on the Law, Privileges, Proceedings and Usage of Parliament* (14th ed. 1946), 41.

to the House itself; the last two may be said to belong to each House as a collective body.[1] We shall touch upon the collective privileges of the American legislature—i.e. that of providing for its own constitution and that of punishing for contempt—in later portions of this chapter. At the moment, we are concerned only with the individual privileges of members of Congress.

As far as such individual privileges are concerned, Article I, section 6, of the American Constitution provides: 'The Senators and Representatives shall...in all Cases, except Treason, Felony and Breach of the Peace, be privileged from Arrest during their Attendance at the Session of their respective Houses, and in going to and returning from the same; and for any Speech or Debate in either House, they shall not be questioned in any other Place.'

This provision of the American Constitution has been construed so that the law of legislative privilege in the United States is not unlike the law on that subject in Britain. Thus, with regard to the privilege of freedom from arrest, it is clear, in both countries, that it is limited to civil causes, and has not been allowed to interfere with the administration of criminal justice.[2] 'Privilege of Parliament', as that body declared in 1641, 'is granted in regard of the service of the Commonwealth and is not to be used for the danger of the Commonwealth.'[3] And Blackstone, writing a century later, was emphatic in his assertion that the privilege was limited to civil actions, stating that 'the claim of privilege hath been usually guarded with an exception as to the case of indictable crimes; or as it has been frequently expressed, of treason, felony and breach (or surety) of the peace'.[4]

The relevant language of the American Constitution, which has already been quoted, parallels this extract from Blackstone. It, too, excepts from the privilege of freedom from arrest 'Treason, Felony, and Breach of the Peace'. Yet, as Blackstone himself points out, the exception tends to eliminate the privilege in criminal cases. 'No privilege was allowable to the members, their families or servants, in any *crime* whatsoever, for all crimes are treated by the law as being *contra pacem domini regis*.'[5] A similar result is reached in the leading American case. The constitutional exception, said the United States Supreme Court there, must be understood 'as excluding from the parliamentary privilege all arrests and prosecutions from criminal offenses; in other words, as confining the privilege alone to arrests in civil cases, the deduction being that when the framers of the Constitution adopted the phrase in question they necessarily must be held to have intended that it should receive its well understood and accepted meaning'.[1] Since arrest of the person is now almost never authorized in American law except for crimes, it follows that the privilege of freedom from arrest given to members of the American Congress is today of little more than theoretical significance.

The legislative privilege of freedom of speech is, on the other hand, still of the greatest consequence on both sides of the Atlantic. 'Freedom of speech', in the words of an American student, 'is inherent in the idea of a deliberative assembly. Speech is the element which gives life and power of action to such a body, as air does to the natural body. And the free and fearless discussion of every plan and purpose, which is essential to wise legislation, would be impossible if members were subjected to the restraints imposed by law with respect to private reputation.'[2]

The American constitutional provision, which has been quoted above, under which members of Congress shall not be questioned in any other place for any speech or debate in either House is clearly derived from the ninth article of the Bill of Rights of 1689. It declared: 'That the freedom of speech, and debates or proceedings in Parliament, ought not to be impeached or questioned in any court or place out of Parliament.' This great and vital privilege, without which all other privileges would be comparatively unimportant or ineffectual,[3] has been construed so as to give members of Parliament an absolute immunity for statements made in the House. Subject to the rules of order in debate, a member may state whatever he thinks fit in debate, however offensive it may be to the feelings, or injurious to the reputation of individuals; and he is protected by his privilege from any action for libel, as well as from any other question or molestation.[4]

The same rule applies to statements made by members of the American Congress. Nor, it should be noted, is the privilege in question, in the American view, confined to debates upon the floor of the House. As we shall see, much of the important work of the American legislature is performed in committees, off the floor of the legislative chamber. Hence, the immunity of American legislators has not been confined to acts within the chamber. If a member be out of the chamber, sitting in a committee, executing the commission of the House, he is still within the immunity.[5] And, since the working of the committee system in the American legislature depends, in large part, upon the information received from witnesses

1 *Williamson* v. *United States*, 207 U.S. 425, 436 (1908).
2 Veeder, 'Absolute immunity in defamation: legislative and executive proceedings', 10 *Columbia L. Rev.* (1910), 131.
3 Story, *Commentaries on the Constitution of the United States* (1833), § 863.
4 May, *op. cit.* 51.
5 Veeder, *loc. cit.* 136.

appearing before congressional committees, the privilege has been extended to such witnesses.[1] Witnesses appearing before legislative committees are entitled to the same immunity as witnesses in American courts.[2] This is true notwithstanding the fact that congressional committees are often composed of persons who do not have the judges' impartial concern with ensuring that proceedings are properly conducted in accordance with the rules of evidence. All too often, in congressional hearings, characters are gravely compromised by evidence that would never see the light of day in a court room. The possibility of injury to individuals is, however, outweighed by the public interest in ensuring that those who appear before the legislature will tender information or advice freely and without fear.

It should be emphasized that the privilege referred to does not extend to the outside publication by members or witnesses of defamatory matter spoken in congressional proceedings. The congressman or witness who repeats a libel over the radio or television is not protected, though he would be wholly immune had the same statement been made only in the proceeding in the legislature. That is why, in the celebrated case of Alger Hiss,[3] it was necessary for Whittaker Chambers to repeat his accusation that Hiss was a Communist on a radio programme, in response to Hiss's challenge to do so in a place other than a congressional proceeding, before Hiss could sue him for libel. While the accusation in question was confined to testimony before a congressional committee, it was wholly immune from legal attack.

ORGANIZATION

Perhaps the basic privilege of any legislative assembly is that of regulating its own constitution and internal affairs. We have already discussed the authority of the American Congress with regard to matters concerning its own composition. It is for that body itself, as we have seen, to determine the qualifications of any of its members. A similar principle applies so far as the rules of its organization and procedure are concerned. According to Article I, section 5, of the Federal Constitution, 'Each House may determine the Rules of its Proceedings'. 'No person', asserts the first great commentator on the American organic instrument, 'can doubt the propriety of the provision authorizing each house to determine the rules of its own proceedings. If the power did not exist, it would be utterly impracticable to transact the business of the nation, either at all, or at least with decency, deliberation, and order. The humblest assembly of men is

---

1 See, similarly, May, *op. cit.* 57.
2 Veeder, *loc. cit.* 137.
3 See Jowitt, *The Strange Case of Alger Hiss* (1953).

understood to possess this power; and it would be absurd to deprive the councils of the nation of a like authority.'[1]

It is true that, in the American system, the Constitution may prescribe rules of legislative organization and procedure, which serve to limit the privilege of Congress with respect to its own constitution. Thus, it is expressly provided by Article I, section 3, that the Vice-President of the United States, who is elected by the people every four years and upon whom the office of the President devolves in case of the death of the latter, is to be the President of the Senate. This constitutional designation of the Vice-President as presiding officer of the Senate must, of course, be respected by that chamber, no matter how reluctant the members of that body may be to be presided over by a particular Vice-President, either as an individual or as a member of a minority political party.

Though a constitutional provision of this type does clearly restrict the authority of the legislature over its own organization, it is not common in the American organic instrument. The existence of a few such sections in the fundamental law does not derogate essentially from the over-all power of the Congress in this respect, though it does, as has been indicated, limit it in details.

Under the Federal Constitution as amended, the American Congress assembles in regular session at noon on the third of January in each year. A new House of Representatives (which is chosen every second year) must first of all organize itself so as to be capable of conducting its legislative business. At its first meeting, the clerk of the previous House calls the members-elect to order and reads the list of those entitled to be members. He then calls for nominations for the presiding officer or Speaker, who is always chosen by the House from among its own members. The choices of the majority and minority parties are then placed in nomination and the roll is called, with the result of the ballot being then announced by the clerk. After the oath of office has been administered to the Speaker by the so-called 'father of the House', i.e. the member oldest in continuous service, the House chooses its other officers—a clerk, sergeant-at-arms, doorkeeper, postmaster and chaplain—none of whom has ever been chosen from the membership of the House and who are, in fact, selected at a caucus of the majority party. The newly elected officers are given the oath of office by the Speaker and the new sergeant-at-arms places the mace on its pedestal. The House is now in session and ready for business.

The picture in the Senate is similar, with the important exception that, as has already been mentioned, its presiding officer is designated by the Constitution, so that that body has no voice in choosing him. The most

1 Story, *Commentaries*, §835.

the senators can do is to designate a president *pro tempore* who serves when the Vice-President of the United States is absent or has succeeded to the presidency.[1] The chief clerk of the Senate is called its Secretary. He and the other officers of that body are elected by the Senate after nomination by a caucus of the majority party. As is the case with the House, these officers are changed when party control of the chamber changes. Until such a change occurs, they usually retain their posts.

RULES

'It is highly important', wrote an acute student of the American legislative process almost half a century ago, 'to the preservation of order, decency, and regularity in a numerous assembly, and not less essential to its power of harmonious and efficient action, that its proceedings should be regulated by established forms and methods; and, with a view to these purposes, it is more material, perhaps, that there should be rules established than that they should be founded upon the firmest basis of reason and argument; the great object being to effect a uniformity of proceeding in the business of the assembly, securing it at once against the caprice of the presiding officer and the captious disputes of members. It is to the observance of regularity and order among the members that the minority look for protection against the power of the majority; and in the adherence to established forms between the different branches, that each finds its security against the encroachments of the other.'[2]

Under the American Constitution, as we have seen, each House of the federal Congress may determine the rules of its proceedings. Acting under this authority, each House has, since the first Congress, which met in New York on 4 March 1789, provided a set of rules for its own governance. The rules of the first Congress were based on those used by the Continental Congress, which had directed the American Revolution, and the various State legislatures, which, in turn, had been modelled upon the procedure then prevailing in the House of Commons.[3] While he served as Vice-President of the United States (1797–1801), Thomas Jefferson prepared for his own use, as presiding officer of the Senate, the work that is known as *Jefferson's Manual of Parliamentary Practice*. This manual, which was an attempt by its learned author to describe the essentials of the English parliamentary practice of his time, still forms the basis for the rules of procedure of the American legislature. In 1837, indeed, the House of

---

1 Walker, *The Legislative Process* (1948), 179.
2 Cushing, *Law and Practice of Legislative Assemblies* (1907), 305.
3 Galloway, *op. cit.* 13.

Representatives adopted a rule, which is still in effect, under which the provisions of *Jefferson's Manual* are to 'govern the House in all cases to which they are applicable and not inconsistent with the standing rules and orders of the House'. The Congress can thus, through *Jefferson's Manual*, trace the lineage of its rules to those of the English Parliament of the eighteenth century. 'However, many changes have occurred since Jefferson's day, not only in the rules of the two houses of Congress but also in those of the House of Commons, so that the relationship between them might be a little difficult to recognize today.'[1]

The first order of business of a newly convened House of Representatives, after it has elected its Speaker and other officers, is the adoption of its rules of procedure. In practice, this normally means the formal adoption by the House of the rules of its predecessor without alteration. 'Each newly-elected House', as Woodrow Wilson pointed out, 'meets without rules for its governance, and amongst the first acts of its first session is usually the adoption of the resolution that the rules of its predecessor shall be its own rules, subject, of course, to such revisions as it may, from time to time, see fit to make.'[2] Changes in the rules of the House are, in actual fact, most difficult to obtain. They require a two-thirds majority and can only be moved on certain specified days.

The American Senate is governed by standing rules, analogous to the Standing Orders of the House of Commons, which remain in operation indefinitely. The present standing rules of the Senate were adopted at the beginning of 1884, and, though there have been numerous amendments, they remain today essentially what they were at that time. Senate rules are adopted and amended by majority vote, but the inherent conservatism of that body makes alterations in its rules well nigh as hard to secure as are changes in those of the House of Representatives.

It should be emphasized that mere familiarity with the written rules of the two Houses will no more enable an outside observer to assert intimacy with congressional procedure than will knowledge of the Standing Orders of the House of Commons permit him to pose as a master of parliamentary practice. 'For the much more important procedure in public business there is, so far as the House of Commons is concerned, no code, not even a partial code; the greater part of its rules are unwritten, to be collected from the Journals or reports of debates, or to be ascertained from personal experience. The written part is merely a pendant to the unwritten part.'[3] The same is true, generally speaking, so far as the American legislature is concerned. The Congress, as an observer has pointed out, has a devotion to

1 Walker, *op. cit.* 193.   2 Wilson, *op. cit.* 104.
3 May, *op. cit.* 1.

precedents as devout as that of the House of Commons. It is difficult to determine the whole meaning, for example, of any rule of the House of Representatives without considering the past rulings which have been made concerning it. So many such rulings have been made up to the present time that it is rare for a matter to arise which has not previously been ruled upon. The published standing rules of the House are annotated by references to these rulings. Collections of these precedents, numbering well over 11,000, have been made from time to time.[1] These constitute the 'parliamentary common law', as it were, of the American legislature.

COMMITTEE SYSTEM

Much of the important work of the American Congress is done through committees. The enormous volume of business which comes before a modern legislature and the limited time at its disposal make it impossible for every measure to be considered at length by that body as a whole. If the work is to be done, the responsibility for investigating in detail matters which come before each House must be entrusted to some other agency in which the House has confidence.[2] In the American legislature, the method devised for this purpose is the standing committee, composed of a small number of the members of the legislative body.

It is well known that the committee system in the American Congress has been developed far more completely than its counterpart in the legislature in Britain. The position of the Government in the British Parliament makes it both unnecessary and unlikely for the standing committees of the House of Commons to play more than a subsidiary part in the process of legislation. In the American legislature, on the other hand, it is the committees of each House which perform *the* vital part of the work of those chambers. All bills and resolutions introduced in Congress are first referred to these committees, considered and screened by them, and those that win favour are then reported back to the chambers with recommendations for action.[3] As it was expressed in 1946 by a Joint Committee of the Congress established to investigate the organization of that body, 'About 90 percent of all the work of the Congress on legislative matters is carried on in these committees. Most bills recommended by congressional committees become laws of the land and the content of legislation finally passed is largely determined in the committees.'[4] Truly, in the words of one writer,

1 Walker, *op. cit.* 197–8. The two authoritative published collections of these precedents are A. C. Hinds, *Parliamentary Precedents of the House of Representatives* (1907), 5 vols.; C. Cannon, *Precedents of the House of Representatives of the United States* (1935), 3 vols.   2 Walker, *op. cit.* 207.   3 Galloway, *op. cit.* 87.
4 *Report of the Joint Committee on the Organization of the Congress* (1946), 2.

the conduct of congressional business would be practically impossible without these organs.[1]

One who looks upon the standing committees of the American Congress as merely the counterparts of those which exist in the Parliament in Britain is bound to get a distorted view of their significance. 'The House of Commons', writes Woodrow Wilson, 'has its committees, even its standing committees, but they are of the old-fashioned sort which merely investigate and report, not of the new American type which originate and conduct legislation.'[2]

The importance of the standing committees of the Congress stems from the fact that every measure introduced in one of its chambers is committed to a committee for its consideration. Unless the measure is reported upon by the committee, it is most unlikely that it will ever come before the consideration of the particular House. 'The fate of bills committed is generally not uncertain. As a rule, a bill committed is a bill doomed. When it goes from the clerk's desk to a committee-room it crosses a parliamentary bridge of sighs to dim dungeons of silence whence it will never return. The means and time of its death are unknown, but its friends never see it again. Of course no Standing Committee is privileged to take upon itself the full powers of the House it represents, and formally and decisively reject a bill referred to it; its disapproval, if it disapproves, must be reported to the House in the form of a recommendation that the bill "do not pass". But it is easy, and therefore common, to let the session pass without making any report at all upon bills deemed objectionable or unimportant, and to substitute for reports upon them a few bills of the Committee's own drafting; so that thousands of bills expire with the expiration of each Congress, not having been rejected, but having been simply neglected.... Of course it goes without saying that the practical effect of this Committee organization of the House is to consign to each of the Standing Committees the entire direction of legislation upon those subjects which properly come to its consideration.'[3]

The standing committees of the American Congress are organized upon the basis of subject-matter. There are fifteen such committees in the Senate[4] and nineteen in the House of Representatives.[5] The organization

1 Walker, *op. cit.* 207. 2 Wilson, *op. cit.* 122.
3 *Ibid.* 69, 70.
4 These are the Committees on Agriculture and Forestry; Appropriations; Armed Services; Banking and Currency; Civil Service; District of Columbia; Expenditures in the Executive Departments; Finance; Foreign Relations; Interstate and Foreign Commerce; Judiciary; Labor and Public Welfare; Public Lands; Public Works; and Rules and Administration.
5 These are the Committees on Agriculture; Appropriations; Armed Services; Banking and Currency; Post Office and Civil Service; District of Columbia; Education

of the committees upon the basis of subject-matter is intended to ensure that there is a standing committee to which any bill may be referred with the assurance that its members, because of their experience with the particular subject-matter, will have special competence to investigate and report upon it. 'To the extent that the same members are re-elected and continue to work on the same committee, year after year, this presumption of special competence may be justified. Certainly the committee members are in a far better position to pass judgment upon a bill in their area of specialization than is the legislature as a whole. For this reason, committee reports are usually approved, the rest of the members feeling that they are not as competent as the committee to reach a sound conclusion.'[1]

In the American Congress, the assignment of members to the different standing committees and the selection of committee chairmen are among the first order of business of each House at the beginning of a new legislative session. In the normal course of events, the Senate and House of Representatives merely ratify the choices which have been made by caucuses of the two parties. The political composition of the committees corresponds roughly to that of the chamber itself, the majority party having a majority of the seats on each standing committee, the minority being represented in proportion to its strength in the particular House.[2]

Seniority in point of service has been the prevailing principle governing both committee assignments and the selection of chairmen since 1846 in the Senate and since 1910 in the House of Representatives.[3] New members are placed on relatively unimportant committees and are appointed to the more significant ones only as vacancies occur in them. And the chairman of each committee, whose position is a cardinal one, is, by congressional convention, always the member of the majority party having the longest service on the committee. 'Under this system', we are told by an eminent American legislator, 'the member of the party in power who has served the longest in any given committee is for practical purposes the *only* person eligible for the chairmanship of that committee regardless of his qualifications, physical fitness, or any other factor that might be weighed, or any other method of trying to pick the best person for the post.'[4]

According to one observer, 'Congress is probably alone among all private or governmental bodies charged with any kind of responsibility

and Labor; Expenditures in the Executive Departments; Foreign Affairs; House Administration; Interstate and Foreign Commerce; Judiciary; Merchant Marine and Fisheries; Public Lands; Public Works; Rules; Un-American Activities; Veterans Affairs; Ways and Means.

2 Galloway, *op. cit.* 186.   1 Walker, *op. cit.* 208.
                                       3 *Ibid.* 187.
4 Kefauver and Levin, *A Twentieth-century Congress* (1947), 133.

which lets leadership depend exclusively upon the accident of tenure.'[1]
It is, however, easier to criticize the principle of seniority as it is applied in
the Congress than to suggest any workable alternative. To throw open
the chairmanship of committees to an open vote of the committee in
question or the House would open the way to internecine disputes which
might well destroy the effective functioning of the committee system.
'The bitter personal feelings engendered by an open dispute for committee
places would complicate party management, and there would be delay in
beginning work . . . until personal and sectional quarrels could be smoothed
out.'[2] The defects of the seniority system, it is often urged, could be
eliminated by its simple abolition.[3] But, as an experienced congressman
has expressed it, those who advocate this solution 'can have had little or
no experience with precisely the same problem in the conduct of every
sizeable business enterprise, or any sort of organization where occasion
arises to promote employees. On the whole, the men who must there
decide find that promotion by seniority conduces most to contentment
and least endangers morale. Exceptions must at times be made, but the
rarer the better for peace and harmony. Then, too, it must be remembered
that though not the only factor in deciding merit, experience is the most
important factor.'[4]

ENACTMENT OF LAWS

'A single volume of 320 octavo pages', Mr Justice Frankfurter informs us,
'contains all the laws passed by Congress during its first five years, when
measures were devised for getting the new government under way;
26 acts were passed in the 1789 session, 66 in 1790, 94 in 1791, 38 in 1792,
63 in 1793. For the single session of the 70th Congress, to take a pre-
depression period, there are 993 enactments in a monstrous volume of
1014 pages—quarto not octavo—with a comparable range of subject
matter. Do you wonder that one for whom the Statutes at Large constitute
his staple reading should have sympathy, at least in his moments of baying
at the moon, with the touching Congressman who not so very long ago
proposed a "Commission on Centralization" to report whether "the
Government has departed from the concept of the founding fathers" and
what steps should be taken "to restore the Government to its original
purposes and sphere of activity"?'[5]

1 Hehmeyer, *Time for Change* (1943), 100.
2 Chamberlain, *Legislative Processes: National and State* (1936), 54.
3 See e.g. Kefauver and Levin, *op. cit.* 137.
4 Luce, *Congress: an Explanation* (1926), 8.
5 Frankfurter, 'Some reflections on the reading of statutes', 47 *Columbia L. Rev.*
(1947), 527.

The prodigious increase in legislative activity, to which the learned justice refers, has placed a tremendous strain upon the congressional machinery for enacting the laws. In large measure, the added burden in this respect has been met by the development of the committee system, which has been discussed. The primary role in the American legislative process is today performed by committees of the Congress, rather than by that body acting as an entity. It should be emphasized that a device like a fully developed committee system is essential in the United States because of the absence of the Government's control over the legislature such as that which prevails in Britain. It is the direction of the Government that is the catalyst in the parliamentary process of legislation. It is difficult for most English students to see how it would be possible, without such governmental management, for a body as large and unwieldy as the House of Commons to get even a small fraction of its legislative work done.

In the House of Commons, the Government, with its majority, can virtually monopolize business. 'In other words, the Government determines what shall be discussed, when it shall be discussed, how long the discussions shall take, and what the decision shall be. So long as its party majority holds, the Government is in complete control of the House of Commons.'[1] In the American Congress, there is nothing like the Government's direction over the law-making process that exists in Britain. There is no distinction there between government bills and private members' bills, such as that which dominates the working of the House of Commons. There is no precedence for bills which originate with a government department. Bills introduced by private members stand upon an equal footing, so far as the allocation of time for debate is concerned. Many of the most important bills enacted by the American legislature are, indeed, bills which are opposed by officers of the executive branch. The fact that the tenure of the executive does not depend upon the continued confidence of the Congress and the consequent lack of strict party discipline in that body make the passage of such bills a not uncommon occurrence in the American legislative process.

It is the precedence of government bills in the House of Commons which ensures that the plethora of bills which may be introduced by private members, for the most part, never sees the light of day on the floor of the House. In the American Congress, it is the committee system which serves to sieve the bills introduced by members. It is in committee, as we have seen, that the real work of the Congress is done. 'A legislature is too large and unwieldy a body and is too unexpert in most of the technical

---

1 Jennings, *Parliament* (1940), 118.

problems presented to it to act in the first instance as a whole. The sifting process is done, therefore by committees.'[1]

Bills in the American legislature must be introduced by members of each House. Since neither the President nor the members of the executive Cabinet are, under the American system, members of the Congress, they cannot introduce proposed legislation directly, as can a minister in Britain. They must act through a member of each House, and that is why, strictly speaking, all bills before the American legislature are private members' bills, with no priority being given to those which originate with the executive departments.

Bills are introduced in the Congress by being filed with the secretary or clerk of the particular House. On introduction, each bill is given a number, by which it is known and identified throughout its progress in the chamber. The first stage in the legislative history of a bill which has been introduced and numbered is its reference to the appropriate committee. Such reference is made by the presiding officer of the House (in practice, all cases except those presenting some difficulty are handled by his clerk), though the wishes of the author of the bill are, if expressed, usually followed.

After a bill has been referred to a particular committee, it is placed upon the list of bills before that committee. Each committee of the Congress is by law required to fix regular meeting days for the transaction of its business. At such meetings, the measures before the committee are considered. If a particular bill is of significance it may be referred to a subcommittee by the chairman for study. Where a matter is deemed to be of sufficient importance, public hearings may be held, at which witnesses may appear to give arguments for and against the bill.[2] The committees of the American legislature are not required to report on all bills referred to them. In practice, it is unusual for bills to be reported to the House unless they are approved by the committees considering them. 'Thus thousands of proposals die in committee pigeon holes at each session.'[3] It is this, as we have already seen, which makes the role of the standing committees such a cardinal one in the American Congress. Unless a bill is reported upon by the committee to which it is referred, it is extremely doubtful that it will ever see the light of day upon the floor of the particular chamber.

When a bill is reported upon from a committee of one of the Houses of the Congress, it is placed upon the calendar of that House. This is a list on which bills are recorded in numerical order to be considered under given

1 Moffatt, 'The legislative process', 24 *Cornell L. Q.* (1939), 223.
2 Galloway, *op. cit.* 162.
3 Walker, *op. cit.* 244.

circumstances at periods fixed in advance.[1] Once on the calendar, a bill will normally come up for the consideration of the House when its turn arises. Appropriation and revenue bills take precedence, as does any bill which the Committee on Rules deems to deserve prompt and special consideration.

In the proceedings on the floor of the chamber, the primary responsibility of leading the debate on a bill rests upon a member designated to represent it for the purpose by the committee which reported the bill. He is usually the chairman of the committee concerned. In the House of Representatives, debate on most measures is severely limited. The duration in particular cases is determined by the importance of the bill and the amount of controversy involved. Owing to its unwieldy size, the House has various rules for restricting debate. It is only in the case of important bills that as much as one or two whole days is allowed for debate, with the time equally divided between the proponents and opponents of the measure. By British standards, even in these days of restriction upon parliamentary discussion, debate in the American House of Representatives appears too limited to enable adequate discussion and consideration of the measures before that chamber. It should, however, be remembered that, in the American system, this deficiency is not felt so much because of the detailed deliberation given each bill by the committee to which it has been referred before it is reported for the consideration of the House itself.

If, to the British observer, debate in the American House of Representatives appears too limited, that in the Senate, on the contrary, appears too free of restrictions. In the Senate, debate is unlimited. It is true that, under a rule adopted in 1917, a motion for closure may be moved by sixteen senators and be adopted if passed by a two-thirds vote. In practice, however, closure is almost never successfully moved. 'Only four times since 1917 has the rule been invoked, since Senators are extremely alert to the preservation of their right to free and unlimited debate.'[2] It is the complete freedom of debate which prevails in the Senate that makes possible the so-called 'filibuster'[3], which, more than anything else, has cast disrepute upon the effectiveness of the American upper House. The way in which a filibuster operates in the Senate has been well described by one of its most

1 Galloway, *op. cit.* 163.   2 *Ibid.* 167.
3 'This fantastic extension of senatorial courtesies has been called legislative piracy, and whoever termed the device a filibuster doubtless had in mind the origins of that word. The Dutch *vrijbuiter*, meaning freebooter, was applied by the English to seventeenth-century buccaneers who plundered Spanish ships in the Caribbean. The Spanish called the same pirates *filibusteros*. *Filibuster* later came to embrace illegal expeditions of international adventurers against the sovereignty of a group or nation for personal gain. Now the word aptly denotes legislative freebooting and buccaneering, with this important exception—in the Senate, it is all very legal.' Kefauver and Levin, *op. cit.* 46.

eminent members: 'A small group, sometimes a single senator, opposes a bill known to be favored by an overwhelming majority.... This small minority plans deliberately to prevent the Senate from ever voting on the measure. One of their number gets control of the floor. This can be done on as flimsy a point as correcting the grammar in the prayer uttered by the Senate chaplain on the previous day—as was done in January, 1946, by Senator John Overton of Louisiana.

'Once in control, so long as the "debate" continues the Senate cannot take a single legislative action except by the grace of those who, under its own rules, are now its master. The presiding officer is powerless, the majority almost so. When this utter negation of democratic procedure is in progress, there exists the parliamentary farce called a filibuster. The power of the filibusterers lies in their ability to hold up all pending legislation, no matter how vital it may be to the nation, until the majority knuckles under and agrees to their point.'[1]

It is difficult to explain to the foreign observer exactly why attempts at closure in the Senate rarely succeed. Perhaps the best explanation is that given by the senator just quoted. 'Why does closure fail so often?' he asks, 'Why do senators time and again vote against invoking the rule that would end a filibuster, even when they favor the bill the minority seeks to kill? The conclusion seems inescapable that they cherish this arbitrary power that lies in every senator's hand, feeling they may wish to filibuster themselves against a measure they oppose. It's a form of senatorial courtesy or, less elegantly: "You scratch my back and I'll scratch yours".'[2]

After the debate comes the last stage in the legislative history of a bill before one of the Houses of the American legislature, namely, the vote upon it by the chamber in question. A vote in the American House of Representatives or Senate normally does not have the dramatic quality that is connected with a division in the House of Commons, where the tenure of the Government may depend upon the result. No matter how the Congress votes, the President and his Cabinet will continue in office, at least until the next presidential election. Most of the votes in the Congress are taken *viva voce*. For the more important measures and those in which the spoken vote may be questioned, a roll-call vote is taken. This involves the calling by the clerk of the name of each member, in alphabetical order, and the recording of his vote, as it is expressed by him. For a vote to be taken on a bill, a quorum of a majority of the members of the

---

1 *Ibid.* The longest one-man filibuster in the history of the Senate was that staged by Senator Morse on 24 and 25 April 1953. It lasted twenty-two hours and twenty-six minutes.

2 *Ibid.* 49.

particular chamber[1] must be present. A majority vote of those present is sufficient to pass an ordinary bill.

When one House of the Congress has passed a bill, it is sent to the other chamber for its consideration. Bills may originate in either House, except revenue bills, which, under the Constitution, must originate in the House of Representatives. If a bill already passed by one chamber is passed without amendment by the other, it has successfully completed its legislative journey. If there are amendments in the second chamber, the bill is sent back to the House of origin for its concurrence. If it refuses to concur, and the second chamber still insists upon its amendments, the bill is sent to a so-called conference committee, which consists of members appointed by each of the Houses. Their job is that of composing the differences between the bills passed by the two chambers. 'The committee nearly always reaches an agreement; and then resubmits the bill to each house for a majority vote. The report of the conference committee is almost invariably confirmed by the vote of the two branches.'[2] When the bill has thus finally been passed by both Houses of the American legislature, it is sent to the President for his approval. As we shall see in the next chapter, under the Federal Constitution, Acts of the Congress become law only upon approval by the chief executive, or re-passage by a two-thirds vote over his veto.

OVERSIGHT OF ADMINISTRATION

As significant as its position as the legislative organ of the Federal Government is the role of the Congress as the overseer of the administration. 'If the Congress is to effectively discharge its full duty', asserted a member of the House of Representatives in 1945, 'it must at the very least supervise each grant of power which it makes with great care, and must assume the function not only of passing legislation, but of seeing that that legislation is carried out in accordance with congressional intent. In the absence of the exercise of this second function, Congress will be only half effective at best, for no law is better than its administration.'[3]

The primary basis of legislative control stems from the fact that all exercises of authority by the administration must find their source in a legislative act. Anglo-American legal theory rejects the notion of inherent or autonomous power in the executive—a rejection which has received striking expression in a significant recent decision of the United States

1 In the Senate 49, and in the House of Representatives 218, is a quorum.
2 Galloway, *op. cit.* 167.
3 Voorhis, in *Hearings before the Joint Committee on the Organization of Congress* (1946), 38.

Supreme Court.[1] And, since the administration, in the common-law countries, acts only as the agent of the legislature, the latter is enabled to exercise continuous control over administrative activities. If the grant of authority is not exercised by the agent in accordance with the desires of the principal, it can at any time be revoked or modified by the latter. The realization of this, more than anything else, tends to ensure against administrative acts which may displease the members of the legislature. This is especially true so far as the American Congress is concerned. The absence of government control over its functioning, such as that which exists in the British Parliament, enables it to revoke or modify delegations of power to the administration even though such revocation or modification is strenuously opposed by the executive branch.

Even more important in this respect is the control exercised by the Congress over expenditures. The financial resources which are essential to the conduct of American government, as of government in Britain, can be obtained only with the authorization of the legislative body. The spending power, as one writer expresses it, is the constitutional birthright of Congress,[2] for Article I, section 9, of that instrument expressly provides that 'No Money shall be drawn from the Treasury, but in Consequence of Appropriations made by Law'. Appropriations are normally made by the American legislature upon a yearly basis, and this enables it to exercise an almost constant supervision over the administration. The latter's activities cannot be carried on unless the necessary funds are authorized by the Congress.

Legislative control over delegations of power and appropriations has, however, hardly proved effective in the great majority of cases. The vast range of modern administrative authority and the innumerable instances in which such authority is constantly being exercised tend to make continuing control by a non-expert legislative body as large as the American Congress more a matter of form than of substance most of the time. What is needed here is control by a compact body of legislative specialists rather than the cumbersome supervision usually wielded by the entire legislative assembly. Something along this line is provided for in the Select Committee on Statutory Instruments—the so-called Scrutinizing Committee— of the House of Commons, which examines the delegated legislation which has been promulgated by the English administration.

A substantial step forward in the direction of providing such specialized legislative control in the American Congress was taken in the Legislative Reorganization Act of 1946. It includes the following provision: 'To assist the Congress in appraising the administration of the laws and in

1 See infra, ch. vii.   2 Galloway *op. cit.* 245.

developing such amendments or related legislation as it may deem necessary, each standing committee of the Senate and the House of Representatives shall exercise continuous watchfulness of the execution by the administrative agencies concerned of any laws, the subject matter of which is within the jurisdiction of such committee; and, for that purpose, shall study all pertinent reports and data submitted to the Congress by the agencies in the executive branch of the Government.' Under this provision, the standing committees of the two chambers of the American legislature, which, as we have seen, have the duty of examining proposed legislation which touches upon the particular subject-matter over which they have competence, are now vested with the additional responsibility of conducting a continual review of the agencies administering the laws originally reported by the committees.[1]

Yet even this scheme of continual oversight by committee, valuable though it doubtless may be, does not wholly resolve the problem of effective legislative supervision of administration. Most American observers of the legislative process would still echo the words of Woodrow Wilson written over half a century ago that 'it is quite evident that the means which Congress has of controlling the departments and exercising the searching oversight at which it aims are limited and defective'.[2] The answer which Wilson gave to the problem—the adoption of the British parliamentary system of which he was an enthusiastic advocate long before his election to the presidency—appears to have little chance at present of being embraced in the American system.

This is true despite proposals in that direction which are now before the federal Congress. The least extreme of these, the so-called Kefauver Resolution, would go no further than to provide for a question period during which members of the executive Cabinet could be questioned on the workings of their department, along the lines which have become so familiar in the legislature in Britain. 'It is difficult', asserts one commentator, 'to see how there can be any objection to this save on the part of those intransigeants who are opposed to anything—however innocuous —that remotely resembles the parliamentary system.'[3] Even if one accepts this view, it should be recognized that the proposal referred to was first introduced in the American House in 1940 and no action of any kind has yet been taken on it. A more drastic alteration in the American system

---

1 In addition joint so-called 'watch dog' committees, made up of members of both Houses, have been set up to scrutinize the work of several specific administrative agencies—notably the Atomic Energy Commission and the National Labor Relations Board. 2 Wilson, *op. cit.* 270.

3 Armstrong, 'Unsolved problems of leadership and powers', 33 *American Bar Association J.* (1947), 417, 420.

would be made by the so-called Fulbright Amendment. Under it, the Constitution would provide for concurrent terms of six years for the President, senators and representatives, with power in the President and in Congress to terminate all incumbencies by ordering a new presidential and congressional election. This plan would go far toward remodelling the American system on parliamentary lines. There is, however, little likelihood that anything like it will be adopted in the United States in the foreseeable future.

POWERS OF INVESTIGATION

One of the most important weapons in the congressional armoury in the legislative struggle to exercise its role as overseer of the administration is the power of investigation. 'In my opinion', declared Harry S. Truman after he had been elected to the vice-presidency, 'the power of investigation is one of the most important powers of the Congress. The manner in which that power is exercised will largely determine the position and prestige of the Congress in the future. An informed Congress is a wise Congress; an uninformed Congress surely will forfeit a large portion of the respect and confidence of the people.'[1]

The proper exercise of the legislative function presupposes the existence of an informed judgment on the part of the members of the particular legislative assembly. Such informed judgment cannot normally exist, as a practical matter, if the members of the legislature do not possess sufficient information about the conditions which their acts are intended to affect. Nor is adequate information usually available within the legislative body itself. The knowledge possessed by its members must necessarily be supplemented by that obtained from outside sources. In obtaining the information which is needed to enable their functions properly to be performed, the legislature in the United States has made an ever-growing use of its powers of investigation. It is, indeed, not too much to say that, under contemporary conditions, investigating committees have become, in large part, the eyes and ears of the American Congress.

In this respect, the situation in the federal Congress must be sharply contrasted with that which prevails in the British Parliament. It is, of course, true that in Britain, as well as in the United States, a committee of inquiry may be established by either House of the legislature to investigate any matter of public interest. Such a method of obtaining information was, indeed, used by the Parliament as early as 1689.[2] And, under the

---

1 Quoted, in *Hearings before the Joint Committee on the Organization of Congress* (1946), 908.
2 Phillips, *The Constitutional Law of Great Britain and the Commonwealth* (1952), 71.

Tribunals of Inquiry (Evidence) Act, 1921, procedure for setting up investigatory committees of a judicial type has been given statutory form. Yet, it cannot be denied that the use of such committees in Britain is comparatively rare. 'I can recall two cases', states Lord Jowitt, 'since I entered political life where this procedure has been adopted.'[1] The cases referred to are the Porter Tribunal appointed in 1936 to inquire into a budget 'leakage' and the Lynskey Tribunal of 1948 which investigated allegations of improper approaches to certain members of the Government. In actual fact, these two cases appear to be the only ones in which tribunals of inquiry have been constituted in Britain under the 1921 Act.

Anyone who is at all familiar with the contemporary functioning of the American Congress realizes that the exercise of legislative investigatory power has become the normal, rather than the exceptional, thing in the United States. That the American Congress should, in practice, make far greater use of its investigatory authority than does the British Parliament results largely from the difference in its constitutional position as compared with that of the legislature in Britain. 'It is inevitable', writes Lord Jowitt, with regard to this subject, 'owing to the fundamental differences in the two constitutions, that the method adopted in the United States must be radically different from that adopted here. In that country, speaking broadly, there is a far greater degree of separation of the executive, of the legislative and of the judicial functions than exists here.'[2] In Britain there must, of necessity, be an intimate relation between the executive and the majority of the House of Commons, for, when the support of the House is withheld, the Government falls. A resolution of the House of Commons to set up an inquiry to investigate matters relating to executive functions will normally be thought of as an expression of no confidence in the Government of the day. Hence the rarity of resort to that procedure in Britain. In the United States, where the tenure of the executive does not depend upon the support of the Congress, the latter need feel no hesitancy in making widespread use of its investigatory authority.

The complete separation between the executive and the legislature in the American system has, indeed, made the role of the Congress as inquisitor a cardinal one, if its functions as the elected representatives of the people are adequately to be carried out. The absence of close *rapports* between the American executive and legislative branches, comparable to those which exist under a parliamentary system, and the non-existence in the Congress of an institution such as the question period, have perforce made reliance by the Congress upon information obtained by its own investigatory efforts essential, if it is intelligently to perform its legislative

1 Jowitt, *The Strange Case of Alger Hiss* (1953), 140.   2 *Ibid.*

tasks. Then, too, the lack of a power in the American legislature to dismiss the Government by a vote of no confidence may make it difficult for the Congress directly to influence the conduct of the administration, especially where it feels that a particular change is called for. By setting up a committee to investigate and report upon what it considers to be an unsatisfactory situation in the administration, it may well, if the facts ferreted out warrant it, be able to marshal public opinion behind its view sufficiently to induce compliance by the administration. 'If the United States legislature', as Lord Jowitt puts it, referring to the most striking recent example of this kind of case, 'thinks that the executive is not being, for example, sufficiently active and astute in investigating or suppressing Communist agencies in the Government, they may appoint a committee to investigate with the intention, if the facts seem to justify it, of enlisting public opinion so that the executive may be forced to take the necessary action.'[1]

The investigatory powers of the American Congress are, in practice, exercised by committees of both Houses. Much of the inquisitorial work of the federal legislature is performed by its standing committees, which have already been discussed in some detail, in connexion with their functions in the process of legislation and in their supervision of administrative agencies whose work involves the subject-matter within their particular jurisdictions. The most spectacular investigating committees of the Congress have, however, been appointed *ad hoc* by the adoption of a formal resolution of the Senate or House of Representatives, or, sometimes, of the two chambers acting jointly. These special committees are set up to make a specific study of a particular problem.[2] In this respect they are comparable to the tribunals contemplated in the Tribunals of Inquiry (Evidence) Act, 1921, though, as has already been indicated, the use by the federal Congress of its authority in this respect is far more common than is that by its counterpart in Britain.[3] The resolution authorizing a special investigation by an *ad hoc* committee in the American Congress normally defines the purpose and subject-matter of the inquiry and fixes a time limit for the undertaking. The committee concerned is customarily given powers similar to those exercised by the federal courts as regards examination of witnesses and production of documents as well as a special appropriation to cover its costs. Its authority is enforced by the power of the Houses of the American legislature to commit for contempt, as well as by a law making it a crime wilfully to refuse to obey the process of a legislative committee.

1 *Ibid.* 141.
2 Carr, *The House Committee on Un-American Activities* (1952), 5.
3 It should also be noted that, in the United States, membership in congressional committees of this type is limited to members of the legislature, while, in Britain, tribunals of inquiry set up under the 1921 Act may have a wider composition.

The investigatory powers of the American Congress have been used for three basic purposes. First, the investigation is a means of supplying the Congress with the accurate and detailed information which is essential to the intelligent exercise of the law-making authority. A good illustration of this motive at work is to be seen in the celebrated so-called Wall Street investigation of 1933, when the Congress sought and obtained information about banking and stock exchange practices that led to the enactment of a series of regulatory statutes, which sought to curb the abuses found to be prevalent in the investment business. Secondly, the investigation is used to supervise the work of administrative agencies. The House of Representatives Committee to Investigate Acts of Executive Agencies beyond the Scope of Their Authority, created in 1943, by its very title, illustrates this motive for investigation. Thirdly, the investigation is used to influence public opinion by giving circulation to certain facts or ideas.[1] The investigations of the Committee on Un-American Activities of the House of Representatives illustrate this motive at work. While the inquiries of that committee have resulted in little actual legislation, as Lord Jowitt has recently expressed it, 'No doubt the Committee did much to make the American people alive to the very real danger of Communist infiltration and to enlighten public opinion as to the extent to which Communist sympathisers had succeeded in getting into federal employment.'[2]

The exact scope of the investigating authority of the federal Congress is a subject about which there has been a great deal of controversy among American jurists, especially during the present generation. That the power to investigate is, in fact, possessed by the American legislature is today beyond question. 'We are of opinion', reads the decision of the United States Supreme Court in the leading case of *McGrain* v. *Daugherty*, 'that the power of inquiry—with process to enforce it—is an essential and appropriate auxiliary to the legislative function....A legislative body cannot legislate wisely or effectively in the absence of information respecting the conditions which the legislation is intended to affect or change; and where the legislative body does not itself possess the requisite information—which not infrequently is true—recourse must be had to others who do possess it.... Thus there is ample warrant for thinking, as we do, that the constitutional provisions which commit the legislative function to the two houses are intended to include this attribute to the end that the function may be effectively exercised.'[3]

It should not, however, be thought that the American court in *McGrain* v. *Daugherty*, in upholding the existence of legislative investigatory authority, intended to go as far as did Mr Justice Coleridge in a famous

1 Carr, *op. cit.* 6.   2 Jowitt, *op. cit.* 145.   3 273 U.S. 135, 174-5 (1927).

English case and assert that such power was unlimited. 'That the Commons are, in the words of Lord Coke, the general inquisitors of the realm, I fully admit', said the learned judge, in the case alluded to, 'it would be difficult to define any limits by which the subject matter of their inquiry can be bounded....I would be content to state that they may inquire into everything which it concerns the public weal for them to know; and they themselves, I think, are entrusted with the determination of what falls within that category.'[1]

American courts have rejected the notion that legislators are the 'general inquisitors of the realm'. Though they have acknowledged the existence of congressional investigatory authority, they have consistently asserted that such authority could properly be exercised only 'in aid of the legislative function'.[2] The difficulty, however, is to determine just what is meant by this limitation. If it renders *ultra vires* any congressional inquiry that is not intended to aid the legislature in the enactment of specific laws, then it would result in the invalidation of investigations intended to supervise the administration and to enlighten the public, whose importance has already been emphasized.

The United States Supreme Court has never given a categorical answer to the question of what, if any, are the precise limits upon the congressional investigatory power. In a case decided in 1880,[3] it did, it is true, hold invalid an investigation by an *ad hoc* committee of the House of Representatives, on the ground that it bore no relation to any contemplated exercise of law-making power. But more recent cases appear to have given up this limitation. The most important of them have involved the work of the Committee on Un-American Activities of the House of Representatives. That committee, which was set up on a permanent basis in 1946 to investigate so-called un-American propaganda activities in the United States, and which has in practice largely concerned itself with Communist activities, has caused much dispute. Especially has this been true of the manner in which it has functioned and its alleged disregard of procedural safeguards. 'In carrying their case against the Un-American Activities Committee to the courts, the committee's opponents have raised virtually every constitutional point that has ever been made against any earlier Congressional committee and have also devised several new arguments.'[4] Not a single final judicial ruling adverse to the committee has, however, as yet been rendered. The recent cases upholding the Un-American

---

1 *Howard* v. *Gossett* (1845), 10 Q.B. 359, 379.
2 The term used in *Kilbourn* v. *Thompson*, 103 U.S. 168, 189 (1880).
3 *Kilbourn* v. *Thompson*, 103 U.S. 168 (1880).
4 Carr, *op. cit.* 422.

Activities Committee and the way in which it has exercised its investigatory authority illustrate, perhaps better than anything else, the present American judicial view with regard to what Mr Justice Frankfurter has termed 'the penetrating and pervasive scope of the investigative power of Congress'.[1]

Under the recent jurisprudence of the American courts, there would seem to be few, if any, practical limitations today upon the scope of congressional investigatory authority. Nor is the legal situation in this respect one which is necessarily to be deplored. The power of investigation is, in the American system of complete separation between the legislative and executive branches at least, a necessary incident of the legislative function. 'Ordinarily legislation cannot be intelligently enacted without previously ascertaining facts from which conclusions can be drawn as to whether need for legislation exists and, if so, what form the legislation should assume.'[2] But the need for broad powers of inquiry in the legislature rests upon something besides the need for information to serve as a basis for enacting laws. The Congress in the United States, like the Parliament in Britain, should be looked upon as a great public forum for the ventilation of popular grievances. The elected representatives of the people, more directly responsible to the citizenry than any other organ of government, should not be restricted by the courts in their efforts to bring to light anything which they feel should be subjected to the public scrutiny. 'It is', as Lord Jowitt has emphasized, 'desirable that a committee of Congress should wield great powers, for otherwise it could never do its job in a complete and satisfactory manner.'[3]

It cannot, of course, be gainsaid that there have been abuses in recent years of the congressional investigatory power. The very method of legislative inquisition in the United States, indeed, seems to involve, in Lord Jowitt's phrase, the risk of unfairness to individuals.[4] An investigative 'committee, if it is fairly to represent Congress, must be comprised in some part of those who support the administration and in some part of those who oppose it. This must give rise to the risk that it will be said, whether truly or not, that some members of such a committee are at least as much concerned with bringing the administration into discredit as with protecting the rights and privileges of an individual citizen.'[5] It is the influence of political considerations upon the conduct of congressional committees vested with the function of investigating the behaviour of government

1 *United States* v. *Rumely*, 345 U.S. 41, 43 (1953). For a review of the recent cases, see Schwartz, 'Legislative powers of investigation', 57 *Dickinson L. Rev.* (1952), 31, 38 *et seq.*
2 *Bryan* v. *United States*, 72 F. Supp. 59, 61 (D.C. 1947).
3 Jowitt, *op. cit.* 142.   4 *Ibid.* 145.   5 *Ibid.* 141.

officials and other individuals which has led to most of the recent misuses of the investigatory power.

The fact that there can be and have, in fact, been substantial abuses by the Congress of its investigatory authority does not, however, affect the legal answer to the questions of the existence and scope of such authority. That the power may be misused, in the words of the American Supreme Court, 'affords no ground for denying the power. The same contention might be directed against the power to legislate, and of course would be unavailing. We must assume, for present purposes, that neither house will be disposed to exert the power beyond its proper bounds.'[1] It is common knowledge to the students of the American system that the behaviour of certain congressional committees has led to widespread criticisms. But such matters are not for the courts in their decisions upon the validity of exercises of the investigatory authority. 'I think it would be an unwarranted act of judicial usurpation', asserted Mr Justice Jackson in 1949, 'to strip Congress of its investigatory power, or to assume for the courts the function of supervising congressional committees. I should... leave the responsibility for the behavior of its committees squarely on the shoulders of Congress.'[2]

So far as the rules of law are concerned, there would seem, and quite properly, as has been indicated, to be few, if any, practical restrictions upon the permissible scope of legislative inquiries in the United States. This is not to deny that there is room for improvement in procedures within the legislative investigatory process. The constant complaints that have been directed against the conduct of certain congressional committees indicate that there is need for legislative self-restraint in this field. 'Friends and supporters of the congressional power may well fear its present exercise here', declared a federal judge, in dissenting from a decision upholding the exercise of investigatory authority by the Un-American Activities Committee of the House of Representatives, 'and find the application of a proper restraint a source of strength in the long run, rather than the reverse.'[3] But this does not change the legal situation with regard to congressional investigatory authority. As even the judge just quoted himself admitted, 'it is true, as many urge, that the force of public opinion and the expression of the electorate at the polls must remain its main source of control'.[4]

1 *McGrain* v. *Daugherty*, 273 U.S. 135, 175 (1927).
2 Dissenting, in *Eisler* v. *United States*, 338 U.S. 189, 196 (1949).
3 Clark, J., dissenting, in *United States* v. *Josephson*, 165 F. 2d 82, 100 (2d Cir. 1947).   4 *Ibid.*

LEGISLATIVE 'EXPERTISE'

'The need for Congress', aptly states an outstanding member of the American Senate, 'is far more vital now than it was when able gentlemen in knee breeches, lace, and three-cornered hats burned midnight candles in Philadelphia and wrote the Constitution. If the reader had lived then, he would hardly have been aware of the existence of the national government in everyday life. Today it regulates even the time: the clocks of the nation are set by the federally operated Naval Observatory in Washington. This relatively obscure fact is only a symbol of the vast expansion in governmental service that the people have demanded their Congress approve as modern science, industry, and education changed ways of living.'[1]

Perhaps the most difficult question which the American legislature has had to face has been that of how to adapt its methods and procedures, born in a leisurely age of knee-breeches and three-cornered hats, to the exigencies of government in the twentieth century. 'How can a group of non-specialists, elected as representatives of the electorate, really function in a specialized and technological age?' plaintively asks an important official of the American Congress.[2] That is the key question which must be answered by those who believe in representative government and seek to preserve it as a flourishing institution even in an atomic age.

An answer to it must proceed along the lines of ensuring that the non-specialist members of the legislative assembly are enabled to acquire the *expertise* or the assistance of experts which will permit them effectively to deal with the innumerable technical problems with which the modern legislature is confronted. For it should not be forgotten that the important problems facing government today are complex to such a degree that the most skilled specialization and the most profound wisdom are none too great to deal with them.[3] 'The great difficulty is not even the fact that in a given session of Congress there are thirty or forty major issues. It is rather what is inherent in the nature of the issues themselves. The measures proposed are generally urgent (especially in foreign affairs); they are almost invariably far-reaching, but obscure in their derivative or secondary effects; they are often drastic in their primary impact, but in a complex and disturbing way; they are highly specialized; they may involve a multitude of principles, often conflicting; they always involve a quantity of facts for background.'[4]

In the committee system developed by it, whose functioning has been

1 Kefauver and Levin, *op. cit.* 17.   2 Griffith, *op. cit.* 53.
3 *Ibid.*   4 *Ibid.* 58.

described above, the American Congress has available to it a ready device to secure adequate division of labour and specialization within its own membership. The legislator who serves upon a standing committee concerned with a particular subject-matter for any length of time can be expected, from the mere force of constant contact with the subject, if from nothing else, to acquire a certain degree of expertness with regard to it. Since all of the members of the Congress are assigned to one or more committees, each of them should, after serving upon them for some time, obtain the specialized knowledge necessary to deal with matters coming up before them.

The realization in practice of such legislative expertness through the committee system has, however, proved most difficult because of the planless way in which that system developed. As is only natural with a system which, like Topsy, just 'growed', the committee system in the American Congress did not evolve in a symmetrical and logical fashion. The result of this was an excessive number of committees (thirty-three in the Senate and forty-eight in the House), whose jurisdiction overlapped and was, in many cases, almost concurrent. This inevitably involved waste and duplication in time and manpower. And, from the point of view of the problem we are concerned with, it meant that many senators served on as many as seven or more standing committees, while House members served on as many as six or more. How could a member of the Congress be expected to become an expert in the work of any one committee, when his time and efforts had to be divided among such a large number?

It was largely for this reason that a joint committee of the two Houses of the American legislature, set up to study the organization of the Congress and to recommend improvements therein, asserted that 'no adequate improvements in the organization of Congress can be undertaken or effected unless Congress first reorganizes its present obsolete and overlapping committee structure....By limiting Members of Congress to service on a few standing committees, they can become more familiar with their committee work. By consolidating many minor committees, a system of major committees for both houses will be created and members will have time properly to weigh and consider legislative matters referred to these consolidated committees.'[1]

The proposals of this joint committee led to the Legislative Reorganization Act of 1946—the first important attempt (though by no means a complete one) by the American legislature to overhaul its structure so as to enable it to meet present-day problems. So far as the committee system is concerned, that Act, in accordance with the most important recommen-

[1] *Report of the Joint Committee on the Organization of the Congress* (1946), 2.

dation of the joint committee, replaced the cumbersome committee structure, which has been described, by fewer and, in the case of the Senate at least, smaller committees. Thus, the number of standing committees in the Senate has been cut down from thirty-three to fifteen and in the House from forty-eight to nineteen. The jurisdiction of each of these newer committees is carefully defined in order to eliminate the conflicts and overlappings that have been referred to above. With the number of committees thus substantially reduced, the average House member finds himself on one or two committees only and the average senator on two or three. This in itself has brought about a higher degree of specialization within the membership of the Congress.[1]

But *expertise* within the members of the legislative body is alone not enough to enable it to deal with the technical problems involved in contemporary legislation. No matter how learned individual legislators may be, they must still have recourse to the technical assistance of others, if they are to perform their tasks adequately. In the past, such assistance has normally been forthcoming from those outside the legislature who are interested in having particular measures enacted. They have been only too willing to supply the legislator with drafts of bills, supported by factual data, statistics, arguments and the like. This has been particularly true of government departments which happen to have been interested in securing the passage or defeat of certain laws.

A legislature which relies wholly upon outside interests, public or private, for the technical and other information necessary for the intelligent carrying on of its work tends, however, to become wholly dependent upon those interests, so far as particular legislation is concerned. Especially is this true with regard to reliance upon administrative *expertise*, for the executive branch has at its disposal investigating and research facilities which tend to overwhelm the individual legislator beneath the mass of information and statistics produced by them.

The obvious answer to all of this is for the legislature itself to establish its own staff agencies to furnish it with the technical information which may be lacking to its individual members. 'The question of adequate and expert staff', as one senator has expressed it, 'is of vital importance. Undoubtedly one of the great contributing factors to the shift of influence and power from the legislative to the executive branch in recent years is the fact that Congress has been generous in providing expert and technical personnel for the executive agencies but niggardly in providing such personnel for itself.'[2]

---

1 Griffith, *op. cit.* 61.
2 Senator La Follette, quoted in Galloway, *op. cit.* 157.

Prior to 1946, the two most important steps which the American legislature had taken in the direction of ensuring competent technical assistance for itself were the creation of an Office of Legislative Counsel, in each House, to assist the members and committees of Congress in the complex process of bill drafting, and of a Legislative Reference Service, to aid the legislators with any problems requiring research which they might have. These staff agencies were, however, far from sufficiently staffed, and, reporting in 1946, the joint congressional committee on the organization of the American legislature, whose work has already been touched upon, was still able to assert that the problem of adequate staff assistance was an acute one. 'The shocking lack of adequate congressional fact-finding services and skilled staffs', reads the committee's report, 'sometimes reaches such ridiculous proportions as to make Congress dependent upon "handouts" from Government departments and private groups or newspaper stories for its basic fund of information on which to reach adequate decisions.'[1]

The Legislative Reorganization Act of 1946, which was based upon the recommendations of the joint committee, sought to deal with the problem referred to in some of its most important provisions. 'This Act', declares the Director of the Legislative Reference Service, 'marked the real birth of a full-fledged Congressional staff.'[2] Under it, greatly increased appropriations were authorized for the Office of Legislative Counsel and the Legislative Reference Service. The expansion of the latter agency has been particularly significant. Its duties, under the law, include the giving of advice and assistance to any committee of either chamber in the analysis, appraisal and evaluation of bills pending before it, or of recommendations submitted to Congress by the President or any executive agency; the gathering, classifying and analysing, upon request or its own initiative, of data having a bearing upon legislation; and the preparing of summaries and digests of public hearings before congressional committees and of public bills and resolutions introduced in either House.

To enable the Legislative Reference Service to perform these duties, it is authorized to appoint senior specialists in the different technical subjects which may have to be dealt with in the course of a legislative session.[3]

---

1 *Report*, 9. 2 Griffith, *op. cit.* 71.

3 Senior specialists are authorized under the Reorganization Act in the following fields: agriculture, American government and public administration, American public law, conservation, education, engineering and public works, full employment, housing, industrial organization and corporation finance, international affairs, international trade and economic geography, labour, mineral economics, money and banking, price economics, social welfare, taxation and fiscal policy, transportation and communications, and veterans' affairs.

These specialists are compensated by salaries comparable to those paid to equivalent senior officials in the executive branch. These provisions for a more adequate professional staff through the Legislative Reference Service are supplemented by other sections of the Act of 1946 which allow each standing committee of the Congress to engage up to four professional staff members at substantial salaries. This is intended to enable the committees to have expert technical assistance at their immediate disposal to aid them in their work. In addition, under a separate Act, each member of the Senate is now empowered to appoint an administrative assistant and the members of both Houses may hire adequate clerical staffs to help them in their duties.

The improvement effected by the Act of 1946 in the technical assistance situation in the American Congress is graphically illustrated in terms of appropriations. From 1944 to 1951, the amount spent upon staff agencies in the Congress multiplied almost fivefold—$5,176,300 for the fiscal year 1951, as compared to $1,193,580 for the fiscal year 1944.[1] The provision by the Congress for hiring a first-class staff commensurate with its grave responsibilities as the legislative assembly of the United States is a development of primary significance. 'It is my sincere conviction', the Director of the Legislative Reference Service has stated, 'based upon many, many more instances than I would ever be at liberty to disclose, that the enlargement and strengthening of the staffs of Congress have in fact been a major factor in arresting and probably reversing a trend that had set in in the United States as well as in every other industrialized nation. This is the trend in the direction of the ascendancy or even the virtually complete dominance of the bureaucracy over the legislative branch through the former's near-monopoly of the facts and the technical and specialized competence on the basis of which decisions are ultimately made. Other legislative bodies—the British Parliament through its Royal Commissions, the Swedish Riksdag through its "remiss" and commission devices—do from time to time tap alternative expert sources. The new Japanese Diet has instituted a legislative reference service on the American model that has great potentialities. Yet by and large the Congress of the United States still remains as yet the only major legislative assembly of which it can unmistakably be said that its independent, creative functioning has grown steadily more effective in the last decade. The time elapsed is naturally still too short to be certain that this will be a permanent achievement.'[2]

1 Griffith, *op. cit.* 72.   2 *Ibid.* 74.

Chapter IV

THE PRESIDENT

'What is the best constitution for the executive department,' states the most famous of *Commentaries* upon the American Constitution, 'and what are the powers, with which it should be entrusted, are problems among the most important, and probably the most difficult to be satisfactorily solved, of all which are involved in the theory of free governments.... No man, who has ever deeply read the human history, and especially the history of republics, but has been struck with the consciousness, how little has been hitherto done to establish a safe depositary of power in any hands; and how often in the hands of one, or a few, or many, of an hereditary monarch, or an elective chief, the executive power has brought ruin upon the state, or sunk under the oppressive burden of its own imbecility.'[1]

There appears to be little doubt but that the framers of the American Constitution were strongly influenced by sentiments such as those which moved the author of this passage. In dealing with the organization of the national executive, the Convention of 1787, which drew up the American organic instrument, was well aware of the dilemma which confronted it. 'The majority of the Framers ardently desired to provide an executive power which should be capable of penetrating to the remotest parts of the Union, not only for the purpose of enforcing the national laws, but also... for the purpose of bringing assistance to the states in grave emergencies of domestic disorders. At the same time, most of them recognized that it was absolutely indispensable that the Convention should avoid stirring up the widespread popular fear of monarchy. Nor did the vast size of the country and the difficulties of travel and transportation make the problem any easier of solution. How could a political force be provided that would be sufficient to overcome these natural obstacles and yet be safe—or at least *thought* safe—from the point of view of popular liberty?'[2]

To set up a national executive which is both potent enough to deal effectively with the problems facing the nation and, at the same time, not so strong that it will tend to overwhelm the other two branches of government—this may seem as impossible a task as the squaring of the circle. The American constitutional system does, however, appear in large measure to have resolved the problem in the presidential office which has been

1 Story, *Commentaries on the Constitution of the United States* (1833), § 1404.
2 Corwin, *The President: Office and Powers* (3rd ed. 1948), 10.

developed under it. Under the Federal Constitution, the executive power possessed by the Government of the United States is vested in a President, who is elected every four years. His ability to perpetuate himself in office is all but eliminated by the provision now contained in the Constitution which prohibits a President from being elected to the term of office more than twice.[1] His authority is circumscribed by the rejection by the American system of the doctrine of inherent power in the executive.[2] His assertions of power must find their source in an express delegation, either in the Constitution or law passed by the Congress. Executive acts, no less than other governmental acts in the American system, are subject to judicial control on the question of their legality.

These are all substantial checks against abuses of authority by the American executive. But it should not be imagined from this that the President of the United States is in the powerless position of a Merovingian monarch. Quite the contrary! The provisions with regard to executive power in the federal Constitution are advisedly drawn in general terms. This has enabled presidential power to expand to meet the needs of emergency, while assuring its contraction on less pressing occasions. In many ways, indeed, the history of the presidency in the United States has been a record of ebbs and flows. And, if the observation of Lord Bryce that 'great men are not chosen Presidents'[3] has often been true, it is never-theless highly inaccurate as a generalization.[4] If mediocrity has all too frequently characterized the American chief magistrate in periods of normalcy, it is none the less a fact that in times of crisis the presidential office has always been occupied by men of stature. Certainly, the consistent ebbs and flows of presidential power speak well of the success of the framers of the American Constitution in their efforts at solving the problem which has been referred to, that of setting up an executive strong enough to contend with the concerns of the nation, but not so strong that the nation will not be able successfully to contend with him.

CONSTITUTIONAL PROVISIONS

'Speculative writers', a leading treatise upon the American presidency informs us, 'have sometimes traced the origins of government to a monarch in the forest who gathered in his person all power. At length wearying of his responsibilities, the hypothetical potentate delegated some of them to followers who eventually became "courts", and shared others

1 See *infra*, p. 95.   2 See *infra*, ch. VII.
3 Bryce, *The American Commonwealth* (1917 ed.), vol. I, 77 *et seq.*
4 See Laski, *The American Presidency, an Interpretation* (1940), 8.

with a more numerous body of subjects who in due time organized themselves into a "legislature". The indefinite residuum, called "executive power", he kept for himself.'[1] Thus it came about, the same treatise tells us, that 'whereas "legislative power" and "judicial power" today denote fairly definable *functions* of government as well as fairly constant *methods* for their discharge, "executive power" is still indefinite as to *function* and retains, particularly when it is exercised by a single individual, much of its original plasticity as regards method'.[2]

The relative vagueness which still inheres in the content of executive power, as contrasted with the authority of the other two branches of government, is seen clearly when one examines the legal position of the President of the United States. The domain of the executive power, as one observer has expressed it, constitutes a sort of 'dark continent' in American jurisprudence, the boundaries of which are still undetermined.[3] The constitutional provisions are among the most skeleton-like in the American organic instrument. 'The most defective part of the Constitution beyond all question', asserted an acute American student over a century ago, 'is that which relates to the Executive Department. It is impossible to read that instrument without being struck with the loose and unguarded terms in which the powers and duties of the President are pointed out.'[4] The language of Article II of the Federal Constitution, which contains the sections dealing with the executive and its powers, is imprecise and indefinite by comparison with the articles defining the authority of the other branches of the Government.

The important provisions of Article II of the American Constitution are contained in but a few sentences. Some of them are comparatively precise, such as those which confer upon the President the power to appoint, with the advice and consent of the Senate, all officers of the United States and to make treaties, provided two-thirds of the Senate concur. But the crucial powers vested in the American executive are conferred by the following sentences, whose terms are so broad as to leave the limits of authority granted by them almost wholly at large: 'The executive Power shall be vested in a President of the United States of America.... The President shall be Commander in Chief of the Army and Navy of the United States.... He shall take Care that the Laws be faithfully executed.'

We shall see in Chapter VII how the indefinite contours of the authority granted by these key provisions have led some American jurists to assert

1 Corwin, *op. cit.* 1.　　　　　　　　　2 *Ibid.*
3 Garner, 'Le pouvoir exécutif en temps de guerre aux États-Unis', *Revue du droit public* (1918), 5, 13.
4 Upshur, *A Brief Inquiry into the Nature and Character of Our Federal Government* (1840), 116.

a doctrine of inherent power in the President analogous to that once possessed by the Crown in England under the royal prerogative. At the moment, it is enough to note that the skeleton-like nature of the provisions in Article II of the American Constitution is hardly enough to prescribe the details of the powers and duties with which the presidential office has become invested. The constitutional provisions, it is true, constitute the base upon which executive power in the United States has been constructed. The structure of presidential authority itself is, however, much larger than the constitutional foundation. It is the composite of the powers asserted by American Presidents during the history of the Republic, which have, by dint of repeated exercise, attained the status of powers authorized by constitutional usage or convention. As is the case in all constitutional systems, the constitutional practice which has grown up is often as significant as the formal provisions of the organic instrument. So far as the presidential office is concerned, indeed, largely because of the rudimentary character of the provisions of Article II in the American Constitution, the unwritten constitutional law is, in many ways, even more important than the written one.

ELECTION

The one portion of Article II of the Federal Constitution which seeks to prescribe the principles which it lays down in some detail is that dealing with the way in which the President is chosen. The method of election which it sets forth with such particularity is, however, today mostly a matter of form; the substance of presidential elections is something entirely unlike that foreseen by the draftsmen of the American organic instrument. 'The founders of the Constitution', as Professor Laski has aptly expressed it, 'were especially proud of the method they adopted for choosing the president; none of their expectations has been more decisively disappointed.'[1]

In the Constitutional Convention of 1787, there had been a sharp dispute on the question of whether the President should be elected directly by the people or be chosen by the legislature. Each system had its strong partisans and, as so often happens when such is the case, the final result was the adoption of a compromise. Under the constitutional provisions governing the election of the American chief executive, 'Each State shall appoint, in such Manner as the Legislature thereof may direct, a Number of Electors, equal to the whole Number of Senators and Representatives to which the State may be entitled in the Congress....The Electors shall meet in their respective States, and vote by Ballot' for President and Vice-

1 Laski, *op. cit.* 41.

President.[1] The President is thus elected, under the Constitution, neither directly by the people nor by the legislature. He is instead chosen by presidential electors appointed for the purpose.

It is to be noted, as the United States Supreme Court has pointed out, that 'The Constitution does not provide that the appointment of electors shall be by popular vote....It...leaves it to the legislature exclusively to define the method of effecting the object.'[2] During the early years under the Constitution, in many of the States, presidential electors were appointed by the legislatures rather than elected by the people. At the present time, however, in all of the States, the electors are chosen by popular vote on a general ticket.

The decision of the draftsmen of the American Constitution not to confide the election of the chief executive to the legislature is one which has rarely, if ever, been criticized. 'The convention of 1787', asserts the Marquis de Chambrun in his well-known treatise on executive power in America, 'was right in withholding from the House of Representatives the right to elect the President. Had it done otherwise, one of two things would have happened—either the House would have received imperative instructions from its constituents—it would itself have been elected, in view of the presidential choice to be made by it, or it would have become a central point of intrigues. Party spirit would have distracted it, and each candidate would have employed every means at his disposal to secure votes. Never would an election have been less free and unbiased.'[3] The experience in European countries like France, where the President has been elected by the legislature, certainly appears to indicate that such a method of election is not the one which is best calculated to ensure that the presidential office will be a strong one.

A more difficult question is that of the wisdom of the framers of the American Constitution in refusing to entrust the selection of the chief executive directly to the electorate. The men of 1787 rejected the notion of immediate choice by the people because they were afraid that the latter were not wholly capable of making a proper selection. 'They feared that the people were not sufficiently enlightened to make an intelligent choice of the executive chief; they also apprehended difficulties as to the manner of execution.'[4] They thus settled upon the solution of the electors— persons, in Hamilton's phrase, chosen for the temporary and sole purpose of electing the President[5]—as an intermediate body upon whom alone

1 Article II, section 1.
2 *McPherson* v. *Blacker*, 146 U.S. 1, 27 (1892).
3 Chambrun, *The Executive Power in the United States* (1874), 44.
4 *Ibid.* 22.   5 *The Federalist*, no. 68.

would devolve the actual duty of selecting the chief executive. 'Being themselves chosen electors on account of their personal merits they would be better qualified than the masses to select an able and honourable man for President.'[1]

There appears to be little doubt but that the draftsmen of the Federal Constitution intended the electors to exercise their individual judgments in casting their votes. 'No one faithful to our history can deny', declares a recent opinion by Mr Justice Jackson, 'that the plan originally contemplated, what is implicit in its text, that electors would be free agents, to exercise an independent and nonpartisan judgment as to the men best qualified for the Nation's highest offices.'[2] As early as 1796, however, with the avowed appearance of political parties upon a national scale, the electors became transmuted into 'party dummies', a character they have retained ever since.[3] 'It has been observed with much point', wrote Joseph Story in 1833, 'that in no respect have the enlarged and liberal views of the framers of the constitution, and the expectations of the public, when it was adopted, been so completely frustrated, as in the practical operation of the system, so far as relates to the independence of the electors in the electoral college. It is notorious, that the electors are now chosen wholly with reference to particular candidates, and are silently pledged to vote for them.... So, that nothing is left to the electors after their choice, but to register votes which are already pledged; and an exercise of independent judgment would be treated, as a political usurpation, dishonourable to the individual, and a fraud upon his constituents.'[4]

The presidential electors have, for over a century, cast their ballots for the nominees of the political party on whose ticket they were elected. In many of the States, indeed, the names of the electors do not even appear on the ballot, and the voters vote only for the party of the presidential candidate whom they favour. It is true that, in theory, the electors still retain their constitutional discretion to vote for any person whom they choose. In practice, however, the power of the electors in this respect is as devoid of practical content as are many of the prerogatives which, in theory, are still possessed by the Crown in Britain. 'An elector who failed to vote for the nominee of his party', a former American President has stated, 'would be the object of execration, and in times of very high excitement might be the subject of a lynching.'[5]

The fate of the electoral plan envisaged by the draftsmen of the American Constitution has been aptly described by Mr Justice Jackson.

1 Bryce, *op. cit.* 41.   2 *Ray* v. *Blair*, 343 U.S. 214, 232 (1952).
3 Corwin, *op. cit.* 51.   4 *Commentaries*, §1457.
5 Benjamin Harrison, quoted in Corwin, *op. cit.* 51.

'This arrangement miscarried', reads his opinion. 'Electors, although often personally eminent, independent, and respectable, officially became voluntary party lackeys and intellectual nonentities to whose memory we might justly paraphrase a tuneful satire: '

> They always voted at their Party's call
> And never thought of thinking for themselves at all.'[1]

In practice, then, the presidential electors in the United States always vote for the candidate of their party. The form of an independent vote by the electors is still gone through, and their ballots are counted and the result announced in Congress with all due ceremony; but the substance is quite another thing. The real election occurs when the voters cast their ballots for electors. Since the latter always adhere to their pledge to vote for the nominees of their party, the voters' choice of electors is, in effect, essentially their choice of a President.

Nevertheless, it should not be thought that the formal method of election prescribed by the Federal Constitution is no longer of any practical significance. Though they no longer retain the freedom of choice which the men of 1787 intended them to have, the intervention of the electors is still often a matter of decisive importance.[2] The system of choosing electors by 'general ticket' over an entire State causes the whole weight of a State to be thrown into the scales of one candidate, that candidate whose list of electors is carried in the given State. The example given by Lord Bryce may still be used to illustrate this. 'In the election of 1884, New York State had thirty-six electoral votes. Each party rán its list or "ticket" of thirty-six presidential electors for the State, who were bound to vote for the party's candidate, Mr Blaine or Mr Cleveland. The Democratic list (i.e. that which included the thirty-six Cleveland electors) was carried by a majority of 1100 out of a total poll exceeding 1,100,000. Thus, all the thirty-six electoral votes of New York were secured for Mr Cleveland, and these thirty-six determined the issue of the struggle over the whole Union, in which nearly 10,000,000 popular votes were cast. The hundreds of thousands of votes given in New York for the Blaine or Republican list did not go to swell the support which Mr Blaine obtained in other States, but were utterly lost.'[3] The result of this has been that the discrepancy between the size of a candidate's electoral vote and that of his so-called

1 *Ray* v. *Blair*, 343 U.S. 214, 232 (1952).

2 Corwin, *op. cit.* 52.

3 Bryce, *op. cit.* 44. In the 1952 election Adlai Stevenson, the Democratic candidate, received 495,729 votes in the State of Kentucky, while President Eisenhower received 495,029. Despite the meagreness of his majority there, Stevenson, of course, received all of Kentucky's ten electoral votes.

popular vote has often been enormous.[1] Several times, indeed, it has even happened that the candidate who secured the majority needed of the votes of the electors has only obtained a minority of the popular vote.[2]

The obvious answer to all of this is to substitute a direct system of choice by popular ballot for the present indirect system of voting by electors. 'The demise of the whole electoral system', a member of the United States Supreme Court has recently declared, 'would not impress me as a disaster. At its best it is a mystifying and distorting factor in presidential elections which may resolve a popular defeat into an electoral victory. At its worst it is open to local corruption and manipulation, once so flagrant as to threaten the stability of the country. To abolish it and substitute direct election of the President, so that every vote wherever cast would have equal weight in calculating the result, would seem to me a gain for simplicity and integrity of our governmental processes.'[3] There are, in fact, a number of proposals before the Congress which aim toward a constitutional amendment accomplishing the suggested result. In view of the normal reluctance of Americans to tamper with the form of their constitutional institutions, it is, however, doubtful whether any of them will be adopted in the immediate future.

Under the design of presidential election conceived by the framers of the Federal Constitution, the most important element was the independent choice to be exercised by the electors. Since the miscarriage of the original plan, with the electors, as we have seen, being reduced to mere automata recording on their ballots the choice of the party on whose tickets they were selected, the focal point has shifted to the methods for nominating presidential candidates of the principal political parties.

The nominating organ of American parties has been a convention composed of representatives of the members of the party. These representatives are normally selected upon a territorial basis. More and more they are coming to be chosen by registered voters of the party in so-called primary elections. The majority of delegates to conventions are, however, still appointed by local political leaders.

The way in which a party convention in the United States operates is as difficult to explain to a non-American observer as it is to elucidate the working of parliamentary government in France to one who is other than an inhabitant of that country. Properly to understand French government, André Malraux has declared, 'one must be married to it, and be frustrated

1 Corwin, *op. cit.* 52.

2 In both 1876 and 1888, the candidates who won received a minority of the popular vote. And the same was true in the case of the first elections of Presidents Lincoln and Wilson, as well as in the 1948 election of President Truman.

3 *Ray v. Blair*, 343 U.S. 214, 234 (1952).

as a man is by a wife with whom he is hopelessly coupled'.[1] Much the
same can be said of the American system of nominating candidates for the
presidency. 'An American presidential convention', writes an acute
English observer, 'is like nothing else in the civilized world; and the critics
of the system—which, in its modern form, is just a hundred years old—
have exhausted the language of vituperation in attacks upon its character.
The power of money; the persuasive power of hidden and corrupt influence; the undue authority of the "doubtful" state; the overt and hidden
prejudices against particular types of candidates, as, for instance, members of the Roman Catholic Church; the "deals" which accompany the
capture of a delegation for one candidate as against another; the mythology
of the "favorite son"; the casual influence, notable in the case of Lincoln's
selection, of the choice of the convention city; the undue impact, as in the
Democratic convention of 1896, of a single speech by a potential nominee;
the operation of the technique of the "dark horse" candidate; the exploita-
tion of the "stalking-horse" behind whom some well-organized group
has its carefully prepared selection whose name is put forward at the right
moment; and, finally, the raucous, complex, and hectic atmosphere of the
convention itself; its well-improvised enthusiasms; its fantastic horse-play;
its immunity to thought; its wild rumors; its incredible conspiracies; all
these characteristics, none of which can ever suffer exaggeration, seem to
the outsider, and especially to the European outsider, about the worst
possible way in which to choose a man to occupy the highest executive
post in a democratic commonwealth.'[2]

The system of nominating presidential candidates by conventions of the
political parties is one which has developed in a wholly extra-constitutional
manner. Yet, it cannot be denied that its development, which was entirely
unforeseen by the framers of the American organic instrument, has completely altered the method of choosing the chief executive which was prescribed in 1787. It was the rise of national parties and their designation of
candidates for the presidency that led to the transformation of the voting
by electors into a mere formal ratification of the choice of the party on
whose ticket they appeared. The salient feature of contemporary American
political life, as in that of all other democratic countries, is thus the
dominance in the political arena of organized parties, through whom alone
the individual can hope to make his weight felt. The major American
parties may seem more like loose coalitions than the closely knit, ordered
parties with which British and European political scientists are familiar.

1 White, 'The three lives of André Malraux', *N.Y. Times Magazine*, 15 February
1953, p. 26.
2 Laski, *op. cit.* 41.

At the same time, it should be recognized that much of the stability of politics in the United States stems from this fact. The reconciliation of diverse views and interests, at least for the purposes of electoral campaigns, under the aegis of the two principal parties has prevented the emergence of the 'splinter' parties so common in European politics.

TENURE

The American Constitution provides that the President shall hold his office during the term of four years. In its original form it says nothing about any limitation upon the number of terms which a President may serve. As Lord Bryce has pointed out, however, in this, as in so many other cases, tradition has supplied the place of law.[1] The Convention of 1787 favoured the indefinite re-eligibility of the President, largely because of the universal expectation that George Washington would be the first person chosen to be President, and would be willing to serve indefinitely.[2] This expectation was disappointed when Washington, after having served a second term, absolutely refused a third. Lord Bryce asserts that he did this to avoid the 'risk to republican institutions of suffering the same man to continue constantly in office'.[3] This may be true, in part, though later students of American history have declared that Washington's decision not to run for a third term was influenced more by personal considerations than by the desire to create a precedent.[4] However that may be, Washington's refusal did, in fact, set a precedent against third terms for a President, which was followed for almost a century and a half.

In stating his reasons for retiring at the end of his second term, in 1807, Thomas Jefferson stressed Washington's example. 'If some termination to the services of the Chief Magistrate be not fixed by the Constitution, or supplied by practice', he contended, 'his office, nominally four years, will in fact become for life, and history shows how easily that degenerates into an inheritance.'[5] The examples of Washington and Jefferson were followed by successive Presidents and, by the middle of the last century, the 'no third-term' tradition had become 'as sacred as if it were written in the Constitution'.[6] The tradition against a third term gained further force by the failure of attempts to break it on the part of Presidents Grant and Theodore Roosevelt, and it appeared as strongly established as are many of the conventions of the British Constitution. As recently as 1940, in the

---

1 Bryce, *op. cit.* 45. 2 Corwin, *op. cit.* 43.
3 Bryce, *op. cit.* 45.
4 See Corwin, *op. cit.* 43; Milton, *The Use of Presidential Power* (1944), 48.
5 Quoted in Corwin, *op. cit.* 388.
6 James Buchanan, quoted *ibid.* 390.

published version of his lectures on the American presidency, Harold J. Laski stated: 'Certainly the pressure of public opinion against a third term is very strong. There is not only the power of tradition, in a country where tradition exercises very great authority. There is an important truth in the argument. . .that "the American people would grow very restive under a long, executive term of office. . .the change for which they so loudly clamor every four years is a safety valve for their prejudices and sentiments".'[1]

Strong though the tradition against a third term for Presidents had thus become, it was, as Lord Bryce so aptly reminded us, nevertheless only a tradition, not sure to be always regarded.[2] And, in the very year in which the statement quoted above by Professor Laski was published, the convention against a third term was broken, for the first time, with the election of President Franklin D. Roosevelt for the third time. 'Today', as a leading treatise on the American chief executive expresses it, 'the anti-third term tradition qua tradition is no more, having succumbed to the late President's successful defiance of it in 1940, which was repeated in 1944.'[3]

Though the election of President F. D. Roosevelt to third and fourth terms marked the end of the anti-third term tradition, it has, since his death, been given renewed vigour, and in a more permanent fashion by the ratification in 1951 of the Twenty-second Amendment to the American Constitution. Under its provision, 'No person shall be elected to the office of the President more than twice.' Thus, the prohibition against more than two terms in office for the American chief executive, which, until 1940, rested upon an unwritten convention which did not prove strong enough to resist the appeal of an enormously popular President, has today been raised to the status of an express constitutional interdiction.

'The wisdom of this amendment', asserts a French student of the American constitutional system, 'may be doubted. It introduces a rigid rule in a domain, where circumstances may require its not being followed.'[4] It is difficult to disagree with this viewpoint. There appears to be little doubt but that the 1951 Amendment to the Federal Constitution was inspired, at least in part, by those seeking to register disapproval of President Roosevelt for seeking a third and then a fourth term. On its merits, its prohibition seems unduly to exclude from office the very person who, by ability and experience, may best be able safely to navigate the ship of state. 'The day may come', stated an American President over a century ago, 'when danger shall lower over us, and when we have a President at the helm of State who possesses the confidence of the country,

1 Laski, *op. cit.* 65. 2 Bryce, *op. cit.* 46.
3 Corwin, *op. cit.* 46.
4 Pinto, *La Crise de l'état aux États-Unis* (1951), 114.

and is better able to weather the storm than any other pilot; shall we, then, under such circumstances, deprive the people of the United States of the power of obtaining his services for a [third] term?'[1]

PRESIDENT AND PRIME MINISTER COMPARED

'As every President has to do', stated former President Taft in 1915, 'I made many addresses, and the gentleman who introduced me, by way of exalting the occasion rather than the guest, not infrequently said that he was about to introduce one who exercised greater governmental power than any monarch in Europe. I need hardly point out the inadequacies of this remark, by comparing the powers of the President of the United States with those of the rulers of countries in which there is not real popular legislative control. The powers of the German Emperor, of the Emperor of Austria, and the Emperor of Russia are far wider than those of the President of the United States.... On the other hand, in really parliamentary governments, the head of the state is less powerful than our President. In England, as it is, the King reigns, but does not govern, and the same thing is true in the Dominion of Canada, of the Governor-General. In France, the President presides, but does not govern. In such parliamentary governments, however, there is a real ruler who exercises in some important respects a greater power than the President of the United States. He is the premier and exercises both executive and legislative functions.'[2]

In President Taft's conception, the position and powers of the American chief executive appear to lie somewhere between those of the Crown and those of the Prime Minister in Britain. To some extent, this concept of the presidential office is an accurate one. Thus, it cannot be denied that the President's part in the legislative process, though far greater than that actually played by the Queen in Britain, is not nearly as large as that of the Prime Minister. The latter can, because of his position as the leader of the majority in the House of Commons, influence the enactment of laws much more directly and effectively than the American President can hope to do.

In many respects, however, the picture painted by President Taft is not an accurate one. The President of the United States is both the head of state and the chief of the executive branch. The fact that his tenure does not depend upon congressional approval enables him to maintain an independence of the legislature which no British Prime Minister could assert

1 James Buchanan, quoted in Corwin, *op. cit.* 390. This statement was made some years before Buchanan's election to the presidency.
2 Taft, *Our Chief Magistrate and his Powers* (1916), 9.

and long remain in office. The election of the President upon a party basis has tended more and more to make him the leader of his party, though, because of the relative laxity of American party discipline, his control in this respect may not be as effective as that exerted by the British Prime Minister. Then, too, the status of the President as a national leader is one to which no Prime Minister in a parliamentary system can pretend. The President alone, of all governmental officials, is elected upon a nation-wide basis, and this enables his actions to be placed upon a basis of popular support such as that which no other individual can assert. In an age of mass communications, the President's position in this respect can easily be made effective by appeals, over the head of the Congress, as it were, for the backing of the electorate, when any part of his programme meets legislative opposition. In Britain too, of course, such appeals to the country can be made. But here, to be truly effective, they involve an election and the consequent risk of loss of office to the Prime Minister who makes them.

In addition, the position of the American President as head of the administration appears, in some ways, more effective than that of the Prime Minister in Britain. To the President alone is delegated all of the executive authority vested in the Federal Government. The Prime Minister in Britain is, in relation to the members of the Cabinet, more or less like a chairman of the board of directors of the governmental enterprise. He is *primus inter pares*; he is as dependent upon his colleagues in the Cabinet as they are upon him. The relationship of the American President to his Cabinet is an entirely different one. He dominates them completely, for they hold their offices entirely at his pleasure. It is he alone who is responsible for ensuring that the laws are faithfully executed. It is he alone who is vested with the power to appoint and remove executive officers, and his authority in this respect enables him to control the government departments in a more efficacious manner than can the British Prime Minister.[1]

Then, too, the President is vested with authority which, in the British system, is still retained by the Crown. It is the President who is the commander-in-chief of the armed forces, and his power in this respect is a real one, as recent American history clearly reveals. Under the Constitution, it is he who exercises the prerogative of pardon. The many formal duties which, in Britain, devolve upon the Crown are, in America, performed by the President. In addition, bills passed by the Congress must be submitted to the President for his signature. The President, unlike the

1 The position of the President is, however, weakened by the existence of the so-called independent regulatory commissions in the American system which are not directly accountable to him. See *infra*, p. 116.

British Sovereign, it should be noted, does possess an effective veto power over legislation. The Crown's power to issue Orders in Council, which is, of course, only a formal power today, finds its counterpart in the United States in the presidential authority to promulgate Executive Orders, an authority which the American chief executive exercises in substance as well as form.

The analogy of the American President as an official whose position lies between that of the Crown and that of the Prime Minister in Britain, which President Taft, as we have seen, drew, is thus not entirely consistent with the facts. A more accurate conception would look upon the President as combining in his hands many of the powers exercised by both the Sovereign and the head of the Government in the British system. It is this combination of the functions of Queen and Prime Minister in his person that makes the office of the President such a significant and powerful one.

LEGISLATIVE ROLE

Under a parliamentary system of government, such as that which prevails in Britain, the Cabinet is characterized not only by its position as head of the administration, but also by its role as leader of the legislature. The position of the American President is an entirely different one. The President is never the leader of Congress in the sense in which the British Prime Minister is of the House of Commons. He rarely has at his disposal the almost automatic legislative majority which is available to the Government in Britain. He cannot hold over the Congress the threat of dissolution; its term of office, like his own, is fixed by the Constitution. He does not have the means available to the British Government to ensure disciplined voting along party lines. Nor does he or any other member of the executive participate immediately in the process of legislation.[1] The President, unlike the Prime Minister, cannot directly ensure that the measures which he desires will be enacted by the Congress. It is these basic differences between the legislative role of the head of the executive on both sides of the Atlantic that led Professor Laski to assert that 'under all normal circumstances it is difficult not to feel that the president of the United States must envy the legislative position of a British prime minister'.[2]

Yet, though it is clear that the legislative role of the President is not as significant as that of the Prime Minister in a parliamentary system, one should not make the mistake of unduly minimizing its importance. In the first place, the President is expressly given a veto power over all legislation

1 Laski, *op. cit.* 112.
2 *Ibid.* 111.

by the Federal Constitution.[1] It provides that, after a bill has passed both Houses, it must be presented to the President; if he approves, he signs it; if not, he returns it, with his objections, to the House in which it originated, which then reconsiders it; if two-thirds of that House vote to pass the bill, it is sent to the other House for reconsideration; if passed by two-thirds of that House, it becomes a law, despite the President's veto. If a two-thirds vote of either House cannot be mustered to override the President's opposition, his veto of a particular bill effectively prevents it from becoming enacted into law.

'The Constitution in giving the President a qualified negative over legislation—commonly called a veto—' the United States Supreme Court has declared, 'entrusts him with an authority and imposes upon him an obligation that are of the highest importance.'[2] The character of the veto power vested in the President is, in President Taft's phrase, purely legislative.[3] 'It is true that the power is one of negation only, but the history of its origin shows that even in its qualified form, it is legislative in its nature, a brake rather than a steam chest, but nevertheless a very important part of the machinery for making laws.'[4] Nor can it be denied that the President, in exercising his veto power, may approach bills presented to him with much the same viewpoint as do the members of Congress when they are called upon to vote upon measures before them. He may, in other words, approve or veto a bill for any reasons which may commend themselves to him. The earlier view that the veto power should be exercised solely to prevent unconstitutional legislation has been definitely repudiated. 'The Constitution makes the President's veto turn on the question whether he approves the bill or not. The term "approve" is much too broad to be given the narrow construction by which it shall only authorize the President to withhold his signature when the reason for his disapproval of the bill is its invalidity. No better word could be found in the language to embrace the idea of passing on the merits of the bill.'[5]

According to Professor Laski, 'On the whole, it cannot be said that the [veto] power is a great one, or that it has been widely used.'[6] Most American jurists would sharply disagree with this statement. 'This Court has emphasized,' Mr Justice Stone (as he then was) has asserted, 'as does the language of the Constitution, the great importance of the veto power and the dominating purpose expressed in the constitutional provision that the power shall not be curtailed.'[7] Actually, as one authority has expressed it, the testimony of statistics is conclusive as to the true effectiveness

---

1 Article I, section 7.   2 *The Pocket Veto Case*, 279 U.S. 655, 677 (1929).
3 Taft, *op. cit.* 14.   4 *Ibid.* 16.   5 *Ibid.*
6 Laski, *op. cit.* 142.   7 *Wright* v. *United States*, 302 U.S. 583, 606 (1938).

of the President's veto.[1] It is only in the relatively rare case that a presidential veto is overridden; the veto is normally effective in well over nine cases out of ten.[2] Nor is Professor Laski's assertion that the veto power is not widely used an accurate one. The tendency, indeed, is for the President's authority in this respect to be exercised with ever-increasing frequency. Thus, the vetoes of Franklin D. Roosevelt during his first two terms represent over thirty per cent of the total measures disapproved since 1792, when the veto was first used (505 out of 1635).[3]

In addition, it should not be overlooked that the veto power is not always merely negative in nature; it is also a positive instrument for the assertion of presidential legislative leadership.[4] The veto power has become an ever-present threat to promoters of bills and has tended to become an instrument of bargaining for other legislation.[5] The threat of presidential disapproval is often enough to restrain congressional action contrary to the executive's desires.

Criticisms of the veto power, such as that enunciated by Professor Laski, strike an American as unfounded. It is true that the President's authority in this respect is weakened by the fact that he must approve or disapprove of a bill as a whole; he cannot veto only a part of a bill. The lack of such a power in the President has enabled Congress at times to bring to bear a pressure on him to permit legislation to go through which otherwise he would veto.[6] This has been done by including a measure disapproved by the President as a so-called rider in a necessary bill, such as an appropriations bill. In such a case, the President cannot veto the rider without vetoing the bill of which it is a part, on which the functioning of the Government may·depend. The obvious answer to this is to give the President the power of partial veto. Though such a power is, in fact, possessed by the Governors of most American States, efforts to secure it for the President have not yet progressed very far.

Important though it may be, it would be erroneous to think that the exercise of the veto power constitutes the sum total of the President's participation in the legislative process. During the present century, the American executive has come to play an ever more important part in the legislative field. 'In theory', as President Theodore Roosevelt expressed it, 'the Executive has nothing to do with legislation. In practice as things now are, the Executive is or ought to be peculiarly representative of the people as a whole. As often as not the action of the Executive offers the only means by which the people can get the legislation they demand and ought to have. Therefore a good Executive under the present conditions

---

1 Corwin, *op. cit.* 342.   2 *Ibid.* 343.   3 *Ibid.* 341.
4 *Ibid.* 343.   5 *Ibid.*   6 Taft, *op. cit.* 25.

of American political life must take a very active interest in getting the right kind of legislation.'[1]

Under the Federal Constitution, the President 'shall from time to time give to the Congress Information of the State of the Union, and recommend to their Consideration such Measures as he shall judge necessary and expedient'.[2] The practice has developed for the President to deliver an annual message to the Congress upon the state of the Union, and also a budget message. In these messages, as well as in others relating to particular subjects which he may transmit, the legislative programme desired by the executive is outlined. Though scarcely vested with the force which inheres in the speech from the throne in which the legislative measures of the British Government are announced at the beginning of each session of Parliament, it cannot be denied that the annual messages do have a great effect upon the passage of legislation. Especially has this been true since the revival by President Wilson of the practice, discontinued since 1801, of delivering such messages in person. When the President personally addresses the Congress, the attention of the nation—and, today, in an era of mass communications, literally its eyes and ears—are focused upon him. How effective such a forum may be in securing support for his programme is well shown in its use by such a consummate orator as Franklin D. Roosevelt.

But the national forum is one which is always available to a President who wishes to secure popular support for his programme. The great Presidents of the past fifty years were, in Franklin D. Roosevelt's phrase, 'moral leaders, each in his own way and for his own time, who used the Presidency as a pulpit'.[3] The President can always counter opposition in Congress by taking his case directly to the people. Describing his constant conflicts with congressional leaders, Theodore Roosevelt writes: 'I was forced to abandon the effort to persuade them to come to my way, and then I achieved results only by appealing over the heads of the Senate and House leaders to the people, who were the masters of both of us.'[4] Today, the effective use of television and radio—which gives the President the whole nation as his audience—offers him the certainty that his case will be heard and known as he wishes it to be heard and known.[5] If the President can marshal public opinion behind his programme, it is a hardy Congress which will continue to resist its enactment into law. It is this which led Harold J. Laski to assert that 'the real source... of presidential power lies, ultimately, in the appeal to public opinion'.[6]

1 Quoted in Corwin, *op. cit.* 321.   2 Article II, section 3.
3 Quoted in Corwin, *op. cit.* 331.   4 Quoted *ibid.* 323.
5 See Laski, *op. cit.* 146.   6 *Ibid.* 144.

Just as significant in the increasing importance of the American executive
in the legislative process has been its emergence as a force in the initiation
and formulation of legislation.[1] 'The House of Commons', states Laski,
'is only formally a legislative assembly; in this context its real business is
to act as the cabinet's organ of registration.... Fundamentally, legislation is
shaped in Whitehall, and not in Westminster. With Congress, this is not
the case.'[2] One of the cardinal facts of contemporary American political
life, however, is that it is more and more coming to be the case. There has
been a growing tendency in recent decades for major legislation to originate
in the executive departments. As administrative problems have become
technical, Congress has turned increasingly to the executive for guidance
in drafting laws.[3] In the ordinary processes of legislation, an outstanding
American jurist informs us, 'the last quarter of a century has witnessed a
tremendous rise of presidential power in initiating legislation, in expediting
its progress through the Congress and in vetoing undesired legislation....
Fully 80 per cent of the important legislation of the administration of
President Franklin D. Roosevelt originated in the White House or in the
executive departments. The habit then formed has not disappeared,
especially in fiscal and economic matters. In these fields the President has
the great advantage of the technical skill and continuous services of the
Bureau of the Budget and of the Council of Economic Advisors, which the
Congress is not equipped to match though legislation in these fields is
peculiarly its responsibility. In effect the President has acquired the powers
of the English Prime Minister over the introduction of legislation without
the correlative duties to the legislative branch imposed on the Prime
Minister under the English practice.'[4] It is, indeed, a far cry from the
attitude of the Senate in 1908 when a furore was created because a cabinet
minister sent to that body the complete draft of a proposed bill.[5] Today,
the drafting of legislation by the executive departments has become
common practice.

FOREIGN AFFAIRS

'Not only...is the federal power over external affairs in origin and
essential character different from that over internal affairs,' the United
States Supreme Court has declared, 'but participation in the exercise of
the power is significantly limited. In this vast external realm, with its

1 See Chamberlain, *The President, Congress, and Legislation* (1946).
2 Laski, *op. cit.* 113.
3 Galloway, *Congress at the Crossroads* (1946), 6.
4 Vanderbilt, *The Doctrine of the Separation of Powers and its Present-day Significance*
(1953), 78.
5 See Galloway, *op. cit.* 7.

important, complicated, delicate and manifold problems, the President alone has the power to speak or listen as a representative of the nation. He *makes* treaties with the advice and consent of the Senate; but he alone negotiates. Into the field of negotiation the Senate cannot intrude; and Congress itself is powerless to invade it. As [John] Marshall said in his great argument of March 7, 1800, in the House of Representatives, "The President is the sole organ of the nation in its external relations, and its sole representative with foreign nations".'[1]

Marshall's dictum has today become a commonplace.[2] The external affairs of the United States are at present carried on almost entirely by the executive branch of the Government. It is the President and his Secretary of State who are primarily responsible for American foreign policy. The range of presidential initiative in this respect is prodigious. It is the President who appoints the architects of the country's foreign policy. From the Secretary of State down, the policy-making officials of the State Department hold office only at his pleasure. He has unlimited discretion in the recognition of foreign Governments. How important this can be is shown by the refusal of the United States to recognize the Government of Communist China, to cite but one recent example. The President alone has the power to negotiate with foreign countries. He may send special agents abroad to deal upon a personal basis with other Governments; the example of Harry Hopkins during the last war shows well how policies can be shaped and understandings secured by this means. He has an undefined power to enter into agreements which do not attain the formal status of a treaty. And it is he who, more than anyone else, gives the lead to the country in matters touching foreign affairs. Moreover, the President is, under the Constitution, the commander-in-chief of the armed forces. In that capacity, he can take action, such as the decision of President Truman to intervene in Korea, which leaves Congress no alternative but to follow the lead which he has given. The action of the American Far Eastern fleet, first in 'neutralizing' Formosa and then in protecting that island from assaults from the mainland of China, has been based entirely upon orders issued by the President, in his capacity as head of the armed forces.[3]

Nor, it should be noted, is presidential authority in the field of foreign affairs subject to judicial control. This is of tremendous importance in a country where all other governmental acts are subject to review by the courts for a determination of their legality. 'The conduct of the foreign relations of our Government', reads an important decision of the American

1 *United States* v. *Curtiss-Wright Export Corp.*, 299 U.S. 304, 319 (1936).
2 Corwin, *op. cit.* 216.　　　3 Compare Laski, *op. cit.* 170–1.

Supreme Court, 'is committed by the Constitution to the Executive and Legislative—"the political"—Departments of the Government, and the propriety of what may be done in the exercise of this political power is not subject to judicial inquiry or decision.'[1]

The extent of judicial abnegation in the field of foreign affairs is well shown by a more recent opinion of the Supreme Court. 'The President,' stated Mr Justice Jackson in that case, 'both as Commander-in-Chief and as the Nation's organ for foreign affairs, has available intelligence services whose reports are not and ought not to be published to the world. It would be intolerable that courts, without the relevant information, should review and perhaps nullify actions of the Executive taken on information properly held secret. Nor can courts sit *in camera* in order to be taken into executive confidences. But even if courts could require full disclosure, the very nature of executive decisions as to foreign policy is political, not judicial. Such decisions are wholly confided by our Constitution to the political departments of the government, Executive and Legislative. They are delicate, complex, and involve large elements of prophecy. They are and should be undertaken only by those directly responsible to the people whose welfare they advance or imperil. They are decisions of a kind for which the Judiciary has neither aptitude, facilities nor responsibility. and which has long been held to belong in the domain of political power not subject to judicial intrusion or inquiry.'[2]

Presidential action relating to the field of foreign affairs is thus free from judicial scrutiny of the type which exists over all other governmental acts in the American system. It should not, however, be thought that the President's authority in this field, broad though it undoubtedly is, is wholly unlimited. Though the executive role in foreign relations is the primary one, it is one which, to be properly performed, must be based upon adequate congressional support. Thus, the President's prerogative to conduct foreign policy through officials of his own choosing is subject to the constitutional power vested in the Senate to confirm or reject his appointees. His power to negotiate with other Governments is restricted by the fact that any treaties agreed upon by him must receive the concurrence of two-thirds of the Senate before they are binding upon the United States. Then, too, the President's authority here is limited by the fact that the implementation of his foreign policy depends upon the existence of sufficient funds voted by the Congress. The legislative body is not bound by anything done by the President in his capacity as organ of foreign relations.[3] It is a free

1 *Oetjen* v. *Central Leather Co.*, 246 U.S. 297, 302 (1918).
2 *Chicago & Southern Air Lines* v. *Waterman S.S. Co.*, 333 U.S. 103, 111 (1948).
3 Corwin, *op. cit.* 213.

agent in voting appropriations, however embarrassing its failure to provide adequate funds may be to the President or the country's relations with other States. And this is true, it should be realized, even with regard to the appropriation of monies needed to carry out the provisions of treaties which have already been ratified. It may well be that, as President Taft has pointed out, the failure of Congress to make the necessary appropriation in such a case is a violation of the plighted faith of the Government.[1] But there is little doubt that, under the American Constitution, the Congress has the legal power to appropriate or not to appropriate, in its discretion.

The constitutional limitation upon the President's authority in foreign affairs that has received the most attention from outside observers is that requiring the adherence of two-thirds of the Senate to the conclusion of treaties.[2] 'The position henceforth to be held in world politics by the American Union', a French student of comparative constitutional law informs us, 'gives a new interest to a study of the institutions and constitutional procedures which determine and control the conduct of foreign affairs.'[3] In making such studies, it is not surprising that outside observers have tended to emphasize the aspect of the American system which has seemed most anomalous to them, namely, the crucial participation of the Senate in the treaty-making power. 'Since the tragic rejection of the Treaty of Versailles and the Covenant of the League of Nations, no one can be unaware of the decisive role of the Senate with regard to treaties.'[4]

To the foreigner, and to many Americans as well, the constitutional provision requiring the concurrence of two-thirds of the Senate before a treaty can be ratified seems inconsistent with the principles of representative democracy for two main reasons. In the first place, under the American system, the chamber of the Congress which is most directly representative of the people, i.e. the House of Representatives, is completely excluded from a share in the treaty-making process. It is only the Senate, in which the States are equally represented regardless of their population,[5] that may determine whether a treaty negotiated by the President shall be ratified or rejected. And perhaps even more important to critics of the present American system is the fact that the Constitution requires a two-thirds vote of the Senate before a treaty can be concluded. The Constitution, as the French jurist quoted above aptly points out, thus permits a minority of senators to checkmate an international policy accepted by the President

---

1 Taft, *op. cit.* 115. 2 Article II, section 2.
3 Pinto, *op. cit.* 60. 4 *Ibid.*
5 Thus, New York, with over 13,000,000 inhabitants, and Nevada, with only 100,000 inhabitants, each represented by two senators, have an equal voice in determining whether a treaty should be approved.

and the majority of the Congress.[1] 'The irreparable mistake of our Constitution', wrote a leading American statesman at the turn of the century, 'puts it into the power of one-third + 1 of the Senate to meet with a categorical veto any treaty negotiated by the president, even though it may have the approval of nine-tenths of the people of the nation.'[2]

Historically, the sharing of the treaty-making power between the President and the Senate is explainable by the desire of the framers of the American Constitution to preserve the rights of the States adhering to the Union, in order to obtain the support of the smaller States, who feared being swallowed up in a strong confederation. The system set up in 1789 may well have suited a young republic, devoted to the conquest of a continent and menaced by the intrigues of powerful States. It has, however, clearly become much less appropriate under contemporary conditions. 'The most significant fact', assert two American jurists, 'about the motives which are supposed to have impelled the Framers to exclude the House of Representatives from the treaty-making process and to require the Senate to give its consent by a two-thirds majority is that none of them have any validity today; most indeed were outmoded within fifty years after the drafting of the Constitution.'[3]

In dealing with the treaty-making power under the Constitution, in his lectures on the presidency, Harold J. Laski concluded that he was 'satisfied to point out that, in [his] own judgment, the case against the Senate has been enormously overestimated'.[4] Despite the defects of the present American system, it would seem desirable, as he points out, to lodge a power of this kind somewhere in the legislature. There is a greater danger in the confinement of the treaty-making power in the executive alone than even those which inhere in the senatorial veto. 'And this view is...reinforced by experience of systems like that of Great Britain where the control of foreign affairs is, in fact, "executive altogether". For the only real control of the House of Commons is of a *post-mortem* nature. It is presented by the cabinet with a *fait accompli*, rejection of which involves the defeat of the government and a subsequent general election. There is no instance in modern times where the government has had an assured majority, upon which its supporters have been willing to take that risk.'[5]

It is thus not participation by the legislature in the treaty-making process that is the great defect of the American system, but the fact that such participation is limited to the Senate, and that, even so far as that chamber is

1 Pinto, *op. cit.* 61.   2 John Hay, quoted in Laski, *op. cit.* 197.
3 McDougal and Lans, 'Treaties and congressional-executive or presidential agreements: interchangeable instruments of national policy. II', 54 *Yale L.J.* (1945), 534, 545.   4 Laski, *op. cit.* 205.   5 *Ibid.* 200.

concerned, participation must be in accordance with the two-thirds rule. The obvious solution here is to associate the House of Representatives in the process of approving treaties, and to require the concurrence of only a majority of both chambers before treaties can be ratified. As in most other cases where constitutional reforms are required, however, it is hardly likely that this solution will be adopted in the foreseeable future.

But, as is often the case where a system set up by a written constitution reveals defects not foreseen by its draftsmen, an attempt has been made to ameliorate the situation by increasing reliance upon methods which do not come precisely within the constitutional provisions in question. In the case of the treaty-making power, the flaws which have been noted in the system set up by the American organic instrument have been avoided in many cases by so-called executive agreements entered into by the President with other Governments which are not submitted to the Senate for its approval. 'The delegation by the Constitution', an American jurist writes, 'to the President and the Senate of the power to make "treaties" does not exhaust the power of the United States over international relations. The will of the nation in this domain may be expressed through other acts than treaties and such acts do not necessarily need to be ratified by the President by and with the advice and consent of the Senate in order to be valid and binding.... Which of the two procedures shall be employed in a given case is a matter of practical convenience or political expediency rather than of constitutional or international law.'[1]

An executive agreement concluded by the President alone has the same legal effect as a treaty ratified by him with the concurrence of two-thirds of the Senate. This has been established since the decision of the United States Supreme Court in 1937 in *United States* v. *Belmont*.[2] That case involved an assignment by the Soviet Government to the American Government of all claims due to that Government from American nationals. The assignment was effected by an exchange of diplomatic correspondence between the two Governments. In an action by the United States to enforce a claim owing to the Soviet Government, the court held that the claim was a valid one, in view of the compact between the two Governments. Such compact, said Mr Justice Sutherland, was valid, even though it had not been submitted to the Senate. 'An international compact, as

1 Garner, 'Acts and joint resolutions of Congress as substitutes for treaties', 29 *American Journal of International Law* (1935), 482, 488.
2 301 U.S. 324 (1937). See, similarly, *United States* v. *Pink*, 315 U.S. 203 (1942). According to *United States* v. *Guy W. Capps, Inc.*, 204 F. 2d 655 (4th Cir. 1953), *affirmed on other grounds*, 378 U.S. 296 (1955), however, an executive agreement, which contravenes the provisions of a prior Act of Congress in an area subject to regulation by Congress under its commerce power, is void.

this was, is not always a treaty which requires the participation of the Senate. There are many such compacts, of which a protocol, a modus vivendi, a postal convention, and agreements like that now under consideration are illustrations.'[1] And, though this might not be a treaty requiring ratification by the Senate, it was a compact negotiated and proclaimed under the authority of the President, and, as such, had the same legal effect as a treaty.

Executive agreements concluded by the President have come to be used interchangeably with treaties in the conduct of the foreign relations of the United States.[2] Thus, such agreements have been used to accomplish the acquisition of territory; the settlement of international claims; the adherence to international organizations; international commercial agreements; control of international communications; and international financial and war debt agreements.[3] Some of the most important moves in the evolution of American foreign policy have, indeed, been brought about by executive agreements, rather than by formal treaties. Thus, the famous 'Open Door' policy, upon which American policy in the Far East has been based during most of this century, was laid down in an agreement concluded by the Secretary of State in 1900 with the principal countries of Europe and Japan. The so-called 'Gentleman's Agreement' entered into between President Theodore Roosevelt and the Japanese ambassador regulated Japanese immigration to the United States for some seventeen years, until it was put an end to by an Act of Congress. And, to take some more recent examples, one has only to cite the celebrated exchange of bases for destroyers between President Franklin D. Roosevelt and the British Government, and the many agreements entered into by him after American participation in the war, such as those concluded at Teheran, Yalta, and (by his successor, President Truman) at Potsdam.

It cannot be denied that, though it enables American foreign policy to operate unhindered by the spectre of senatorial veto, the tendency to rely upon executive agreements concluded by the President alone has its dangers as well as its advantages. Legislative control ensures against overaudacious executive adventures in this field. A self-willed President of dominant personality, as Professor Laski has aptly expressed it, 'might easily have taken the United States into dubious foreign adventures for which public opinion was unprepared, for which, also, there would have been little justification, had it not been for the knowledge that the Senate

1 301 U.S. at 330.
2 McDougal and Lans, 'Treaties and congressional-executive or presidential agreements: interchangeable instruments of national policy. I', 54 *Yale L. J.* (1945), 181, 290.
3 See *ibid.* 262–82.

would ultimately review the results of their activities.... A president eager for imperialist adventure, or concerned to exercise influence in Europe in a particular direction, might easily, in the absence of Senate control, be a source of grave danger to the American people.'[1]

ADMINISTRATIVE HEAD

The functions of a chief executive of a sovereign State, generally speaking, fall into two categories—political and administrative. In different countries, the emphasis laid upon each of these functions varies. In some, the powers and influence of the head of the executive are almost entirely political. In others, such as Switzerland, the chief importance is upon the administrative side.[2]

In the United States it was probably intended that the President should be primarily a political chief and that he should not, except as to political matters, be the administrative head of the Government.[3] Perusal of the early Acts of the Congress organizing the American administrative system shows that the first Congress did not have the idea that the President had any power of direction over matters not political in character.[4] The legislative intent in organizing the administrative departments was to place them under congressional control rather than under the direction of the President. That this was also the general view in the early years of the American Republic is shown by a case decided by a federal court in 1837. 'The President,' stated the opinion there, 'in the execution of his duty to see that the laws be faithfully executed, is bound to see that the postmaster-general discharges "faithfully" the duties assigned to him by law; but this does not authorize the President to direct him how he shall discharge them.'[5]

Yet, though thus denying at first any presidential power of direction, the courts have uniformly recognized the existence of authority in the President to remove the heads of the executive departments from office. In practice, the power of removal thus recognized has easily enabled the President to ensure that administrative action would be taken only in accordance with his directions. Since department heads who do not follow his instructions can be removed from office by him at will, he can, in effect, dictate the policies to be followed by the administration.

It was largely the President's possession of the removal power, first used effectively to compel administrative obedience to presidential directions

---

1 Laski, *op. cit.* 200.
2 Willoughby, *Principles of the Constitutional Law of the United States* (2nd ed. 1935), 619.   3 *Ibid.* 620.
4 Goodnow, *The Principles of the Administrative Law of the United States* (1905), 78.
5 *United States v. Kendall*, 5 Cranch C.C. 163, 272 (D.C. 1837).

in 1833 by President Jackson, that led to the development of the modern conception of the President as the administrative chief of the nation. The present-day notion of the President as the responsible head of the national administration was well stated in an official report issued in 1937, just a century after the judicial opinion taking a narrow view of presidential authority which has been quoted above. 'The President', reads the report referred to, 'is the general manager of the United States. The very purpose of an Executive Department under the Constitution is to center upon a unified and powerful Executive responsibility for a coordinated policy of administration and its efficient execution. Congress, by its very nature, is incapable either of doing administrative work or of holding accountable in any effective way the many officers or agencies engaged in administration. The President's duties and responsibilities in this field are not routine in nature, but carry with them broad discretionary powers.'[1]

THE CABINET

The position of the President as the effective head of the administration is thus maintained consistently by his removal powers, at least so far as the executive departments of the Government are concerned. There are, at present, ten such departments in the Federal Government,[2] each headed by a minister (usually termed a Secretary in the American system), who is a member of the President's Cabinet.[3] Like its British namesake, the American Cabinet is entirely extra-constitutional.[4] But it is important to realize at once that the American Cabinet hardly corresponds to the classic idea of a Cabinet to which parliamentary government in Britain has accustomed us.[5] There is, as Lord Bryce aptly pointed out, in the government of the United States no such thing as a Cabinet in the English sense of the term.[6] Because of his unfettered power of removal over them and the fact that his tenure of office is not in any way dependent upon the effect which his dismissal of Cabinet members may have upon the Congress, the President is able to dominate his Cabinet to an extent which would be almost impossible in the case of a British Prime Minister.

1 *Report of the President's Committee on Administrative Management* (1937), 219.

2 These are the Departments of State, the Treasury, Defense, Justice, the Post Office, the Interior, Agriculture, Commerce, Labor, and Health, Education, and Welfare. The last of these was established in 1953 by a Presidential Reorganization Plan.

3 The ministers who are the members of the Cabinet are the Secretaries of State, the Treasury, Defense, the Interior, Agriculture, Commerce, Labor, and Health, Education, and Welfare, and the Attorney-General and Postmaster-General.

4 Corwin, *op. cit.* 98.

5 Laski, *op. cit.* 70.   6 Bryce, *op. cit.* 85.

The Prime Minister in Britain is, after all, one who may be described as *primus inter pares* rather than as an autocrat.[1] Though he usually stands out as the chief of his colleagues, he cannot govern effectively without their aid and too many resignations may cause the fall of a Government.[2] 'A prime minister in England or in France, hazards his head when he dispenses with a powerful colleague; Lord John Russell did not long survive his dismissal of Palmerston in 1851.'[3] The same is clearly not true of an American President. The ejection of a member of his Cabinet can have no adverse effect upon his authority or tenure, both of which are expressly provided for in the Constitution. Nor are the decisions of the American Government anything like the collective decisions taken by the Cabinet in Britain. There is no such thing in the American system as the principle of collective responsibility of the Cabinet. The American Cabinet is a body of advisers to the President; it is not a council of colleagues with whom he has to work and upon whose approval he depends.[4] 'In England, we blame an anonymous entity "the Government" if things go wrong, or a mistake is made; in the United States it is the president. A decision of the Supreme Court is regarded as adverse to *his* policy; a defeat in Congress is a blow to *his* prestige; the mid-term congressional elections affect *his* policy, for good or ill. No one thinks of them in terms of their effect upon his cabinet. For the purpose of action, it is he alone who is fundamentally involved.'[5]

The basic fact about the relation of the President to his Cabinet is his complete predominance. The members of the Cabinet are merely the instruments by which the policy of the President is carried out. They are not members of Congress; they are not accountable to it, but only to the President, their master.[6] The decisions which the Cabinet may reach in the weekly meetings which are normally held are only in the nature of advice to the President. The ultimate decisions are still exclusively his to take. Even a united Cabinet cannot prevail against his will. 'He is a court of appeal from them all, and his verdict is decisive against them.'[7] This is well illustrated by the story, perhaps apocryphal, told of President Lincoln's submission of the draft of his famous Emancipation Proclamation to his Cabinet. After calling for a vote, in which the entire Cabinet voted against the issuing of the Proclamation, which the President had decided upon, Lincoln stated the result of the vote as follows: 'Seven against; one for. The ayes have it.'

It is, of course, true that the relation between President and Cabinet varies from President to President. A Franklin D. Roosevelt will himself

1 Wade and Phillips, *Constitutional Law* (4th ed. 1950), 143.
2 *Ibid.* 3 Laski, *op. cit.* 72. 4 *Ibid.* 73.
5 *Ibid.* 90. 6 Bryce, *op. cit.* 93. 7 Laski, *op. cit.* 73.

take the initiative in all major matters; a Harry S. Truman will place far more reliance upon the advice of his Cabinet. But, in both cases, it is the President alone who has the decisive voice, if he chooses to exercise it. It was this which led Lord Bryce to assert that 'In this state of things one cannot properly talk of the cabinet apart from the President. An American administration resembles not so much the cabinets of England and France as the group of ministers who surround the Czar or the Sultan or who executed the bidding of a Roman emperor like Constantine or Justinian.'[1]

EXECUTIVE DEPARTMENTS

The members of the President's Cabinet are important not so much because of their role as advisers to the chief executive, but because of their position as administrative heads of the ten executive departments in the Federal Government. The government departments themselves in the United States are organized in a manner which should not seem unduly strange to the outside observer. The departments are set up to perform certain connected governmental functions, and each has as its sphere one of the important aspects of modern governmental activity. Thus, the State Department is charged with conducting the foreign affairs of the country, while the Treasury Department administers the fiscal affairs of the Government. Each American department is divided into divisions, bureaux, offices and services (the terms are used interchangeably)[2] which specialize in the particular tasks performed. Added specialization is often attained within each such division by its further partition into subdivisions, along lines which should be familiar to any student of public administration.

Each department has its central offices in Washington, which formulate its policies and its agents to execute those policies throughout the country. The details of field organization vary from department to department, but, in general, it is customary for each of the department's divisions to be divided into a number of regional offices located in each of the more important population centres. It is these offices in the field, to borrow the expression of a leading French jurist, who are the 'combattants' in the actual tasks of administration, but, as is always the case, they are dependent upon the 'non-combattants' in the department, i.e. those in the central offices in Washington.[3]

Under Article II, section 2, of the Federal Constitution, the President

1 Bryce, *op. cit.* 94.

2 The recent report of the Hoover Commission, whose work will be discussed *infra*, p. 122, recommended that the internal organization of each department should follow a standard nomenclature as follows: 'Service; Bureau; Division; Branch; Section; Unit.' *The Hoover Commission Report* (1949), 28.

3 Hauriou, *Précis de droit administratif* (12th ed. 1933), 160.

'shall nominate, and by and with the Advice and Consent of the Senate, shall appoint Ambassadors, other public Ministers and Consuls, Judges of the supreme Court, and all other Officers of the United States...: but the Congress may by Law vest the Appointment of such inferior Officers, as they think proper, in the President alone...or in the Heads of Departments.' Under this provision, the power to appoint 'Officers of the United States' is vested exclusively in the President, subject to the confirmation of the Senate and, in the case of 'inferior Officers', as provided by law, in the President alone or, as has been usual, in the heads of the executive departments. It is this power of appointment vested either in the President or in the members of his Cabinet, who are wholly subject to his will, which enables the American chief executive to staff the administration with officials of his own inclination and choosing.

It should, however, be noted that the presidential authority in this respect is subject to significant restrictions. Except in the case of so-called inferior officers, the President's appointee must receive senatorial confirmation. And, even more important, perhaps, is the limitation which results from the fact that, in creating an office, Congress may stipulate the qualifications of appointees thereto.[1] 'A multitude of laws', as Mr Justice Brandeis once expressed it, 'have been enacted which limit the President's power to make nominations, and which through the restrictions imposed, may prevent the selection of the person deemed by him to be best fitted. Such restriction upon the power to nominate has been exercised by Congress continuously since the foundation of the Government.'[2] The most important of the restrictions imposed by Congress upon the appointing power has been that contained in the Civil Service Law of 1883 and subsequent civil service legislation, under which the Federal Government has attempted to build a permanent career civil service, such as that which exists in Britain. The Civil Service Law was intended to curb the abuses of the so-called 'spoils system',[3] which had developed with the growth of party government in the United States. Under that system, public offices and their emoluments were regarded as in the nature of plunder to be distributed among the members of the party victorious at the polls. 'Since the induction into office of President Jackson', wrote Joseph Story in 1833, shortly after the system referred to came into being, 'a system of removals and new appointments to office has been pursued so extensively, that it has reached a very large proportion of all the offices of honour and profit in the civil departments of the country.'[4]

1 Corwin, *op. cit.* 88.
2 Dissenting, in *Myers* v. *United States*, 272 U.S. 52, 265 (1926).
3 *Ibid.* 276.   4 *Commentaries*, §1537.

The spoils system, which led to an almost complete change in the personnel of the Government departments whenever the opposition party was returned to office, was hardly compatible with the development of an expert and efficient civil service. The Civil Service Law of 1883 sought to remedy the situation by providing for appointment only from among those who had attained the highest grade upon open, competitive examinations. And, since that time, the concept of appointment by merit, as demonstrated by the satisfaction of educational and other tests, has been extended to cover most of the employees of the American Government. In addition, the civil service laws have attempted to give security of tenure to those appointed under them. The unfettered removal power which the President and department heads might otherwise have is limited to removal only for specified causes and in accordance with the procedures outlined in the relevant Acts.

The existence of a permanent civil service in the American system, however, should not lead the outside observer to assume that it is exactly like the civil service which exists in Britain. The outstanding fact about the British permanent civil service system is that it extends to all but the very highest levels of the Government departments. A change in government thus means a change only at the very apex of the administrative hierarchy. But the administration, as such, continues, and it is its continuity which makes the administration so important a factor in the life of the nation. In Continental countries, like France, indeed, it is the higher permanent civil servants, rather than the political heads of the Government, who wield much of the substance of governmental authority. It is they who 'possess the substance of administrative power, with the ministers exercising only a political control'.[1] The political life expectancy of a French minister being as short as it is, it is not to be wondered at if his influence upon administration tends to be more or less ephemeral.

This is not at all the situation in the United States. By British or European standards, the number of American public officers who are appointed by patronage remains surprisingly large.[2] Though the percentage not covered by the civil service system may not be very great, it tends to include every administrative policy-making office. The American student, even today, tends to think of a change in Government as being necessarily accompanied by a veritable upheaval of the employees in the upper levels

1 Hauriou, *op. cit.* 159.
2 According to the Seventieth Annual Report of the Civil Service Commission, the agency charged with administering the civil service laws in the United States, there was, as of June 1953, a total of 2,290,610, civilian federal employees in the Continental United States. Of these, 2,102,921, or 92%, were subject to the competitive requirements of the civil service laws, while 187,689, or 8%, were not subject to them at all.

of the administration. The President retains a wide power of removal over officers appointed by him, who are not part of the permanent civil service. And American Presidents have not hesitated to use their removal authority upon their accession to office.

That the President does have a broad removal power over officers of the executive departments who are not appointed under the civil service laws is shown by the celebrated case of *Myers* v. *United States*.[1] 'The vesting of the executive power in the President', stated Mr Chief Justice Taft, himself a former chief executive, in his opinion there, 'was essentially a grant of the power to execute the laws. But the President alone and unaided could not execute the laws. He must execute them by the assistance of subordinates....As he is charged specifically to take care that they be faithfully executed, the reasonable implication, even in the absence of express words, was that as part of his executive power he should select those who were to act for him under his direction in the execution of the laws. The further implication must be, in the absence of any express limitation respecting removals, that as his selection of administrative officers is essential to the execution of the laws by him, so must be his power of removing those for whom he can not continue to be responsible.'[2]

The *Myers Case* established the principle that the President could remove at will all officers of the executive departments who did not have security of tenure under the civil service laws. It is this principle which ensures the effectiveness of the President's position as administrative chief of the nation. It is almost a truism that the doctrine of ministerial responsibility in the British sense, i.e. in the sense of executive accountability to the supreme legislature, is not a part of the American governmental system. 'Our principal executive and administrative officers, on the other hand, are responsible to the President, the executive head of the nation. They are his agents, the instruments through whom he works.'[3] The President has an absolute power of removal over the higher echelons of the executive departments, and he can consequently ensure that the policies administered by them are not in conflict with his views. The basic principle of ordinary governmental administration in the United States is thus that of the executive hierarchy, with the President at its head, possessing complete powers of supervision and control. 'There is no independence here; the accountability of these officers is absolute.'[4]

1 272 U.S. 52 (1926).   2 *Ibid.* 117.
3 Cushman, *The Independent Regulatory Commissions* (1941), 667.
4 *Ibid.*

INDEPENDENT REGULATORY COMMISSIONS

An analysis only in terms of the ordinary executive departments, headed by members of the Cabinet, will, however, hardly give a complete picture of the administrative machinery of the American Government. For there are in the Federal Government a large number of agencies which are not within any of the regular departments. Of these, the most significant are the so-called independent regulatory commissions. There are eight important agencies of this type in the Federal Government whose functions involve the regulation of particular aspects of the American economic system.[1] 'The independent regulatory commission', stated a recent report on the organization of the executive branch in the United States, 'is a comparatively new feature of the Federal Government. It consists of a board or commission, not within an executive department, and engaged in the regulation of some form of private activity.'[2] The type of regulatory authority vested in these bodies falls into two general categories. Some, like the Interstate Commerce Commission, the first of these agencies, which was established in 1887, are granted broad powers of control over a given industry, such as the transportation industry. Others are given extensive authority to prevent certain abusive practices anywhere in the economy which are conceived to be injurious to the working of a system of free competition. Thus, the Federal Trade Commission is empowered to prohibit unfair methods of competition on the part of business men engaged in interstate commerce.

To enable these independent commissions adequately to perform their regulatory tasks, they have been vested with both administrative and quasi-judicial authority. In addition, most of them have been given broad powers of delegated legislation. 'If in private life we were to organize a unit for the operation of industry, it would scarcely follow Montesquieu's lines.'[3] Nor can the regulation of industry be carried out effectively under a rigid separation of powers. Industrial power must be controlled by governmental power similarly concentrated. Regulatory commissions, such as the Interstate Commerce Commission, have consequently been made the repositories, as it were, of all three types of governmental power. In these bodies, the various stages of making and applying law,

---

1 These are the Interstate Commerce Commission, Federal Power Commission, Federal Trade Commission, Securities and Exchange Commission, Federal Communications Commission, Civil Aeronautics Board, Federal Reserve Board, and National Labor Relations Board. For a more detailed account of these agencies, see Schwartz, *American Administrative Law* (1950), ch. 1.

2 *The Hoover Commission Report* (1949), 429.

3 Landis, *The Administrative Process* (1938), 10.

traditionally separate in Anglo-American polity, 'have been telescoped into a single agency'.[1]

The members of the regulatory commissions which have been established in the United States are appointed by the President for a fixed term of years, subject to the confirmation of the Senate. Because of their possession of quasi-judicial authority, however, it has been widely felt that they should not be directly subject to presidential direction in the performance of their duties. In the case of agencies possessing such authority, as Professor Laski has pointed out, 'the object of legislation is to offer the citizen a guarantee that the official is independent of the political executive in the view he forms upon its policies. It is as legitimate to safeguard that guarantee as it is to secure the tenure of a judge from executive interference.'[2]

That the regulatory commissions in the American system are largely independent of the President is a result of the *Humphrey Case*, which was decided by the Supreme Court in 1935.[3] That case arose out of the removal from office by President Roosevelt of a member of the Federal Trade Commission, who had been appointed by his predecessor in office in 1931 for a term of seven years, on the ground 'that the aims and purposes of this Administration with respect to the work of the Commission can be carried out most effectively with personnel of my own selection'. The applicable statute provided that members of the commission were to hold office for terms of seven years and that 'any commissioner may be removed by the President for inefficiency, neglect of duty, or malfeasance in office'.

The American court in the *Humphrey Case* held that the President did not possess the wide removal power over members of the commission which he had over officers appointed by him in the ordinary executive departments. Pointing to the quasi-judicial functions of the commission, Mr Justice Sutherland asserted that freedom from presidential control was vital to their successful execution. 'The authority of Congress', reads his opinion, 'in creating quasi-legislative or quasi-judicial agencies, to require them to act in discharge of their duties independently of executive control cannot well be doubted; and that authority includes, as an appropriate incident, power to fix the period during which they shall continue in office, and to forbid their removal except for cause in the meantime. For it is quite evident that one who holds his office only during the pleasure of another, cannot be depended upon to maintain an attitude of independence against the latter's will.'[4]

That the *Humphrey* decision tends to make the role of the President as the

1 *Report of the United States Attorney-General's Committee on Administrative Procedure* (1941), 204.   2 Laski, *op. cit.* 226.

3 *Humphrey's Executor* v. *United States*, 295 U.S. 602 (1935).   4 *Ibid.* at 629.

administrative chief of the American Government a difficult one cannot be doubted. The recognition by the court of the independence of the regulatory commissions helps to make the administration in the United States anything but the fully co-ordinated executive branch which is the desideratum of the efficient administrator. 'These independent commissions have been given broad powers to explore, formulate, and administer policies of regulation; they have been given the task of investigating and prosecuting business misconduct; they have been given powers, similar to those exercised by courts of law, to pass in concrete cases upon the rights and liabilities of individuals under the statutes. They are in reality miniature independent governments set up to deal with the railroad problem, the banking problem, or the radio problem. They constitute a headless "fourth branch of the Government", a haphazard deposit of irresponsible agencies and uncoordinated powers.'[1]

The great weakness of the American independent regulatory commission, to a student of public administration, is that it is a hybrid organism, set up to perform basically incompatible functions, whose very incompatibility makes it impossible for them to be performed properly. In the first place, the commission is vested with the positive duties of implementing its enabling Act, usually laid down in broad and general (or even 'skeleton') terms, by the exercise of powers of delegated legislation, and of administering its provisions. Especially significant in this respect is the affirmative duty imposed upon most of these bodies themselves to ensure that the terms of the enabling Act are in fact complied with and to ferret out violators. These are basically executive functions, and the effectiveness with which they are exercised must, of necessity, have repercussions, often drastic, upon the policy and measures of the President at the head of the executive branch of the Government. The very independence of these agencies is such, however, as almost inevitably to hamper the effective execution of the President's policies and measures in the fields committed to them. A new President may thus, for example, desire to relax or make more stringent the enforcement of the anti-trust laws. But his policy in either direction may be thwarted if the majority of the Federal Trade Commission is committed to a contrary policy followed by his predecessor.

Why not then, one might ask, remove from these agencies their independent character and place them within the structure of the executive branch, subject to the complete hierarchical control of the President? Such a solution is precluded by the fact that the regulatory commissions, in addition to their functions of implementing and administering their enabling legislation, which are essentially executive in nature, are vested

[1] *Report of the President's Committee on Administrative Management* (1937), 39.

with the duty of deciding cases in which alleged violators of the legislation are proceeded against. This latter duty is basically judicial in nature—that of trying defendants brought before the bar of justice (administrative rather than judicial justice, it is true, but that does not change the primarily judicial nature of the function). The exercise of a function of this type is one which, under Anglo-American conceptions, is deemed to be best exercised in an atmosphere of independence, rather than as part and parcel of the very process of execution of the laws, exposed to all of the political pressures which play upon the political branches of government. Hence the independence of these agencies from the chief executive, which was underlined by the *Humphrey Case*. But the purpose of securing truly independent judicial determinations is subverted by the possession by the commissions of the executive functions referred to above. The commissions cannot be expected to decide cases before them with that 'cold neutrality of an impartial judge' of which Burke speaks, when it is they who have instituted the proceedings against the private party and they who have the burden of presenting the case against him.

Here, then, is the great paradox of the American regulatory commission. It is entrusted with executive functions because it is felt that only then can it be expected effectively to administer a scheme of governmental regulation. At the same time, however, it is placed in a position of independence *vis-à-vis* the President, to ensure that its judicial functions will be performed free from political pressures and prejudices. What is not generally realized is that the combination of these functions in the one agency renders the effective execution of either most difficult. The merger of the duties of investigator, prosecutor and judge in the one organ makes the exercise of the latter's function in a truly judicial manner almost impossible to achieve. In addition, the vesting of judicial duties in the organ charged with administering the law renders the proper exercise of the administrative function a hard one. From the point of view of the public interest, indeed, this aspect of the problem is, in many ways, the more important. Adequate executive co-ordination is rendered difficult by the vesting of vital administrative duties in these organs, which are free from accountability to the President, because such independence is deemed necessary to the proper exercise of their judicial functions.

The key to the problem of the American regulatory commission is thus the merger in it of administrative and judicial duties—not only because such merger militates against proper exercise of the role of quasi-judge but, just as significant, because it prevents the administrative work of the commissions from being effectively co-ordinated into the policy and measures of the executive branch as a whole.

ADMINISTRATIVE REORGANIZATION

The analysis of the independent regulatory commissions which has just been given indicates that, from the point of view of effective administration, the organization of the executive branch of the Federal Government still leaves something to be desired. But the problem of the regulatory commission is only one aspect of the question of effective organization of the executive branch of the Government. And the larger question is one with which American students of government have been much concerned in the past generation. The problem of executive reorganization is, of course, a recurrent one in any system of government. The American Constitution, as has been seen, refers neither to the details of structure nor to the operational methods of the executive branch. Consequently both have changed markedly over the years and both have been the subject of numerous investigations and proposals for reform, inspired by the widespread desire to increase efficiency and to economize in the expense of the Government.[1] Especially during the past twenty years, as a French comparative lawyer informs us, has the problem of the general reorganization of the American governmental structure been on the political agenda.[2]

Effective reorganization of the administration must be based upon careful studies by experts of the existing executive machinery. The first important study of this type was undertaken in 1937 by the President's Committee on Administrative Management, three distinguished public administrators appointed by President Roosevelt to investigate the problem. That committee, in its report, asserted that no enterprise could operate effectively if set up as the Federal Government was. 'There are over 100 separate departments, boards, commissions, corporations, authorities, agencies, and activities through which the work of the Government is being carried on. Neither the President nor the Congress can exercise effective supervision and direction over such a chaos of establishments, nor can overlapping, duplication, and contradictory policies be avoided.'[3]

The primary concern of the President's committee was to ensure that the President possessed adequate supervisory authority over the administration. To this end it made several recommendations. The most important of these sought to deal with the problem of the independent regulatory commissions, which has been discussed. 'Any program to restore our constitutional ideal of a fully coordinated Executive Branch', declared the

1 Note, 48 *Columbia L. Rev.* (1948), 1211, 1212.
2 Pinto, *op. cit.* 84.
3 *Report of the President's Committee on Administrative Management* (1937), iv.

committee, 'must bring within the reach of that responsible control all work done by these independent commissions which is not judicial in nature.'[1] To accomplish this end, the committee proposed to replace the independent commissions with two sorts of agencies, both to be organized within the appropriate executive departments, whose heads are, as we have seen, subject to the presidential power of removal at will. In one of the agencies would be vested the 'quasi-judicial' functions of the present commissions, and it would exercise these just as the present commissions do, wholly independent of the department and the President with respect to its work and its decisions. The other agency, which would exercise all of the non-judicial functions now vested in the commissions, would be directly responsible to the minister at the head of the department and, through him, to the President.[2]

To enable the President to carry out its recommendations, the President's committee suggested that the chief executive be vested with broad powers to reorganize the administration. The Congress responded to this proposal by the passage of the Reorganization Act of 1939. That Act did give the President authority to promulgate so-called reorganization plans, which were to provide for the regrouping, transfer or reassignment of the functions of the executive agencies at the discretion of the President. It did not, however, in the words of one commentator, 'put into the President's hands the means of sundering at one fell blow the "Gordian knot" of the problem of administrative organization'.[3] The reorganization plans prepared by the President had to be laid before Congress and were to take effect sixty days after such laying only if, during that period, there had not been passed a concurrent resolution of both Houses disapproving the plan.[4] And, even more important, the Act of 1939 expressly exempted the independent regulatory commissions and a number of other agencies from its provisions. Nor was the President authorized to abolish any of the functions of agencies affected by his reorganization plans. The authority given by the Act was to expire at the end of two years.

The war intervened to divert attention from the question of administrative reorganization.[5] After it was won, however, it was widely felt that the time had arrived for a definitive study of the whole problem. It was this which led the Congress, in 1947, to provide by law for the establishment of the Commission on Organization of the Executive Branch of the Government. This commission, popularly known as the Hoover Commission,

1 *Ibid.* 40. 2 Corwin, *op. cit.* 116. 3 *Ibid.* 120.

4 This, it should be noted, is one of the rare examples in the American system of legislative control of delegated legislation by the 'negative resolution' technique.

5 Reorganization powers to deal with problems arising out of the war were granted to the President under statutes enacted in 1941 and 1945.

after its chairman,[1] former President Hoover, was directed to 'study and investigate the present organization and methods of operation of all... agencies...of the executive branch of the Government'. The commission was bipartite in nature, with six members chosen from each party. Four commissioners each were chosen by the President, the Speaker of the House of Representatives, and the President *pro tempore* of the Senate.

The work of the Hoover Commission represents the most ambitious attempt yet made to study the organization of the American administration.[2] The commission's approach to its investigatory task was a most thorough one. It began by defining some twenty-four of the principal problems of government and management. These included such things as personnel, budgeting and accounting, the Post Office, foreign affairs, and many other matters of this type. Special research committees, termed 'task forces', were then created. Composed of some 300 eminent specialists, these task forces inquired into each field and, after about a year, returned to the commission with their findings. 'The result was the most imposing collection of facts, figures, and opinions on Government that has ever been assembled. It amounted, in fact, to some 2,500,000 words of basic data of the most valuable sort.'[3] This massive material was then considered by the commission itself for the better part of a year. The commission then issued a series of nineteen reports which appeared during the first half of 1949. These reports, as an outside observer has expressed it, taken as a whole, constitute an incomparable source of information on the organization and functioning of the American Government.[4]

The approach of the Hoover Commission was essentially that of the so-called efficiency expert, whose role has become so important in modern American industrial management. 'To put it another way, Herbert Hoover and associates, as consulting engineers, have presented the American people with a blueprint for good government.'[5] The details of this blue-print do not concern us here. It is enough, for our purposes, to note that the Hoover Commission, like the President's Committee on Administrative Management a decade earlier, was concerned primarily with rendering effective the position of the President as the administrative chief of the Government. The President, and under him his chief lieutenants, the department heads, declares the commission, clearly must be held responsible and accountable to the people and the Congress for the conduct of the executive branch. At the same time, 'responsibility and accountability are impossible with-

1 Its vice-chairman was Dean Acheson.
2 48 *Columbia L. Rev.* (1948), 1211.
3 *The Hoover Commission Report* (1949), vii.
4 Pinto, *op. cit.* 86.
5 *The Hoover Commission Report*, vii.

out authority—the power to direct. The exercise of authority is impossible without a clear line of command from the top to the bottom, and a return line of responsibility and accountability from the bottom to the top.'[1] Any systematic effort to improve the organization and operation of the Government must establish such a clear line of control from the President down to the various agencies in the federal administration.

The Hoover Commission, like the President's Committee on Administrative Management before it, felt that effective reorganization of the executive branch could be accomplished only upon the primary initiative of the President. And, like the earlier body, it recommended that the President be given the authority to promulgate reorganization plans. The commission felt, however, that limitations such as those contained in the Reorganization Act of 1939, discussed above, would be unwise. 'The Commission recommends that such authority should be given to the President and that the power of the President to prepare and transmit plans of reorganization to the Congress should not be restricted by limitations or exemptions. Once the limiting and exempting process is begun it will end the possibility of achieving really substantial results.'[2] Specifically, the commission disapproved of the exemption from the reorganization power of the independent regulatory commissions contained in the 1939 Act. The only limitation which the commission did not oppose was a provision for the laying of reorganization plans before the legislature.

The Reorganization Act of 1949, which was enacted in response to the commission's recommendation, largely followed that body's desires. Essentially like the Act of 1939, in that it gave the President the authority to promulgate reorganization plans, it did not contain that law's restrictions. The President was expressly authorized to abolish any functions of the agencies as well as the agencies themselves. Even more important was the fact that no agency—either the independent regulatory commissions or any other—was exempted from the Act. The only limitation imposed was that of legislative disapproval. Reorganization plans were to be laid before the Congress for sixty days and were to become effective only if not rejected by a vote of either House.[3] It should be mentioned also that the power given to the President under the 1949 Act was to extend only for four years. An Act giving similar authority to President Eisenhower, however, was quickly passed by the Congress which convened at the beginning of 1953.

1 *Ibid.* 3.   2 *Ibid.* xv.
3 Each House was thus given a veto power, instead of the power being given to the Congress as a whole, as was the case with the 1939 Act. This, it should be pointed out, is a step closer to the 'negative resolution' technique in Britain.

Acting under the power vested in him by the Act of 1949, the President submitted over thirty reorganization plans to the Congress during the life of the Act. In one of them, the Maritime Commission, one of the independent regulatory commissions, was placed within the Department of Commerce and its administrative functions split off from its quasi-judicial regulatory functions.[1] This, it should be noted, has been the first implementation in practice of the solution of the problem of the independent commission recommended, as we have seen, by the President's Committee on Administrative Management.[2]

The exercise of his authority under the Reorganization Acts of 1949 and 1953 has enabled the President to extend and consolidate his position as chief of the American administration. At the same time, from the point of view of effective management, it cannot be denied that the problem of effective organization of the federal executive still remains. Especially significant in this respect is the question of the independence of the regulatory commissions which, apart from the Maritime Commission, has hardly been touched thus far by presidential reorganization plans. The unaccountability to him of these agencies still greatly impairs the position of the President as general manager of the administration. 'Placed by the Constitution at the head of a unified and centralized Executive Branch, and charged with the duty to see that the laws are faithfully executed, he must detour around powerful administrative agencies which are in no way subject to his authority and which are, therefore, both actual and potential obstructions to his effective over-all management of national administration.'[3]

1 Reorganization Plan, no. 21 of 1950. Perhaps the most striking use of his reorganization power thus far was the creation by the President under the 1953 Act of a new executive department, the Department of Health, Education, and Welfare: Reorganization Plan, no. 1 of 1953.

2 A half-way measure concerning the National Labor Relations Board was taken in the Taft-Hartley Act of 1947. It separated the quasi-judicial functions of that agency from its other tasks. It did not, however, place the divided agency within an executive department, as the President's committee had proposed.

3 *Report of the President's Committee*, 40. That the problem of effective executive organization is still considered an acute one is shown by the constitution under a law of 1953 of a second Commission on Organization of the Executive Branch of the Government. Like its predecessor, which reported in 1949, this commission has been presided over by former President Hoover and is, hence, generally known as the second Hoover Commission. Its reports were issued during the first part of 1955.

Chapter V

THE COURTS

The position of the courts in a country is of crucial importance to one seeking to comprehend its constitutional institutions. The proper function of the constitutional lawyer, according to A. V. Dicey, is to show what are the legal rules (i.e. rules recognized and enforced by the courts) which are to be found in the several parts of the constitution.[1] Adequate performance of this function presupposes an understanding of the organization and functioning of the judiciary. This is especially true for one interested in the study of the law of the American Constitution. For it has become almost a commonplace that the courts in the United States—and especially the Supreme Court—are the fulcrum upon which the American constitutional system turns. 'In no country in the world today has the lawyer a standing remotely comparable with his place in American politics. The respect in which the federal courts and, above all, the Supreme Court are held is hardly surpassed by the influence they exert on the life of the United States. If it is excessive to say that American history could be written in terms of its federal decisions, it is not excessive to say that American history would be incomplete without a careful consideration of them.'[2]

Ever since de Tocqueville, outside observers have emphasized the primordial role of the judge in American society.[3] Nor is this role based exclusively upon the fact that the Constitution of the United States, unlike that in Britain, is a written instrument. Most of the countries of Continental Europe have written constitutions; yet in none of them has the judge attained anything like the status of his American confrère. From a practical point of view, the situation in such Continental countries is basically like that in Britain because of the lack in their system of any effective judicial control of the constitutionality of the laws enacted by the legislature. The restrictions placed upon the legislature under most Continental constitutions are not, in reality, laws since they are not rules which in the last resort will be enforced by the courts. Their true character is that of maxims of political morality, which have more a moral than a legal basis.[4]

The Continental experience shows that a constitution which cannot be

---

1 Dicey, *Law of the Constitution* (9th ed. 1939), 31.
2 Laski, *The American Democracy* (1948), 110.
3 Pinto, *La Crise de l'état aux États-Unis* (1951), 120.   4 Dicey, *op. cit.* 136.

judicially enforced contains but empty words. It is the failure of Continental courts to assert a power of review over legislative and executive acts that has made most European constitutions mere paper instruments. The assertion by the American courts of such a power of review ensures that the Federal Constitution does not suffer a similar fate. It is thus not the existence alone of a written organic instrument which makes the constitutional role of the judge in the United States of greater consequence than it is in Britain. It is rather the fact that the American judiciary is looked upon as one of the three co-ordinate branches of the Federal Government, not as dependent upon the legislature or the executive, that has enabled it to assert the power of review which so sharply differentiates the American constitutional system from those which have prevailed in Britain and the Continent. 'The judiciary', declares a leading American judge, 'owes its place in American government in large measure to its having been established in our federal and state constitutions in accordance with the doctrine of separation of powers as an independent, coordinate branch of government, and also in part to its being so often called on (in contrast with the English and French judiciary, though for different reasons in each of these countries) to decide what is the "supreme law of the land" and thus on occasion to override legislative or executive action. Because of this high responsibility the independence of the judiciary from both the legislative and executive branches is the keystone of American constitutional government.'[1]

ORGANIZATION

In a system of parliamentary government, such as that which prevails in Britain, the constitutional questions of the extent and limits of judicial power and its freedom from legislative control do not arise. Although it cannot be doubted that British judges have manifested a considerable degree of independence, it is a political fact that in Britain the courts depend entirely upon Acts of Parliament for their existence, jurisdiction and powers. The same is true in other countries whose constitutional system is dominated by the doctrine of parliamentary sovereignty.[2] That doctrine implies judicial subordination in the sense that it tends to make the courts, like the executive, wholly subject, in constitutional theory at least, to the will of the supreme legislature.

The situation in the United States, in many ways, is a different one. 'Under the aegis of a written constitution, which vaguely apportions the powers of government among the three great departments and incorporates

[1] Vanderbilt, *The Doctrine of the Separation of Powers and its Present-day Significance* (1953), 98.

[2] Harris, *The Judicial Power of the United States* (1940), 1.

by construction the theories of dual federalism and the separation of powers, the courts have achieved a degree of independence from statutory regulation and control that exists in no other country.'[1] It is more by the Constitution than by an act of the legislature that the federal courts have been vested with judicial authority. 'The judicial Power of the United States', declares Article III of the American Constitution, 'shall be vested in one supreme Court, and in such inferior Courts as the Congress may from time to time ordain and establish.... The judicial Power shall extend to all Cases, in Law and Equity, arising under this Constitution, the Laws of the United States, and Treaties made, or which shall be made, under their Authority.'

Under these provisions, it should be noted, only the Supreme Court itself is expressly provided for in the organic instrument. All other federal courts are established under Acts of the Congress, though it should be noted that, once established, they immediately have vested in them *the* judicial power delegated by Article III of the Constitution. It is their possession of such authority, delegated to them directly by the Constitution, that has enabled them to assert an independence of the legislature so much greater than that possessed by the judiciary in other countries. Apart from the Supreme Court, however, though to some extent also with regard to it, as we shall see, the extent of legislative control in the judicial field is much larger in the United States than most students of comparative law realize.

Acting under the implied mandate in Article III of the Federal Constitution to ordain and establish courts inferior to the Supreme Court provided for expressly in that document, the Congress has created a federal judicial system, whose structure should not seem unduly strange to the English jurist. The federal courts in the United States are organized in the pyramid-like manner usual in most contemporary legal systems. Original jurisdiction is conferred upon a large number of tribunals of territorial competence located throughout the country. From them there is an appeal to a smaller number of intermediate appellate courts, whose jurisdiction is also defined territorially. At the apex of the system is a central court, with ultimate appellate jurisdiction in certain cases.

General original jurisdiction in the federal judicial system in the United States is vested in the United States district courts. The United States is by law divided into some eighty-four judicial districts. There is at least one district for each State. No district includes territory in more than one State, though about half the States are divided into more than one district.[2] In each of these judicial districts, there is established a federal district court.

1 *Ibid.* 2 Two States, New York and Texas, are divided into four judicial districts.

The actual composition of a given district court depends upon its individual importance, in terms of the size and population of its territorial unit. Thus, the district court of a small State like Utah may consist of one judge, while that in the Southern District of New York is composed of some eighteen judges. The district courts are essentially trial courts—that is, courts of original jurisdiction. Litigation in them is normally presided over by a single judge. In some cases of special importance, however, it is provided by statute that a specially organized court of three judges shall sit, of which one must be a judge of a higher federal court. Among the class of cases thus triable are those arising under the federal anti-trust laws.[1]

Since the whole United States has been divided into federal judicial districts, and each district has within it a district court, the territorial extent of the federal judicial power is nation-wide. Indeed, it includes even areas outside the continental United States.[2] The legal jurisdiction of the district courts was formerly a limited or special, rather than a general, jurisdiction, much as is that of the county courts in England. Since 1911, however, when the federal judicial system was substantially reorganized, the district courts have been vested with general original competence in cases involving the exercise of federal judicial power.[3] In this respect they are now comparable to the High Court in the English system, though it should, of course, be remembered that, unlike that tribunal whose competence extends throughout the country, that of the American district courts is limited to the territorial confines of the districts in which they sit. In the exercise of their general federal jurisdiction, the district courts apply the rules of common law and equity in appropriate cases,[4] and also sit as courts of admiralty and courts of bankruptcy.

Above the district courts in the federal judicial system are the United States courts of appeals. While the United States is, as we have seen, divided into federal judicial districts, the districts are in turn organized into larger judicial units known as circuits. There are at present ten circuits designated by number, and one in the District of Columbia, where most governmental litigation is concentrated. In general, there is a rough attempt to include in each numbered circuit sufficient districts to furnish approximately the same amount of judicial work for one circuit that arises for other circuits.[5] The result of this is that the courts of appeals which are

---

1 The decisions of such three-judge district courts may, it should be noted, be appealed against directly to the Federal Supreme Court.

2 Kinnane, *A First Book on Anglo-American Law* (2nd ed. 1952), 479. There is, for example, a district court in Hawaii and one in Puerto Rico.   3 *Ibid*. 480.

4 As has been the case in England since 1875, there has been a merger of law and equity in the federal trial courts since the beginning of their existence.

5 Kinnane, *op. cit.* 484.

located in each circuit do not vary in size as much as do the district courts. Most of these appellate tribunals are composed of six or seven judges, though two of them—the courts for the First and Fourth Circuits—consist of only three members, while, at the other extreme, the courts of appeals for the District of Columbia and the Ninth Circuit, contain nine judges.

Cases before the federal courts of appeals are usually heard before a tribunal composed of three members of the court (a practice, it should be noted, not unlike that followed in the hearing of cases by the Court of Appeal in England), though important cases may be heard before the entire court *in banc*. The courts of appeals in the American system have no original jurisdiction and are strictly appellate tribunals. Their appellate jurisdiction is an extensive one—all final decisions of the district courts may be appealed against to them[1]—and, since only the most important cases can be taken from a court of appeals to the Supreme Court, these courts, in effect, perform much of the ultimate appellate work in the federal judicial system. In addition, though the courts of appeals are normally thought of as having appellate jurisdiction only over the lower federal courts, it should be pointed out that, with the increased use of administrative agencies in the federal system, the courts of appeals have been given appellate jurisdiction over many administrative decisions.[2] Thus, orders of most of the independent regulatory commissions in the federal administration, whose work has already been dealt with,[3] are subject to review in the appropriate court of appeals.

At the apex of the federal judicial system is the United States Supreme Court. As is well known, this is a central court which sits in Washington and is composed of a Chief Justice and eight associate justices. It meets every year in a term beginning on the first Monday in October and lasting normally until the beginning of June. Although the name of the highest court suggests that it is solely an appellate tribunal, it nevertheless has some original jurisdiction, notably in cases coming within the federal judicial power in which a State may be a party. To a student of comparative law, however, the original jurisdiction of the American court is of slight importance and, for our purposes, it can be treated exclusively as an appellate body. As the highest court in the land, the Supreme Bench in Washington is clearly the most important tribunal in the American system, especially in the field of constitutional law. In that field, indeed, the relevant law is almost entirely made up of the significant decisions of the Supreme Court. It is true that all such decisions have been based upon the written text of the Federal Constitution. But, as Chief Justice Hughes once so candidly

---

1 In certain rare cases, district court decisions may be appealed against directly to the Supreme Court.   2 *Ibid*.   3 *Supra*, p. 116.

remarked, 'the Constitution is what the judges say it is'.[1] And it is as the authoritative expounder of the American organic instrument that the role of the federal Supreme Court is of such cardinal significance.[2]

SELECTION

The outstanding feature of the polity of the common-law countries, we are informed by Roscoe Pound, is that it is a legal polity. 'Thus the courts necessarily play a part in the polity of an English-speaking country which they do not play elsewhere. In Great Britain, the United States, Canada, and Australia the judge is a figure of the first magnitude. The English and the American *Who's Who*? contain sketches of the judges of the important courts. In the equivalent books on the Continent one will hardly find the name of a single judge.'[3]

The appreciation in the Anglo-American countries of the importance of the judicial function has naturally led to a focusing of attention upon the securing of proper personnel in the courts. 'It has been eloquently argued', writes an American jurist in a treatise devoted to the problem of judicial personnel, 'that the one factor most likely to provoke revolution is a feeling of injustice in the mass of the people. The kind of men who are on the bench must necessarily have much to do with the presence or absence of that feeling.'[4] It is almost a truism that the quality of justice depends more upon the quality of the men who administer the law than on the content of the law they administer.[5] Unless those appointed to the bench are competent and upright and free to judge without fear or favour, a judicial system, however sound its structure may be on paper, is bound to function poorly in practice. That is why the problem of judicial selection and tenure is the pivotal one in all discussions of the proper administration of justice.

It should be noted that the approach to this problem in the Anglo-American countries is wholly different from that which is followed in civil-law countries. 'In continental countries judgeship is a career. The young judge starts his career in one of the lowest courts and hopes to advance through judicial office and other posts under the Ministry of Justice to the highest courts.'[6] That being the case, it is not surprising that

1 Hendel, *Charles Evans Hughes and the Supreme Court* (1951), 11.
2 In addition to the courts which have been described, there are a number of so-called legislative courts in the federal system, with jurisdiction over particular kinds of litigation. These include the Court of Claims, the Court of Customs and Patent Appeals, the Tax Court, and the Court of Military Appeals.
3 Introduction to Haynes, *The Selection and Tenure of Judges* (1944), ix.
4 *Ibid.* 3.   5 *Ibid.* 5.
6 Wade and Phillips, *Constitutional Law* (4th ed. 1950), 232.

the method of appointment to the Continental judiciary is one which the Anglo-American jurist would consider more appropriate for the recruitment of civil servants than for the selection of judges. 'Judges are civil servants (*fonctionnaires*) of the State,' declares a recent French treatise, 'recruited by means of a competitive examination.'[1]

The common-law conception of judicial office is an entirely different one. The Anglo-American jurist tends to think of such office as a reward for service at the bar. He looks upon promotion to the bench as the culmination of a distinguished professional career. 'In England judges—both of inferior and superior courts—are appointed from practising members of the Bar. They have thus a tradition of independence and their affinities are with the Bar rather than the Executive and its servants.'[2]

The method of selection in the federal judicial system in the United States is, in a general way, similar to that followed in England. Appointment to the federal bench, under the relevant constitutional provision,[3] is made by the President, subject to confirmation by the Senate. One American writer has asserted that the power vested in him to appoint the judges of the federal courts makes of the President a sort of American Lord High Chancellor.[4] This analogy, of course, overlooks the role of the Crown and the Prime Minister in making judicial appointments in Britain. In reality, the authority of the President in this respect is a combination of the formal appointing power of the Crown plus the real power exercised by the Lord Chancellor in the case of puisne judges of the High Court and that exerted by him and the Prime Minister in the case of the other judges of the superior courts.

In some ways, indeed, the appointing authority of the President over the federal courts is greater than that wielded by the Lord Chancellor and Prime Minister in Britain. The latter are restricted in their choice to barristers of at least ten years' standing, for puisne judges, and to barristers of at least fifteen years' standing or High Court judges, for members of the Court of Appeal. In the United States, there are no such limitations upon the presidential appointing authority. It is true that, as a practical matter, only members of the legal profession may be chosen for judicial office. It should, however, be remembered that the bar in the United States is nothing like the relatively restricted group which makes up the English bar. The lack of the sharp division between barristers and solicitors in the American system means that the presidential choice is not limited to that

---

1 Brethe de la Gressaye and Laborde-Lacoste, *Introduction générale à l'étude du droit* (1947), 428.
2 Wade and Phillips, *op. cit.* 232.   3 Article II, section 2.
4 Patterson, *Presidential Government in the United States* (1947), 182.

portion of the legal profession engaged only in the tasks of advocacy. Nor is the President required to appoint only from among those who are actually active at the bar. In fact, a growing number of judicial appointments are being made from among lawyers whose work does not at all resemble that performed by the active English barrister, such as members of the executive, the legislature or of law faculties, who have not engaged in legal practice for many years. Thus, in the 1954 Supreme Court, eight of its members were appointed from among the groups just mentioned,[1] while the ninth was elevated from his seat on a court of appeals.

Perhaps the greatest weakness, in practice, of the system of selecting federal judges in the United States arises from the fact that, all too often, the presidential power of appointment has been used for political purposes. 'The President', states one author in discussing appointments to the Supreme Court, 'can hardly be expected to appoint men, however outstanding they may be, whose views on matters of public policy are known to be radically different from his own. He has personal and political obligations, which being human, he will be tempted to fulfill through appointment to the Court. Besides being President, he is the leader of a political party, and partisan considerations will be borne in mind.'[2] It is true that, in Britain also, similar remarks have been made in the past with regard to the appointment of judges upon a political basis. Thus, as late as 1929, Lord Sankey thought it worth while to deprecate the idea that judges should be chosen from among the members of the party in power.[3] Happily, however, the situation is quite otherwise in Britain today, for the defect referred to has been largely remedied.

In the federal judicial system, on the other hand, it cannot be denied that political considerations still play a primary part in the choice of members of the bench. Thus, to take the highest court of the nation as an example, at the beginning of 1953, after twenty years of Democratic government, the Supreme Court was composed of eight Democrats and one Republican. And, of the eight belonging to the party in power, five had been active members of the Government at the time of their elevation to the court. The tendency to appoint those active in the administration to high judicial office—and there is a similar tendency in the lower federal courts—is a development which has been much deplored among American jurists. It is to be feared that men who have been part and parcel of the executive

1 Of these, four were appointed directly from positions in the executive branch, two from the Senate, one from a law faculty, and one, the Chief Justice, from the governorship of the State of California.

2 Bates, *The Story of the Supreme Court* (1936), 42.

3 *The Times*, 11 November 1929, p. 8, cited in Haynes, *op. cit.* 148. See also Laski, *Studies in Law and Politics* (1932), 168.

will be too favourable to its point of view. Though there may be no conscious effect, there is always the danger of bias in favour of administration forming in the mind of such future judge. This is especially significant in view of the extent to which issues of public law now constitute the stuff of federal and particularly of Supreme Court litigation.[1] A Supreme Court, whose majority is made up (as was that of the American court at the beginning of 1953) of two former Attorneys-General, one ex-Solicitor-General, an ex-Secretary of the Treasury, and a former Chairman of the Securities and Exchange Commission, is bound to feel more friendly toward administration than former courts, whose members were mostly selected from the practising bar, as judges still are, in major part, in Britain.[2]

Though one may thus deprecate the method of appointment in the federal judicial system, it should be realized that, by American standards, it is not as bad as it might look to the student of comparative law. Certainly, the federal manner of choice is far superior to the way in which judges are selected in the great majority of American States. In most States, judges are still chosen for short terms by the method of popular election, against which the strictures of Lord Bryce were so justly directed.[3] That choice by popular election lowers the character of the judiciary cannot be denied. 'The mere statement of the attributes of a good judge', declares a prominent American jurist, 'is in itself perhaps the most effective way of exposing the inherent weakness of the elective system of selecting judges.'[4]

In dealing with the appointment of federal judges by the President, one should consequently recognize that, even with its weaknesses, it is still much better than the mode of selecting judges followed in most of the American States. And, even with the tendency which has been noted to appoint federal judges primarily upon a political basis, it is surprising how high the over-all calibre of the federal judiciary has been. 'While it is true', writes a British observer who was not over friendly toward American institutions, 'that there have been judges of poor quality in each of the three tiers of the federal courts, it is also true that they have been able to attract into their service men whose ability, taken as a whole, rivals that of the men who

1 Frankfurter and Landis, 'The Supreme Court under the Judiciary Act of 1925', 42 *Harvard L. Rev.* (1928), 1, 18.

2 One should note that there has been a somewhat similar convention in Britain, that the principal law officers of the Government have a first claim on the higher judicial posts, though one may doubt whether it now has much force.

3 Bryce, *The American Commonwealth* (1917 ed.), vol. 1, 512.

4 Vanderbilt, *Cases and Materials on Modern Procedure and Judicial Administration* (1952), 1167.

have sought to win the ultimate prize of the presidency.'[1] At the same time, however, it cannot be denied that, though this comment may be accurate taking a wide range of view, the quality of judicial personnel in the federal system has been waning in recent years. The observations of a French jurist on this point with regard to the highest federal tribunal aptly illustrate this. 'In the past ten years, the prestige of the Supreme Court has markedly declined. The present judges are of very minor stature, compared with Holmes, Brandeis, Cardozo, or Charles Evans Hughes. The systematic political appointments of recent Presidents, aggravated by the mediocrity of the judges selected by Mr Truman, has without any doubt contributed to the decline.'[2]

Just as important as the tendency to make appointments on a political basis in lowering the calibre of the federal judiciary has been the relatively low salary paid to federal judges. That the compensation received by members of the judiciary in the United States has been inadequate, as compared with the financial rewards open to the successful practising lawyer, was noted by Lord Bryce almost seventy years ago.[3] This unhappy situation, if anything, became aggravated after he wrote his celebrated study of American government. While it is true that the dollar salary of federal judges has substantially increased during the present century,[4] this formal rise in compensation has hardly done more than keep pace with the decline in the value of the dollar due to inflationary trends. In addition, it should be borne in mind that the salary of American judges is, at present, subject to substantial income taxes, which was not at all true in Lord Bryce's day. If one bears these factors, i.e. the fall in the value of the dollar and the payment of income taxes, in mind, there is little doubt but that judicial salaries in the United States are relatively not higher today than they were in Lord Bryce's time. 'The most important effect on the federal judiciary of . . . inadequate judicial salaries', declares a recent article, 'is the difficulty of getting good men to accept appointment at present salaries and the inevitable decline of the calibre of the federal judiciary unless salaries are substantially increased.'[5] The successful practising lawyer, who can earn more than the salary paid to a federal district judge, is bound to hesitate before accepting judicial office, despite the prestige of such position. Indeed, in recent years, there have been cases where district judges resigned

1 Laski, *op. cit.* 110.   2 Pinto, *op. cit.* 126.

3 Bryce, *op. cit.* 272, 512.

4 Today, district court judges receive $22,500, as against $6000 in Lord Bryce's day; judges of the courts of appeals $25,500 as against $7000; and Supreme Court justices $35,000, as against $12,500.

5 Mitchell, 'The judicial salary crisis: an increase is urgently needed', 39 *American Bar Association J.* (1953), 197, 198.

to return to private practice because the rise in the cost of living made it too difficult for them to make ends meet on their salaries. An Act passed early in 1955 has made for some improvement, for it provided for substantial increases in the compensation of federal judges. Even under it, however, the situation is not entirely satisfactory, since, even with the increases provided by this Act, the net spendable salaries of the judges have lower purchasing power than those which they received before the last war.

TENURE

The Anglo-American jurist rightly looks upon security of tenure as one of the cardinal safeguards to ensure that judicial functions will be properly performed. 'It is quite evident', as the United States Supreme Court has asserted, 'that one who holds his office only during the pleasure of another cannot be depended upon to maintain an attitude of independence against the latter's will.'[1] It is only when tenure during good behaviour became the accepted practice that the independence of the judiciary in Britain was effectively secured.

In the federal judicial system in the United States, as in Britain, the established rule is that of tenure during good behaviour[2]—a rule which is expressly provided for in the article on the judiciary in the American Constitution.[3] It is true that judges, like other officers of the Federal Government, can be removed by impeachment proceedings in cases of 'Treason, Bribery, or other high Crimes and Misdemeanors'.[4] These provisions clearly do not, as such, constitute any infringement of judicial independence, for they do not permit the removal of a judge for political reasons or because the Congress disapproves of his decisions. In the early days of the American Republic, they were, in fact, used for political ends, with the attempt, in 1805, by the Jeffersonian party, dominant in the executive and legislative branches of the Government, to impeach a justice of the Supreme Court with whose views it disagreed. Fortunately, the attempt failed when a split in the Jeffersonian ranks led to the acquittal of the justice in question.[5] The danger of removal upon political grounds was dispelled with the miscarriage of this endeavour. 'The Senate's verdict of

1 *Humphrey's Executor* v. *United States*, 295 U.S. 602, 629 (1935).
2 It should be noted that this is not true so far as the district courts in Hawaii and Puerto Rico are concerned. Their judges hold office for terms of six and eight years only. Compare *Terrell* v. *Secretary of State for the Colonies*, [1953] 2 Q.B. 483, where Lord Goddard, C.J., held that a superior judge in a colony was removable at the pleasure of the Crown.
3 Article III, section 1.   4 Article II, section 4.
5 For a vivid account, see Beveridge, *The Life of John Marshall* (1919), vol. III, ch. 4.

"Not Guilty" put an end to a theory of judicial tenure that would have meant the annihilation of an independent judiciary.'[1] Since 1805, though impeachment proceedings have been brought against nine other federal judges,[2] in none of these cases was the effort to secure removal based upon political reasons.

Just as important as security of tenure as a *sine qua non* of judicial independence is provision for compensation of the judiciary to be independent of the political branches of the Government. The framers of the American Declaration of Independence, itself, were fully aware of this. 'He has made judges dependent on his will alone', reads the ninth specification of that document, 'for the tenure of their offices, and the amount and payment of their salaries.' It is for this reason that the draftsmen of the Federal Constitution inserted in it an express provision that the compensation received by the judges appointed under it 'shall not be diminished during their Continuance in Office'.[3] The lack of a similar enforceable constitutional safeguard in Britain led to a reduction of judicial salaries under the National Economy Act, 1931. The restoration of the cuts by the Inland Revenue in deference to public opinion did prevent the difficulty arising out of the 1931 Act from becoming more than a theoretical one.[4] Yet the experience of American States which do not have a constitutional prohibition such as that which protects the federal judges does indicate that there is a danger that the power to reduce judicial compensation may be used to impair the independence of the courts. Thus, it is said that in one State the legislature, enraged at a decision of its highest court, reduced the judges' annual salaries to twenty-five cents.[5] This may be an extreme case whose occurrence today would be unthinkable on either side of the Atlantic. That it did happen does, however, show the peril which may inhere in unrestricted legislative control over judicial compensation.

1 Vanderbilt, *op. cit.* 125.
2 Of these nine proceedings, three resulted in acquittal, one was dismissed, one was abandoned, and four resulted in convictions and removal. For a recent discussion of these proceedings by a member of the highest American Court, see Burton, 'An independent judiciary: the keystone of our freedom', 39 *American Bar Association J.* (1953), 1067.
3 Article III, section 1.
4 Phillips, *The Constitutional Law of Great Britain and the Commonwealth* (1952), 447.
5 Haynes, *op. cit.* 95.

JURISDICTION

To the student of comparative law, the existence in the American system of a separate set of federal courts alongside the courts established in each of the States may seem like a needless duplication of judicial machinery and personnel. Yet, as Lord Bryce aptly pointed out, a federal judicature is needed in the United States to interpret and apply the laws enacted by the Federal Congress, and to compel obedience to them. 'The alternative would have been to entrust the enforcement of the laws to State courts. But State courts were not fitted to deal with matters of a quasi-international character, such as admiralty jurisdiction and rights arising under Treaties. They supplied no means for deciding questions between different States. They could not be trusted to do complete justice between their own citizens and those of another State. Being under the control of their own State governments, they might be forced to disregard any Federal law which the State disapproved; or even if they admitted its authority, might fail in the zeal or the power to give due effect to it. And being authorities coordinate with and independent of one another, with no common court of appeal placed over them to correct their errors or harmonize their views, they would be likely to interpret the Federal Constitution and statutes in different senses, and make the law uncertain by the variety of their decisions.'[1]

These reasons, which led to the establishment of a separate series of federal courts in the United States, also explain the jurisdiction which is conferred upon these tribunals. Since the primary purpose of the federal courts is to ensure the proper interpretation and enforcement of federal laws, their basic competence is in cases arising under them. Thus, the first section of the American Judicial Code, dealing with the jurisdiction of the federal courts, provides that the district courts shall have original jurisdiction of all civil actions, wherein the amount in controversy exceeds $3000, which arise under the Constitution, laws or treaties of the United States. In addition, in order to avoid the possibility of bias on the part of the State courts where actions before them are between their own citizens[2] and those of another State, the federal judiciary is expressly declared competent in actions involving such diversity of citizenship. The district courts, states the Judicial Code, shall have original jurisdiction of all civil actions, where the matter in dispute exceeds the sum of $3000, which are between

---

[1] Bryce, *op. cit.* 229.
[2] Though the term 'citizen' is used in American law in this connexion, what is actually meant is 'resident', for citizenship is common throughout the Union and does not vary from State to State.

citizens of different States or between citizens of a State and foreign States or citizens or subjects thereof. These two classes of cases—those arising under federal laws and those where there is a diversity of citizenship among the parties—constitute the bulk of litigation brought before the federal district courts.

It has already been indicated that the courts of first instance in the federal judicial system are the district courts. It is they who exercise the original jurisdiction conferred upon the federal courts. The courts of appeals, who are above them in the judicial hierarchy, are exclusively appellate tribunals. They have jurisdiction of appeals from all final decisions of the district courts. In addition, they are vested with appellate authority over the decisions of many administrative agencies. It should be noted, however, that this administrative-law competence of the courts of appeals exists only where it is expressly provided by statute. In the absence of statute, authority to review administrative action exists in the district courts, which, in the American system, have inherited the supervisory authority over inferior tribunals exercised in England by the Court of King's Bench for centuries, and the High Court since the Judicature Acts.[1]

The Federal Supreme Court, as has been pointed out, is almost entirely an appellate tribunal. The need for such a central court at the apex of the judicial system to unify the law expounded and applied by lower courts seems clear. At the same time, in a country as large as the United States, the right of appeal to the highest tribunal must be restricted, lest the court be swamped with more appeals than it can properly dispose of. If private litigants were allowed to appeal their case to the Supreme Court whenever they desired, the cases would be too numerous for the court to handle expeditiously. This would result in cases of wide general importance being unduly delayed in coming to decision, while the court frittered away its time on cases of slight importance.[2]

A similar problem in England with regard to the ultimate appellate tribunal led to the provision of the Administration of Justice (Appeals) Act, 1934, under which no appeal lies from the Court of Appeal to the House of Lords save by leave of the one or the other tribunal. The American Congress has gone even further in its attempt to restrict the right of appeal to the highest federal court. Under an Act of 1925, the former right to appeal to the Supreme Court as a matter of course was destroyed. Instead, the court itself was, in most cases, made the judge of whether or not it

1 Compare Farwell, L.J., in *Rex* v. *Board of Education*, [1910] 2 K.B. 165, 178.
2 Kinnane, *op. cit.* 486.

would receive an appeal to it.[1] If it feels that the question involved is not one of sufficient importance, it may refuse to hear the case.[2]

The theory of the 1925 Act, in transferring most cases from the obligatory to the discretionary jurisdiction of the Supreme Court, as Chief Justice Taft has told us, 'is that litigants have their rights sufficiently protected by a hearing or trial in the courts of first instance, and by one review in an immediate appellate Federal Court. The function of the Supreme Court is conceived to be, not the remedying of a particular litigant's wrong, but the consideration of cases whose decision involves principles, the application of which are of wide public or governmental interest, and which should be authoritatively declared by the final court.'[3] The discretionary authority of the Supreme Court to hear or refuse to hear appeals is thus based primarily upon public, rather than private, interest. Its reviewing power, to quote the words of another Chief Justice, is exercised 'in the interest of the law, not the interest of the particular parties. It is not the importance of the parties or the amount involved that is controlling, but the need of securing harmony of decision and the appropriate settlement of questions of general importance so that the system of federal justice may be appropriately administered.'[4] It is thus erroneous to think of the American Supreme Court as only an ultimate appellate tribunal. Its discretionary power to determine the cases which shall be heard by it has resulted in its ceasing to be merely an ordinary judicial body. It is a court of special resort for the settlement only of such questions as it deems to involve a substantial public concern, rather than the concerns only of private persons as such.[5]

LEGISLATIVE CONTROL

'No feature in the government of the United States', reads a celebrated passage by Lord Bryce, 'has awakened so much curiosity in the European mind, caused so much discussion, received so much admiration, and been more frequently misunderstood, than the duties assigned to the Supreme Court and the functions which it discharges in guarding the ark of the Constitution.'[6] To the jurist in Britain, whose conceptions of judicial power are much more limited than those of his American confrère, the

1 In most cases, appeals to the Supreme Court are in the form of a petition for a writ of certiorari. It should be noted, that, though the name is the same, this proceeding bears little resemblance to the proceeding for certiorari before the High Court in England.

2 Kinnane, *op. cit.* 487.

3 Taft, 'The jurisdiction of the Supreme Court under the Act of February 13, 1925', 35 *Yale L. J.* (1925), 1, 2.

4 Hughes, Address, 20 *American Bar Association J.* (1934), 341.

5 Kinnane, *op. cit.* 487.   6 Bryce, *op. cit.* 242.

constitutional competence of the federal courts seems, indeed, to be a most redoubtable one. Looking at the power exercised by the Supreme Court to invalidate statutes on the ground of their unconstitutionality, he not unnaturally tends to conclude that the court is, in fact, a third chamber in the United States.[1] And, if anything, it is a chamber superior to the two Houses of the Congress, for it possesses an absolute veto over the laws enacted by them.

What non-American observers of the federal system tend to overlook, however, is that the position of the courts in the United States is not nearly as powerful as it may appear, at first glance, to be. 'The judiciary', wrote Alexander Hamilton in the *Federalist Papers*, in a passage which has recently been re-echoed by a distinguished American jurist, 'is beyond comparison the weakest of the three departments of power.... [It] has no influence over either the sword or the purse; no direction either of the strength or the wealth of the society; and can take no active resolution whatever. It may truly be said to have neither FORCE nor WILL, but merely judgment.'[2]

That the federal judiciary does not occupy the all-powerful position which comparative students assign to it may be seen from the fact that its very organization and jurisdiction depend, in large part, upon statutory provisions. Except for the Supreme Court itself, none of the federal courts is provided for expressly in the American Constitution. The federal judicial power, under Article III of that instrument, is, as has already been mentioned, vested in the Supreme Court 'and in such inferior Courts as the Congress may from time to time ordain and establish'. The federal district courts and courts of appeals have been established by the Congress under this provision, and they owe their direct existence, not to the organic instrument, but to the statutes which set them up. There is no constitutional reason why the Congress cannot, if it sees fit, abolish any or all of the lower federal courts and transfer their jurisdiction to a set of newly created tribunals. It is true that this cannot be done with regard to the Supreme Court, whose establishment is provided for expressly in the Constitution. Yet, even with regard to it, as we shall see, the details of its organization and jurisdiction are dependent directly upon legislative provisions.

The very existence of all federal courts but the Supreme Court is thus based primarily upon statute rather than constitutional law. The Congress has drastically altered the structure of the federal judicial system several times in the past, and it can do so in the future without constitutional hindrance. And what is true of the federal judicial structure is also true of the jurisdiction vested in the federal courts. Except for the original juris-

---

1 Laski, *op. cit.* 11.   2 *The Federalist*, no. 78, quoted in Vanderbilt, *op. cit.* 97.

diction of the Supreme Court, which is today of little practical importance, the American Constitution is silent with regard to the competence of the federal courts. The result is that the jurisdiction of the federal judiciary, except for the original jurisdiction of the Supreme Court, is subject to legislative control, and the Congress has, in fact, not hesitated to impose such jurisdictional restrictions as it has deemed the exigencies of particular situations to require.[1] Since the Constitution did not establish the inferior federal courts, one of two consequences must result, stated the American Supreme Court over a century ago, '...either that each inferior court created by Congress must exercise all the judicial powers not given to the Supreme Court, or that Congress having the power to establish the courts, must define their respective jurisdictions. The first of these inferences has never been asserted, and could not be defended with any show of reason, and if not, the latter would seem to follow as a necessary consequence. And it would seem to follow also that, having a right to prescribe, Congress may withhold from any court of its creation jurisdiction of any of the enumerated controversies. Courts created by statute can have no jurisdiction but such as the statute confers.'[2]

What the congressional authority in this respect can mean in practice is shown by the so-called Norris-LaGuardia Act of 1932. That law was enacted because of the abuses which were widely felt to have resulted from the wholesale use by the federal courts of their injunctive power in cases involving labour disputes. The 1932 Act sought to curb these abuses by drastically limiting the authority of the federal courts to issue injunctions in such cases. 'No court of the United States', it declared, 'shall have jurisdiction to issue a temporary or permanent injunction in any case involving or growing out of a labor dispute, as herein defined', except subject to restrictions which made the granting of such relief impractical in almost all cases. There were those who argued, at the time of the Norris-LaGuardia Act, that it was an unconstitutional infringement of the authority of the federal courts. The power to restrain by injunction, contended one congressional opponent of the law, is inherent in equity courts and is of the very essence of judicial power; the legislature could not so impinge upon the inherent equity powers of the courts 'as to destroy altogether the power of the court to vindicate its existence and discharge its exalted functions'.[3] Arguments such as these proved, however, to be of little avail in view of the established congressional authority over the jurisdiction of the federal courts. When the question of the constitutionality of the anti-injunction provisions of the Norris-LaGuardia law came before it, the

1 *Ibid.* 109.　　2 *Sheldon* v. *Sill*, 8 How. 441, 448 (U.S. 1850).
3 Congressman Beck, quoted in Vanderbilt, *op. cit.* 110.

Supreme Court found little difficulty in finding them valid.[1] 'There can be no question', asserts the court's opinion in summarily disposing of this point, 'of the power of Congress thus to define and limit the jurisdiction of the inferior courts of the United States.'[2]

The Norris-LaGuardia Act, just discussed, is, according to a noted American judge, but one example of how the Congress, in the exercise of its power over the federal courts, can restrict or eliminate the right of persons directly concerned to secure the relief that the courts were designed to afford them.[3] If the Congress can interfere with the injunctive process in this manner, he goes on, one might well ask whether there is any limit to congressional interference with the federal courts.[4]

Nor, it should be noted, is the congressional authority over judicial jurisdiction limited entirely to the lower federal courts. The details of Supreme Court competence as well are subject to legislative control. The congressional power over the highest tribunal may doubtless be more limited than it is in the case of the other federal courts, for the existence of the Supreme Court and its original jurisdiction are expressly provided for by the Constitution. The same is not, however, true of that tribunal's appellate competence, which covers, as has been indicated, by far the greatest part of its work. It may well be, in the words of the Chief Justice of the Supreme Court in an important case, 'that the appellate jurisdiction of this court is not derived from Acts of Congress. It is, strictly speaking, conferred by the Constitution. But it is conferred "with such exceptions and under such regulations as Congress shall make".'[5] And in the case referred to, *Ex parte McCardle*,[6] the court sustained an Act of Congress which deprived the court of jurisdiction to decide certain appeals, among them being McCardle's, which had already been argued before it.

That the American courts are not nearly as all-powerful as most students of comparative law think results from the principles which have just been discussed. The congressional authority over the organization and jurisdiction of the lower federal courts and the appellate competence of the Supreme Court, in many ways, is comparable to the control over the judiciary exercised by the legislature in a parliamentary system of government. It is true that the analogy may not be an entirely accurate one, for the existence of the Supreme Court in the American system is expressly provided for in the Constitution and consequently cannot be affected by legislative fiat. And, with regard to the lower federal courts, it is from the

1 Vanderbilt, *op. cit.* 110.
2 *Lauf* v. *E. G. Shinner & Co.*, 303 U.S. 323, 330 (1938).
3 Vanderbilt, *op. cit.* 111.   4 *Ibid.*
5 Chase, C.J., in *Ex parte McCardle*, 7 Wall. 506, 512 (U.S. 1868).
6 7 Wall. 506 (U.S. 1868).

Constitution also that they derive 'the judicial power', once they are established. Yet, as the Norris-LaGuardia Act shows, the details of the judicial authority possessed by the federal courts are subject to drastic congressional restriction. Even the appellate jurisdiction of the Supreme Court can be limited, for its details also depend upon legislative prescriptions.

CONFLICTS WITH EXECUTIVE

The present august position of the federal courts in the United States is thus, as the above analysis indicates, dependent in large part upon legislative sufferance. The Congress could, if it wished, by the exercise of its authority over the structure and competence of the courts, drastically limit the scope of the judicial power vested in them. It should, however, be noted that the danger of congressional action of this type has, up till now, proved more theoretical than real. The Congress has not, in fact, used its authority over judicial organization and jurisdiction in order unduly to control the functioning of the courts.

The relation between the federal courts and the executive has, on the contrary, not always been a harmonious one. Here, too, the power of the American judiciary has been weaker than most non-Americans suppose. The courts themselves do not directly command the force of politically organized society. It is the executive, as Alexander Hamilton aptly pointed out, which holds the sword of the community. The judiciary must ultimately depend upon the aid of the executive arm even for the efficacy of its judgments.[1]

From the time of Thomas Jefferson, at the beginning of the last century, to that of Franklin D. Roosevelt, in the present one, there have been a number of conflicts between the President and the courts. And, if the latter have emerged triumphant from most of them, their margin of victory has often been a slender one. In his efforts to control the federal judiciary, Jefferson, soon after his second election in 1804, resorted to attempted impeachment of a justice of the Supreme Court, an effort which, as we have seen,[2] failed because of a split in the ranks of the Jeffersonian party in Congress. Since Jefferson's time, there have been no open attempts by the executive to remove federal judges for political reasons. Later Presidents have not, however, hesitated to try to control the political aspects of the work of the courts by a judicious use of their power to appoint members of the federal judiciary. In this respect, probably the most extreme case was the appointment in 1871 by President Grant of two Supreme Court justices solely in order to obtain the reversal by the court

1 *The Federalist*, no. 78.   2 *Supra*, p. 135.

of an important 1870 decision[1] with which he violently disagreed, which had been rendered by a bare majority of one. Since the two Grant appointees were men whose views on the matter coincided with those of the President, it is not surprising that the court repudiated its earlier decision soon after their appointment.[2] Of course, in the words of one commentator, practically every President has made judicial appointments with a view to influencing constitutional construction, but generally there was no specific case in mind, only a long-range proposition. The Grant appointments, on the other hand, were made for the purpose of reversing a specific decision of the court and involved a case of presidential 'packing' of the court for that purpose.[3]

The most notable conflict that has occurred between the federal courts and the executive since the time of Jefferson arose out of the repeated invalidation by the Supreme Court of the basic measures upon which the 'New Deal' programme of President Franklin D. Roosevelt was based. The President, who saw his legislative plans invalidated by what he deemed to be the over-narrow constitutional construction of a majority of the court, was unwilling to wait for the law of mortality to furnish him with the opportunity to appoint men of his viewpoint to the highest tribunal. Instead, he sought to deal with the problem of a recalcitrant court by proposing a drastic shake-up in its membership. Shortly after his second triumphant inauguration, the President sent to the Congress his so-called Court Reorganization Plan. The President's solution was to give a Supreme Court justice over seventy years of age six months in which to retire. If he failed to do so he could continue in office, but the chief executive could appoint an additional justice—presumably younger and better able to carry the heavy load of Supreme Court work. As there were six justices in the over-seventy category at that time, President Roosevelt would at once have had six appointments to make, which would have enabled him to staff the court with a majority of his own choice.[4]

From the constitutional point of view, it should be emphasized, President Roosevelt's 'court-packing' plan, if once it had been passed by the Congress, could not have been assailed. Though the Federal Constitution does, as has been indicated, expressly provide for the existence of the Supreme Court, it does not in any way specify the composition of that tribunal. That is determined by the Congress, and the composition of the Supreme Court has been fixed by statute since the beginning of the Re-

1 *Hepburn* v. *Griswold*, 8 Wall. 603 (U.S. 1870).
2 *Legal Tender Cases*, 12 Wall. 457 (U.S. 1871).
3 Patterson, *op. cit.* 214.
4 See Mason, 'Harlan Fiske Stone and FDR's Court Plan', 61 *Yale L. J.* (1952), 791, 796.

public. The present membership of nine justices, which is the number which the court has contained since 1869, has no constitutional basis; it merely happens to be the number fixed in the Judicial Code, by which the organization and jurisdiction of the federal courts are regulated. And, in fact, the membership of the court has varied from six, the number of justices at the time of its creation, to eight, then ten, then eight again, and, finally, to the present membership of nine.

It cannot be denied that the failure to fix the membership of the Supreme Court in the Constitution constitutes a dangerous lacuna in the American organic instrument.[1] An unscrupulous President, whose party is dominant in the Congress, whose measures are declared unconstitutional by the court, has the way open to achieve his ends by securing legislation increasing the membership of the court and then 'packing' that tribunal with his own appointees.[2] Thus, in 1869, the number of justices on the court was enlarged to nine, in part at least in order to enable President Grant to appoint a member of his own choice who would vote in accordance with his view in an important case. And the court reorganization plan of Franklin D. Roosevelt was clearly intended to lead to a reversal in the constitutional jurisprudence of the highest court, by a drastic alteration in the composition of that tribunal.

Against attempts of this type by the executive, the Supreme Court is, constitutionally speaking, helpless. From the point of view of purely legal protection, then, judicial control, such as that exercised by the Supreme Court in the United States, may well prove ineffectual as the sole safeguard against attempts to establish a totalitarian system of government. It is not, however, the Supreme Court alone, but the Supreme Court, backed by the force of informed public opinion, that has made judicial control of constitutionality so important a factor in the working of the American governmental system. 'There is no modern community', writes Professor Laski, 'in which respect for the principle of judicial review goes deeper than it does in the United States, with the result that acceptance of the Court's authority by all persons or institutions affected is taken for granted.'[3] It was the pressure of public opinion that caused President Roosevelt's plan to 'pack' the Supreme Court to miscarry, and that despite the unprecedented majority which the President's party then had in both Houses of Congress. 'From the very start', as a recent commentary puts it, 'the President's Reorganization Proposal ran into over-

1 On May 11, 1954, the Senate passed, with the required two-thirds majority, a proposed constitutional amendment fixing the membership of the Supreme Court at nine, but the 83rd Congress adjourned without any action being taken on the measure by the House of Representatives.

2 Cf. Bryce, *op. cit.* 276.   3 Laski, *op. cit.* 112.

whelming public opposition. Overnight Supreme Court Justices were pictured as demigods far above the sweaty crowd, weighing public policy in the delicate scales of the law. The same Congressmen who, prior to FDR's message, had demanded the scalps of reactionary Justices, were "shocked beyond measure" and turned upon Roosevelt in an attitude of anguished surprise. Closing ranks with Bar Associations, the newspapers lined up...solidly against Court-packing....The press and bar had hit a responsive chord. Said Walter Lippman: "No issue so great or so deep has been raised in America since secession."'[1]

In its conflicts with the executive, the federal judiciary has at times suffered from the fact that the execution of its will is almost entirely dependent upon the concurring will of the executive. 'Everybody knows', stated a leading article in a Pennsylvania newspaper in 1936, 'there will be nothing the Court can do about it when elected officials finally say to it: "Your ruling is stupid and doesn't make sense, according to our opinion.... Therefore we shall ignore you."'[2] In actual fact, such defiance of judicial authority by the executive has occurred several times in American history. Thus, there is the celebrated refusal of President Jackson to enforce a Supreme Court decision, in which he is reported to have said, 'Well, John Marshall has made his decision; now let him enforce it!'[3] And, during the Civil War, a writ of habeas corpus issued by Chief Justice Taney was defied by the military authorities, acting upon the express orders of President Lincoln. In the face of such executive disregard of its authority, there is little that the judiciary can do. 'In these encounters the judiciary has no weapons other than the shield of its own integrity and such support as may rally to it from an aroused public fearful of the peril to its liberties.'[4] That these weapons, though mainly moral, are, indeed, powerful ones is shown by the fact that examples of direct executive defiance of the courts, such as those just cited, are relatively rare in the history of American law, and, fortunately, none of any consequence has occurred in almost a century. Acceptance of the Supreme Court and its authority in the constitutional sphere is today as ingrained in the American consciousness as is the acceptance of the competence of the courts in matters of private law in Britain. The celebrated steel seizure case, which will be discussed in Chapter VII, illustrates this as well as anything else. The court's decision there, which drastically restricted the scope of executive power, might well have given rise to strong conflict with the executive branch. But the court's authority in the matter was accepted without question by the

---

1 Mason, *loc. cit.* 796.   2 Quoted *ibid.* 792.
3 According to Corwin, *The President: Office and Powers* (3rd ed. 1948), 77, this may be only a legend.   4 Vanderbilt, *op. cit.* 126.

entire country, from the President down. 'All observers of the American scene', declares an English observer, 'should have noted, with respect, the most impressive fact. This is that the Supreme Court, although it does not possess and never has possessed any means of enforcing its decisions, has once more brought to heel the mighty: the President, the union, the industry, and Congress. All that was needed to produce this effect was the knowledge that the Court had seen and was ready to do its constitutional duty.'[1]

JUDICIAL SELF-LIMITATION

It may be seen from the above that the basic support of the federal judiciary in the United States is not in its constitutional position, which is, in many ways, inherently a weak one in comparison with that of the legislative and executive branches, but in the acceptance by public opinion of its role as guardian of the American Constitution. 'In a representative, democratic government such as ours', writes a noted American judge, 'the power of the judiciary depends largely on its reputation for independence, integrity and wisdom.'[2] The Supreme Court has been able to maintain its role as the ultimate expounder of constitutional law only because it has by and large continued to retain its reputation in these respects in the public eye. When its place in public esteem has tended to go down and there has been danger of its losing its status, it has sooner or later remoulded its jurisprudence to accord with public demands. The analysis in Chapter VIII of the post-1937 change in the role of the highest American tribunal should serve to show this. Where public acceptance of the Supreme Court's authority is called into question, to quote Harold J. Laski, 'as over the Dred Scott case before the Civil War, or, rather less emphatically, in the generation from the election of McKinley to the second election of Franklin D. Roosevelt, it is legitimate to assume that the Court has lost the support of that public upon which its status depends; and there will then follow either a change in the postulates upon which its policy is built, or, sooner or later, such changes in its membership as will lead to a change in those postulates.'[3]

That the Supreme Court itself has recognized the inherent weakness of its position unless it is supported by public sentiment is not unnatural. 'The Supreme Court feels the touch of public opinion. Opinion is stronger in America than anywhere else in the world, and judges are only men. To yield a little may be prudent, for the tree that cannot bend to the blast may be broken.'[4] Realizing this, the American court has, so far as possible,

1 *The Economist*, 10 May 1952, p. 371.   2 Vanderbilt, *op. cit.* 140.
3 Laski, *op. cit.* 112.   4 Bryce, *op. cit.* 274.

tried to minimize the possibility of conflicts between it and the other two branches of government. It has done this by refusing to pronounce decisions upon constitutional questions unless it has been absolutely compelled to do so in the particular case. And it has ensured that constitutional pronouncements would not be rendered in many cases by evolving a number of self-imposed limitations on judicial review of issues of constitutionality.

'CASE' OR 'CONTROVERSY'

'In endowing this Court with "judicial power",' Mr Justice Frankfurter has asserted, 'the Constitution presupposed an historic content for that phrase and relied on assumption by the judiciary of authority only over issues which are appropriate for disposition by judges.'[1] In the view of the Supreme Court, 'courts are not charged with general guardianship against all potential mischief in the complicated tasks of government'.[2] The judicial function is a more limited one. Judicial power, however large, has an orbit more or less strictly defined.[3] It 'could come into play only in matters that were the traditional concern of the courts at Westminster and only if they arose in ways that to the expert feel of lawyers constituted "Cases" or "Controversies".... Even as to the kinds of questions which were the staple of judicial business, it was not for courts to pass upon them as abstract, intellectual problems but only if a concrete, living contest between adversaries called for the arbitrament of law.'[4]

Under Article III of the Federal Constitution, the judicial power vested in the federal courts may be exercised only for the determination of so-called 'cases' or 'controversies'. 'By the express terms of the Constitution,' the highest American court has stated, 'the exercise of the judicial power is limited to "cases" and "controversies". Beyond this it does not extend, and unless it is asserted in a case or controversy within the meaning of the Constitution, the power to exercise it is nowhere conferred.'[5]

As a practical matter, the 'case' or 'controversy' requirement, as it has been construed by the federal courts, has resulted in what has aptly been termed 'government by lawsuit'[6] as the outstanding characteristic of the American polity. Fundamental constitutional issues in the United States

1 *Coleman v. Miller*, 307 U.S. 433, 460 (1939).
2 *Federal Communications Commission v. Pottsville Broadcasting Co.*, 309 U.S. 134, 146 (1940).
3 Frankfurter and Fisher, 'The business of the Supreme Court at the October terms, 1935 and 1936', 51 *Harvard L. Rev.* (1938), 577, 621.
4 *Coleman v. Miller*, 307 U.S. 433, 460 (1939).
5 *Muskrat v. United States*, 219 U.S. 346, 356 (1911).
6 Jackson, *The Struggle for Judicial Supremacy* (1941), 286.

are ultimately determined through the technical forms of the lawsuit. 'By cases and controversies are intended the claims of litigants brought before the courts for determination by such regular proceedings as are established by law or custom for the protection or enforcement of rights, or the prevention, redress, or punishment of wrongs.'[1] It is only when a constitutional issue is presented to it in the form of an action at law or equity between two adverse parties that a federal court can attempt to dispose of it. No matter how important the issue may be, or how pressing its resolution may be for the nation, its decision by the courts, and ultimately the Supreme Court, must await the presentation to them of an actual suit for settlement.

The insistence by the American Supreme Court on the presence of a real case before federal judicial power can come into play has prevented it from performing an advisory role analogous to that performed by courts in other legal systems, notably, in France, where the Conseil d'État, the supreme administrative-law court, is the consultative organ of the administration as well as the reviewer of the legality of administrative acts.[2] That the need for expert judicial advice has often been felt by Anglo-American administrators is shown by the attempts they have made to introduce advisory opinion procedures by which the validity of administrative action could be tested at the outset, the best known of which is that which was contained in the English Rating and Valuation Bill, 1928.[3] In a system such as the American one, where an entire legislative scheme can be invalidated by the courts, *ex post facto* as it were, years after it has been put into operation, an advisory opinion technique might prove particularly helpful. It would enable the legislature or executive to obtain an advance decision by the courts on the constitutionality of proposed action and thus avoid many of the inconveniences of the present system.

Such an anticipatory judgment technique is, however, precluded in the federal judicial system by the consistent insistence of the Supreme Court upon the presence of an actual 'case' or 'controversy' before constitutional issues can be judicially decided. *Muskrat* v. *United States*,[4] where the court refused to determine in the abstract the validity of a statute, in the absence of an actual case between adverse litigants, is the leading case. 'Is such a determination within the judicial power conferred by the Constitution', asked Mr Justice Day there, 'as the same has been interpreted and defined in the authoritative decisions to which we have referred? We think it is

1 *Muskrat* v. *United States*, 219 U.S. 346, 357 (1911).
2 See Schwartz, *French Administrative Law and the Common-Law World* (1954), 33–5.   3 See Schwartz, *Law and the Executive in Britain* (1949), 202–4.
4 219 U.S. 346 (1911).

not. That judicial power, as we have seen, is the right to determine actual controversies arising between adverse litigants, duly instituted in courts of proper jurisdiction.'[1]

The judicial refusal in the United States to allow the courts to act in an advisory capacity stems from the feeling that it would be unwise for judges, whose authority under the Constitution has such significant impact upon the work of the political departments of the Government, to exercise such authority except when it is absolutely imperative for the decision of a case between hostile parties presented to them for decision. In such a case, the federal courts pronounce upon the validity of a statute or of executive action as part of their duty of deciding the case before them in accordance with the law of the land. If a statute relied upon by one of the parties is alleged by the other to be contrary to the organic instrument, the American courts must determine the correctness of that claim. Yet they do so only in order properly to decide the actual case before them. As an acute English observer aptly expressed it, 'while the judges of the United States control the action of the constitution, they nevertheless perform purely judicial functions, since they never decide anything but the cases before them. It is natural to say that the Supreme Court pronounces Acts of Congress invalid, but in fact this is not so. The court never directly pronounces any opinion whatever upon an Act of Congress. What the court does is simply to determine that in a given case A is or is not entitled to recover judgment against X; but in determining that case the court may decide that an Act of Congress is not to be taken into account, since it is an Act beyond the constitutional powers of Congress.'[2]

It may well be, in the words of Lord Birkenhead, that this view is 'a little subtle', for 'when an issue challenged by an individual raises the question whether a law is constitutional or not the decision of the Supreme Court decides this question for all time, and if the decision is against the legislature the attempted law is stripped of its attempted authority'.[3] However that may be, the insistence of the Supreme Court upon an actual case before a constitutional issue can be decided has enabled Americans to assert that, august as are the functions of the court, 'surely they do not go one step beyond the administration of justice to individual litigants'.[4] For the federal courts to intervene in other than actual cases brought before them, as, for example, to decide the validity of legislative or executive action in advance by an advisory opinion procedure, would be for them to act more

1 219 U.S. at 361.   2 Dicey, *op. cit.* 163.
3 Birkenhead, 'Development of the British Constitution in the last fifty years', 9 *American Bar Association J.* (1923), 578, 579.
4 Davis, 'Present-day problems', *ibid.* 557.

directly in a purely political manner. They would then be part and parcel of political controversies, and, lacking the sword of the executive, the purse of the legislature, and the authority of both which comes from their direct election by the people, they would soon be in a wholly untenable position. It is the realization of this that has made the American courts refuse to exercise their power in other than 'cases' or 'controversies', where, however much their action might bear upon the activity of the political departments, they could still be said to be exercising purely judicial power.

'STANDING'

Federal judicial power in the field of constitutional law extends, we have just seen, only to the resolution of actual controversies between opposed litigants. In the view of the American courts, there can be no real 'case' or 'controversy', in the sense required, if the individual bringing the particular action does not have a personal interest in having the governmental act which he challenges declared unconstitutional. Unless he is adversely affected personally, as an individual, he is seeking only a judgment in the abstract upon the constitutionality of such act. Such a proceeding is not enough to call for the exercise of federal judicial power. Its exercise is 'legitimate only in the last resort, and as a necessity in the determination of real, earnest and vital controversy between individuals'.[1] The action to review the constitutionality of a law in the federal courts is thus clearly not the *actio popularis* of the Roman law; citizens cannot bring it in the interest of the community as a whole to see that the rule of law is respected by the legislative and executive branches.[2] Unless the action is brought by one who has a direct personal interest, he does not have the 'standing' required to bring the suit.

What this requirement of 'standing' can mean in practice is shown by the celebrated case of *Massachusetts* v. *Mellon*,[3] which challenged the constitutionality of a federal law providing for appropriations of money to be allotted among the States for the purpose of reducing maternal and infant mortality. The allotment to each State, in accordance with the formula of federal grants-in-aid which, as we shall see,[4] has been developed during the present century, was made conditional upon acceptance by the States of the terms of the statute, and the States were also to contribute financially. Massachusetts claimed that the statute in question was unconstitutional as a usurpation of power reserved to the States under the Tenth Amendment.

---

1 *Chicago & Grand Trunk Railway Co.* v. *Wellman*, 143 U.S. 339, 345 (1892).
2 Cf. Alibert, *Le Contrôle juridictionnel de l'administration* (1926), 96.
3 262 U.S. 447 (1923).   4 *Infra*, p. 175.

It was argued that, even though the State had not accepted the Act, its constitutional rights were infringed by the imposition of an option either to yield part of its reserved rights to the Federal Government or to lose its share of the appropriation.[1] The court held, however, that the case must be dismissed for want of jurisdiction 'without considering the merits of the constitutional questions'.[2] The statute in question did not require the plaintiff to do or yield anything, and no burden was imposed upon it. No direct interest of the State was involved, since it was not adversely affected by the statute. Hence, it did not have the 'standing' required to bring the action. 'No rights of the State falling within the scope of the judicial power have been brought within the actual or threatened operation of the statute,' reads the court's conclusion on the matter, 'and this court is. . . without authority to pass abstract opinions upon the constitutionality of acts of Congress.'[3]

In a companion case, the same statute was attacked by an individual taxpayer, but the court held that he also did not have a sufficient interest to bring the action. 'The party who invokes the [judicial] power', said the court, 'must be able to show, not only that the statute is invalid, but that he has sustained or is immediately in danger of sustaining some direct injury as the result of its enforcement, and not merely that he suffers in some indefinite way in common with people generally.'[4] The interest of a taxpayer was declared to be too remote to justify his bringing of such an action. 'His interest in the moneys of the treasury—partly realized from taxation and partly from other sources—is shared with millions of others; is comparatively minute and indeterminable; and the effect upon future taxation of any payment out of the funds, so remote, fluctuating and uncertain, that no basis is afforded for appeal to the preventive powers of a court.'[5]

According to a distinguished American jurist, in a recent comment upon *Massachusetts* v. *Mellon*, 'the net result is that notwithstanding the fact that the constitutional issue was raised by the only parties who could possibly object to the act, the United States Supreme Court avoided deciding it and thereby left unanswered one of the most important constitutional questions ever presented to it. By an act of self-imposed judicial deference the court has rendered immune from attack the flood of legislative appropriations that have created an imbalance between the states and federal government never dreamed of by the Founding Fathers or the judges who spoke of an indestructible Union, composed of indestructible States.'[6]

---

1 See Vanderbilt, *op. cit.* 135–6.   2 262 U.S. at 480.
3 *Ibid.* at 485.   4 *Frothingham* v. *Mellon*, 262 U.S. 447, 488 (1923).
5 *Ibid.* at 487.   6 Vanderbilt, *op. cit.* 137.

In a case like *Massachusetts* v. *Mellon*, unless the State or a taxpayer is permitted to challenge the constitutionality of the statute, it is unlikely that its validity will ever be reviewed. In a practical sense, then, such legislative act would be placed in a conclusive position, for it would never be challenged by the only other party involved, i.e. the Federal Government, which enacted the law. It is incorrect to assume that one who seeks judicial review of the constitutionality of a governmental act is vindicating only his own personal interest. It may, it is true, be to his benefit to have an unconstitutional act, which adversely affects him, ruled invalid. But, even more important, he is vindicating the public interest, for it is clearly in the interest of the community that illegal governmental action be not left untouched.

If one looks at the suit to obtain judicial review of constitutionality in the American system in this manner, he can easily conclude that it should be treated as was the *actio popularis* of the Roman law, with no restrictions upon the 'standing' of those who seek to bring it. If such actions vindicate the public interest in preventing the legislative and executive branches from acting in excess of their constitutional authority, is it not in the public interest that they should be able to be brought as freely as possible?

It should, however, be recognized that the fear of the American courts lest they be accused of acting in a non-judicial manner has led them to impose the 'case' or 'controversy' restriction upon their competence which has already been discussed. So long as that restriction exists, it is most unlikely that the requirement of 'standing' in petitioners seeking review of constitutionality will be done away with. As it was expressed by the court in its *Massachusetts* v. *Mellon* opinion, for it to grant relief in such a case, where plaintiff was not adversely affected by the challenged statute, 'would be not to decide a judicial controversy, but to assume a position of authority over the governmental acts of another and coequal department, an authority which plainly we do not possess'.[1]

POLITICAL QUESTIONS

The 'case' or 'controversy' restriction and the requirement of 'standing', which have been discussed, bar consideration by the American courts of constitutional issues unless they arise in the course of actual litigation between interested adverse parties. Yet, even in true cases presented to them for decision, not all constitutional issues will be determined by the federal courts. For certain questions have, by their very nature, been considered inappropriate for decision by courts. These are questions which

1 262 U.S. at 489.

have been felt to be suitable for final determination by the political branches of the Government. The judiciary has kept its hands off them because it has feared the consequences of interfering in matters which are deemed to be primarily political. As it has been expressed by one member of the American court, 'Courts ought not to enter this political thicket'.[1]

The reluctance of the American courts to handle these so-called 'political questions' is, it is to be noted, one which has been shared by courts in the common-law countries from an early time. In 1460, the Duke of York brought suit to have himself declared the rightful heir to the throne. But the judges decided that they 'durst not enter into any communication thereof, for it perteyned to the Lorde's of the Kyngs blode and th'apparage of this his lond, to have communication and medle in such maters'.[2] Ever since that time, Anglo-American courts have refused to exercise jurisdiction in cases where it has been felt that the exercise of judicial power was inappropriate.

'What are these political questions?' asks one observer. 'To what matters does the term apply? It applies to all those matters of which the court, at a given time, will be of the opinion that it is impolitic or inexpedient to take jurisdiction.'[3] As it was expressed by Chief Justice Hughes in an important case, 'In determining whether a question falls within that category, the appropriateness under our system of government of attributing finality to the action of the political departments and also the lack of satisfactory criteria for a judicial determination are dominant considerations.'[4]

The American doctrine of political questions is, in many ways, analogous to the British doctrine of 'acts of State', from which it is, in part at least, derived. Like the British act of State, the action of the American Government which relates to political questions is wholly immune from judicial control. The 'decision of a "political question" by the "political departments" to which the Constitution has committed it "conclusively binds the judges, as well as all other officers, citizens and subjects of... government"'.[5]

Unlike the British doctrine, however, the American one is not limited in operation to the field of foreign affairs. A list of the matters which the American courts have considered to be political questions not subject to any judicial control would consequently contain a number of matters relating to the government of internal affairs. A striking recent illustration is furnished by an important 1946 decision of the Federal Supreme Court.[6]

1 *Colegrove* v. *Green*, 328 U.S. 549, 556 (1946), *per* Frankfurter, J.
2 The Duke of York's Claim to the Crown (1460), Rotuli Parl. v, 375, quoted in Weston, 'Political questions', 38 *Harvard L. Rev.* (1925), 296, 303.
3 Finkelstein, 'Judicial self-limitation', 37 *Harvard L. Rev.* (1924), 338, 344.
4 *Coleman* v. *Miller*, 307 U.S. 433, 454 (1939).   5 *Ibid.* at 457.
6 *Colegrove* v. *Green*, 328 U.S. 549 (1946).

It involved an action to invalidate an Illinois law governing the apportionment of the seats of that State in the Federal House of Representatives. The effect of the law at issue was to give the citizens in some voting districts a vote disproportionate to that given citizens in other districts, for changes in the distribution of population in the almost half a century since it had been enacted had altered the approximate equality which originally prevailed between the districts.[1] Despite the claim that this prevented citizens of Illinois from obtaining their full voting right and hence violated the provision of the Fourteenth Amendment of the Federal Constitution guaranteeing all persons the equal protection of the laws, the Supreme Court dismissed the action on the ground that it involved a political question beyond judicial cognizance. 'The Constitution', stated Justice Frankfurter, 'has left the performance of many duties in our governmental scheme to depend on the fidelity of the executive and legislative action and, ultimately, on the vigilance of the people in exercising their political rights.'[2] In these two cases, aptly states a leading American critic of this decision and a later case reaffirming its doctrine,[3] in a comment which well shows the drastic effect of the doctrine of political questions, 'out of judicial deference to the action of the two state legislatures, the equal protection clause faded out of the Constitution and with it fundamental rights of citizens of Georgia and Illinois'.[4]

It should, however, be noted that, important though cases like this relating to internal government may be, the doctrine of political questions has been employed most widely by the American courts in the field of foreign affairs. The American doctrine, like the doctrine of acts of State in Britain, thus emphasizes the autonomy of the political departments in the conduct of external relations. We have already noted that the acts of the President in that field are, as a practical matter, immune from judicial control.[5] The federal courts have designedly abjured authority in the sphere of external affairs because of their feeling that the exercise of judicial power is peculiarly inappropriate with regard to it. The conduct of foreign relations, declared the United States Supreme Court at the very beginning of its history, involves 'considerations of policy, considerations of extreme magnitude, and certainly entirely incompetent to the examination and decision of a Court of Justice'.[6]

That there must be some judicial self-limitation in cases which bear directly upon the carrying on of the foreign affairs of a country cannot be

---

1 The population of the election districts in the State, each of which elected one congressman, ranged, at the time of the case, from 112,000 to over 900,000.
2 328 U.S. at 556.   3 *South* v. *Peters*, 339 U.S. 276 (1950).
4 Vanderbilt, *op. cit.* 138.   5 *Supra*, p. 103.
6 *Ware* v. *Hylton*, 3 Dall. 199, 260 (U.S. 1796).

denied. At the same time, one wonders whether the American courts have not gone too far in this direction. In the recent jurisprudence of the Federal Supreme Court, one can note a tendency to hold that judicial review is barred, not only when the conduct of foreign affairs is immediately involved, but also whenever the governmental act at issue is seen to have some repercussions upon international relations.

As good an illustration as any of a case exemplifying this tendency in the highest tribunal is *Chicago & Southern Air Lines* v. *Waterman Steamship Co.*[1] It concerned the power of the Civil Aeronautics Board to license those seeking to engage in aerial transport. The board is the administrative agency authorized to grant licences to engage in both domestic and foreign air transportation, though, in the latter case, its decision is subject to the approval of the President. The relevant statute provides for review by the federal courts of any order of the board, 'except any order in respect to any *foreign* air carrier subject to the approval of the President'.[2] This statutory exception did not expressly cover the instant case, which concerned an application by a citizen carrier to engage in overseas transportation. Despite this, the court held that review was precluded of the board's decision, because of the effect which it might have upon the field of foreign affairs.

Although Mr Justice Jackson, who delivered the opinion, conceded that a literal reading of the statute would subject the administrative decision to re-examination by the courts, he asserted that the letter of the statute need not govern here. Because of the impact of the board's order on foreign relations, the courts should not intervene. Decisions such as this 'are wholly confided by our Constitution to the political departments of the government.... They are decisions of a kind for which the Judiciary has neither aptitude, facilities nor responsibility and which has long been held to belong in the domain of political power not subject to judicial intrusion or inquiry.'[3]

In the *Chicago & Southern Air Lines Case*, the Supreme Court held that it could not exercise jurisdiction even though the challenged governmental action clearly affected adversely the property of the individual seeking review. Even in such a case, review is precluded because of the foreign affairs aspects of the board's decision. As stated by the dissenting justices, 'no matter how extreme the action of the Board, the courts are powerless to correct it under today's decision'.[4] The individual affected might doubtless find it difficult to comprehend why he is in a worse position than if he were applying only for a licence to engage in domestic

1 333 U.S. 103 (1948). 2 *Emphasis* added.
3 333 U.S. at 111. 4 *Ibid.* at 118.

transport. The effect upon him of a refusal by the board is essentially the same, whether he is applying for a domestic or an overseas licence; yet, so far as judicial review is concerned, the court's decision does make for a substantial difference in his rights. If his licence relates to overseas traffic, the administration can act in a lawless way,[1] without fear of restraint by the courts.

Here, indeed, is the great weakness of both the American and British doctrines of political questions and acts of State. It is all very well to assert that the Government should be free from judicial interference in its conduct of foreign affairs. But when the action at issue has immediate effect upon the person or property of particular citizens, is it not opening the door to governmental lawlessness to free such action wholly from judicial control? 'If you make only one exception to the principle of legality', as a French jurist has aptly declared, 'you cannot tell where it may lead you.... To make only one exception to the principle of legality, is to take the fatal first step toward the German doctrine and say... with Jellinek: "The State is above every particular rule of law."'[2]

'STARE DECISIS' IN CONSTITUTIONAL LAW

The above analysis has dealt with the self-limitations imposed by the federal courts upon the exercise of their authority in the field of constitutional law. Cognizant of their exposed position, if they act in what seems to be an unjudicial manner, they have consistently refused to decide constitutional issues except where necessary for the resolution of an actual litigable controversy before them. And, even with regard to such controversies, they have followed a strict policy of *noli tangere* where so-called 'political questions' have been at issue.

Yet, even admitting these limitations upon judicial power in the United States, it cannot be denied that the federal courts play a far more important role in the field of constitutional law than do the courts in Britain. The authority to review the constitutionality of governmental acts is one which is possessed without question by American judges, and, unless a case before them is characterized as involving a political question, it will be exercised by them whenever that is necessary for the disposition of litigation. Until relatively recently, indeed, the power of the Federal Supreme Court over the constitutionality of laws was exercised so widely that students of the American system could properly speak of it as involving 'government by judiciary'.[3] During the past two decades, however, as Chapter VIII will

1 The term used by Douglas, J., dissenting, *ibid.* at 117.
2 Duguit, *Traité de droit constitutionnel* (3rd ed.), vol. III, 738.
3 See Lambert, *Le Gouvernement des juges* (1921).

show, the role of the American Supreme Court in this respect has undergone a fundamental change. In order to understand how that tribunal can have so drastically altered its position in constitutional law cases, a word will have to be said first about the place of the doctrine of *stare decisis* in American constitutional law.

In England, as is well known, the principle of adherence to precedent is rigidly followed. The question whether the House of Lords is bound by its own decisions has not been raised since 1898, and at that time Lord Halsbury considered the answer in the affirmative so clear that he gave his opinion in a few lines and without citing authority.[1] The English principle is founded on the theory that it is essential for the law to be certain, and that, to attain this certainty, it is worth while to sacrifice justice in occasional cases.[2] 'Of course I do not deny', stated Lord Halsbury in the case referred to, 'that cases of individual hardship may arise, and there may be a current of opinion in the profession that such and such a judgment was erroneous; but what is that occasional interference with what is perhaps abstract justice as compared with the inconvenience—the disastrous inconvenience—of having each question subject to being reargued and the dealings of mankind rendered doubtful by reason of different decisions, so that in truth and fact there would be no real final Court of Appeal?'[3]

According to an authoritative treatise on English constitutional law, the result of its self-limitation in favour of the certainty of the law is that legislation is necessary to avoid the results of a bad decision of the House of Lords.[4] In order to understand the eclipse of the doctrine of *stare decisis*[5] in American constitutional law, one must bear in mind that, while legislation can cure a bad decision of the House of Lords, the same is not true of a bad decision by the highest American court in its interpretation of the federal organic instrument. 'In cases involving the Federal Constitution', reads a famous opinion of Mr Justice Brandeis, 'the position of this Court is unlike that of the highest court of England, where the policy of *stare decisis* was formulated and is strictly applied to all classes of cases. Parliament is free to correct any judicial error; and the remedy may be promptly invoked.'[6]

Cases before the American courts, upon which the working of the

1 *London Street Tramways Co.* v. *London County Council*, [1898] A.C. 375. See Phillips, *op. cit.* 467.
2 Goodhart, 'Case law in England and America', 15 *Cornell L. Q.* (1930), 173, 178.
3 [1898] A.C. at 380.
4 Phillips, *op. cit.* 467. For a recent American discussion, see *Mazza* v. *Cavicchia*, 105 A. 2d 545, 557–8 (N.J. 1954).
5 The term used in Goodhart, *loc. cit.* 193.
6 *Burnet* v. *Coronado Oil & Gas Co.*, 285 U.S. 393, 409 (1932).

federal organic instrument turns, stand upon a different footing from the cases which normally come before the House of Lords. In private-law cases, the chief desideratum is that the law remain certain. Where the question is one of constitutional construction, the matter is otherwise. An error in the construction of a statute may easily be corrected by legislative act, but a written constitution can be amended with great difficulty. Hence a mistake in its construction can, for all practical purposes, be corrected only by the judicial repudiation or modification of the prior decision.[1] 'Stare decisis', to quote Justice Brandeis again on this point, 'is usually the wise policy, because in most matters it is more important that the applicable rule of law be settled than that it be settled right....But in cases involving the Federal Constitution, where correction through legislative action is practically impossible,[2] this Court has often overruled its earlier decisions. The Court bows to the lessons of experience and the force of better reasoning, recognizing that the process of trial and error, so fruitful in the physical sciences, is appropriate also in the judicial function.'[3]

There is little doubt but that the attitude of the federal courts toward the doctrine of *stare decisis* would strike an English judge as revolutionary.[4] The post-1937 reversal in the jurisprudence of the United States Supreme Court, which is described in Chapter VIII[5], could not, in truth, have occurred if the American Supreme Court were faithfully wedded to the English principle of adherence to precedent. The freedom of the American tribunal in this respect has enabled it almost completely to repudiate its earlier attitude toward questions of constitutional law. This has involved the specific overruling by the Supreme Court, in recent years, of a great many of its earlier decisions, some of which had been regarded as settled in American law for the better part of a century.

Most American jurists have looked without regret upon the refusal of their courts rigidly to follow precedent in constitutional-law cases. 'It is refreshing', writes one commentator, 'to see a court willing to admit its error openly. When once a court has reached the conclusion that a prior decision is wrong it is much better to overrule it expressly than to purport to follow it and yet construct subtle distinctions every time the general principle involved arises.'[6] At the same time, while recognizing that the

1 Willoughby, *Principles of the Constitutional Law of the United States* (2nd ed. 1935), 52.

2 In only two instances has the process of constitutional amendment been successfully employed to correct decisions of the American Supreme Court.

3 *Burnet* v. *Coronado Oil & Gas Co.*, 285 U.S. 393, 406–8 (1932).

4 Goodhart, *loc. cit.* 180.

5 Other drastic recent changes in Supreme Court case law are discussed in Chapters VI and IX.

6 Note, 34 *Harvard L. Rev.* (1920), 74, 76.

doctrine of the House of Lords with regard to its precedents should not be slavishly followed by the United States Supreme Court, one may wonder whether the American tribunal has not gone too far to the other extreme. Scarcely a term of the American court goes by without the repudiation by that tribunal of one or more of its earlier decisions. The situation had, indeed, become such that a justice of the Supreme Court was led, a few years ago, to assert that the proneness of the court to reverse decisions deemed to be erroneous 'tends to bring adjudications by this tribunal into the same class as a restricted railroad ticket, good for this day and train only'.[1]

The recent American experience in this respect indicates that Lord Halsbury was correct in his view that there could be no *finis litium* if it were possible for a court to overrule its decisions.[2] 'The evil resulting from overruling earlier considered decisions must be evident', affirmed a dissenter from the tendency of the American Supreme Court to reverse precedents deemed erroneous. 'In the present case, the court below naturally felt bound to follow and apply the law as clearly announced by this court. If litigants and lower federal courts are not to do so, the law becomes not a chart to govern conduct but a game of chance; instead of settling rights and liabilities it unsettles them. Counsel and parties will bring and prosecute actions in the teeth of the decisions that such actions are not maintainable on the not improbable chance that the asserted rule will be thrown overboard. Defendants will not know whether to litigate or to settle for they will have no assurance that a declared rule will be followed. But the more deplorable consequence will inevitably be that the administration of justice will fall into disrepute. Respect for tribunals must fall when the bar and the public come to understand that nothing that has been said in prior adjudication has force in a current controversy.'[3]

1 Roberts, J., dissenting, in *Smith* v. *Allwright*, 321 U.S. 649, 669 (1944).
2 *London Street Tramways Co.* v. *London County Council*, [1898] A.C. 375, 380.
3 Roberts, J., in *Mahnich* v. *Southern S.S. Co.*, 321 U.S. 96, 112 (1944).

PART TWO
MODERN DEVELOPMENTS

Chapter VI

THE NEW FEDERALISM

'What is the fundamental characteristic of the United States considered as
an association of states?' asks the leading English study of federal government.[1] The answer, according to the author, is the principle under which
the general and the regional governments are co-ordinate and independent
in their respective spheres. 'The answer seems to be that the Constitution
of the United States establishes an association of states so organized that
powers are divided between a general government which in certain
matters...is independent of the governments of the associated states, and,
on the other hand, state governments which in certain matters are, in their
turn, independent of the general government.'[2]

There is little doubt but that this answer accords with the structure of
the American Union that was contemplated by the framers of the Federal
Constitution. Their dominant concern was to ensure that the national
Government which they were creating would not be so powerful that it
would, in practice, swallow up the States out of which the nation was to
be composed. They sought to accomplish this by limiting the Federal
Government to a specific list of enumerated powers which were essential
to its effective functioning, while reserving all other authority to the
States, which were to continue unaltered as separate sovereignties, except
for whatever powers they had surrendered to the nation. The concept of
federalism which pervaded the governmental philosophy of the founders
of the American Union was based upon the co-ordinate and independent
position of the different centres of government. What was necessary, in
their view, was that each government should be limited to its own sphere
and, within that sphere, should be independent of the other.[3]

'In the classical Anglo-American doctrine of federalism,' a French
student of American public law has declared, 'the division of powers
between the federal State and the member-States guarantees, to the one
and to the others, full sovereignty in the domain appropriate to each. The
exercise of federal powers should not infringe upon the area of powers
reserved to the member-States. And vice versa.'[4] This classical concept of
federalism, however, upon which the American system was based, has not

1 Wheare, *Federal Government* (3rd ed. 1953), 2.
2 *Ibid.*   3 Cf. *ibid.* 15.
4 Pinto, *La Crise de l'état aux États-Unis* (1951), 7.

been able successfully to withstand the stresses of twentieth-century political evolution. Government in the United States, no less than government in other parts of the world, has followed a trend toward consistent concentration of authority in the centre of the political structure. The development in this direction has, indeed, progressed so far that it is not amiss today to term the American system the *new federalism*,[1] to distinguish it from the concept of federalism upon which the original distribution of authority between nation and States in the United States was based.

'NEW DEAL'

The federal system put into operation by the Constitution of 1787, has, as we have seen,[2] been dominated by the doctrine of so-called *dual federalism*. And, as interpreted by the federal Supreme Court in decisions like that in the *Child Labor Case*,[3] dual federalism required a complete dichotomy of State and federal power. A line had to be drawn, in cases such as those involving the regulation of commerce, dividing the area in which the national Government could operate from that over which the States had exclusive jurisdiction. In the latter area, federal power could not be exerted at all. And this was true, even though, as, for example, in the field of regulation of child labour, only federal controls could prove effective in practice to deal with a situation nation-wide in scope.

The concept of dual federalism, thus applied by the highest American court, has been seen to be wholly inconsistent with an era of ever-expanding governmental authority. It could, as a practical matter, be maintained only when the exercise of State power was dominated by the doctrine of *laissez-faire*. 'Leviathan hath two swords: war and justice', stated Hobbes in a famous passage. It has, however, become almost a commonplace that, during the present century, the armoury of the State has come to include much more than these two elementary weapons. 'The scope and character of government have changed enormously in the last fifty years. Formerly, government was chiefly regulatory and negative: its main task (apart from defence) was to keep the ring and maintain fair play while private interests asserted themselves freely. Today, government is largely concerned with the administration of social services and has become positive in a new sense. A century ago, the State acted mainly as policeman, soldier and judge. Today, the State acts also as doctor, nurse, teacher, insurance

---

1 See Clark, *The Rise of a New Federalism* (1938).   2 *Supra*, p. 42.

3 *Hammer* v. *Dagenhart*, 247 U.S. 251 (1918), *supra*, p. 45. In that case, it will be recalled, it was held that the Federal Government could not prohibit the shipment in interstate commerce of goods produced by child labour because the effect of such prohibition was to regulate manufacturing carried on within the individual States.

organiser, house builder, sanitary engineer, chemist, railway controller, supplier of gas, water and electricity, town planner, pensions distributor, provider of transport, hospital organiser, road maker, and in a large number of other capacities.'[1]

If the State is effectively to execute the manifold functions which modern public opinion has required it to assume, it can do so only by intervention in social and economic affairs upon a national scale. Governmental action limited to the local level would hardly prove efficacious where problems which are national in scope have to be dealt with. In the United States, however, action on the part of the Federal Government was rendered difficult by the doctrine of dual federalism, as it was applied by the Supreme Court in cases like the *Child Labor Case*. The result in that case 'sprang from a conception of the federal relationship which regards the National Government and the states as rival governments bent on mutual frustration, and on a conception of the judicial role which makes it the supreme duty of the Court to maintain the two centers of government in theoretical possession of their accustomed powers, however incapable either might be in fact of exercising them'.[2] For the Government in Washington to be able to exercise regulatory authority upon the national scale demanded by contemporary conditions, the abandonment of the concept of dual federalism was required.

The doctrine of *laissez-faire*, upon which the operation of governmental authority in the United States had been essentially based since the founding of the Republic, proved wholly inadequate to meet the problems presented by the great economic depression which began in 1929. It was widely felt that the national economy could be resuscitated only by the extended intervention of the Federal Government. And the procedure of the 'New Deal' of the Roosevelt administration meant the very negation of *laissez-faire*. The legislative measures enacted by the federal Congress sought to regulate most of the critical aspects of the economic system—most of which had heretofore been thought to be beyond the scope of federal regulatory power. The 'New Deal' involved a degree of governmental control on the part of Washington far greater than any which had previously been attempted in the American system. If the country was to go forward, said President Roosevelt in his inaugural address in 1932, 'we must move as a trained and loyal army willing to sacrifice for the good of a common discipline, because without such discipline no progress is made, no leadership becomes effective'.[3]

---

1 Robson, in *Committee on Ministers' Powers, Minutes of Evidence* (1932), 52.
2 Corwin, *Constitutional Revolution, Ltd.* (1941) 99.
3 Quoted in Swisher, *American Constitutional Development* (2nd ed. 1954), 878.

The most important of the regulatory measures enacted under the 'New Deal' was the National Industrial Recovery Act of 1933. As it has been described by an outstanding American constitutional lawyer, 'This grandiose statute—a veritable legislative Colossus, meant to bestride the entire business structure of the United States, from pants-pressing to the production of steel—was the original incarnation of the New Deal. The opening section of the act asserted the existence of "a national emergency productive of widespread unemployment and disorganization of industry which" burdened "interstate and foreign commerce", affected "the public welfare", and undermined "the standards of living of the American people". To effect the removal of these conditions the President was authorized, upon the application of industrial or trade groups, to approve "codes of fair competition", or to prescribe the same in cases where such applications were not duly forthcoming. Among other things such codes, of which eventually more than 700 were promulgated, were required to lay down rules of fair dealing with customers and to furnish labor certain guarantees respecting hours, wages, and collective bargaining. For the time being, business and industry were to be cartelized on a national scale.'[1]

It is not difficult to see that a law such as this was utterly inconsistent with the concept of dual federalism. Under it, the Federal Government asserted regulatory authority over well-nigh every detail of the American economic system. In doing so, it sought to control local trade and production in the manner which had been held invalid in the *Child Labor Case*.[2] This, at any rate, was the opinion of the Supreme Court in *Schechter Poultry Corp.* v. *United States*,[3] where the constitutionality of the 1933 Act was at issue. In that case, the defendant company, wholesale poultry dealers in New York City, were charged with having violated the Live Poultry Code, both with respect to its minimum wage and maximum hour requirements, and by according preferential treatment to favoured customers. For the Federal Government to regulate the business of the defendant, said the court, was for it to attempt to exercise a power reserved exclusively to the States. 'Where the effect of intrastate transactions upon interstate commerce is merely indirect, such transactions remain within the domain of state power. If the commerce clause were construed to reach all enterprises and transactions which could be said to have an indirect effect upon interstate commerce, the federal authority would embrace practically all the activities of the people and the authority of the State over its domestic concerns would exist only by sufferance of the federal government.'[4]

---

1 Corwin, *op. cit.* 46. 2 *Supra*, p. 45.
3 295 U.S. 495 (1935). 4 *Ibid.* at 546.

ABANDONMENT OF DUAL FEDERALISM

Although it was not generally realized at the time, it seems clear today that the *Schechter Case* involved one of the last important applications by the American court of the concept of dual federalism. The need for national regulation of the economic system, which had induced the legislative and executive branches of the Federal Government to discard the *laissez-faire* policies that had controlled their action prior to 1929, was bound also to have its effect upon the jurisprudence of the Supreme Court. It is true that there was a certain delay before the court began to adjust its case law to the changes demanded by the great depression. Thus, while the 'New Deal' measures to deal with the economic crisis were enacted as early as 1933, it was not until 1937—two years after the *Schechter* decision—that the American court began to remove the restrictions upon federal action which had been imposed by its strict adherence to dual federalism. Such a lag appears to be inherent in the functioning of any judicial tribunal which is compelled by changing external conditions to make fundamental modifications in its case law. It constitutes perhaps the prime weakness of the American system of judicial review, for the basic conservatism of the judiciary often makes it difficult for its members to make the necessary accommodation before it is too late.

It was in 1937, as has been indicated, that the American court began to remove the limitations which the concept of dual federalism had placed upon federal action. Early in that year, that tribunal upheld a federal statute regulating labour relations, as against the contention that it conflicted with the constitutional authority reserved to the States.[1] And, in 1940, the court, in deciding that an act of Congress regulating the coal industry was valid, stated that 'Congress under the commerce clause is not impotent to deal with what it may consider to be dire consequences of laissez-faire. It is not powerless to take steps in mitigation of what in its judgment are abuses of cut-throat competition.'[2]

In 1941, the American tribunal went even further and expressly overruled its decision in the *Child Labor Case*,[3] which, as we have seen, had strictly applied the concept of dual federalism to restrict federal action which might infringe upon State regulatory authority. The Fair Labor Standards Act, enacted by the Congress in 1938, provides for the fixing of minimum wages and maximum hours by an agency of the Federal Government. It prohibits the shipment in interstate commerce of goods manu-

---

1 *National Labor Relations Board* v. *Jones & Laughlin Steel Corp.*, 301 U.S. 1 (1937).
2 *Sunshine Anthracite Coal Co.* v. *Adkins*, 310 U.S. 381, 396 (1940).
3 *Supra*, p. 45.

factured by employees whose wages are less than the prescribed minimum or whose hours of labour are more than the prescribed maximum. As such it is not unlike the law at issue in the *Child Labor Case*, which had prohibited the transportation in interstate commerce of goods which were produced by child labour. In that case, it will be recalled, the Supreme Court had held such a statute to constitute an unconstitutional attempt by the Congress to regulate the manner in which production was carried on, a matter reserved exclusively to the individual States. In its 1941 decision, *United States* v. *Darby*,[1] the Supreme Court refused to follow its *Child Labor* decision. Instead, it declared specifically that its prior decision rested upon a conception of federal-State power which was now outmoded and the decision itself must be considered as overruled. 'The reasoning and conclusion of the Court's opinion there cannot be reconciled with the conclusion which we have reached, that the power of Congress under the Commerce Clause is plenary to exclude any article from interstate commerce subject only to the specific prohibitions of the Constitution.'[2]

The court went on to state that the Tenth Amendment to the Constitution, under which all powers not granted by that instrument to the Congress are reserved to the States, did not really have any effect upon the question at issue. 'The amendment states but a truism that all is retained which has not been surrendered. There is nothing in the history of its adoption to suggest that it was more than declaratory of the relationship between the national and state governments as it had been established by the Constitution before the amendment or that its purpose was other than to allay fears that the new national government might seek to exercise powers not granted, and that the states might not be able to exercise fully their reserved powers.'[3]

To look upon the Tenth Amendment as a mere 'truism' is to destroy the basis upon which the concept of dual federalism was based. Under the present view of the Supreme Court, that amendment no longer requires the complete dichotomy of federal and State power, with the exclusive authority of the States serving to limit the area in which federal action may be taken. To take the regulation of commerce as an example, the dual federalism doctrine demanded the division of commerce into two mutually exclusive categories: State and national. Only the latter was subject to federal control. Under the recent jurisprudence of the Supreme Court, on the other hand, this rigid division, which served to preclude federal regulation of local economic activities, has been abandoned.

'The power of Congress over interstate commerce', declared the Supreme Court in its opinion in the *Darby Case*, 'is not confined to the

1 312 U.S. 100 (1941).   2 *Ibid.* at 116.   3 *Ibid.* at 124.

regulation of commerce among the states. It extends to those activities intrastate which so affect interstate commerce or the exercise of the power of Congress over it as to make regulation of them appropriate means to the attainment of a legitimate end, the exercise of the granted power of Congress to regulate interstate commerce.'[1] What this means in practice is shown by the subsequent case law. Since the *Darby* decision in 1941, the federal law regulating wages and hours has been held to be constitutionally applicable to employees engaged in the maintenance and operation of a building in which large quantities of goods for interstate commerce were produced;[2] to the employees of a window-cleaning company, which cleaned windows of people who were engaged in interstate commerce;[3] to the employees of a local newspaper with a limited circulation;[4] and to women doing embroidery work for pay in their own homes.[5]

The activities regulated in these cases appear clearly to have been local in character. Congressional action with regard to them was none the less sustained because of the court's opinion that they might have some effect upon interstate commerce. It would seem, however, that, under contemporary conditions, the economic system is so interconnected in its parts that there are few, if any, even purely local business activities which may not have at least some repercussions upon commerce which extends beyond State lines. And, if that is true, the federal regulation of local commerce is no longer prohibited in the American system. This, at any rate, appears to be the view now followed by the United States Supreme Court. Thus, in a 1942 case involving the constitutionality of federal regulation of the price of milk produced and sold entirely within the State of Illinois, the regulation was upheld because the intrastate milk was sold in competition with milk transported from outside the State. 'The marketing of a local product in competition with that of a like commodity moving interstate may so interfere with interstate commerce or its regulation as to afford a basis for Congressional regulation of the intrastate activity. It is the effect upon the interstate commerce or its regulation, regardless of the particular form which the competition may take, which is the test of federal power.'[6]

If it is the effect upon interstate commerce which is now the test, it is difficult to see what limitations exist upon federal regulatory power. 'If the commerce clause were construed to reach all enterprises and transactions which could be said to have an...effect upon interstate commerce,

1 *Ibid.* at 118.
2 *Kirschbaum Co.* v. *Walling*, 316 U.S. 517 (1942).
3 *Martino* v. *Mich. Window Cleaning Co.*, 327 U.S. 173 (1946).
4 *Mabee* v. *White Plains Pub. Co.*, 327 U.S. 178 (1946).
5 *Gemsco, Inc.*, v. *Walling*, 324 U.S. 244 (1945).
6 *United States* v. *Wrightwood Dairy Corp.*, 315 U.S. 110, 120 (1942).

the federal authority would embrace practically all the activities of the people and the authority of the State over its domestic concerns would exist only by sufferance of the federal government.'[1] Since even purely local economic activity may have at least an indirect effect upon interstate commerce, there appears to be little, if anything, in the American economic system that is today beyond the regulatory authority of the Congress. In an important case decided by it in 1942, the Supreme Court upheld a federal law extending federal regulation of wheat production to wheat not intended in any part for commerce but solely for consumption on the farm. 'Even if appellee's activity be local,' asserted the opinion of Mr Justice Jackson, 'and though it may not be regarded as commerce, it may still, whatever its nature, be reached by Congress if it exerts a substantial economic effect on interstate commerce, this irrespective of whether such effect is what might at some earlier time have been defined as "direct" or "indirect".... Congress may properly have considered that wheat consumed on the farm where grown, if wholly outside the scheme of regulation, would have a substantial effect in defeating and obstructing its purpose to stimulate trade therein at increased prices.'[2]

Decisions like those just discussed illustrate the extent to which the Supreme Court has departed from the concept of dual federalism which had previously governed its approach to cases involving the relationship of federal and State authority. For the older view that the federal power over commerce could not be exercised over local transactions, which were within the exclusive area of State authority, has been substituted the notion of a plenary power of the national Government over commerce. If wheat production intended by the farmer solely for his domestic consumption can be regulated by Congress because of its possible effect upon interstate commerce, however indirect it may be, there are, in practice, no restrictions upon federal regulation of even so-called purely local commerce. And, if this is true, the American system is clearly no longer one of dual federalism. The American Union today is not based upon a division of sovereignty between governmental equals. It is, instead, characterized by the predominance of federal over State power. There is no longer an exclusive area of State authority over commerce within which federal authority cannot be exerted. The cases just discussed show that federal regulatory power is now all-pervasive. It can be exerted over any subject chosen by the Congress and it is no objection to its exercise that it may come into conflict with the accustomed powers of the States.

1 Hughes, C.J., in *Schechter Poultry Corp.* v. *United States*, 295 U.S. 495, 546 (1935).
2 *Wickard* v. *Filburn*, 317 U.S. 111, 125, 129 (1942).

GENERAL WELFARE

The authority of the Federal Government in the American system has also been expanded greatly in recent years by the use which has been made by Congress of its taxing and spending power. Under Article I, section 8, of the American Constitution, 'The Congress shall have Power To lay and collect Taxes, Duties, Imposts and Excises, to pay the Debts and provide for the common Defence and general Welfare of the United States.'

It has been argued by some that the power to provide for the general welfare vested under this section is an independent grant of authority, and not a mere qualification of the taxing power. Under this view, the provision in question can be construed as a comprehensive grant of power to the Federal Government to take any action which may promote the general welfare of the people of the United States.[1] This extreme position has been consistently repudiated by American constitutional lawyers. As it was expressed by perhaps the greatest of them—Joseph Story—over a century ago, to follow such a view would be to create 'a general authority in congress to pass all laws, which they may deem for the common defence or general welfare. Under such circumstances, the constitution would practically create an unlimited national government. The enumerated powers would tend to embarrassment and confusion; since they would only give rise to doubts, as to the true extent of the general power, or of the enumerated powers.'[2]

It may thus be seen that the 'general welfare' clause of the American organic instrument is not an independent grant of authority, but rather a qualification of the taxing power.[3] Congress, in other words, is not empowered by the provision under discussion to do anything it pleases to provide for the general welfare, but only to impose taxes for that purpose.[4]

Yet even looked at in this way, the 'general welfare' clause appears to confer tremendous powers upon the Government in Washington. If Congress may impose taxes to promote the general welfare, it means, because of the broadness of the term used, that its taxing authority is practically unlimited. Its power to impose taxes is consequently not limited to imposition for the purpose of securing revenue. And its power of expenditure would certainly seem to be as broad as its authority to tax.

1 Willoughby, *Principles of the Constitutional Law of the United States* (2nd ed. 1935), 64. For a recent strong exponent of this view, see Crosskey, *Politics and the Constitution in the History of the United States* (1953).

2 Story, *Commentaries on the Constitution of the United States* (1833), §906.

3 Corwin, 'The spending power of Congress—apropos the Maternity Act', 36 *Harvard L. Rev.* (1923), 548, 552.

4 Story, *op. cit.* §923, quoting Thomas Jefferson.

These propositions are now firmly established in the jurisprudence of the United States Supreme Court, and they appear to vest well-nigh unrestricted taxing and spending power in the Federal Government. The limitation of the authority to tax to taxes imposed for the general welfare is, in fact, no limitation at all, as is shown by a leading Supreme Court decision. That Congress may tax and spend in aid of the general welfare is settled, said Mr Justice Cardozo in that case. 'Yet difficulties are left when the power is conceded. The line must still be drawn between one welfare and another, between particular and general. Where this shall be placed cannot be known through a formula in advance of the event. There is a middle ground or certainly a penumbra in which discretion is at large. The discretion, however, is not confided to the courts. The discretion belongs to Congress.... Nor is the concept of the general welfare static. Needs that were narrow or parochial a century ago may be inter-woven in our day with the well-being of the Nation.'[1]

It is because, in effect, it vests Congress with the authority to impose taxes as it will that the general welfare clause of the American Constitution is of such significance. The power to tax, reads one of the most famous statements of Chief Justice John Marshall, involves the power to destroy.[2] But the power to tax also involves the power to regulate, as is shown by the recent practice of the American Congress. If any tax may be imposed which promotes the general welfare, exercise of the authority to tax is not limited to cases involving the need to secure revenue. The taxing power may serve as the basis for governmental regulation, with the imposition of taxes serving as the sanction behind the regulatory scheme.

One of the most important regulatory measures of the 'New Deal'— the Agricultural Adjustment Act of 1933—was based entirely upon the taxing power. That law sought primarily to eliminate over-production of farm products, such as that which had so greatly depressed prices in the post-1929 period. The legislative idea was to furnish the American farmer with a sufficient inducement for curtailing his production. Under the Act, a processing tax was levied upon different agricultural commodities, and the proceeds from this tax were used to compensate farmers who agreed beforehand to raise less or none of such commodities. It seems obvious that the prime purpose of this exercise of the power to tax was the regulation of agricultural production, rather than the securing of revenue. It was for this reason that the Act in question was held unconstitutional in 1936 by the Supreme Court. The Act attempted to regulate local production under the guise of an exercise of the taxing power, said the court. 'If the

1 *Helvering* v. *Davis*, 301 U.S. 619, 640, 641 (1937).
2 *McCulloch* v. *Maryland*, 4 Wheat, 316, 431 (U.S. 1819).

act before us is a proper exercise of the federal taxing power, evidently the regulation of all industry throughout the United States may be accomplished by similar exercises of the same power. It would be possible to exact money from one branch of an industry and pay it to another branch in every field of activity which lies within the province of the states. The mere threat of such a procedure might well induce the surrender of rights and the compliance with federal regulation as the price of continuance in business.'[1]

There was a strong dissenting opinion by Mr Justice Stone (as he then was), joined in by Justices Brandeis and Cardozo. The decision of the court, asserted the dissent, was contradictory and destructive of the power to tax for the general welfare. 'The limitation now sanctioned must lead to absurd consequences. The government may give seeds to farmers, but may not condition the gift upon their being planted in places where they are most needed or even planted at all. The government may give money. to the unemployed, but may not ask that those who get it shall give labor in return, or even use it to support their families. It may give money to sufferers from earthquake, fire, tornado, pestilence or flood, but may not impose conditions—health precautions designed to prevent the spread of disease, or induce the movement of population to safer or more sanitary areas. All that, because it is purchased regulation infringing state powers, must be left for the states, who are unable or unwilling to supply the necessary relief.'[2]

There appears to be little doubt that the view expressed in Justice Stone's dissent is that which is now followed by the Supreme Court. Thus, the Agricultural Adjustment Act of 1938, which differed only in details from that held unconstitutional in 1936, was upheld by the Court in 1939. The motive of Congress in exerting the power, said the Court in that case, is irrelevant to the validity of the legislation.[3] And, in a 1937 case in which it was claimed that the exercise of the federal taxing power was invalid since the main purpose of the Congress was regulation of a particular industry, the court declared that 'Every tax is in some measure regulatory. To some extent it interposes an economic impediment to the activity taxed as compared with others not taxed. But a tax is not any the less a tax because it has a regulatory effect...; and it has long been established that an Act of Congress which on its face purports to be an exercise of the taxing power is not any the less so because the tax is burdensome or tends to restrict or suppress the thing taxed.'[4]

1 *United States* v. *Butler*, 297 U.S. 1, 75 (1936).   2 *Ibid.* at 85.
3 *Mulford* v. *Smith*, 307 U.S. 38, 48 (1939).
4 *Sonzinsky* v. *United States*, 300 U.S. 506, 513 (1937).

A more recent case which strikingly illustrates the way in which the congressional power to tax may now be used for regulatory purposes is *United States* v. *Kahriger*.[1] At issue in it was the constitutionality of a federal statute which levied a tax of $50 per year upon persons engaged in the business of accepting wagers, and required such persons to register with the Federal Collector of Internal Revenue their names, addresses and places of business. Though ostensibly a revenue measure, the primary purpose of the wagering tax law appears clearly to have been to aid in the suppression of gambling. 'The context of the circumstances which brought forth this enactment', declared Mr Justice Frankfurter, '—sensationally exploited disclosures regarding gambling in big cities and small, the relation of this gambling to corrupt politics, the impatient public response to these disclosures, the feeling of ineptitude or paralysis on the part of local law-enforcing agencies—emphatically supports what was revealed on the floor of Congress, namely that what was formally a means of revenue for the Federal Government was essentially an effort to check if not to stamp out professional gambling.'[2] The law in question was intended to place the professional gambler on the horns of a legal dilemma. If he were not to register and pay the tax required by the law, he would commit a federal offence for which he could be punished judicially. On the other hand, if he were to come forward to register and, in effect, confess that he was engaged in the business of gambling, he would lay himself open to prosecution by local law-enforcement authorities, for there are anti-gambling laws on most State statute books. The Act at issue, in the words of one member of the Supreme Court, 'creates a squeezing device contrived to put a man in federal prison if he refuses to confess himself into a state prison as a violator of state gambling laws'.[3]

Although the object of the wagering tax law was thus the regulation of professional gambling rather than the securing of revenue, it was held by the court that this did not render it unconstitutional. 'A federal excise tax does not cease to be valid', said Mr Justice Reed, 'merely because it discourages or deters the activities taxed. Nor is the tax invalid merely because the revenue obtained is negligible. ...The instant tax has a regulatory effect. But regardless of its regulatory effect, the wagering tax produces revenue.'[4] Or, to put it another way, the court will not go behind what is formally a revenue measure to determine whether the raising of revenue is, indeed, its primary purpose. The fact that the taxing power is used as an instrument of regulation does not, in the present view of the Supreme Court, affect the validity of its exercise. 'It is axiomatic that the

1 345 U.S. 22 (1953).   2 Dissenting, *ibid.* at 39.
3 Black, J., dissenting, *ibid.* at 36.   4 *Ibid.* at 28.

power of Congress to tax is extensive and falls with crushing effect on businesses deemed unessential or inimical to the public welfare....As is well known, the constitutional restraints on taxing are few.'[1]

Under a decision like that in the *Kahriger Case*, just discussed, the Federal Congress is provided with a ready means in its power to tax of asserting authority over matters that were formerly deemed to be wholly within the competence of the States. We can take the regulation of professional gambling, at issue in *Kahriger*, as a good example. Such regulation would appear to fall within the reserved powers of the States, at least where purely local gambling is involved. And, even under the expanded concept of the national commerce power which, as we have seen, now dominates the jurisprudence of the Supreme Court, it is doubtful whether such local gambling can be considered to have any effect upon interstate commerce so as to be subject to federal regulatory authority. Yet, by framing its regulatory law in the form of a nominal taxing measure, the Congress is, under the *Kahriger* decision, enabled to make what might otherwise be an inadmissible intrusion into a domain of legislation reserved for the States. Clearly, as Mr Justice Frankfurter pointed out in dissenting in the *Kahriger Case*, the court's decision there gravely affects the balance of powers within the federal system. 'To allow what otherwise is excluded from congressional authority to be brought within it by casting legislation in the form of a revenue measure could...offer an easy way for the legislative imagination to control "any one of the great number of subjects of public interest, jurisdiction of which the States have never parted with...".'[2]

FEDERAL GRANTS-IN-AID

Closely related to the use of the federal taxing power for regulatory purposes is that of the use of federal bounties or grants-in-aid to attain a similar end. The grant of subventions by the Federal Government to the States is not a new thing in the American system. During the early days of the United States, the central Government gave vast amounts of public lands to the States for the development of schools and universities, for roads, canals and railroads, and reclamation purposes. Federal generosity reached a climax in 1837, when a $28 million surplus that had accumulated in the federal treasury was given to the States in proportion to their representation in Congress.[3] These early cases involved simple grants without conditions; there was no attempt to regulate even the manner in which the federal subventions might be used.

A fundamental change in approach came with a federal law of 1862

1 *Ibid.*   2 *Ibid.* at 38.   3 Clark, *op. cit.* 140.

granting public lands to the States on condition that they establish colleges teaching agricultural and mechanical studies. This law was a milestone on the road of federal grants-in-aid, for, under it, such grants were given only in return for the fulfilment of certain conditions by the States receiving them.[1] Since 1862, the grant of federal subventions upon condition has become common in the American system. This has been especially true since the economic crisis of 1929. Many of the individual States did not possess the resources required for the undertaking of the vast measures of relief and rehabilitation which were necessary for the resuscitation of their economies. Only the Government in Washington, which alone could levy taxes throughout the country, could muster the needed funds.

An extensive system of federal grants-in-aid to enable the States to re-habilitate their economies and give aid to individuals unable to take care of themselves was a major part of the 'New Deal' measures. But the largesse of the Federal Government was no longer granted without qualifi-cations. Substantial conditions were imposed by Washington upon States which accepted its subventions, which, in effect, amounted to stringent federal supervision of the schemes of economic revival undertaken by the States.

As good an example as any of a 'New Deal' statute which made exten-sive use of the grant-in-aid device was the Social Security Act of 1935. Under it, the Federal Government made grants to the States for immediate old-age assistance, administration of State unemployment compensation laws, aid to dependent children, maternal and child welfare, public health, and assistance to the blind. Federal control was, however, imposed upon State activities in return, for State legislation and machinery and methods of administration had to conform to standards prescribed by the federal statute and the Social Security Board, the agency set up to administer it. An old-age insurance fund was established. The money paid into the fund was to be derived from income taxes on employees and excise taxes on their employers. For unemployment compensation, a federal tax was levied upon employers alone. Employers in States which enacted satis-factory unemployment compensation laws were to receive credit up to ninety per cent of the federal tax. Payments of unemployment compensa-tion were to be made only in States having unemployment compensation laws. Since the federal tax was to be collected whether or not any such State law existed, pressure was put, at least indirectly, upon each State to enact unemployment compensation legislation. The money collected under approved unemployment compensation laws was to be put in a trust fund administered by the Federal Government.[2]

1 Clark, *op. cit.* 141. 2 Swisher, *op. cit.* 913-4.

The federal law in question was sustained in a series of cases in 1937 by the American Supreme Court, as against the contention that it constituted an unconstitutional attempt by the Federal Government to coerce and control the States in the manner in which they dealt with the problem of unemployment. 'Even though it be assumed', declared Mr Justice Stone in one of the cases referred to, 'that the exercise of a sovereign power by a state, in other respects valid, may be rendered invalid because of the coercive effect of a federal statute enacted in the exercise of a power granted to the national government, such coercion is lacking here.... The United States and the State of Alabama are not alien governments. They coexist within the same territory. Unemployment within it is their common concern. Together the two statutes now before us embody a cooperative legislative effort by state and national governments, for carrying out a public purpose common to both, which neither could fully achieve without the cooperation of the other.'[1] And the language of Mr Justice Cardozo in another of these cases was even stronger in its assertion of the validity of the federal regulatory scheme. 'Who then is coerced', he asked, 'through the operation of this statute? Not the taxpayer. He pays in fulfilment of the mandate of the local legislature. Not the state. Even now she does not offer a suggestion that in passing the unemployment law she was affected by duress.... For all that appears she is satisfied with her choice, and would be sorely disappointed if it were now to be annulled.... Every rebate from a tax when conditioned upon conduct is in some measure a temptation. But to hold that motive or temptation is equivalent to coercion is to plunge the law in endless difficulties.'[2]

During the past generation, the federal provision of grants-in-aid to the States has grown by leaps and bounds. Today, to quote an important study, grants-in-aid are part of the warp and woof of the American governmental system.[3] Indeed, it has been estimated that about fifteen per cent of all funds expended by State Governments in the United States are derived from federal subventions; and this trend toward using grants-in-aid for supporting public services is definitely on the increase.[4] Thus, an extensive programme of federal aid to the States for educational purposes appears likely to be enacted in the near future. And the same is true of similar expansion of federal grants-in-aid in the field of public health.

What is the significance of the growth of the grant-in-aid system upon American federalism? It cannot be denied that there are great advantages

1 *Carmichael* v. *Southern Coal Co.*, 301 U.S. 495, 525, 526 (1937).
2 *Steward Machine Co.* v. *Davis*, 301 U.S. 548, 589 (1937). See also *Helvering* v. *Davis*, 301 U.S. 619 (1937).
3 *The Hoover Commission Report on Organization of the Executive Branch of the Government* (1949), 493.   4 *Ibid*.

to be obtained from the extension of federal assistance to the States. 'The cooperative system based on grants-in-aid has provided needed standards of public services throughout the country in many fields—services that many States would be unable to supply. It has provided for some re-distribution of resources from States that have superior means to those that lack them.'[1] Though it has been argued that the policy of federal subventions tends to break down State initiative and to paralyse State policies, its actual effect has, in many instances, been just the opposite.[2] As it was expressed by Mr Justice Cardozo, in upholding the old-age assistance provisions of the Social Security Act, 'States and local governments are often lacking in the resources that are necessary to finance an adequate program of security for the aged.... Apart from the failure of resources, state and local governments are at times reluctant to increase so heavily the burden of taxation to be borne by their residents for fear of placing themselves in a position of economic disadvantage as compared with neighbors or competitors.'[3] It is only because of federal aid that many of the States have been able to initiate the necessary measures of old-age relief.

At the same time it must be admitted that the growth of the federal grant-in-aid system has helped to alter the balance between State and national Governments in the United States. Federal aid has been extended only at the price of ever-increasing control by Washington over State legislation and administration. 'It cannot be denied that all federal grants for administrative expenses drive stakes of important federal control into state administration.... The old adage that he who pays the piper calls the tune contains an element of truth in relation to grant-in-aid services.'[4] From the point of view of the maintenance of vigorously functioning federalism, this is the great objection to the extension of the grant-in-aid system, or system of 'co-operative federalism', as it is often termed, in the United States. Further expansion of that system, in practice, means further aggrandizement of federal power. 'Unquestionably it does, for when two cooperate, even though they be a Hitler and a Mussolini, it is the stronger member of the combination who calls the tune. Resting as it does primarily on the superior fiscal resources of the National Government, Cooperative Federalism has been, to date, a short expression for a constantly increasing concentration of power at Washington.'[5]

1 *The Hoover Commission Report,* 493.   2 Corwin, *op. cit.* 101.
3 *Helvering* v. *Davis,* 301 U.S. 619, 644 (1937).
4 Clark, *op. cit.* 152, 303.   5 Corwin, *op. cit.* 101.

INTERGOVERNMENTAL TAX IMMUNITIES

What has been said thus far indicates that federalism in the United States is no longer controlled by the concept of equality between States and nation. More and more, the American system is coming to be characterized by the supremacy of the Government in Washington. We have analysed this development in the fields of regulation of commerce, taxing power and grants-in-aid. In all of them the dominant theme has been the magnification of federal authority, accompanied by a corresponding diminution of the reserved powers of the States. It remains now to discuss the similar trend in a field which Americans consider to be of fundamental importance to the functioning of a federal system, namely, that of so-called intergovernmental tax immunities.

'For one hundred and twenty years', stated Mr Justice Frankfurter in 1939, 'this Court has been concerned with claims of immunity from taxes imposed by one authority in our dual system of government because of the taxpayer's relation to the other. The basis for the Court's intervention in this field has not been any explicit provision of the Constitution. The States, after they formed the Union, continued to have the same range of taxing power which they had before, barring only duties affecting exports, imports, and on tonnage.[1] Congress, on the other hand, to lay taxes in order "to pay the Debts and provide for the common Defense and general Welfare of the United States," Art. I, § 8, can reach every person and every dollar in the land with due regard to Constitutional limitations as to the method of laying taxes. But, as is true of other great activities of the state and national governments, the fact that we are a federalism raises problems regarding these vital powers of taxation. Since two governments have authority within the same territory, neither through its power to tax can be allowed to cripple the operations of the other. Therefore state and federal governments must avoid exactions which discriminate against each other or obviously interfere with one another's operations.'[2]

The starting-point for the doctrine of intergovernmental tax immunities in the American system was the celebrated case of *McCulloch* v. *Maryland*,[3] where the court held that the State of Maryland could not levy a tax upon an agency of the Federal Government operating within the State. The power to tax, declared the opinion of Chief Justice Marshall, involves the power to destroy. To permit the States to tax federal agencies would be to

1 The States are expressly forbidden to impose such duties without the consent of the Congress by Article I, section 10 of the Constitution.
2 *Graves* v. *New York ex rel. O'Keefe*, 306 U.S. 466, 488 (1939).
3 4 Wheat. 316 (U.S. 1819).

place in their hands the power to nullify the operations of such agencies. 'The question is, in truth, a question of supremacy; and if the right of the states to tax the means employed by the general government be conceded, the declaration that the constitution, and the laws made in pursuance thereof, shall be the supreme law of the land, is empty and unmeaning declamation.'[1]

Though *McCulloch* v. *Maryland* was thus based upon the national supremacy clause of the Federal Constitution,[2] later cases held that implicit in its holding was a broad doctrine of intergovernmental immunity which protected the States as well as the national Government. 'The fear that one government may cripple or obstruct the operations of the other early led to the assumption that there was a reciprocal immunity of the instrumentalities of each from taxation by the other. It was assumed that there was an equivalence in the implications of taxation by a State of the governmental activities of the National Government and the taxation by the National Government of State instrumentalities. This assumed equivalence was nourished by the phrase of Chief Justice Marshall that "the power to tax involves the power to destroy".'[3]

Under the cases following *McCulloch* v. *Maryland*, the Supreme Court, in Professor Wheare's phrase,[4] set rigid limits to the use of the taxing power in any way which might permit the general Government to interfere with the operation of the State Governments within their own allotted sphere. The maintenance of the federal system was seen to require that both States and nation be wholly immune from taxation by the other. 'If the means and instrumentalities employed by that [i.e. the national] government to carry into operation the powers granted to it are, necessarily, and, for the sake of self-preservation, exempt from taxation by the States, why are not those of the States depending upon their reserved powers, for like reasons, equally exempt from Federal taxation? . . .' asked the Supreme Court in a leading case. 'In both cases the exemption rests upon necessary implication, and is upheld by the great law of self-preservation; as any government, whose means employed in conducting its operations, if subject to the control of another and distinct government, can exist only at the mercy of that government. Of what avail are these means if another power may tax them at discretion?'[5]

If one theme dominated the decisions made after the *McCulloch* v. *Maryland Case*, like that just cited, it was that of equality as between States and

---

1 4 Wheat. at 433.   2 See *supra*, p. 39.
3 *New York* v. *United States*, 326 U.S. 572, 576 (1946).
4 Wheare, *op. cit.* 114.
5 *The Collector* v. *Day*, 11 Wall. 113, 127 (U.S. 1870).

nation so far as tax immunity was concerned. But this, as we have seen,[1] was precisely the governing principle of the doctrine of dual federalism which, until 1937, was that upon which the working of American federalism was grounded. With the abandonment by the Federal Supreme Court of that concept, it was to be expected that the notion of intergovernmental equality should give way in the field of tax immunity, just as it has in the other fields which have been discussed in earlier portions of this chapter. And this, in fact, is what has happened in the recent jurisprudence of the Supreme Court.

The rule of *McCulloch* v. *Maryland*,[2] that the States may not impose any tax upon a federal agency, has not, of course, been altered by the rejection of dual federalism. It is, indeed, seen to be an essential element of the national supremacy which is, more and more, coming to be the hallmark of American federalism. The equivalent immunity of the States from federal taxation is, however, quite another thing. As Mr Justice Frankfurter expressed it in 1946, 'The considerations bearing upon taxation by the States of activities or agencies of the federal government are not correlative with the considerations bearing upon federal taxation of State agencies or activities. The federal government is the government of all the States, and all the States share in the legislative process by which a tax of general applicability is laid. "The taxation by the State governments of the instruments employed by the general government in the exercise of its powers...is a very different thing. Such taxation involves an interference with the powers of a government in which other States and their citizens are equally interested with the State which imposes the taxation."'[3]

New York v. *United States*[4] is a good case to illustrate the present situation in American law with regard to State immunity from federal taxation. Under the relevant federal revenue law, a tax is imposed on all mineral waters sold in the United States. The *New York Case* arose out of an action by the Federal Government to recover taxes assessed against the State of New York on the sale of mineral waters taken from springs on State-owned land at Saratoga Springs and bottled and sold by a State agency. The State claimed immunity from the federal tax, but this claim was rejected by the Federal Supreme Court. 'In the older cases', states Justice Frankfurter's opinion, 'the emphasis was on immunity from taxation. The whole tendency of recent cases reveals a shift in emphasis to that of limitation upon immunity.'[5] In a case like this, the nation may tax the State activity upon the same basis as it does private individuals engaged in that activity.

---

1 *Supra*, p. 42. 2 4 Wheat. 316 (U.S. 1819).
3 *New York* v. *United States*, 326 U.S. 572, 577 (1946).
4 326 U.S. 572 (1946). 5 *Ibid.* at 581.

'If Congress...taxes all vendors of mineral water alike, whether State vendors or private vendors, it simply says, in effect, to a State: "You may carry out your own notions of social policy in engaging in what is called business, but you must pay your share in having a nation which enables you to pursue your policy."' [1]

It should be pointed out that, under a decision like that in *New York* v. *United States*, State immunity from federal taxation is not entirely done away with. There are certain activities which are so essential to the existence of State government that to permit the Federal Government to tax them would be to allow it to interfere unduly with the States' performance of their sovereign functions of government. [2] 'There are, of course, State activities and State-owned property that partake of uniqueness from the point of view of intergovernmental relations. These inherently constitute a class by themselves. Only a State can own a Statehouse; only a State can get income by taxing. These could not be included for purposes of federal taxation in any abstract category of taxpayers without taxing the State as a State.' [3] State immunity is, however, now limited to those activities which are considered as basically governmental in nature. When the State engages in an activity not essential to government as we have traditionally known it, then the activity can be taxed by the nation. 'So long as Congress generally taps a source of revenue by whomsoever earned and not uniquely capable of being earned only by a State, the Constitution of the United States does not forbid it merely because its incidence falls also on a State.' [4]

The law of intergovernmental tax immunity in the American federal system is thus no longer characterized by the equivalent immunity of States and nation. The States are now immune from federal taxation only so far as activities deemed essential to their continuance as independent governments are concerned. But the Congress can clearly tax all functions considered to be 'non-governmental'—such as the sale of mineral waters —even though they may be exercised by a State. The Federal Government, on the other hand, remains wholly immune from taxation by the States. The immunity of federal agencies does not turn on their nature or the nature of their activities. [5] Whether their functions be considered as essential to government or not, they are still completely beyond the reach of State taxing power.

The implications for the development of American federalism of the subordinate position of the individual States in the field of tax immunity

1 326 U.S. at 582.   2 *Ibid.* at 587.
3 *Ibid.* at 582.   4 *Ibid.*
5 *Carson* v. *Roane-Anderson Co.*, 342 U.S. 232, 234 (1952).

are of great consequence. If federal power to tax the States is conceded, they no longer have the independence which they have always been assumed to have. 'They are relegated to a more servile status. They become subject to interference and control both in the functions which they exercise and the methods which they employ. They must pay the federal government for the privilege of exercising the powers of sovereignty guaranteed them by the Constitution.'[1]

It is true, as has been pointed out, that the States still retain a certain amount of tax immunity—i.e. so far as their essential governmental activities are concerned. But the area of State activity from which immunity has been removed is precisely that of especial significance to modern government, which is more and more undertaking social functions that half a century ago were thought to be beyond the sphere of government. 'A State's project is as much a legitimate governmental activity whether it is traditional, or akin to private enterprise, or conducted for profit....A State may deem it as essential to its economy that it own and operate a railroad, a mill, or an irrigation system as it does to own and operate bridges, street lights, or a sewage disposal plant. What might have been viewed in an earlier day as an improvident or even dangerous extension of state activities may today be deemed indispensable.'[2]

Recognition of federal taxing power over State so-called non-governmental activities gives to Washington a ready means of controlling the social service functions of the States. And that is why the removal of State tax immunity with regard to such functions has been, like the other developments dealt with in this chapter, an important step in the magnification of federal authority that has occurred in the American system. 'A tax', as a dissenting member of the Supreme Court has asserted, 'is a powerful, regulatory instrument.... If the federal government can place the local governments on its tax collector's list, their capacity to serve the needs of their citizens is at once hampered or curtailed. The field of federal excise taxation alone is practically without limits. Many state activities are in marginal enterprises where private capital refuses to venture. Add to the cost of these projects a federal tax and the social program may be destroyed before it can be launched.'[3]

1 Douglas, J., dissenting, in *New York* v. *United States*, 326 U.S. at 595.
2 *Ibid.* at 591.   3 *Ibid.* at 593.

FUTURE OF AMERICAN FEDERALISM

'The question of the relation of the States to the federal government is the cardinal question of our time', wrote Woodrow Wilson in 1908,[1] and his conclusion was reiterated in 1949 by an important official study.[2] The analysis which has been given above indicates that, to an ever-growing extent, that question is being resolved in favour of federal authority. The starting-point of the American system, as we have seen, was the concept of dual federalism, under which State and nation were looked upon as equals, with each having reserved to it an exclusive area of authority in which it could act. This concept was maintained in its essential aspects for over a century by a series of Supreme Court decisions invalidating attempts by the Federal Government to encroach upon the field reserved to the States. The equilibrium between State and federal power has, however, been drastically altered during the past generation. The need for the exertion of national power to meet the requirements of present-day government has led to the abandonment of the notion of governmental equality as the keystone of the structure of American federalism.

'Under a federal as under a unitarian system', states Dicey with his customary eloquence, 'there exists a sovereign power, but the sovereign is in a federal state a despot hard to rouse. He is not, like the English Parliament, an ever-wakeful legislator, but a monarch who slumbers and sleeps. The sovereign of the United States has been roused to serious action but once during the course of more than a century. It needed the thunder of the Civil War to break his repose, and it may be doubted whether anything short of impending revolution will ever again rouse him to activity.'[3]

The events which have occurred in the half-century that has passed since this statement was written have proved how greatly Dicey underestimated the strength of federal power in the United States. During the past two generations, the American sovereign has roused himself to participate in two world conflicts, to deal with a disastrous economic depression, and to assume world leadership during a period of 'cold war'. Nor has he shown any sign of returning to his repose with the passing of the emergencies that have called forth the exercise of his power. The aroused state of the federal sovereign appears, on the contrary, to be a normal condition of the contemporary American scene.

The 'new federalism' in the United States is characterized by the predominance of federal authority. The American social and economic system

1 Wilson, *Constitutional Government in the United States* (1908), 173.
2 *Hoover Commission Report*, 491.
3 Dicey, *Law of the Constitution* (9th ed. 1939), 149.

is more and more being subjected to regulation and control by Washington. The national Government's power over commerce is construed so as to subject even enterprises which have the most remote effect upon the national economy to detailed federal regulation. And, as the authority of the nation in this respect has grown, that of the States has suffered a corresponding decrease, for State action, in the American system, is barred where federal power inconsistent therewith has validly been exerted. National authority has also been greatly expanded by recent reliance upon the federal power to tax and spend to promote the general welfare. And the position of the States has deteriorated further by the constantly increasing reliance of State Governments upon subventions granted by Washington, which are normally accorded only upon conditions which subject the recipients to varying degrees of federal control. It is the importance of federal grants-in-aid that led an important official study to conclude in 1949, with regard to federal-State relations in the American system: 'Prior to 1900, the question was largely a legal problem. Since that time, it has become increasingly an economic problem.'[1]

The development of the 'new federalism', which has been described, in the United States, poses the problem of the future of the American States. Is the trend toward federal aggrandizement likely to continue with the eventual substitution of a unitarian form of government for the federal system as its probable ultimate phase? An answer to this question is not an easy one. Mere logical considerations would appear to demand an affirmative reply. The existence of the American States often involves a needless and wasteful duplication of governmental structures and services. And, even if organs of local government are considered necessary, they would be better organized if the United States were divided along regional lines, rather than according to the present State boundaries, which were normally chosen for anything but considerations of governmental efficiency.

Yet, though the trend toward increasing federal authority is likely to continue unabated in the United States, it is most unlikely that it will lead in the foreseeable future to the complete curtailment of the State Governments. Much more than claims of governmental effectiveness is involved here. To most Americans, their States are as much a part of their political system as is the Government in Washington. Each State has its own particular features, and some of them can look back upon a history of which they are entitled to be proud.[2] Local patriotism and sentimental attach-

1 *Hoover Commission Report,* 491. See Vanderbilt, *The Doctrine of the Separation of Powers and its Present-day Significance* (1953), 59.
2 Laski, *The American Democracy* (1948), 138.

ment to the particular State have lost none of their vigour.[1] 'The states', aptly declares Harold J. Laski, 'are provinces of which the sovereignty has never, since 1789, been real. But they are provinces which, with all their limitations, have something of the magic of Athens and of Rome, of London and of Paris and of Florence. They breed in most of their citizens an undeniable parochialism; but the states are few in which there is not something akin to loveliness in their parochialism.'[2]

Though the American States appear likely to decline even more from the position of independent sovereigns which they possessed upon the founding of the Republic, their continuance as separate governmental entities seems assured. It is certainly not yet reasonable to expect their status to become similar to that of an English county or, still less, of a French department. Even if State power continues to decrease and federal control to grow, the American States will continue to possess authority to which no organ of local government in Britain can pretend. They will still possess an initiative in law-making which can be exercised in the absence of federal action in the field. It is they who will still be responsible for the functioning of local administrative and judicial machinery. Education, police, public health, welfare, and a host of other functions appear likely, at least on the local level, to continue to be administered by State officials. It is true that their activities may be subject to ever-increasing federal control. But their role will still be a large one, as compared with English organs of local government. The American States may be under constantly growing féderal control; yet it is unlikely that they will ever have to look to Washington in determining their behaviour, as every area of local government in England and Wales must look to Whitehall and Westminster if it becomes possessed of the desire to embark upon innovations.[3]

1 Pinto, *op. cit.* 23.   2 Laski, *op. cit.* 139.   3 Cf. *ibid.* 138.

Chapter VII

PRESIDENTIAL PREROGATIVE AND THE STEEL SEIZURE CASE

'At the first sound of a new argument over the United States Constitution and its interpretation the hearts of Americans leap with a fearful joy. The blood stirs powerfully in their veins and a new lustre brightens their eyes. Like King Harry's men before Harfleur, They stand like greyhounds in the slips, straining upon the start.'[1]

On 8 April 1952, 'the old bugle-note rang out, clear and thrilling, calling Americans to a fresh debate on the Constitution'.[2] For, on that day, the Secretary of Commerce was directed by President Truman to take possession of and operate the plants and facilities of the nation's steel industry. The President had acted in order to head off a steel strike which was to have begun on 9 April. The indispensability of steel as a component of substantially all weapons and other war materials led the President to believe that the proposed work stoppage would jeopardize the national defence of the United States and that governmental seizure of the steel mills was necessary in order to assure the continued availability of steel.

But, though the President's action in ordering seizure of the steel industry was motivated by his conception of what was necessitated by the public interest, he had acted without any statutory authorization to do what he did. And, under the American constitutional system, the question whether the President's action in such circumstances was valid was a judicial question, to be resolved ultimately by the federal Supreme Court.

To the student of comparative law, the judicial resolution of a case like the steel seizure illustrates, in a striking manner, the key position of the judiciary in the American scheme of things. It was the American Supreme Court which determined the legality of the President's action in seizing the steel industry, and its resolution of the issue was accepted without question by the other branches of the Government. It is as an outstanding example of the role of the federal judiciary in the constitutional sphere that the decision of the American courts in the steel seizure case is of primary interest. A constitution is a mere paper instrument unless the guarantees contained in it are adequately safeguarded by the courts. It is judicial enforcement that makes a constitutional right a thing of meaning, for rights without remedies to enforce them are denuded of practical content.

1 *The Economist*, 10 May 1952, p. 370.   2 *Ibid.*

It is true, as one of the great opinions of Chief Justice John Marshall pointed out, that we must never forget that 'it is a *constitution* we are expounding'[1]—a living instrument which must be construed so as to meet the practical necessities of present-day government. The courts would be remiss in their duty if they allowed their individual political, economic and social theories to lead them to invalidate exercises by the executive branch of powers needed to cope with contemporary conditions. One familiar with the background of judicial supremacy in the United States during the last century cannot help but feel sympathetic toward assertions of judicial self-restraint, so far as the invalidation of governmental action is concerned. But even self-restraint must have its limits if the provisions of a constitution are to be more than mere maxims of political morality.[2] Judicial abnegation and judicial abdication are two entirely different things.

FACTS AND BASIC ISSUE

In the latter part of 1951, a dispute arose between the major steel companies in the United States and the union representing their employees—the United Steelworkers of America—over terms and conditions that should be included in new collective bargaining agreements. Long-continued conferences failed to resolve the dispute. On 18 December 1951, the union gave notice of an intention to strike when the existing bargaining agreements expired on 31 December. Further efforts to get labour and management to agree having failed, President Truman then referred the dispute to the Federal Wage Stabilization Board, an agency set up to deal with certain aspects of the field of labour relations, to investigate and make recommendations for fair and equitable settlement. The board held lengthy public hearings and, on 20 March 1952, submitted its report and recommendations. These met, in substantial part, the union's demands and were rejected by the steel companies. This the latter had a perfect right to do, for the board's recommendations were advisory only. They were intended to aid labour and management in the collective bargaining process and had no binding effect unless accepted by both sides.

After the President referred the dispute to the Wage Stabilization Board, the union had deferred the strike which had previously been set. But when the steel companies refused to accept the board's recommendations, the union issued a call for a nation-wide strike in the steel industry, which was scheduled to begin on the morning of 9 April 1952. It was the fear of the effects on the nation's economy of such a strike that caused President

1 *McCulloch* v. *Maryland*, 4 Wheat. 316, 407 (U.S. 1819).
2 The term used in Dicey, *Law of the Constitution* (9th ed. 1939), 135.

Truman to take the drastic action that led to the steel seizure case. A few hours before the strike was to have begun, the President issued an executive order directing the Secretary of Commerce to take immediate possession of the plants, facilities and other properties of more than eighty named steel companies and 'to operate or to arrange for the operation thereof and to do all things necessary for, or incident to, such operation'. The President, in his order, asserted that steel was an essential component of substantially all the weapons used by the armed forces and that its supply was also indispensable for the maintenance of the civilian economy upon which American military strength depended. 'A work stoppage', declared the order, 'would immediately jeopardize and imperil our national defense and the defense of those joined with us in resisting aggression, and would add to the continuing danger of our soldiers, sailors, and airmen engaged in combat in the field.' In order to avert these dangers 'it is necessary that the United States take possession of and operate the plants, facilities, and other properties of the said companies'.[1]

Soon after the announcement of the President's seizure order, the steel companies filed suit in the appropriate United States district court against the Secretary of Commerce for declaratory judgments holding the seizure illegal and for injunctions against the enforcement of the President's order. The Government, in opposing the action, asserted that a strike disrupting steel production for even a brief period would so endanger the well-being and safety of the nation that the President had 'inherent power' to do what he had done—power 'supported by the Constitution, by historical precedent, and by court decisions'.[2]

The issue was thus squarely joined upon a question as important as any ever decided by the American courts under their authority as arbiters of constitutional disputes. The question is one which has never before been authoritatively determined by the American judiciary, although it is one which is fundamental in modern government. It is the question of the extent of inherent executive power—one which is as important in other countries as it is under the American constitutional system.

INHERENT EXECUTIVE POWER

In 1950, a study of French administrative law was published in England entitled *Government by Decree*.[3] This title was intended to emphasize the fact that, in a Continental country like France, government is carried on as

---

1 The full text of the President's Order is printed in *Youngstown Sheet & Tube Co.* v. *Sawyer*, 343 U.S. 579, 589–92 (1952).
2 *Ibid.* at 584.   3 Sieghart, *Government by Decree* (1950).

much by exercises of inherent executive power as it is by administrative exercises of authority delegated by the legislature. This is particularly apparent so far as the administrative rule-making power is concerned. The common lawyer who examines the rule-making power in France is immediately struck by the fact that, in the French system, the administration is vested with the inherent authority to promulgate rules which have the force of law.[1] This is something which is foreign to Anglo-American conceptions of executive power; for, in our theory, the administration possesses only the rule-making authority which has been delegated to it by the legislature.

It is true that, even in the common-law countries, the extent of administrative rule-making power has been drastically altered in the last fifty years. If, as the *Report of the United States Attorney-General's Committee on Administrative Procedure* pointed out, 'the promulgation of general regulations by the Executive, acting under statutory authority, has been a normal feature of federal administration ever since the Government was established',[2] the area of administrative authority has certainly increased by leaps and bounds since the founding of the American Republic. In mere point of view of volume, indeed, the amount of administrative rule-making completely dwarfs the number of statutes enacted by the Federal Congress. And what is true of volume is true also of degree of authority. Anglo-American legislatures are tending more and more to enact legislation of the 'skeleton' type, which lays down only the broadest standards to limit the administrative rule-making power. In such cases, the flesh and the blood—not to mention the soul—of the scheme of legislative regulation have to be provided by the rules promulgated by the administration.[3]

Yet, even though the administrative rule-making power is an enormous one today in the common-law countries, it is still one which has its source in delegations by the legislature. In Anglo-American theory, it is only the elected representatives of the people who have been vested with the inherent power to legislate. Other governmental organs may exercise legislative authority only by virtue of an express grant of such authority from the legislature. It is in this sense that the common lawyer has become accustomed to the term 'delegated legislation', as indicating the exercise by the administration of rule-making authority which has been delegated to it.

American constitutional theorists, however, have not been slow to claim for the executive an inherent power similar to that which has existed in

---

1 See Schwartz, *French Administrative Law and the Common-Law World* (1954), 89–92. 2 *Final Report* (1941), 97.
3 Compare Allen, *Law and Orders* (1945), 122.

the executive in Continental countries, like France. Their theories which involve, in effect, a readaptation of the English notion of prerogative to contemporary American conditions, appear inconsistent with the basic Anglo-American theory of administrative authority as delegated, rather than inherent. Yet it has been difficult tó assert categorically that they are wholly incorrect, because of the lack of clarity in the provisions relating to executive power in the American Constitution.

ABSOLUTE PREROGATIVE

The language of Article II of the Federal Constitution, which contains the sections dealing with the executive and its powers, is, as was pointed out in Chapter IV[1], vague and indefinite by comparison with the articles defining the authority of the other branches of the government. Its important provisions are contained in the following sentences: 'The executive Power shall be vested in a President of the United States of America. ... The President shall be Commander in Chief of the Army and Navy of the United States, and of the Militia of the several States when called into the actual Service of the United States. ... He shall take Care that the Laws be faithfully executed.'

One American school of constitutional construction—of which the outstanding adherent was former President Theodore Roosevelt—has derived a theory of inherent executive power from the differences in the language used in Article II from that employed in Article I of the American Constitution. The latter, which deals with the Congress and its powers, reads: 'All legislative Powers herein granted shall be vested in a Congress.' The absence of such express limitation in the general grant of '*the* executive power' to the President has led to the assertion that the authority vested in the President includes all powers executive in nature, though not specifically enumerated in Article II. Advocates of this view have maintained, in the words of its leading exponent, that 'the executive power was limited only by specific restrictions and prohibitions appearing in the Constitution or imposed by Congress under its constitutional powers'. They have denied 'that what was imperatively necessary for the Nation could not be done by the President unless he could find some specific authorization for it'.[2]

The advocates of such power in the executive have, indeed, gone even further, and claimed for the President what amounts to an unlimited prerogative. 'The present claim of the Executive', asserted the steel companies

1 *Supra*, p. 87.
2 T. Roosevelt, *Autobiography* (1927), 57.

in their argument before the American Supreme Court, 'to an inherent right to do whatever he considers necessary for what he views as the common good—without consulting the legislature and without any authority under law—is not a new claim. It is precisely that which was made more than three centuries ago by James I of England when he claimed for himself the right to make law by proclamation and asserted that it was treason to maintain that the King was under the law. It is precisely the claim for which Charles I lost his life and James II his throne.'[1]

In many ways, the claims of the American Government in the steel seizure case are but a modern echo of those made for the Crown in the celebrated *Ship Money Case*.[2] In that case, too, the Crown lawyers based their contentions squarely upon the claims of 'national emergency', 'common defence', and 'inherent powers' of the King. As is well known, a majority of the judges accepted the King's views in the *Ship Money Case*. 'It doth appear by this record', stated Mr Justice Crawley, in words to which the contentions advanced on behalf of the American Government in the steel seizure case have been said to be surprisingly similar, 'that the whole kingdom is in danger, both by sea and land, of ruin and destruction, dishonour and oppression, and that the danger is present, imminent and instant, and greater than the king can, without the aid of his subjects, well resist: whether must the king resort to parliaments? No. We see the danger is instant and admits of no delay.'[3]

The decision in the *Ship Money Case* involved the judicial acceptance of the theory of what has been called the absolute or extraordinary prerogative of the Crown.[4] Under it, there is in the executive an unlimited discretionary authority to do what it thinks necessary for the good of the realm. In essence, it is this theory of absolute prerogative, dead in the country of its origin since the defeat of Stuart attempts at absolutism, that was resurrected by American advocates of inherent power in the President to do what he did in the steel seizure case. That this theory is, in fact, the basis for their claims is shown by the following extracts from the official transcript of the oral argument of Mr Baldridge, the Assistant Attorney-General, before the district court:

'*The Court:* So you contend the Executive has unlimited power in time of an emergency?

'*Mr Baldridge:* He has the power to take such action as is necessary to meet the emergency.

---

1 Brief for plaintiff companies in the steel seizure case, p. 30.
2 *Rex* v. *Hampden* (1637), 3 State Tr. 826.
3 *Ibid.* at 1087.
4 Wade and Phillips, *Constitutional Law* (4th ed. 1950), 131.

'*The Court:* If the emergency is great, it is unlimited, is it?

'*Mr Baldridge:* I suppose if you carry it to its logical conclusion, that is true....

'*The Court:* Then, as I understand it, you claim that in time of emergency the Executive has this great power.

'*Mr Baldridge:* That is correct.

'*The Court:* And that the Executive determines the emergencies and the Courts cannot even review whether it is an emergency.

'*Mr Baldridge:* That is correct.'

The extreme nature of the American Government's position in the steel case is perhaps even better illustrated by another portion of the argument:

'*The Court:* So, when the sovereign people adopted the Constitution, it enumerated the powers set up in the Constitution, but limited the powers of the Congress and limited the powers of the judiciary, but it did not limit the powers of the Executive. Is that what you say?

'*Mr Baldridge:* That is the way we read Article II of the Constitution.'

REJECTION OF ABSOLUTE PREROGATIVE THEORY

If the decision of the American courts in *Youngstown Sheet & Tube Co.* v. *Sawyer*,[1] the steel seizure case, means anything, it means that they have rejected the theory of absolute prerogative in the executive. In that case, it will be recalled, the steel companies had brought proceedings in the district court, the court of general jurisdiction in the federal judicial system, to enjoin the Secretary of Commerce from taking any action under the President's steel seizure order. The case was heard before David A. Pine, a jurist on the bench of the district court in the nation's capital. 'Up to that moment only a minute part of the population had ever heard of Judge Pine, though there were many lawyers and others in Washington who knew him, or knew of him, and held him in respect. But overnight his place in the history books became secure.'[2]

On 29 April 1952, Judge Pine, in a now famous decision, seized hold of the constitutional issue and ruled that the President's steel seizure order was illegal.[3] Referring to the provisions of Article II of the American Constitution, which have already been quoted, the learned jurist asserted: 'Neither singly nor in the aggregate do they grant the President, expressly or impliedly,...the "residuum of power" or "inherent" power which authorizes him, as defendant claims, to take such action as he may deem to

1 343 U.S. 579 (1952).
2 *The Economist,* 10 May 1952, p. 370.
3 *Youngstown Sheet & Tube Co.* v. *Sawyer,* 103 F. Supp. 569 (D.C. 1952).

be necessary, including seizure of plaintiffs' properties, whenever in his opinion an emergency exists requiring him to do so in the public interest.[1] ...The President can exercise no power which cannot be fairly and reasonably traced to some specific grant of power or justly implied and included within such express grant as proper and necessary to its exercise.'[2] And, alluding to the Theodore Roosevelt theory of inherent executive power, which has been discussed above, Judge Pine felt compelled to declare, 'with all due deference and respect for that great President of the United States, I am obliged to say that his statements do not comport with our recognized theory of government, but with a theory with which our government of laws and not of men is constantly at war'.[3]

The normal procedure in the federal judicial system is for decisions of the district courts to be appealed against to the appropriate court of appeals, the tribunal of intermediate appellate jurisdiction, before they are reviewed by the Supreme Court, the tribunal of last resort in the hierarchy of federal courts. In important cases, however, where expedition in making a final decision is desirable, the Supreme Court may decide to hear appeals directly from the district court. This was the procedure which was followed in the steel seizure case, and it enabled that controversy to be resolved by the nation's highest court less than two months after the proceedings were originally instituted.

It was on 2 June 1952 that the Supreme Court announced its decision in *Youngstown Sheet & Tube Co. v. Sawyer*.[4] 'The nine Justices of the U.S. Supreme Court', reads a journalist's account, 'filed out from behind their velour curtain on "decision Monday" this week and took their seats with routine solemnity. Chief Justice Fred Vinson looked out across the crowded chamber and announced that routine business would be postponed until after the reading of opinions in "the steel case". At his words, the chamber buzzed with electric anticipation. On Vinson's right, Justice Hugo Lafayette Black put on his thick-rimmed glasses and picked up a sheaf of papers. In his Alabama half-drawl, he began reading the majority decision.'[5]

The Supreme Court, in a decision concurred in by six of its nine members, affirmed the judgment of the district court. 'It is clear', stated Mr Justice Black, in delivering the court's opinion, 'that if the President had authority to issue the order he did, it must be found in some provision of the Constitution. And it is not claimed that express constitutional

1 103 F. Supp. at 573.
2 *Ibid.* at 574, quoting Taft, *Our Chief Magistrate and his Powers* (1916), 139.
3 103 F. Supp. at 575.   4 343 U.S. 579 (1952).
5 *Time*, 9 June 1952, p. 17.

language grants this power to the President.'[1] It was, however, contended that presidential power should be implied from the aggregate of his powers under Article II of the American Constitution. This contention was unequivocally rejected by the majority of the court. As it was expressed by Mr Justice Burton, in his concurring opinion, 'Does the President, in such a situation, have inherent constitutional power to seize private property which makes congressional action in relation thereto unnecessary? We find no such power available to him under the present circumstances.'[2]

Advocates of the doctrine of inherent power in the American executive, as has been pointed out, have urged that the delegation to the President of '*the* executive power' in Article II of the Federal Constitution constitutes a 'grant of all of the executive powers of which the Government is capable'.[3] This view was repudiated by the majority of the Supreme Court, as it had been by Judge Pine in the district court. 'The example of such unlimited executive power that must have most impressed the forefathers', eloquently asserts the concurring opinion of Mr Justice Jackson, 'was the prerogative exercised by George III, and the description of its evils in the Declaration of Independence leads me to doubt that they were creating their new Executive in his image. Continental European examples were no more appealing. And if we seek instruction from our own times, we can match it only from the executive powers in those governments we disparagingly describe as totalitarian. I cannot accept the view that this clause is a grant in bulk of all conceivable executive power but regard it as an allocation to the presidential office of the generic powers thereafter stated.'[4]

COMMANDER IN CHIEF

Two of the generic powers specifically accorded in Article II of the American Constitution have been particularly relied upon by those who have affirmed the existence of inherent authority in the President to act as he did in the steel seizure case, even in the absence of statutory authorization. These have been the grant to the President of the role of commander-in-chief of the armed forces and of the authority to take care that the laws be faithfully executed. The Supreme Court in the steel seizure case held, however, that these are not sufficiently substantial supports for so significant a power in the executive.

The court was careful to state that its decision was not intended to circumscribe the legitimate military role of the President as head of the armed forces. The widest latitude of interpretation should be indulged in to

1 343 U.S. at 587.   2 *Ibid.* at 659.
3 *Ibid.* at 640.   4 *Ibid.* at 641.

sustain his function to command the instruments of national force, at least when turned against the outside world for security reasons. But, when they are turned inward, not because of rebellion but because of a lawful economic struggle between industry and labour, there should be no such indulgence.[1] 'The Constitution did not contemplate that the title Commander in Chief *of the Army and Navy* will constitute him also Commander-in-Chief of the country, its industries and its inhabitants.'[2]

The military powers of the American executive as head of the nation's armed forces do not thus extend to such an interference with the civilian life of the country as that involved in the President's steel seizure order. 'His command power is not such an absolute as might be implied from that office in a militaristic system but is subject to limitations consistent with a constitutional Republic whose law and policy-making branch is a representative Congress.'[3] It is not a military prerogative to seize persons or property because they are essential for the military establishment. 'The order cannot properly be sustained as an exercise of the President's military powers as Commander in Chief of the Armed Forces...', declared Mr Justice Black. 'Even though "theatre of war" be an expanding concept, we cannot with faithfulness to our constitutional system hold that the Commander in Chief of the Armed Forces has the ultimate power as such to take possession of private property in order to keep labor disputes from stopping production.'[4]

EXECUTION OF THE LAWS

The Supreme Court gave a similar answer to the contention based upon the provision in Article II of the Federal Constitution directing the President to 'take Care that the Laws be faithfully executed'. American advocates of the doctrine of inherent executive power have urged that this 'faithful execution' clause implies a vast residue of authority in the President. As it has been put by one jurist, 'It would seem to include the power to take all steps "which shall be necessary and proper for carrying into Execution" the laws of the United States, except those which conflict with Constitution or statute. The Executive power is thus not limited to specific constitutional or statutory grants, but includes the power to take measures and exercise authority not specifically conferred.'[5]

This, it should be noted, is precisely the view which has prevailed in Continental countries, like France, with regard to the question of inherent

---

1 343 U.S. at 645.   2 *Ibid.* at 643.
3 *Ibid.* at 645.   4 *Ibid.* at 587.
5 Schwartz, 'The war power in Britain and America', 20 *New York University L. Q. Rev.* (1945), 465, 486.

executive power. In the French system, the grant to the executive of the power to ensure the execution of the laws has been construed to imply a delegation of autonomous rule-making authority. This includes the power to promulgate any rule which is considered necessary to promote public order, safety, health and tranquillity, even though specific powers of delegated legislation may not have been accorded by the legislature in the particular case.[1]

It may well be that the worst abuses inherent in a system such as that in France are avoided by the existence there of a parliamentary system of government. The executive in France, as in Britain, is wholly responsible to the Parliament and can be dismissed by the legislature if its exercise of inherent authority is disapproved of. In the United States, on the other hand, as is well known, there is nothing like the direct accountability of the executive to the legislature which prevails in countries governed by a parliamentary system. The American executive, as we have seen, is elected directly by the people for a fixed term of four years, during which he holds office, regardless of whether he is supported by a majority of the legislature. In a system like the American one, where the executive is almost entirely independent of legislative control, the recognition of inherent executive power like that acknowledged to exist in the executive in France, in virtue of its constitutional charge to ensure the execution of the laws, could be much more dangerous than it is in a parliamentary system.

All the same, it must be admitted that the argument advanced by the Government in the American steel seizure case, based upon the constitutional direction to the President to 'take Care that the Laws be faithfully executed', has great force in its application to executive action taken in connexion with the prosecution of a formally declared war. Under the American Constitution, it should be realized, it is the Congress alone which is given the power to declare war.[2] A declaration of war is hence as much a part of the statute book as those other laws whose faithful execution the President is exhorted to attend to. As Mr Justice Story pointed out almost a century and a half ago, the power to see that this law is faithfully executed carries with it the authority to take all steps necessary for such execution.[3]

The exercise of inherent executive power in execution of a declaration of war, however, does not present the case of the greatest difficulty. That case occurs when the executive relies upon inherent power to deal with an emergency when the nation is not formally at war. If assertions of unrestricted executive power are valid in such cases, then the American

1 See Schwartz, *French Administrative Law and the Common-Law World*, 91.
2 Article I, section 8.
3 *Brown* v. *United States*, 8 Cranch 110, 145, 149 (U.S. 1814).

constitutional system is not as different from Continental systems, for instance, the French, as one would have hoped. Exercises of inherent power which are not in execution of a declaration of war, run counter to the basic principle that executive power, in the common-law countries, is delegated, rather than independent. It is in such cases that the constitutional shoe really 'pinches'.

As it was expressed by Mr Justice Jackson, concurring in an important case: 'No one will question that this power is the most dangerous one to free government in the whole catalogue of powers. It usually is invoked in haste and excitement when calm legislative consideration of constitutional limitation is difficult.... Always, as in this case, the Government urges hasty decision to forestall some emergency or serve some purpose and pleads that paralysis will result if its claims to power are denied or their confirmation delayed.'[1]

One nurtured upon common-law constitutional traditions must reject the view that the American executive possesses authority as vast as that of its counterpart in a Continental country, such as France. Reliance upon the constitutional grant of the power to take care that the laws be faithfully executed can be of little avail if, in the particular case, the executive action which is at issue does not find its source in a law . In war-time, as has been pointed out, executive acts related to the war effort are carried out in execution of the declaration of war enacted by the legislature. But, in the absence of such a formal declaration, the executive action must find its source in some other law passed by the Congress. For, if the action is not taken in execution of a law, it cannot be justified by reliance upon the 'faithful execution clause'.

This was clearly the view of the majority of the Supreme Court in the steel seizure case. 'In the framework of our Constitution,' reads Mr Justice Black's opinion, 'the President's power to see that the laws are faithfully executed refutes the idea that he is to be a lawmaker. The Constitution limits his functions in the lawmaking process to the recommending of laws he thinks wise and the vetoing of laws he thinks bad. And the Constitution is neither silent nor equivocal about who shall make laws which the President is to execute.... This is a job for the Nation's lawmakers, not for its military authorities.'[2]

1 *Woods* v. *Cloyd W. Miller Co.*, 333 U.S. 138, 146 (1948).
2 343 U.S. at 587.

PREROGATIVE AND STATUTE LAW

'Nothing better could be devised by human wisdom', reads a famous passage from the writings of Edmund Burke, 'than argued judgments, publicly delivered, for preserving unbroken the great traditionary body of the law, and for marking, whilst that great body remained unaltered, every variation in the application and the construction of particular parts.'[1]

One who is at all familiar with the practice of the English courts realizes that Burke's praise of reasoned judgments extends not only to the articulation by the tribunal as a whole of the bases of its decision but also to the presentation of their views by the individual judges who compose the court. The situation in the English courts in this respect is, however, wholly unlike that which prevails in their American counterparts. Where an English lawyer is habituated to an individual expression of views by each judge who is a member of an appellate tribunal, his confrère in the United States is normally accustomed to the explanation of a judicial decision by a single opinion of the court.

In the United States Supreme Court, the practice of delivering judgments through an opinion of the court as a whole has been established for over a century and a half. To the American jurist, the refusal of his highest court to follow the English custom of the delivery of opinions by each individual judge in turn has been of basic importance. The change from the individual to the court opinion has, in his view, been admirably suited to strengthen the power and prestige of the Supreme Court. The needed authority and dignity of the court could be attained only if the principles it proclaimed were pronounced by a united tribunal. For conclusiveness and fixity to be won for its constructions, a court with a single voice was greatly to be desired.

In the steel seizure case, as in other cases, the decision was announced in an opinion of the court, delivered in that case by Mr Justice Black. The case itself was, however, felt to be of such importance that it merited more than a single majority opinion to explain its disposition. As Thomas Jefferson once expressed it, with regard to decisions of the Supreme Court in his day, 'Some of these cases...have been of such importance, of such difficulty,....as to have merited the fullest explanation.'[2] If ever a case was of this type, it was the steel seizure case. And, in such a case, it was not unwarranted for each of the six justices who concurred in the judgment of the court to deliver a separate opinion, expressing his individual views.

1 Quoted in Vanderbilt, *Studying Law* (1945), 551.
2 Quoted in Levin, 'Mr Justice William Johnson, creative dissenter', 43 *Michigan L. Rev.* (1944), 497, 514.

In a case of such consequence, stated Mr Justice Frankfurter, in explaining why this practice was followed, it was inevitable that the judges differed individually on the exact application of the governing principle of the separation of powers. 'Even though such differences in attitude toward this principle may be merely differences in emphasis and nuance, they can hardly be reflected by a single opinion for the Court. Individual expression of views in reaching a common result is therefore important.'[1]

The opinion of the court in the steel seizure case, as has been shown, rejected the claim that the President had prerogative power to seize the steel industry, in the absence of statutory authorization. In several of the concurring opinions, however, there is also discussion of a question of basic importance to students of the prerogative power of the executive, namely, that of the relationship between prerogative and statute law.

That question was presented in the steel seizure case because of the provision by the Congress of a procedure alternative to seizure which the President could have followed to deal with the threat of a steel strike. The Labor-Management Relations Act of 1947, commonly known as the Taft-Hartley Act, includes provisions adopted for the purpose of dealing with nation-wide strikes. They establish a procedure whereby the President may appoint a board of inquiry and thereafter, in proper cases, seek relief by injunction from a district court for an eighty-day period against a threatened work stoppage. The President can invoke that procedure whenever, in his opinion, 'a threatened or actual strike...affecting an entire industry...will, if permitted to occur or to continue, imperil the national health or safety'. At the time when the Taft-Hartley Act was passed, the Congress specifically rejected a proposal to empower the President to seize any 'plant, mine, or facility' in which a threatened work stoppage would, in his judgment, 'imperil the public health or security'. Instead, the Act directed the President, in the event of a strike not being settled during the eighty-day injunction period, to submit to Congress 'a full and comprehensive report...together with such recommendations as he may see fit to make for consideration and appropriate action'.

Although the opinion of Mr Justice Black in the steel seizure case did not deal directly with the effect of the provisions of the Taft-Hartley Act upon the President's prerogative powers, there are, in some of the concurring opinions, clear indications that, even if the President had been held to have a common-law prerogative to act as he had, such prerogative power would have been superseded by the statutory procedure. The provisions of the Taft-Hartley Act, said Mr Justice Burton, 'distinguish this emergency from one in which Congress takes no action and outlines no governmental

1 343 U.S. at 589.

policy. In the case before us, Congress authorized a procedure which the President declined to follow.'[1] In such a case, there can be no excuse for presidential reliance upon prerogative rather than upon the procedure which the legislature has provided. 'I conclude', declared the concurring opinion of Mr Justice Clark, 'that where Congress has laid down specific procedures to deal with the type of crisis confronting the President, he must follow those procedures in meeting the crisis;...I cannot sustain the seizure in question because here...Congress had prescribed methods to be followed by the President in meeting the emergency at hand.'[2]

The concurring opinions just quoted deal with the question of the relationship between executive prerogative and statute law much as it was dealt with in the leading English case of *Attorney-General* v. *De Keyser's Royal Hotel*.[3] In that case, too, it was held that the executive could not choose whether it would proceed under its prerogative power or under a statutory procedure enacted to meet the case. The enactment by the legislature of statutory provisions covering the same ground as the prerogative power must be deemed *pro tanto* to suspend the prerogative. 'The Legislature,' as Lord Sumner put it, 'by appropriate enactment, can deal with such a subject-matter as that now in question in such a way as to abate such portions of the prerogative as apply to it. It seems also to be obvious that enactments may have this effect, provided they deal directly with the subject-matter, even though they enact a modus operandi for securing the desired result, which is not the same as that of the prerogative.'[4] This, it should be noted, was, in the view of the concurring opinions already quoted, precisely what was involved in the steel seizure case. There, too, the relevant provisions of the Taft-Hartley Act did deal directly with the subject-matter which the President sought to deal with by his asserted prerogative power of seizure, though by a wholly different *modus operandi*.

It may well be that, since the opinion of the court in the steel seizure case held that the President did not have any prerogative power of seizure in the circumstances of the case, what was said in the concurring opinions just referred to was only *obiter dictum*. But *obiter dicta* in the United States Supreme Court, like those in the House of Lords, usually have a 'persuasive' force almost equivalent to binding authority.[5] And, in this instance, there appears to be little doubt that the *dicta* in question will be followed by the Supreme Court if a case involving an existing presidential prerogative which has been modified or suspended by statute should arise.[6] The

---

1 *Ibid.* at 659. 2 *Ibid.* at 662. 3 [1920] A.C. 508.
4 *Ibid.* at 561. 5 Compare Allen, *op. cit.* 139.
6 Compare *United States* v. *Guy W. Capps, Inc.*, 204 F. 2d 655 (4th Cir. 1953), *affirmed on other grounds*, 348 U.S. 296 (1955), where an executive agreement between

supremacy of the statute in such a case is the only principle consistent with a polity in which all legislative power has been vested in the legislature. To hold otherwise is to ignore what Lord Atkinson has termed the 'unanswerable question' posed by the Master of the Rolls in the *De Keyser's Royal Hotel Case*: 'Those powers which the executive exercises without Parliamentary authority are comprised under the comprehensive term of the prerogative. Where, however, Parliament has intervened and provided by statute for powers previously within the prerogative, being exercised in a particular manner and subject to the limitations and provisions contained in the statute, they can only be so exercised. Otherwise, what use would there be in imposing limitations, if the Crown could at its pleasure disregard them and fall back on prerogative?'[1]

REVIEW OF PRESIDENTIAL ACTION

Many American jurists have become disturbed by a tendency which has become apparent in the jurisprudence of the American courts to refuse to review directly action of the President. While American courts have never hesitated to review the action of officers in the executive branch, they have been most reluctant to control the legality of acts of the head of the executive branch himself. 'The President,' stated a majority of the Supreme Court in 1948, 'both as Commander-in-Chief and as the Nation's organ for foreign affairs, has available intelligence services whose reports are not and ought not to be published to the world. It would be intolerable that courts, without the relevant information, should review and perhaps nullify actions of the Executive taken on information properly held secret.'[2]

The leading case is *Mississippi* v. *Johnson*, decided in 1866.[3] That case involved an action to enjoin the President from carrying into effect an Act of Congress alleged to be unconstitutional. The Supreme Court held that such an action could not be maintained. 'We are fully satisfied', reads the opinion, 'that this court has no jurisdiction of a bill to enjoin the President in the performance of his official duties; and that no such bill ought to be received by us.'[4] Since this case, it has generally been assumed, as a basic principle of American law, that a federal court may not issue an injunction against the President. This principle tends to place presidential action in an unreviewable position, for the action for an injunction is the basic remedy, in the absence of statutory provisions, for review of

the United States and Canada which contravened the provisions of an earlier statute was held invalid.

1 [1920] A.C. at 538.
2 *Chicago & Southern Airlines* v. *Waterman S.S. Co.*, 333 U.S. 103, 111 (1948).
3 4 Wall. 475 (U.S. 1866).   4 *Ibid.* at 501.

executive action by the federal courts in the United States.[1] As it has been expressed by Mr Justice Jackson, the presidential office is 'relatively immune from judicial review'.[2]

The reluctance of American courts to review the legality of acts of the President stems from a perverted construction of the doctrine of the separation of powers. 'The Congress', the United States Supreme Court has stated, 'is the legislative department of the government; the President is the executive department. Neither can be restrained in its action by the judicial department.'[3] For the courts to attempt to control the legality of presidential action would, in this view, amount to undue interference by the judiciary with the workings of a co-ordinate, independent branch of the Government.

The separation of powers interpreted in this way is, in effect, the opening wedge to a system of government foreign to Anglo-American conceptions. It places the head of the executive beyond judicial control, which, in practice, means that his acts are not subject to law. Such a construction of the separation-of-powers doctrine is neither desirable nor justified. It is erroneous to assert that the American courts are interfering unduly in the operation of another department when they review the legality of presidential action. The essence of judicial power is the application of the law in cases presented to the courts for decision. The fact that the head of the executive happens to be a party in a given case does not mean that a court, in deciding that case, is exercising other than purely judicial power.

The decision of the Supreme Court in the steel seizure case indicates that it is becoming aware of the need for avoiding the dangers inherent in the doctrine that acts of the head of the executive cannot be reviewed. It is true that the court did not expressly repudiate the principle that the federal courts cannot enjoin the President. But, even though the court continued to pay lip service to that principle, it did none the less assert an effective review power over the chief executive by a liberal application of the doctrine of an earlier case, *Williams* v. *Fanning*.[4] In that case, the court held that the American Postmaster-General was not an indispensable party in an action to enjoin a local postmaster from carrying out the provisions of an order not to deliver mail to plaintiff, although all that the postmaster was doing was to carry out the orders of his departmental superior. The President, like the Postmaster-General, acts in practice through subordinate

1 Certiorari and prohibition, which are the basic common-law remedies in this field, are not available in the federal courts for the review of executive action under *Degge* v. *Hitchcock*, 229 U.S. 162 (1913). See *infra* p. 298.
2 *Youngstown Sheet & Tube Co.* v. *Sawyer*, 343 U.S. at 654.
3 *Mississippi* v. *Johnson*, 4 Wall. 475, 500 (U.S. 1866).
4 332 U.S. 490 (1948).

officials. Under *Williams* v. *Fanning*, the subordinates through whom the President acts can be enjoined from executing illegal presidential orders. This enables the American courts to review the legality of acts of the President, without the need for formally ordering the head of the executive to do, or to refrain from doing, anything.

This is, in fact, the approach which was followed by the American courts in the steel seizure case. The action in that case, it will be recalled, was brought against the Secretary of Commerce to restrain him from carrying out the President's order. The defendant claimed that the federal courts were without power to nullify action of the President, relying upon the principle that the judiciary would not attempt directly to control the President. 'But', said Judge Pine, in his now famous opinion in the district court, 'in this case the President has not been sued. Charles Sawyer is the defendant, and the Supreme Court has held on many occasions that officers of the Executive Branch of the Government may be enjoined when their conduct is unauthorized by statute.... There is no doubt, therefore, that the defendant is subject to an injunction, and the President not only is not a party but he is not an indispensable party to this action, as held in Williams *v.* Fanning.'[1] In upholding Judge Pine's decision, the majority of the Supreme Court clearly appears to have agreed with his opinion on this point. Indeed, even the dissenting justices did not question the propriety of the injunction action against the Secretary of Commerce.

NEED FOR JUDICIAL CONTROL

To constitutional and administrative lawyers, the steel seizure case will remain of primary importance as an illustration of the basic principle that, in the American system, assertions of executive power are subject to judicial control. Though American courts may accept the existence of some inherent authority in the executive to deal with emergencies, that does not eliminate the need for judicial control. When executive action 'directs interferences with liberty or property—measures normally beyond the scope of governmental power, which are lawful if at all only because an abnormal situation has made them necessary and appropriate—it is of the very essence of the rule of law that the executive's *ipse dixit* is not of itself conclusive of the necessity'.[2]

The American approach in this respect should be compared with that of the House of Lords in the celebrated case of *Liversidge* v. *Anderson*.[3] That

1 103 F. Supp. 569, 576 (D.C. 1952).
2 Fairman, 'The law of martial rule and the national emergency', 55 *Harvard L. Rev.* (1942), 1266, 1272.   3 [1942] A.C. 206.

case involved an action by a person detained under the notorious Regulation 18B against the Home Secretary for damages for false imprisonment. Appellant applied for particulars of the grounds on which the Secretary had reasonable cause to believe him a person of hostile associations, over whom it was necessary to exercise control under the regulation. The question for the House of Lords was whether such disclosure could be compelled or whether the order of the Home Secretary was conclusive proof of the legality of his action.

As is well known, the House of Lords in the *Liversidge Case* adopted the latter view, despite the vigorous dissent of Lord Atkin. What is especially significant from our point of view is the complete preclusion of any judicial control over the legality of executive action which results from their Lordships' opinions. Such exclusion of all judicial control is not merely implicit in those opinions but is candidly expressed as their underlying purpose. 'To my mind', asserted Viscount Maugham, 'this is so clearly a matter for executive discretion that I cannot myself believe that those responsible for the Order in Council could have contemplated for a moment the possibility of the action of the Secretary being subject to the discussion, criticism and control of a judge in a court of law.'[1]

The *Liversidge* v. *Anderson* approach, which renders executive emergency action immune from judicial control, has been rejected by the American courts. Thus, even the dissenting justices in the steel seizure case recognized the propriety of review on the question of whether the President's action was, in fact, justified by the necessities of emergency.[2]

To assert that executive emergency power should not be subject to judicial control is, in the words of one American jurist, to advance an argument as untenable today as when it was cast in the language of the Plantagenets, the Tudors and the Stuarts.[3] 'If this position could be deemed well taken', the United States Supreme Court has declared, 'it is manifest that the fiat of [the Executive], and not the Constitution of the United States, would be the supreme law of the land.... There is no such avenue of escape from the paramount authority of the Federal Constitution.'[4]

It thus seems clear that, even if we were to accept the assertions of those who assert authority in the executive to cope with emergencies, we should,

1 *Ibid.* at 220. For a more complete discussion of the *Liversidge Case*, see Schwartz, *Law and the Executive in Britain* (1949), 329 *et seq.* An interesting case involving a similar problem is *Gopalan* v. *State of Madras* (1950), *Indian Supreme Court Journal*, XIII, 174. See Schwartz, 'A comparative view of the Gopalan case', 4 *Indian L. Rev.* (1950), 276.

2 343 U.S. at 709.

3 Murphy, J., in *Duncan* v. *Kahanamoku*, 327 U.S. 304, 329 (1946).

4 *Sterling* v. *Constantin*, 287 U.S. 378, 397 (1932).

at the same time, constantly have to reiterate the need for judicial control. Executive action must not be proof of its own necessity, nor must executive judgment be conclusive that its action was justified by exigency. In the American system, as Mr Chief Justice Hughes stated in a landmark case, 'What are the allowable limits of [executive] discretion, and whether or not they have been over-stepped in a particular case, are judicial questions.'[1]

It is the existence of judicial control over exercises of executive authority that minimizes the danger of 'government by decree' in the United States, such as that which has occurred so often in countries where the judicial safeguard has been absent. It should not be forgotten that it was the recognition in the Weimar Constitution of unrestrained power in the executive to deal with emergencies that helped pave the way for the downfall of the German Republic. And it was the existence of similar authority in the French executive that eased the transition to the régime of Vichy in 1940. It is not enough to say that executive freedom of action is essential to deal with exigencies, as the executive is the only branch of government that can act efficaciously to protect the public in emergency. 'From time immemorial', as Mr Justice Murphy has eloquently pointed out, 'despots have used real or imagined threats to the public welfare as an excuse for needlessly abrogating human rights. That excuse is no less unworthy of our traditions when used in this day of atomic warfare or at a future time when some other type of warfare may be devised.'[2]

1 *Sterling* v. *Constantin* 287 U.S. at 400.
2 *Duncan* v. *Kahanamoku*, 327 U.S. 304, 330 (1946).

Chapter VIII

THE CHANGING ROLE OF THE
SUPREME COURT

In 1948, Professor Friedmann called attention to what he termed the 'fundamental changes of legal ideology reflected in the jurisdiction of the Supreme Court of the United States during the past ten years'.[1] That such changes have occurred must be evident to anyone who has observed the work of that tribunal. What is perhaps not so apparent to the British observer is the extent of such change, which has been characterized by a leading American constitutional lawyer as 'Constitutional Revolution, Ltd.'[2]

To the outsider, the most striking characteristic of the American constitutional system is the doctrine of judicial supremacy. 'No feature in the Government of the United States', writes Lord Bryce, 'has awakened so much curiosity in the European mind, caused so much discussion, received so much admiration, and been more frequently misunderstood, than the duties assigned to the Supreme Court and the functions which it discharges in guarding the ark of the Constitution.'[3] Under the doctrine of judicial supremacy, it has been the American Supreme Court that has determined conflicts between acts of government and the Constitution, and it has done so through the technical forms of the lawsuit. 'These lawsuits', states a justice of the Supreme Court, 'are the chief instruments of power in our system. Struggles over power that in Europe call out regiments of troops, in America call out regiments of lawyers.'[4]

It is precisely this aspect of the American system—what has been termed 'government by lawsuit'[5]—that is most difficult for the foreigner to comprehend. In February 1935, the federal Supreme Court by a bare majority, in effect, upheld the power of the Congress to lower the gold content of the dollar.[6] The holder of a railroad bond bearing an interest coupon payable in gold of face value of $22.50 which had been issued before the gold content of the dollar had been lowered, demanded $38.10 in payment after devaluation, but the court held that he was required to accept

1 Friedmann, Book Review, 64 *L. Q. Rev.* (1948), 545, 547.
2 Corwin, *Constitutional Revolution, Ltd.* (1941).
3 Bryce, *The American Commonwealth* (1917 ed.), vol. 1, 242.
4 Jackson, *The Struggle for Judicial Supremacy* (1941), xi.
5 *Ibid.* 286.
6 *Norman* v. *Baltimore & O. R. Co.*, 294 U.S. 240 (1935).

the face value of the coupon in the new dollars. When Robert H. Jackson, afterwards a member of the highest American court, went abroad that summer, he was asked by Swedish lawyers and bankers: 'How could you Americans let your national monetary and economic policy be dependent on the outcome of a lawsuit between private parties over a difference of $15.60? How could American business intelligently function while such basic questions were pending in the Court? Why could you not learn the answer earlier? Why should within one of a majority of your court hold that a private contract between two citizens should deprive the nation of power to change its monetary policy? And why, anyway, should lawyer-judges be supreme over the national parliament, the President, the Treasury, and the whole government in a matter so vital to economic life?'[1]

PRE-1937 JUDICIAL SUPREMACY

The doctrine of judicial supremacy in its present form did not come into being full-grown upon the establishment of the American Republic. Although the doctrine was first enunciated in the celebrated case of *Marbury* v. *Madison* in 1803,[2] through most of the first century under the Constitution, important questions of national governmental power were settled in the Cabinet and on the floors of Congress. 'The fact of the matter is that judicial review as exercised by the United States Supreme Court did not become an important factor of national legislative power till about 1890 and to a lesser degree this is so even as to state legislative power. And in both instances the augmentation of the Court's role was the outgrowth of its acceptance of the laissez-faire theory of governmental function.'[3]

The classic case illustrating the approach of the American Supreme Court during the period from 1890 to 1937 in cases involving judicial review of legislative action is *Lochner* v. *New York*,[4] in which the constitutionality of a New York statute fixing maximum hours for bakers furnished the issue. In holding the statute invalid, Mr Justice Peckham, speaking for the majority of the court, stated the question to be determined in this class of cases as follows: 'In every case that comes before this court... where legislation of this character is concerned and where the protection of the Federal Constitution is sought, the question necessarily arises: Is this a fair, reasonable and appropriate exercise of the police power of the State, or is it an unreasonable, unnecessary and arbitrary interference with the right of the individual to his personal liberty or to enter into those contracts in

---

1 Jackson, *op. cit.* 103. 2 1 Cranch 137 (U.S. 1803).
3 Corwin, *op. cit.* 10. 4 198 U.S. 45 (1905).

relation to labor which may seem to him appropriate or necessary for the support of himself and his family?'[1]

In applying a test as vague and indefinite as the above—i.e. is the statute unreasonable, unnecessary and arbitrary?—was not the court virtually exercising the functions of a 'super-legislature',[2] in effect determining upon its own judgment whether particular legislation was desirable? This was, however, vigorously denied by the court in the *Lochner Case*. 'This is not a question', asserted the court's opinion, 'of substituting the judgment of the court for that of the legislature.'[3] The court's function was seen to be simply that of interpreting the law. This view, that the Supreme Court is not the master of the Federal Constitution, but merely its interpreter, was well expressed by Lord Bryce over half a century ago. 'It is ...no mere technicality', he wrote, 'to point out that the American judges do not, as Europeans are apt to say, "control the legislature", but simply interpret the law. The word "control" is misleading, because it implies that the person or body of whom it is used possesses and exerts discretionary personal will. Now the American judges have no discretionary will in the matter any more than has an English court when it interprets an Act of Parliament. The will that prevails is the will of the people expressed in the Constitution they enacted. All that the judges have to do is to discover from the enactments before them what the will of the people is, and apply that will to the facts of a given case.'[4]

Lord Bryce's almost mechanical conception of the constitutional role of the American Supreme Court is one which found an echo in the pre-1937 opinions of that tribunal itself. 'It is sometimes said', declared the Supreme Court as late as 1936, 'that the court assumes a power to overrule or control the action of the people's representatives. This is a misconception. The Constitution is the supreme law of the land ordained and established by the people. All legislation must conform to the principles it lays down. When an act of Congress is appropriately challenged in the courts as not conforming to the constitutional mandate the judicial branch of the Government has only one duty,—to lay the article of the Constitution which is invoked beside the statute which is challenged and to decide whether the latter squares with the former.'[5]

How does the above view of the court's function square with the result in the *Lochner Case*, under which a State maximum-hour law was held unconstitutional? There is nothing in the Federal Constitution which provides

---

1 *Ibid.* at 56.
2 Brandeis, J., dissenting, in *Burns Baking Co.* v. *Bryan*, 264 U.S. 504, 534 (1924).
3 198 U.S. at 56.   4 Bryce, *op. cit.* 253.
5 *United States* v. *Butler*, 297 U.S. 1, 62 (1936).

that there shall be no power to regulate hours of labour. Such a prohibition was, however, deduced by the Supreme Court from the due process clauses of the Fifth and Fourteenth Amendments, which provide that no person shall be deprived of life, liberty, or property without 'due process of law'. 'The statute', reads the *Lochner* opinion, 'necessarily interferes with the right of contract between the employer and employés, concerning the number of hours in which the latter may labor in the bakery of the employer. The general right to make a contract in relation to his business is part of the liberty of the individual protected by the Fourteenth Amendment.... Under that provision no state can deprive any person of life, liberty or property without due process of law. The right to purchase or to sell labor is part of the liberty protected by this amendment.'[1]

The statute at issue in the *Lochner Case* was thus held invalid on the ground of deprivation of freedom of contract. 'What is this freedom?' asks Mr Chief Justice Hughes in a later case. 'The Constitution does not speak of freedom of contract. It speaks of liberty and prohibits the deprivation of liberty without due process of law. In prohibiting that deprivation the Constitution does not recognize an absolute and uncontrollable liberty.'[2] It would appear that the *Lochner* court was reading its own notion of freedom from government restraints into the 'due process' clause—a notion derived from the then dominant *laissez-faire* theory of governmental function. That notion is, to say the least, somewhat outmoded at the present day. 'There is grim irony in speaking of the freedom of contract of those who, because of their economic necessities, give their services for less than is needful to keep body and soul together.'[3] As stated by a justice of the High Court of Australia, the doctrine of modern economists of all schools is that 'freedom of contract is a misnomer as applied to a contract between an employer and an ordinary employee'.[4]

REJECTION OF LOCHNER TEST

Even at the time of the *Lochner Case*, Mr Justice Holmes, dissenting, could assert: 'This case is decided upon an economic theory which a large part of the country does not entertain.'[5] Today that theory has been repudiated by the entire Supreme Court. But the present court has done more than reject the economic doctrine behind the *Lochner* decision. It has, in effect,

1 198 U.S. at 53.
2 *West Coast Hotel Co.* v. *Parrish*, 300 U.S. 379, 391 (1937).
3 Stone, J., dissenting, in *Morehead* v. *New York ex rel. Tipaldo*, 298 U.S. 587, 632 (1936).
4 Higgins, 'A new province for law and order', 29 *Harvard L. Rev.* (1915), 13, 25.
5 198 U.S. at 75.

shifted the balance which had previously existed between the court and the other branches of the Federal Government. The primacy of the Supreme Court which had prevailed under the 1890–1936 interpretation of the doctrine of judicial supremacy has been replaced by a more subdued position. In this respect, the present court has more or less adopted the view of Mr Justice Holmes as to what its function should be *vis-à-vis* the legislature. The Holmesian view is pithily expressed in his comment to Chief Justice Stone: 'About seventy-five years ago I learned that I was not God. And so, when the people of the various states want to do something I can't find anything in the Constitution expressly forbidding them to do, I say, whether I like it or not, "Goddammit, let 'em do it!"'[1]

In this comment is expressed the essence of the doctrine of judicial self-restraint which prevails among the present Supreme Court. Unless the statute at issue violates an express constitutional provision, it will be held constitutional. Clearly, under such a view, there is no place for extreme concepts such as absolute freedom of contract, about which the Federal Constitution says nothing. According to Justice Holmes, a statute should not be held invalid 'unless it can be said that a rational and fair man necessarily would admit that the statute proposed would infringe fundamental principles as they have been understood by the traditions of our people and our law'.[2]

In the Holmesian view, the test to be applied is whether a rational legislator—the congressional version of the 'reasonable man'—could have adopted a statute like that at issue. Is the statute as applied so clearly arbitrary or capricious that legislators acting reasonably could not have believed it to be necessary or appropriate for the public welfare?[3] But, under this approach, which the present Supreme Court has adopted, the court has very rarely had occasion to declare statutes unconstitutional. Under the *Lochner* decision, it will be recalled, the test was whether the court itself thought the statute was reasonable. Now, the court looks only to see whether there was a rational basis for the legislative action. Under the *Lochner Case*, the reasonableness of a statute was determined as an objective fact by the court on its own independent judgment. Today a more subjective test is applied, i.e. could rational legislators have regarded the statute as a reasonable method of reaching the desired result?[4]

A court which applies the more subjective test of constitutionality should,

1 Quoted in Curtis, *Lions under the Throne* (1947), 281.
2 *Lochner* v. *New York*, 198 U.S. at 76.
3 Brandeis, J., dissenting, in *Burns Baking Co.* v. *Bryan*, 264 U.S. 504, 534 (1924).
4 Holmes, J., dissenting, in *Meyer* v. *Nebraska*, 262 U.S. 390, 412 (1923).

as a practical matter, not invalidate statutes very often, for there is almost always some rational basis for a statute. If such a basis is found, the statute must be upheld unless it contravenes an express prohibition of the Constitution. And the latter case is not a common occurrence, especially in so far as federal statutes are concerned.

JUDICIAL SELF-RESTRAINT

The above analysis is confirmed by the manner in which the Federal Supreme Court has dealt with cases of claimed unconstitutionality since 1937. Perhaps the outstanding characteristic of the Supreme Court today is the restraint with which it exercises its power of judicial review in dealing with Acts of Congress.[1] As stated by Mr Justice Frankfurter: 'It is not for us to find unconstitutionality in what Congress enacted although it may imply notions that are abhorrent to us as individuals or policies we deem harmful to the country's well-being....Particularly when Congressional legislation is under scrutiny, every rational trail must be pursued to prevent collision between Congress and Court. For Congress can readily mend its ways, or the people may express disapproval by choosing different representatives. But a decree of unconstitutionality by this Court is fraught with consequences so enduring and far-reaching as to be avoided unless no choice is left in reason.'[2]

Since 1937, in only one case—*United States* v. *Lovett*[3]—has an Act of Congress been declared unconstitutional. The respondents in the *Lovett Case* were three federal employees who had been working for the Government for several years. The Government agencies which had lawfully employed them were fully satisfied with the quality of their work and wished to keep them employed on their jobs. They had, however, been reported as 'unfit' to continue in Government service and guilty of 'subversive activities' by a committee of the House of Representatives. When the two agencies employing these men refused to discharge them, the House adopted a rider[4] to the 1943 appropriations law forbidding the use of money appropriated in the statute to pay respondents' salaries. The Senate refused to adopt this rider six times, but finally under pressure of the close of the fiscal year concurred in a compromise which provided that, after 15 November 1943, no salary or compensation should be paid respondents out of any monies then or thereafter appropriated, unless the

1 Fellman, 'Recent tendencies in civil liberties decisions of the Supreme Court', 34 *Cornell L. Q.* (1949), 331, 332.
2 *United States* v. *Lovett*, 328 U.S. 303, 319 (1946).
3 328 U.S. 303 (1946).   4 See *supra*, p. 100.

President again appointed them to jobs and the Senate confirmed them. President Roosevelt, unable to veto the rider without killing the entire Act, signed it with the following statement: 'The Senate yielded, as I have been forced to yield, to avoid delaying our conduct of the war. But I cannot so yield without placing on record my view that this provision is not only unwise and discriminatory, but unconstitutional.'

The Supreme Court agreed with the President on this point. 'We hold', reads the opinion in the *Lovett Case*, 'that § 304 falls precisely within the category of congressional actions which the Constitution barred by providing that "No Bill of Attainder...shall be passed".'[1] A bill of attainder, said the court in an earlier case which was cited with approval, 'is a legislative act which inflicts punishment without a judicial trial. If the punishment be less than death, the act is termed a bill of pains and penalties. Within the meaning of the Constitution, bills of attainder include bills of pains and penalties.'[2] According to Mr Justice Black, who delivered the opinion in the *Lovett Case*, the present rider to the appropriations Act came within this definition.

'Section 304...', he declared, 'clearly accomplishes the punishment of named individuals without a judicial trial. The fact that the punishment is inflicted through the instrumentality of an Act specifically cutting off the pay of certain named individuals found guilty of disloyalty, makes it no less galling or effective than if it had been done by an Act which designated the conduct as criminal. No one would think that Congress could have passed a valid law, stating that after investigation it had found Lovett, Dodd, and Watson "guilty" of the crime of engaging in "subversive activities",...and sentenced them to perpetual exclusion from any government employment. Section 304, while it does not use that language, accomplishes that result. The effect was to inflict punishment without the safeguards of a judicial trial and "determined by no previous law or fixed rule". The Constitution declares that that cannot be done either by a State or by the United States....Much as we regret to declare that an Act of Congress violates the Constitution, we have no alternative here.'[3]

As has been stated, the statutory provision at issue in the *Lovett Case* is the only congressional Act which has been declared unconstitutional since 1937 by the American Supreme Court. And that provision, as interpreted by the court, was seen to violate the express constitutional injunction

1 328 U.S. at 315.
2 *Cummings* v. *Missouri*, 4 Wall. 277, 323 (U.S. 1866). It should be noted that this differs from the old English concept of attainder, under which a judgment of death was necessary to attaint and the consequences of attainder were forfeiture and corruption of blood. See Chitty, *Criminal Law* (1836 ed.), vol. 1, 724.
3 328 U.S. at 316, 318.

against bills of attainder. Unless there is a specific constitutional prohibition of this character which is contravened, the present court will not invalidate challenged legislation. It may be going too far to conclude from this, as one commentator did, that 'the scope of national authority has become a question of governmental policy, and has substantially ceased to be one of constitutional law'.[1] But the attitude of the court today with regard to its power to declare statutes unconstitutional certainly represents a drastic change from that of its predecessors. No longer can the Supreme Court be accused of exercising the functions of a super-legislature, which decides upon the desirability of legislation according to its own notions of reasonableness. If anything, the pendulum has swung to the opposite extreme. As expressed by a member of the present court, the determination of whether particular legislation is desirable is not for the court. 'A century and a half of constitutional history and government admonishes this Court to leave that choice to the elected legislative representatives of the people themselves, where it properly belongs both on democratic principles and the requirements of efficient government.'[2]

ARBITER OF FEDERAL SYSTEM

As a practical matter, then, the Federal Supreme Court has largely abandoned its role as controller of Congress. The reluctance to exercise the most striking feature of its jurisdiction does not, however, mean that the court does not still exercise important constitutional functions. With regard to certain of its functions, indeed—notably those involving the safeguarding of civil liberties—the post-1937 court has gone further than any of its predecessors in the direction of asserting its jurisdiction. Much of the court's work in this respect has involved a supervisory power over the action of State legislative and executive officials.

American constitutional law, as Lord Bryce pointed out, is complicated by the fact that 'the United States is a federation of commonwealths, each of which has its own constitution and laws. The Federal Constitution not only gives certain powers to Congress, as the national legislature, but recognizes certain powers in the States, in virtue whereof their respective peoples have enacted fundamental State laws (the State constitutions) and have enabled their respective legislatures to pass State statutes. However, as the nation takes precedence of the States, the Federal Constitution, which is the supreme law of the land everywhere, and the statutes duly made by

---

1 Dodd, 'The United States Supreme Court, 1936–1946', 41 *American Political Science Rev.* (1947), I, 9.
2 Black, J., dissenting, in *Southern Pacific Co.* v. *Arizona*, 325 U.S. 761, 789 (1945).

Congress under it, are preferred to all State constitutions and statutes; and if any conflict arises between them, the latter must give way.'[1] It is the Federal Supreme Court which determines whether there is such a conflict in particular cases. The importance of the court's role as arbiter of the federal system was well stated by Mr Justice Holmes: 'I do not think the United States would come to an end if we lost our power to declare an Act of Congress void. I do think the Union would be imperilled if we could not make that declaration as to the laws of the several states. For one in my place sees how often a local policy prevails with those who are not trained to national views and how often action is taken that embodies what the Commerce Clause was meant to end.'[2]

The cases involving the exercise of the court's function of striking a balance between national and State authority which have arisen before the present court have in the main involved claimed interferences by the States with interstate commerce. These have been of two kinds, those concerned with State taxes which were unduly burdensome upon interstate commerce and those dealing with State regulatory measures which hindered the free flow of commerce between the States. It should not be forgotten that one of the principal reasons for the growth and continued prosperity of American industry has been the existence of a continental market, unobstructed by local tariffs and customs regulations. The work of the court in this respect ensures that national commerce will continue free from crippling state interference. 'It is essential today, as at the time of the adoption of the Constitution, that commerce among the States and with foreign nations be left free from discriminatory and retaliatory burdens imposed by the States.'[3]

As an illustration of the Supreme Court's vital task of preserving interstate commerce from State obstructions, we can take *Southern Pacific Co. v. Arizona.*[4] That case involved an Arizona train-limit law which made it unlawful for any person or corporation to operate within the State a railroad train of more than fourteen passenger, or seventy freight, cars in length. This statute, said the court, 'imposes a serious burden on the interstate commerce conducted by appellant. It materially impedes the movement of appellant's interstate trains through that state and interposes a substantial obstruction to the national policy proclaimed by Congress to promote adequate, economical and efficient railway transportation service'.[5] It should be obvious that such State statutes would seriously

---

1 Bryce, *op. cit.* 248.
2 Quoted in Pritchett, *The Roosevelt Court* (1948), 82.
3 *Gwin, etc., Inc.* v. *Henneford*, 305 U.S. 434, 455 (1939).
4 325 U.S. 761 (1945).   5 *Ibid.* at 773.

impede interstate rail traffic, for the carrier might have to conform to 'a crazy-quilt of State laws'[1] which imposed different regulations in each State. 'Compliance with a state statute limiting train lengths requires interstate trains of a length lawful in other states to be broken up and reconstituted as they enter each state according as it may impose varying limitations upon train lengths. The alternative is for the carrier to conform to the lowest train limit restriction of any of the states through which its trains pass, whose laws thus control the carriers' operations both within and without the regulating state.'[2]

It is interesting to note that the doctrine of the *Southern Pacific Case* was applied the next year to a Virginia statute which required all motor-vehicle carriers, both interstate and intrastate, to separate the white and coloured passengers in their motor buses travelling in the State. 'It seems clear to us', said Mr Justice Reed, 'that seating arrangements for the different races in interstate motor travel require a single, uniform rule to promote and protect national travel. Consequently, we hold the Virginia statute in controversy invalid.'[3]

GUARDIAN OF CIVIL LIBERTIES

Cases like the *Southern Pacific Case* are illustrative of the American Supreme Court's function in holding State authority within the limits of the federal system. Of even more importance, perhaps, has been the court's role in the safeguarding of civil liberties. It is in its performance of this function more than in any other respect that the post-1937 court has differed from its predecessors. While most of the work of previous courts had concerned the protection of *property* rights as against what were conceived as legislative and executive violations of due process, in the present court the emphasis has shifted to *personal* rights. If, in 1921, a federal judge could assert 'that of the three fundamental principles which underlie government, and for which government exists, the protection of life, liberty, and property, the chief of these is property',[4] the judicial emphasis today has shifted in favour of the other two. Thus, the Supreme Court has stressed the 'preferred place given in our scheme' to the personal liberties protected by the Bill of Rights. 'That priority gives these liberties a sanctity and a sanction not permitting dubious intrusions.'[5]

1 Frankfurter, J., concurring, in *Morgan* v. *Virginia*, 328 U.S. 373, 388 (1946).
2 325 U.S. at 773.
3 *Morgan* v. *Virginia*, 328 U.S. 373, 386 (1946).
4 *Children's Hospital* v. *Adkins*, 284 Fed. 613, 622 (App. D.C. 1922).
5 *Thomas* v. *Collins*, 323 U.S. 516, 530 (1945). But compare Frankfurter, J., concurring, in *Kovacs* v. *Cooper*, 336 U.S. 77, 89 (1949). See Freund, *On Understanding the Supreme Court* (1949), 10–16.

The civil liberties cases which have been decided by the present court have generally involved the protection of the specific rights safeguarded in the Bill of Rights which are contained in the first eight amendments to the Federal Constitution. Those amendments prohibit Congress from making any laws respecting an establishment of religion, or prohibiting the free exercise thereof; or abridging freedom of speech or of the Press; or the right of the people peaceably to assemble, and to petition the Government for a redress of grievances. They prohibit violation of the right of the people to be secure in their persons, houses, papers and effects against unreasonable search and seizure. They preserve the right to be held to answer for an infamous crime only on indictment by a grand jury, prohibit double jeopardy for the same offence, and compulsory self-incrimination. They prevent deprivation of life, liberty or property without due process of law, and taking of private property for public use without just compensation. They give an accused the right to a speedy trial by an impartial jury in the district where the offence was committed, the right to be informed of the nature of the accusation, to be confronted with the witnesses against him, to have compulsory process for witnesses in his favour, and to have the assistance of counsel for his defence. Trial by jury is preserved in civil cases, and excessive bail or fine, or cruel and unusual punishments, are prohibited.[1]

It should be noted that the Bill of Rights contains limitations upon the Federal Government. After the Civil War, the Fourteenth and Fifteenth Amendments to the Constitution provided federal judicial protection for the citizen against his State Government as well. States were forbidden to 'abridge the privileges or immunities of citizens of the United States; nor shall any State deprive any person of life, liberty or property, without due process of law; nor deny to any person within its jurisdiction the equal protection of the laws.' Nor could the right of United States citizens to vote be denied or abridged on account of race, colour or previous condition of servitude.

From the point of view of the average American citizen, the danger of abridgment of his civil rights arises largely on the level of State or local government. That is why most of the cases involving infringement of those rights which have been brought before the federal courts have dealt with the action of State, rather than federal, legislative or executive officials. And that is why the interpretation by the Federal Supreme Court of the Fourteenth and Fifteenth Amendments, which limit the power of the States in this field, has been of such great practical importance.

A development worthy of note in understanding why the present

1 See Jackson, *op. cit.* 22.

Supreme Court has intervened in so many cases involving State abridgments of civil liberties has been its abandonment of the normal presumption of constitutionality of governmental action in personal liberty cases. Through the years, the Supreme Court has followed the rule that legislation which is challenged as to constitutionality must be presumed to be valid unless its violation of the organic instrument is proved beyond all reasonable doubt. 'In the last decade, however, the Court has announced a new doctrine that when a law appears to encroach upon a civil right—in particular, freedom of speech, press, religion, and assembly—the presumption is that the law is invalid, unless its advocates can show that the interference is justified because of the existence of a "clear and present danger" to the public security.' [1]

The protection of civil liberties by the American Supreme Court has been strengthened by its use of the so-called 'clear and present danger' test of Mr Justice Holmes. 'The question in every case', wrote Justice Holmes in a case involving freedom of speech, 'is whether the words used are used in such circumstances and are of such a nature as to create a clear and present danger that they will bring about the substantive evils that [the legislature] has a right to prevent.' [2] In the Supreme Court today, the Holmes doctrine is applied as the test in determining the validity of infringements upon civil liberties. Nor, as we shall see in Chapter x, has the constitutional position in this respect been changed by the pressures caused by the so-called 'cold war', even though they have, in practice, been held to validate important legislative restrictions upon civil liberties. 'Any attempt to restrict those liberties', stated the Supreme Court in 1945, 'must be justified by clear public interest, threatened not doubtfully or remotely, but by clear and present danger. The rational connection between the remedy provided and the evil to be curbed, which in other contexts might support legislation against attack on due process grounds, will not suffice. These rights rest on firmer foundation. Accordingly, whatever occasion would restrain orderly discussion and persuasion, at appropriate time and place, must have clear support in public danger, actual or impending. Only the gravest abuses, endangering paramount interests, give occasion for permissible limitation.' [3]

The solicitude of the American Supreme Court for civil liberties—at least in cases which do not involve seditious or subversive activities [4]—has resulted in a striking increase in the number of cases involving them

1 'To secure these Rights', *The Report of the President's Committee on Civil Rights* (1947), 113. See *Thomas* v. *Collins*, 323 U.S. 516, 530 (1945).
2 *Schenck* v. *United States*, 249 U.S. 47, 52 (1919). See *infra*, p. 248.
3 *Thomas* v. *Collins*, 323 U.S. 516, 530 (1945).
4 These cases are discussed in Chapter x.

which have been heard by that tribunal. Thus, in more than a score of cases since 1938, the court has dealt with charges that States or cities have violated the religious liberty of the sect known as Jehovah's Witnesses. In the majority of these cases, the Supreme Court held that the action complained of was invalid. The question of religion and its place under the American Constitution has, indeed, been a key one in a number of recent cases before the highest federal court. Among the important problems with which that tribunal has been concerned has been that of the extent to which the American organic instrument bars State aid for religious education. The First Amendment to the Federal Constitution provides that 'Congress shall make no law respecting an establishment of religion, or prohibiting the free exercise thereof'. Does this provision for religious disestablishment ordain a watertight division between Church and State, or may the latter assist and encourage religious education, provided there is no discrimination between denominations?

According to a case decided in 1948, the constitutional clause against the establishment of religion by law was intended to erect a wall of separation between Church and State.[1] 'Neither a state nor the Federal Government can set up a church. Neither can pass laws which aid one religion, aid all religions, or prefer one religion over another.'[2] And, in the case referred to, the Supreme Court held invalid an Illinois scheme under which religious instruction was given by representatives of the different denominations in State-operated schoolrooms during the regular hours set apart for secular teaching under the compulsory education law of the State. According to the court, this was a utilization of the tax-established and tax-supported State school system to aid religious groups to spread their faith, and hence it fell squarely within the ban of the First Amendment. On the other hand, in a more recent case, a New York scheme which permitted its schools to release students during the school days so that they might leave the school buildings and go to religious centres for religious instruction or devotional exercises was upheld, for here there was neither religious instruction in State school classrooms nor the expenditure of public funds.[3]

These cases on religion and its relation to the State have aroused a tremendous amount of controversy in the United States. 'Probably few opinions from this Court in recent years', stated Mr Justice Black, with regard to one of them, 'have attracted more attention or stirred wider debate.'[4] The controversy caused by these cases illustrates, as well as anything, the crucial role of the Supreme Court today in the field of civil

1 *Illinois ex rel. McCollum* v. *Board of Education*, 333 U.S. 203, 211 (1948).
2 *Ibid.* at 210.
3 *Zorach* v. *Clauson*, 343 U.S. 306 (1952).   4 *Ibid.* at 317.

rights and the practical impact of its decisions in that field. Equally important in that tribunal's jurisprudence in this field have been its recent decisions ameliorating the status of the negro, which will be dealt with in the next chapter, and those dealing with freedom of speech and of the Press. Of particular significance, in so far as the latter are concerned, is a 1952 decision holding that expression by means of motion pictures is included within the free speech and free Press guarantees of the Federal Constitution.[1] It may well be that, in certain fields, notably that of seditious and subversive activity, the present Supreme Court has not been as militant as some might have hoped. But the cases just discussed show that it is erroneous to think of that tribunal as anything but solicitous of American civil liberties. Indeed, as the President's Committee on Civil Rights concluded, 'It is not too much to say that during the last 10 years, the disposition of cases of this kind has been as important as any work performed by the Court. As an agency of the federal government, it is now actively engaged in the broad effort to safeguard civil rights.'[2]

CONCLUSION

What has been said above should indicate sufficiently how the role of the Federal Supreme Court in the American scheme of government has been changing in the past decade and a half. From an organ that had been mainly interested in safeguarding property rights and the preservation of a system of *laissez-faire*, it has become one that is primarily concerned with the personal rights guaranteed in the Bill of Rights. In addition, as we have seen, there is the vital work which the court performs as arbiter of the federal system.

A question that naturally arises relates to the permanence of the changes we have been discussing. More specifically: Is the change in role one that has been caused only by a change in its members, so that there may be another swing back to the pre-1937 view of the court's functions now that the Roosevelt-Truman Court is beginning to give way to one appointed by a more conservative President?[3]

It is believed that the change in the role of the Supreme Court is one that rests on something more permanent than the political beliefs of the Presidents who have appointed its judges. The changing jurisdiction of the Supreme Court reflects changes in legal ideology which are common

1 *Joseph Burstyn, Inc.*, v. *Wilson*, 343 U.S. 495 (1952).
2 *The Report of the President's Committee on Civil Rights* (1947), 113.
3 Thus far, there have been two appointments—those of Warren, C.J. and Harlan, J.—by President Eisenhower to the Supreme Court.

to the American legal profession as a whole. It must not be forgotten that the members of the pre-1937 court had been brought up under the influence of an extreme individualist philosophy, whose foundations have been severely shaken in the present century. Spencerian *laissez-faire* has given way on the bench to the judicial pragmatism of Mr Justice Holmes. It is not to be assumed that a new court will easily abandon the judicial self-restraint in cases other than those involving civil liberties which was Justice Holmes's principal tenet. If that is the case, the doctrine of judicial supremacy as it was applied by the pre-1937 court is now a thing of the past. The court's chief functions in the future will continue to be, as they are today, to hold the balance between national and State authority and to serve as the judicial guardian of the Bill of Rights.

Chapter IX

THE NEGRO AND THE LAW

An American travelling outside the United States cannot help but be struck
by the vast interest displayed in the position of the Negro in his country.
The reason for that interest is not hard to find. 'Our American heritage
of freedom and equality has given us prestige among the nations of the
world, and a strong feeling of national pride at home. There is much
reason for that pride. But pride is no substitute for steady and honest performance, and the record shows that at varying times in American history
the gulf between ideals and practice has been wide.'[1] To the foreigner, the
position of the Negro in the United States indicates that the American
ideal of freedom and equality for all men is still far from complete
realization.

For this gap between ideal and reality, American law must take a portion
of the blame. It is true that discrimination against the Negro in the United
States has roots deeper than the actions of legislatures and courts. Historical
causes reaching far back into North American origins have placed the
Negro race in the position of 'second-class' citizens. 'The Civil War gave
the Negro legal equality with his former masters, but it could not and did
not give him either the experience in the exercise of freedom or the moral
status in the sight of his white fellow citizens to make the freedom of the
Negro an acceptable and workable relationship for them.'[2] Discrimination against the Negro is still embedded in the customs of a large part of
the United States.

It is, however, inevitable that the law should play a pivotal role in a
country whose political and legal institutions are British in origin. This is
especially true under the American constitutional system, where the work
of the courts is of such significance. Discrimination against the Negro
could not have as great an effect without the condonation of the legal order.
The consent of the courts has been necessary for the subordinate status of
the Negro to become of more than extra-legal consequence.

That the American courts have condoned, if not encouraged, discriminatory practices should not be a source of surprise. It is not unusual for
law courts, like other organs of government, to mirror the dominant pre-

[1] 'To secure these Rights' *The Report of the President's Committee on Civil Rights*
(1947), 9.
[2] Tannenbaum, *Slave and Citizen* (1947), 111.

judices of their time. Even a tribunal as far removed from political pressure as the United States Supreme Court cannot help but be swayed by popular sentiment. As was aptly pointed out by Lord Bryce, 'The Supreme court feels the touch of public opinion.... Of course, whenever the law is clear, because the words of the Constitution are plain or the cases interpreting them decisive on the point raised, the court must look solely to those words and cases, and cannot permit any other consideration to affect its mind. But when the terms of the Constitution admit of more than one construction, and when previous decisions have left the true construction so far open that the point in question may be deemed new, is a court to be blamed if it prefers the construction which the bulk of the people deem suited to the needs of the time?'[1]

In so far as the legal position of the American Negro is concerned, the attitude of the federal Supreme Court has been of cardinal importance. Under the American constitutional system, it has been the court that has determined whether particular discriminatory practices have violated the Thirteenth, Fourteenth and Fifteenth Amendments to the Federal Constitution. Those amendments were adopted after the Civil War to guarantee to the emancipated Negro a full and equal status in American society. The Thirteenth Amendment prohibited slavery and involuntary servitude, except as a punishment for crime. 'But that amendment having been found inadequate to the protection of the rights of those who had been in slavery, it was followed by the Fourteenth Amendment, which added greatly to the dignity and glory of American citizenship, and to the security of personal liberty, by declaring that "all persons born or naturalized in the United States and subject to the jurisdiction thereof, are citizens of the United States and of the State wherein they reside", and that "no State shall make or enforce any law which shall abridge the privileges or immunities of citizens of the United States; nor shall any State deprive any person of life, liberty or property without due process of law, nor deny to any person within its jurisdiction the equal protection of the laws".'[2] Nor, under the Fifteenth Amendment, could the right of United States citizens to vote be denied or abridged on account of race, colour or previous condition of servitude.

These amendments, said Mr Justice Harlan, 'if enforced according to their true intent and meaning, will protect all the civil rights that pertain to freedom and citizenship.... Our Constitution is color-blind, and neither knows nor tolerates classes among citizens'.[3] Yet, as interpreted by

1 Bryce, *The American Commonwealth* (1917 ed.), vol. 1, 274.
2 Harlan, J., dissenting, in *Plessy* v. *Ferguson*, 163 U.S. 537, 555 (1896).
3 *Ibid.* at 555, 559.

the Supreme Court, it is clear that these amendments have not till now been adequate to place the American Negro on a footing of full legal equality with other citizens. The gulf between the letter of the amendments and their practical effect was well expressed by a dissenting member of the Supreme Court, in a case where the validity of a State segregation statute was at issue: 'We boast of the freedom enjoyed by our people above all other peoples. But it is difficult to reconcile that boast with a state of the law which, practically, puts the brand of servitude and degradation upon a large class of our fellow-citizens, our equals before the law.'[1]

A student of the work of the Supreme Court cannot, however, but observe that there has been a profound change in recent years in the attitude of that tribunal toward racial discrimination. 'Distinctions based on color and ancestry', asserted a member of the court during the last war, 'are utterly inconsistent with our traditions and ideals. They are at variance with the principles for which we are now waging war. We cannot close our eyes to the fact that for centuries the Old World has been torn by racial and religious conflicts and has suffered the worst kind of anguish because of inequality of treatment for different groups.'[2] It is, indeed, mostly in its positive approach to the problem of safeguarding the rights of minority groups that the Supreme Court today differs from its predecessors. The fundamental changes in the jurisprudence of the Supreme Court during the past decade and a half,[3] which were discussed in the last chapter, have profoundly affected the attitude of the court in cases involving racial discrimination. The approach of the present court in such cases was well stated by Mr Justice Black in 1944. 'It should be noted, to begin with, that all legal restrictions which curtail the civil rights of a single group are immediately suspect. That is not to say that all such restrictions are unconstitutional. It is to say that courts must subject them to the most rigid scrutiny. Pressing public necessity may sometimes justify the existences of such restrictions; racial antagonism never can.'[4]

The change in attitude of the Supreme Court toward the problem of racial discrimination has been reflected in an improvement of the legal position of the American Negro. That such improvement has in fact occurred will be seen from the remainder of this chapter, which will be devoted to a discussion of the present legal position, derived from recent Supreme Court decisions, with regard to three of the most important manifestations of discrimination against the Negro, i.e. restrictions upon

1 163 U.S. at 562.
2 Murphy, J., concurring, in *Hirabayashi* v. *United States*, 320 U.S. 81, 110 (1943).
3 See Friedmann, Book Review, 64 *L.Q.R.* (1948), 545, 547.
4 *Korematsu* v. *United States*, 323 U.S. 214, 216 (1944).

the right to vote, restrictions upon the use of land, and enforced segregation.

That legally condoned discrimination against the Negro exists in the United States is evident to most observers. What is, perhaps, not so apparent even to the informed British observer is the extent to which the legal position has been improving in recent years. It may be that one should not overemphasize the immediate practical consequences of Supreme Court decisions in a field such as this. At the same time, one should beware of minimizing their effect, especially from the prospective point of view. One of the things which has made anti-Negro discrimination in the United States of such moment is the fact that it has been sanctioned by the law. With the legal prop removed, the discrimination itself can more easily be eliminated.

SUFFRAGE

Ever since *Ashby* v. *White*,[1] it has been assumed that the right to vote is one of the primary attributes of citizenship. 'The right of voting...', asserted Lord Chief Justice Holt in that case, 'is a thing of the highest importance, and so great a privilege that it is a great injury to deprive the plaintiff of it. ...It is denying him his English right, and if this action be not allowed, a man may be for ever deprived of it. It is a great privilege to choose such persons, as are to bind a man's life and property by the laws they make.'[2]

As far as the American Negro is concerned, the suffrage question has been a key one, for, as a disfranchised minority, the Negro would have little hope of exerting political pressure to bring about an end to discriminatory practices. It was in recognition of the importance of the vote to the emancipated Negro that the Fifteenth Amendment to the Federal Constitution was adopted after the Civil War, prohibiting interferences with the right of United States citizens to vote because of their race, colour or previous condition of servitude. The constitutional amendment has not, however, of itself, automatically given the Negro the ballot. 'The Southern white people have always viewed the Fifteenth Amendment in much the same way in which patriotic Germans after the [First World War] regarded the harsher provisions of the Versailles Treaty. It was a form of compulsion imposed by victors upon the defeated.'[3] Accordingly, they have resorted to many devices to defeat the intent of the amendment. The Southern attitude is well illustrated in a remark made to Lord Bryce by a

1 (1703), 2 Ld. Raym. 938.
2 *Ibid.* at 953, 958.
3 Cushman, 'The Texas "white primary" case', 30 *Cornell L.Q.* (1944), 66.

leading Southern politician in 1881: 'We like the Negro, and we treat him well. We mean to continue doing so. But we vote him.'[1]

It seems clear that the Fifteenth Amendment automatically put an end to all State constitutional and statutory provisions expressly limiting the franchise at general elections to persons of the white race. 'Beyond question', declared the Supreme Court in 1880, 'the adoption of the Fifteenth Amendment had the effect, in law, to remove from the State Constitution, or render inoperative, that provision which restricts the right of suffrage to the white race.'[2] But the Southern States have sought to use methods other than those of such express constitutional or statutory discrimination to disfranchise the Negro. A typical case is *Guinn* v. *United States*,[3] where the validity of the so-called 'grandfather clause' of the Oklahoma Constitution was at issue. That portion of the State's organic law provided that anyone who could vote on 1 January 1866, or a descendant of such person, would be able to qualify as a permanent voter without submitting to certain educational tests. Since the date specified was at a time when the Negro could not legally vote, the effect of the provision was clearly to discriminate against the Negro. It was because of this that it was held invalid by the federal Supreme Court. 'It is true', said the court, 'it contains no express words of an exclusion from the standard which it establishes of any person on account of race, color, or previous condition of servitude prohibited by the Fifteenth Amendment, but the standard itself inherently brings that result into existence since it is based purely upon a period of time before the enactment of the Fifteenth Amendment and makes that period the controlling and dominant test of the right of suffrage.'[4] As explained by Mr Justice Frankfurter in a more recent decision, in so far as voting in a general election is concerned the 'Amendment nullifies sophisticated as well as simple-minded modes of discrimination. It hits onerous procedural requirements which effectively handicap exercise of the franchise by the colored race although the abstract right to vote may remain unrestricted as to race.'[5]

The prohibition of discrimination in voting in general elections has not, however, of itself, been enough to ensure the effective participation of the American Negro in the electoral process. As Lord Bryce pointed out, in discussing American elections, 'There are two stages in an election campaign. The first is to nominate the candidates you desire; the second to carry them at the polls. The first of these is often the more important,

1 Bryce, *The American Commonwealth* (1889 ed.), vol. 2, 279.
2 *Neal* v. *Delaware*, 103 U.S. 370, 389 (1880).
3 238 U.S. 347 (1915).   4 *Ibid.* at 364.
5 *Lane* v. *Wilson*, 307 U.S. 268, 275 (1939).

because in many [areas] the party majority inclines so decidedly one way..., that nomination is in the case of the dominant party equivalent to election.'[1] The best example of an area such as that referred to is the American South, which in the main has been a solid supporter of the Democratic party. In the South, for all practical purposes, to bar the Negro from participation in the nomination of Democratic candidates is effectively to preclude his participation in the electoral process.

Since the time when Lord Bryce wrote his study of American government, the so-called primary election has become the general method employed by political parties in the United States to nominate candidates for office. The primary election is held before the holding of a general election to enable the voters who are registered as members of a particular party to choose the candidates of that party whose names are to find a place on the ballot at the general election. A primary is thus a 'nominating' as distinguished from an 'electing' election.[2]

In recent years, efforts aimed at disfranchising the Southern Negro have made use of the so-called 'white primary', by which participation in the primary election of the Democratic party is limited to white citizens. Since the Democratic primary has been the only election of real significance in the Southern States, the device of the white primary has resulted in effective exclusion of the Negro from the process of government in those States. As expressed by the Federal Supreme Court, with regard to a primary election for a congressman in Louisiana, 'Interference with the right to vote in the Congressional primary in the Second Congressional District for the choice of Democratic candidate for Congress is thus, as a matter of law and in fact, an interference with the effective choice of the voters at the only stage of the election procedure when their choice is of significance, since it is at the only stage when such interference could have any practical effect on the ultimate result, the choice of the Congressman to represent the district.'[3]

Does discrimination against the Negro in primary elections come within the prohibition of the Fifteenth Amendment? The answer to this question depends upon whether State action is involved in such discrimination, for it is only such State action which is affected by the Fifteenth Amendment and that portion of the Fourteenth Amendment which guarantees to all persons the 'equal protection of the laws'.

In *Nixon* v. *Herndon*,[4] the court dealt with a Texas statute which provided that 'in no event shall a Negro be eligible to participate in a Demo-

1 Bryce, *op. cit.* 105.
2 *Strecker* v. *Smith*, 164 P. 2d 192, 193 (Idaho 1945).
3 *United States* v. *Classic*, 313 U.S. 299, 314 (1941).   4 273 U.S. 536 (1927).

cratic party primary election held in the State'. The discrimination against the Negro in this case was clearly caused by the action of the State legislature, and the statute was consequently held to violate the constitutional prohibition. 'The statute of Texas', reads the court's opinion, 'in the teeth of the prohibitions referred to assumes to forbid negroes to take part in a primary election the importance of which we have indicated, discriminating against them by the distinction of color alone.'[1]

Nothing daunted, the Texas legislature enacted a new statute which gave the State executive committee of a political party the power to prescribe the qualification of its members for voting or other participation. The State executive committee of the Democratic party then adopted a resolution that white Democrats and no others might participate in the primaries of that party. The Supreme Court held that this, too, transgressed the constitutional command, for whatever power of exclusion had been exercised by the members of the Democratic executive committee had come to them, 'not as the delegates of the party, but as the delegates of the State'.[2]

The decision in this case was based upon the theory that the Texas statute vested in the executive committee an authority independent of the will of the party as a whole, and that, therefore, its discriminatory acts amounted to State action within the constitutional prohibition. Three weeks after the decision of the court, a State convention of the Democratic party in Texas adopted a resolution to the effect that in the future only white citizens might vote in the party primaries. A Negro who had been refused a ballot in the Democratic primary brought an action for damages, and the case having been carried to the Supreme Court, that tribunal held in *Grovey* v. *Townsend*[3] that the convention resolution was not State action within the meaning of the Fourteenth and Fifteenth Amendments but was only the action of the political party in exercising its inherent right to determine its own policies and membership. The court thus held that the Democratic party was in a position similar to that of any ordinary voluntary association, with power to determine the qualifications of its own membership 'and that qualifications thus established are as far aloof from the impact of constitutional restraint as those for membership in a golf club or for admission to a Masonic lodge'.[4] Here the matter seemed to rest, and the Southern States appeared to have found a legally condoned method of precluding the Negro from effectively exercising his right to vote.

Yet it soon became clear that the constitutional guarantee of suffrage was an empty form if it did not extend to participation in primary elections.

1 273 U.S. at 541.   2 *Nixon* v. *Condon*, 286 U.S. 73, 85 (1932).
3 295 U.S. 45 (1935).
4 Cardozo, J., in *Nixon* v. *Condon*, 286 U.S. 73, 83 (1932).

'There is not the slightest doubt that the purpose of the "white primary" rule was to disfranchise the Negro.... There was something strangely anomalous and unrealistic about a result which, in spite of the Fourteenth and Fifteenth Amendments, left the one agency in the State of Texas which completely dominates the choice of State and federal officials just as free to bar Negroes from participation in that choice as though it were a Greek letter fraternity or an association of private business men.'[1]

The Federal Supreme Court itself recognized this in 1944, when it over-ruled *Grovey* v. *Townsend* in *Smith* v. *Allwright*,[2] which arose on similar facts. The court said in the *Smith Case* that, while the privilege of membership in a political party may be no concern of the State in certain circumstances, when that privilege is made a necessary qualification for voting in a primary to select candidates for a general election, the State makes the action of the party the action of the State. 'The United States', stated Mr Justice Reed, 'is a constitutional democracy. Its organic law grants to all citizens a right to participate in the choice of elected officials without restriction by any State because of race. This grant to the people of the opportunity for choice is not to be nullified by a State through casting its electoral process in a form which permits a private organization to practice racial discrimination in the election. Constitutional rights would be of little value if they could be thus indirectly denied.'[3] The Supreme Court has thus come over to the view that a primary election is a vital part of the machinery of government. 'It may now be taken as a postulate that the right to vote in such a primary for the nomination of candidates without discrimination by the State, like the right to vote in a general election, is a right secured by the Constitution.'[4]

Smith v. *Allwright* did not, of itself, definitively put an end to attempts on the part of the Southern States to disfranchise the Negro. But it seems clear that, ever since the Supreme Court in that case decided that the action of a State convention of the Democratic party in excluding Negroes from the primary election was State action within the constitutional prohibition against discrimination, the handwriting has been on the wall. The present situation in the American South has been described as follows: 'A few States continue to tinker with their primary systems with the forlorn hope of producing a sophisticated rather than simple-minded mode of discrimination;[5] others are relying on new forms of registration;[6] and an

---

1 Cushman, *loc. cit.* 67, 71.   2 321 U.S. 649 (1944).
3 *Ibid.* at 664.   4 *Ibid.* at 661.
5 That their hope is, indeed, a 'forlorn' one is shown by *Terry* v. *Adams*, 345 U.S. 461 (1953); *Perry* v. *Cyphers*, 186 F. 2d 608 (6th Cir. 1951); *Baskin* v. *Brown*, 174 F. 2d 391 (4th Cir. 1949); and *Rice* v. *Elmore*, 165 F. 2d 387 (4th Cir. 1947).
6 See *Davis* v. *Schnell*, 81 F. Supp. 872 (S.D. Ala. 1949), affirmed 336 U.S. 933 (1949).

increasing number, recognizing the essentials of democracy, are doing all in their power to follow the rules of the game.'[1] This does not mean that the full franchise for the Negro has become a complete practical reality throughout the South. In the past, as 'legal devices for disfranchising the Negro have been held unconstitutional, new methods have been improvised to take their places. Intimidation and the threat of intimidation have always loomed behind these legal devices to make sure that the desired result is achieved.'[2] Attempts at continuing disfranchisement are, as has been indicated, still being made. But *Smith* v. *Allwright* has at least forced abandonment of group disfranchisement of the Negro through the 'white primary' and has opened the door to gradual improvement of the political status of the Southern Negro by ensuring that attempts at disfranchisement will no longer be legally condoned.

RESTRICTIVE COVENANTS

The doctrine laid down by Lord Cottenham in *Tulk* v. *Moxhay*[3] has in America been employed as a means of restricting the use of real property by the Negro. 'That this court has jurisdiction to enforce a contract between the owner of land and his neighbour purchasing a part of it, that the latter shall either use or abstain from using the land purchased in a particular way, is what I never knew disputed', asserted the Lord Chancellor in the *Tulk Case*.[4] And he went on to hold that such covenant between vendor and purchaser, on the sale of land, that the purchaser and his assigns should use or abstain from using the land in a particular way, would be enforced in equity against all subsequent purchasers with notice, independently of the question whether it was one which ran with the land so as to be binding upon subsequent purchasers at law. 'That the question does not depend upon whether the covenant runs with the land is evident from this, that if there was a mere agreement and no covenant, this court would enforce it against a party purchasing with notice of it; for if an equity is attached to the property by the owner, no one purchasing with notice of that equity can stand in a different situation from the party from whom he purchased.'[5]

Under Lord Cottenham's doctrine, a court exercising equitable powers will enforce a restriction upon the use of land contained in a contract of sale both against the original covenantor and any subsequent holder of the land taking with notice of the restriction. There is nothing in the doctrine to prevent its employment as a means of restricting the use of real property

---

1　Bischoff, 'Civil rights', *Annual Survey of American Law* (1949), 148.
2　*Report of the President's Committee on Civil Rights*, 35.
3　(1848), 2 Ph. 774.
4　*Ibid.* at 777.　　　　　　　　　5　*Ibid.* at 778.

to members of a specific race, and, in the United States, restrictive covenants which have as their purpose the exclusion of persons of the Negro
race from the occupancy of real property have been widely used.

Attempts at restricting the use of land have, indeed, gone even further
in the Southern States. Thus, in *Buchanan* v. *Warley*,[1] there was in issue the
provisions of a municipal ordinance which denied to coloured persons the
right to occupy houses in blocks in which the greater number of houses
were occupied by white persons, and imposed similar restrictions on white
persons with respect to blocks in which the greater number of houses were
occupied by coloured persons. This type of direct restriction by State
authorities—which amounted to governmentally enforced segregation of
the races—was struck down by the Federal Supreme Court as violating
the equal protection clause of the Fourteenth Amendment. 'The Fourteenth
Amendment and these statutes enacted in furtherance of its purpose operate
to qualify and entitle a colored man to acquire property without state
legislation discriminating against him solely because of color.'[2]

But this did not dispose of the question of the use of restrictive covenants,
which under the doctrine of *Tulk* v. *Moxhay* create an equity in the land in
favour of the covenantee and his successors which will be enforced by the
courts against the covenantor and his successors. For, as the Supreme
Court has stated, 'the principle has become firmly embedded in our constitutional law that the action inhibited by the first section of the Fourteenth
Amendment is only such action as may fairly be said to be that of the
States. That Amendment erects no shield against merely private conduct,
however discriminatory or wrongful.'[3]

If restrictions against the use of real property by Negroes could be considered as involving merely the action of the individuals concerned, the
constitutional prohibition would not be violated. This was the approach
of the Supreme Court in *Corrigan* v. *Buckley*,[4] which was decided in 1926.
The constitutional prohibitions, said the court there, 'have reference to
State action exclusively, and not to any action of private individuals. . . .
It is State action of a particular character that is prohibited. Individual
invasion of individual rights is not the subject-matter of the Amendment.
. . . It is obvious that none of these Amendments prohibited private individuals from entering into contracts respecting the control and disposition
of their own property.'[5]

There is, however, an obvious weakness in the Supreme Court's holding
that such restrictions upon the use of land involve merely individual, not

1 245 U.S. 60 (1917).   2 *Ibid.* at 79.
3 *Shelley* v. *Kraemer*, 334 U.S. 1, 13 (1948).
4 271 U.S. 323 (1926).   5 *Ibid.* at 330.

State, action. It is true that the restrictive covenants themselves come into being through the voluntary action of private individuals. Yet they derive their force and effect primarily through the application of the doctrine of *Tulk* v. *Moxhay*, and that doctrine is applied and enforced by organs of the State—by the courts. The sanction behind restrictive covenants is the possibility of legal or injunctive relief if they are violated. The holding of the court in *Corrigan* v. *Buckley* ignores the fact that such covenants are enforced through State action.

This was seen by the American Supreme Court itself, in 1948, in *Shelley* v. *Kraemer*,[1] where the court held that the Fourteenth Amendment forbids the enforcement by State courts of restrictive covenants which have as their purpose the exclusion of persons of designated race or colour from the ownership or occupancy of real property. The petitioners there, who were Negroes, had acquired property in a tract subject to a covenant restricting use or occupancy to persons of the Caucasian race, and respondents, as owners of property subject to the terms of the restrictive agreements, brought suit for injunctive relief in the appropriate State courts.

The opinion of the court in the *Shelley Case* differs from that which had been rendered in *Corrigan* v. *Buckley*, in the court's recognition that these cases involve more than the action of merely private individuals. The action of a State court of equity in enforcing a restrictive covenant, said Mr Chief Justice Vinson, is clearly to be regarded as action of the State within the meaning of the Fourteenth Amendment. 'It has been the consistent ruling of this court that the action of the States to which the Amendment has reference includes action of state courts and state judicial officials.'[2] Under *Buchanan* v. *Warley*, which has been discussed above, restrictions of the sort involved here 'could not be squared with the requirements of the Fourteenth Amendment if imposed by state statute or local ordinance.'[3] Since enforcement by the courts is treated as State action in the same sense in which a statute is, 'We hold that in granting judicial enforcement of the restrictive agreements in these cases, the States have denied petitioners the equal protection of the laws and that, therefore, the action of the state courts cannot stand'.[4]

Shelley v. *Kraemer* has dealt a death blow to the application of the doctrine of *Tulk* v. *Moxhay* by American courts in cases involving racial restrictive covenants. It is true that Chief Justice Vinson was careful not to rule upon the validity of the restrictive covenants themselves. The American court did not go as far as did the Ontario High Court in holding such covenants void as against public policy. 'If the common law of

---

1 334 U.S. 1 (1948).   2 *Ibid.* at 18.
3 *Ibid.* at 11.   4 *Ibid.* at 20.

treason encompasses the stirring up of hatred between different classes of His Majesty's subjects', asserted Mackay, J., speaking for that court, 'the common law of public policy is surely adequate to void the restrictive covenant which is here attacked.'[1] Chief Justice Vinson, on the contrary, implied that the covenants themselves were not invalid. 'So long as the purposes of those agreements are effectuated by voluntary adherence to their terms, it would appear clear that there has been no action by the State and the provisions of the Amendment have not been violated.'[2]

But, in denying the possibility of judicial enforcement, the court has surely removed the 'teeth' from such restrictive covenants and has taken a most important step toward a breakdown of racial restrictions upon the use of property. At least in so far as the use of land is concerned, *Shelley* v. *Kraemer* indicates that equal protection of the laws will be more than a mere slogan for the American Negro.

Today, indeed, there is more even than the constitutional guaranty which is violated by the enforcement of restrictive covenants. Such enforcement would seem to be an obstacle to the free accomplishment of American policy in the international field. For, as a member of the Supreme Court has expressed it, 'we have recently pledged ourselves to co-operate with the United Nations to "promote. . . universal respect for, and observance of, human rights and fundamental freedoms for all without distinction as to race, sex, language, or religion". How can this nation be faithful to this international pledge if [covenants] which bar land owner-ship and occupancy. . . on account of race are permitted to be enforced?'[3]

SEGREGATION

'Legally enforced segregation has been followed throughout the South since the close of the Reconstruction era. In these States it is generally illegal for Negroes to attend the same schools as whites; attend theatres patronized by whites; visit parks where whites relax; eat, sleep or meet in hotels, restaurants or public halls frequented by whites. This is only a partial enumeration—legally imposed separation of races has become highly refined. In the eyes of the law, it is also an offence for whites to attend "Negro" schools and similar places. The result has been the familiar system

1 *Re Drummond Wren*, [1945] 4 D.L.R. 674, 679. But compare *Re Noble and Wolfe*, [1948] 4 D.L.R. 123, 139.
2 334 U.S. at 13. Under the more recent case of *Barrows* v. *Jackson*, 346 U.S. 249 (1953), a court may not award damages for breach of a racial restrictive covenant, such judicial action also being treated as State action forbidden by the Fourteenth Amendment.
3 Black, J., concurring, in *Oyama* v. *California*, 332 U.S. 633, 649 (1948).

of racial segregation in both public and private institutions which cuts across the daily lives of Southern citizens from the cradle to the grave.'[1]

Perhaps the best-known examples of laws providing for such segregation have been the so-called 'Jim Crow' laws, which have made it unlawful for any common carrier to transport white and coloured passengers in the same vehicle or the same portion thereof. The result of these laws has been the enforced separation of the races in public conveyances which has become prevalent in the Southern States.

The Fourteenth Amendment to the United States Constitution, as we have seen, forbids a State to deny to any person within its jurisdiction 'the equal protection of the laws'. How can these 'Jim Crow' laws be considered consistent with the constitutional guaranty of equality of legal status?

Before 1954, the American Supreme Court answered this question by asserting that segregation, as such, was not discriminatory. The leading case was *Plessy* v. *Ferguson*,[2] where it was claimed that a Louisiana statute requiring separate railroad accommodations for Negro and white passengers denied equal protection of the laws. Mr Justice Brown, speaking for the court, in upholding the Act, rejected 'the assumption that the enforced separation of the two races stamps the colored race with a badge of inferiority. If this be so, it is not by reason of anything found in the act, but solely because the colored race chooses to put that construction upon it.'[3] Or, to express it another way, 'Laws permitting, and even requiring, their separation in places where they are liable to be brought into contact do not necessarily imply the inferiority of either race to the other'.[4] So long as laws requiring segregation did not establish unequal facilities for the Negro, the court's doctrine held, there was no unreasonable discrimination and therefore no denial of equal protection under the law.

There was a vigorous dissent by Mr Justice Harlan, which has been characterized as 'one of the most vigorous and forthright dissenting opinions in Supreme Court history'.[5] In his opinion, he attacked the very basis of the court's decision, i.e. that segregation alone was not discriminatory. 'It was said in argument that the statute of Louisiana does not discriminate against either race, but prescribes a rule applicable alike to white and colored citizens. But this argument does not meet the difficulty. Everyone knows that the statute in question had its origin in the purpose, not so much to exclude white persons from railroad cars occupied by

1 *Report of the President's Committee on Civil Rights*, 79.
2 163 U.S. 537 (1896).
3 *Ibid.* at 551.   4 *Ibid.* at 544.
5 *Report of the President's Committee on Civil Rights*, 81.

blacks, as to exclude colored people from coaches occupied by, or assigned to, white persons.... The arbitrary separation of citizens, on the basis of race, while they are on the public highway, is a badge of servitude, wholly inconsistent with the civil freedom and the equality before the law established by the Constitution.... The thin disguise of "equal" accommodations for passengers in railroad coaches will not mislead anyone, nor atone for the wrong this day done.'¹

To the present-day observer, who has, of course, the advantages of half a century of retrospect, it would seem that the merits of the case are all with Justice Harlan's dissent. Segregation, such as was legally condoned by the Supreme Court in the *Plessy Case*, has been the cornerstone of the structure of discrimination against the American Negro.² And the court's assertion that segregation of itself does not mean discrimination appears manifestly unsound. 'The core of Mr Justice Brown's argument is in his assumption that segregation is not a white judgment of colored inferiority. This would be so palpably preposterous as a statement of fact that we must assume Mr Justice Brown intended it as a legal fiction. The device of holding a despised people separate, whether by confinement of the Jew to the ghetto; by exclusion of the lowest caste in India from the temple; or by the slightly more refined separate [accommodations], is clearly expression of a judgment of inferiority.'³

From 1896, when it was first enunciated, to 1954, the doctrine of *Plessy* v. *Ferguson* was consistently adhered to by the highest American court. The fact that the federal Supreme Court did not during that period go so far as to overrule the *Plessy* decision did not, however, mean that it was not able to take important steps toward improving the legal position of the Negro within the limits of that case. It will be recalled that, in *Plessy* v. *Ferguson*, the court held that segregation of the races did not violate any constitutional prohibition where the laws requiring segregation did not establish unequal facilities. But implicit in this holding was the rule that legally enforced segregation was valid only if the separate facilities provided for the Negro were substantially equal to those provided for members of the white race. In actual practice, the American Negro has received far from equal treatment so far as the separate facilities provided for him have been concerned. Strict enforcement of the requirement of equality in facilities could consequently make for a substantial improvement in the status of the Negro even if segregation as such were still constitutionally condoned.

1 163 U.S. at 556, 562.   2 *Report of the President's Committee on Civil Rights*, 81.
3 'Segregation and the equal protection clause', 34 *Minnesota L. Rev.* (1950), 289, 305.

The American Supreme Court in recent years has placed ever-increasing emphasis upon judicial implementation of the requirement of equality in facilities. Its decisions have been aimed at ensuring that the separate facilities provided for Negroes have in fact been substantially equal to those afforded to the white race. Perhaps the best cases to illustrate this are those dealing with educational opportunities, where the inferior position of the Negro in the past has been clearly manifest. The status of the Negro with regard to education—especially in the field of higher education—has been of cardinal significance. This has been recognized by the Supreme Court in cases involving claims of inequality in educational facilities. 'Our society grows increasingly complex,' stated the court in 1950, 'and our need for trained leaders increases correspondingly. Appellant's case represents, perhaps, the epitome of that need, for he is attempting to obtain an advanced degree in education, to become, by definition, a leader and trainer of others. Those who will come under his guidance and influence must be directly affected by the education he receives. Their own education and development will necessarily suffer to the extent that his training is unequal to that of his classmates.'[1]

Nor has the Supreme Court, in dealing with assertions of inequality in educational facilities, been bound by formal attempts to comply with the requirement of equality. In a case decided in 1948, the court had held that Negro applicants for a course in legal education must be admitted to the law schools which had heretofore been reserved to the white race unless equivalent facilities were provided for them.[2] In the State of Texas, a separate law school for Negroes was, indeed, opened. A first-rate law school cannot, however, come into being full-grown, like Minerva from the head of Jove. The facilities afforded by the newly opened law school for Negroes could not, in actual fact, equal those which were available to white students at the University of Texas.

That the Negro seeking a legal education in Texas was still in reality in a position of inequality, despite the compliance in form with the constitutional requirement, was the basis of the 1950 decision of the Supreme Court in *Sweatt* v. *Painter*.[3] Comparing the facilities offered by the new law school for Negroes with those available to white students at the University of Texas, Chief Justice Vinson asserted that 'we cannot find substantial equality in the educational opportunities offered white and Negro law students by the State. In terms of number of the faculty, variety of courses and opportunity for specialization, size of the student

---

1 *McLaurin* v. *Oklahoma State Regents*, 339 U.S. 637, 641 (1950).
2 *Sipuel* v. *Board of Regents*, 332 U.S. 631 (1948).
3 339 U.S. 629 (1950).

body, scope of the library, availability of law review and similar activities, the University of Texas Law School is superior. What is more important, the University of Texas Law School possesses to a far greater degree those qualities which are incapable of objective measurement but which make for greatness in a law school. Such qualities, to name but a few, include reputation of the faculty, experience of the administration, position and influence of the alumni, standing in the community, traditions and prestige. It is difficult to believe that one who had a free choice between these law schools would consider the question close.'[1] Under these circumstances, petitioner in the *Sweatt Case* had been denied a legal education equivalent to that offered to students of other races. 'We hold that the Equal Protection Clause of the Fourteenth Amendment requires that petitioner be admitted to the University of Texas Law School.'[2]

In the *Sweatt Case*, the Supreme Court was able to hold for petitioner without reaching his 'contention that *Plessy* v. *Ferguson* should be re-examined in the light of contemporary knowledge respecting the purposes of the Fourteenth Amendment and the effects of racial segregation'.[3] The court's decision did, however, come very close to holding that segregation as such, at least in the field of higher education, was contrary to the Constitution. In view of the court's reasoning, it is difficult to see how, in that field, segregated facilities for the Negro can ever come up to the demands of equality. What was said in the *Sweatt Case* of the University of Texas Law School applies with equal force to all long-established white educational institutions. Though the doctrine of *Plessy* v. *Ferguson*[4] has permitted segregation, provided the requirement of equality in facilities was met, the court's approach in *Sweatt* v. *Painter* means, in practice, that that requirement can never be met in the field of higher education.

But what is true of segregation in higher education is, in reality, also true of segregation as such. There can never be real equality in separated facilities, for the mere fact of segregation makes for discrimination. The arbitrary separation of the Negro, solely on the basis of race, is a 'badge of servitude'[5] and must generate in him a feeling of inferior social status, regardless of the formal equality of the facilities provided for him.

That the American Supreme Court itself has come to realize that segregation as such is discriminatory and hence a denial of the equal protection of the laws demanded by the Constitution is shown by its 1954 decision in *Brown* v. *Board of Education*.[6] Petitioners there, minors of the Negro race,

1 *Ibid.* at 633.   2 *Ibid.* at 636.
3 *Ibid.*   4 *Supra*, p. 234.
5 The term used by Harlan, J., dissenting, in *Plessy* v. *Ferguson*, 163 U.S. at 562.
6 347 U.S. 483 (1954).

through their legal representatives, sought the aid of the federal courts in obtaining admission to the public schools[1] of their community on a non-segregated basis. They had been denied admission to schools attended by white children under laws requiring segregation according to race. What made this case of such importance was the fact that the lower courts had found expressly that the Negro and white schools involved were equalized, or were being equalized, with respect to buildings, curricula, qualifications and salaries of teachers, and other 'tangible' factors. Because of these findings, the lower courts had denied relief on the doctrine of *Plessy* v. *Ferguson*. 'Under that doctrine, equality of treatment is accorded when the races are provided substantially equal facilities even though these facilities be separate.'[2] In the Supreme Court, petitioners argued that, even if the findings below were correct, they should be given judgment, contending that '"segregated" public schools are not "equal" and cannot be made "equal" and that, hence, they are deprived of the equal protection of the laws'.[3] Petitioners' argument was based upon the claim that segregation as such was inherently discriminatory and consequently contrary to the constitutional command of equality. In effect, they were asking the court to overrule *Plessy* v. *Ferguson*, which, as we have seen, had held the other way.

Few cases decided by it have been more carefully considered by the highest American court than *Brown* v. *Board of Education*. The case was first argued before the court in December 1952. Desiring further clarification before reaching a decision, the court ordered rearguments in 1953, and the case was argued for the second time in December of that year. It was not until May 1954, almost two years after the case first came to it, that the Supreme Bench announced its decision.

For a unanimous court, Mr Chief Justice Warren proclaimed that the segregation of petitioners violated the constitutional guaranty of equality. 'Does segregation of children in public schools solely on the basis of race, even though the physical facilities and other "tangible" factors may be equal, deprive the children of the minority group of equal educational opportunities? We believe that it does.'[4] The mere fact of segregation, according to the opinion, discriminates against petitioners. 'To separate them from others of similar age and qualifications solely because of their race generates a feeling of inferiority as to their status in the community that may affect their hearts and minds in a way unlikely ever to be undone.'[5]

1 It should be borne in mind that, in the United States, the term 'public schools' is used to designate the free elementary and secondary schools maintained by local governmental authorities.

2 *Brown* v. *Board of Education*, 347 U.S. at 488.

3 *Ibid.*   4 *Ibid.* at 493.   5 *Ibid.* at 494.

The finding of the court that segregation as such is discriminatory is, as its opinion recognizes, contrary to *Plessy* v. *Ferguson*. 'Whatever may have been the extent of psychological knowledge at the time of *Plessy* v. *Ferguson*, this finding is amply supported by modern authority. Any language in *Plessy* v. *Ferguson* contrary to this finding is rejected.'[1] The doctrine of the *Plessy Case*, under which separate but equal facilities were held valid, was thus overruled. 'We conclude that in the field of public education the doctrine of "separate but equal" has no place. Separate educational facilities are inherently unequal.'[2]

It is true that the decision in the *Brown Case* applies directly only to cases involving public education. It is, however, difficult to see why it should be limited to that field. On the contrary, the court's reasoning and its unequivocal rejection of the doctrine of *Plessy* v. *Ferguson* should directly apply to all forms of segregation. If that is true, *Brown* v. *Board of Education* is indeed a landmark decision. It will mean the end of legally enforced segregation in the United States—an institution which, more than anything else, has prevented the American Negro from attaining a status of full equality.

It can, of course, be asserted that decisions such as that in *Brown* v. *Board of Education* are in reality of little practical effect, for they do not reach the heart of the problem, the feelings of racial prejudice which still exist in the Southern American States. 'It may be argued that appellant will be in no better position when these restrictions are removed, for he may still be set apart by his fellow students.'[3] Yet, though the removal of the legal condonation of segregation will not necessarily abate individual and group predilections and prejudices, it cannot be denied that there is a vast difference between restrictions imposed by the State which prohibit the commingling of Negroes and members of the white race and the refusal of individuals to commingle where the State presents no bar.[4] It has been the fact that segregation has had behind it the force of the law that has made it of such moment to the American Negro. It is because it eliminates the legal sanction that the decision of the Supreme Court in the *Brown Case* is so important. Without the support of the law, segregation itself can hardly continue to be of such widespread consequence in the United States.

1 *Ibid.*   2 *Ibid.* at 495.
3 *McLaurin* v. *Oklahoma State Regents*, 339 U.S. 637, 641 (1950).
4 Paraphrasing *ibid.*

Chapter X

CIVIL LIBERTIES AND THE 'COLD WAR'

Security and liberty, in their pure form, are antagonistic poles. The one pole represents the interest of politically organized society in its own self-preservation. The other represents the interest of the individual in being afforded the maximum right of self-assertion, free from governmental and other interference.[1] Neither can be given the absolute protection, to the exclusion of the other, which its devotees desire. 'Absolute rules would inevitably lead to absolute exceptions, and such exceptions would eventually corrode the rules.'[2]

Both security and liberty are essential elements in the functioning of any polity, and their co-existence must somehow be reconciled. The right of a government to maintain its existence—self-preservation—has been characterized as the most pervasive aspect of sovereignty.[3] 'To preserve its independence, and give security against foreign aggression and encroachment, is the highest duty of every nation,' declared the United States Supreme Court in 1889, 'and to attain these ends nearly all other considerations are to be subordinated.'[4] But, as a member of that tribunal has more recently pointed out, even the all-embracing power and duty of self-preservation is not absolute.[5] The problem is more one of striking a proper balance between the claims of both liberty and security than of seeking wholly to vindicate the one or the other. 'The demands of [liberty] in a democratic society as well as the interest in national security are better served by candid and informed weighing of the competing interests... than by announcing dogmas too inflexible for the non-Euclidean problems to be solved.'[6]

In their balancing of security and liberty, it cannot be denied that the Founders of the American Republic gave a preferred position to the latter. 'The American Bills of Rights', an outstanding student of comparative constitutional law informs us, 'drew up the inventory—since become classic, of modern liberties.'[7] The Bill of Rights of the Federal Constitution

1 Compare Bodenheimer, *Jurisprudence* (1940), 28.
2 Frankfurter, J., in *Dennis* v. *United States*, 341 U.S. 494, 524 (1951).
3 *Ibid.* at 519.
4 *Chinese Exclusion Case*, 130 U.S. 581, 606 (1889).
5 Frankfurter, J., in *Dennis* v. *United States*, 341 U.S. 494, 520 (1951).
6 *Ibid.* at 524.
7 Mirkine-Guetzévitch, *Les Constitutions européennes* (1951), 127.

is contained in the first eight amendments to that instrument, which were adopted almost immediately after the Constitution went into effect, in order to meet widespread popular criticism resulting from the absence of such specific safeguards in the original organic instrument. Of the guarantees afforded by the Federal Bill of Rights, none is more important than those contained in the First Amendment to the Constitution. It categorically provides that 'Congress shall make no law respecting an establishment of religion, or prohibiting the free exercise thereof; or abridging the freedom of speech, or of the press; or the right of the people peaceably to assemble, and to petition the Government for a redress of grievances.'

The limitation in favour of freedom of speech imposed upon the Federal Government by the First Amendment is one which has always been regarded as fundamental by American constitutional lawyers. 'Full and free discussion', Mr Justice Douglas has eloquently stated, 'has indeed been the first article of our faith. We have founded our political system on it. It has been the safeguard of every religious, political, philosophical, economic, and racial group amongst us. We have counted on it to keep us from embracing what is cheap and false; we have trusted the common sense of our people to choose the doctrine true to our genius and to reject the rest. This has been the one single outstanding tenet that has made our institutions the symbol of freedom and equality. We have deemed it more costly to liberty to suppress a despised minority than to let them vent their spleen. We have above all else feared the political censor. We have wanted a land where our people can be exposed to all the diverse creeds and cultures of the world.'[1]

'Whoever travels in the United States', wrote de Tocqueville over a century ago, 'is involuntarily and instinctively so impressed with the fact that the spirit of liberty and the taste for it have so pervaded all the habits of the American people, that he cannot conceive of them under any but a Republican government.'[2] It has, however, become a commonplace that the freedoms guaranteed by the Federal Bill of Rights have been becoming more restricted in recent years than they have been since almost the founding of the American Republic. 'It is still not too late', asserts an English commentary, 'for Americans to stop the drift towards totalitarian conformity and to restore decent standards of controversy.'[3] This characterization of the contemporary American scene is doubtless extreme; still, it cannot be denied that, since the end of the last war, the response of the Federal

1 *Dennis v. United States*, 341 U.S. 494, 584 (1951).
2 Quoted in Dicey, *Law of the Constitution* (9th ed. 1939), 186.
3 *New Statesman and Nation*, 28 March 1953, p. 359.

Government to the threat posed by the expansion of world communism has included some suppression of the liberties safeguarded by the Bill of Rights.

How can such suppression of civil liberties be reconciled with the unqualified demands of the Bill of Rights, and especially those of the First Amendment? That is perhaps the most difficult question which the American Supreme Court has been called upon to answer during the past decade. The validity of the restrictions upon civil liberties caused by the 'cold war' is, like other matters in the American constitutional system, ultimately a judicial question. 'Scarcely any political question arises in the United States', Mr Justice Frankfurter, quoting from de Tocqueville tells us, 'that is not resolved, sooner or later, into a judicial question. And so it was to be expected that conflict of political ideas now dividing the world more pervasively than any since this nation was founded would give rise to controversies for adjudication by this Court.'[1]

To the student of comparative constitutional law, the attempt made by the highest American tribunal to reconcile the rights guaranteed by the Bill of Rights with the legislative demand for security articulated in recent restrictive legislation is of primary significance. It indicates that the safeguards of the federal organic instrument are far from the unqualified absolutes which their categorical language implies. 'Just as there are those who regard as invulnerable every measure for which the claim of national survival is invoked, there are those who find in the Constitution a wholly unfettered right of expression. Such literalness treats the words of the Constitution as though they were found on a piece of outworn parchment instead of being words that have called into being a nation with a past to be preserved for the future. The soil in which the Bill of Rights grew was not a soil of arid pedantry. The historic antecedents of the First Amendment preclude the notion that its purpose was to give unqualified immunity to every expression that touched on matters within the range of political interest.'[2]

ANTI-SEDITION LAWS

Activity deemed to be seditious or subversive has given the American Congress sporadic concern almost from the founding of the Republic. Apart, however, from the enactment of laws defining such specific offences as treason, espionage, sabotage, and conspiracy, this concern has largely been limited to the present century. The one important example of an earlier interest occurred in 1798 when Congress, confronted with the

---

1 *American Communications Assn.* v. *Douds*, 339 U.S. 382, 415 (1950).
2 Frankfurter, J., in *Dennis* v. *United States*, 341 U.S. 494, 521 (1951).

threat of a war with France, and badly frightened by the seeming spread of the doctrines of the French Revolution—facts that have a familiar sound today—enacted the now notorious Alien and Sedition Laws.[1] The Alien Law allowed the President to compel the departure of aliens whom he considered dangerous or suspected of treasonable or secret machinations against the Government. The Sedition Law criminally punished those publishing false, scandalous, or defamatory writings with an intent to discredit the Government, the President, or the Congress, or to excite the hatred of the people against them, or to stir up sedition, to excite resistance to law, or to aid any hostile designs of any foreign nation against the United States. Persons convicted under this Act could be fined up to $2000 and imprisoned for a maximum of two years.[2]

In the year or two after its adoption, the Sedition Law was vigorously enforced by the Federalist party then in power.[3] The lengths to which such enforcement went are well shown by cases like the following: 'A New Jersey editor...was fined $100 for hoping in print that the wad of a cannon fired in a presidential salute might hit President Adams on the seat of the pants. A Vermont Jeffersonian, who accused the President of "unbounded thirst for ridiculous pomp, foolish adulations, and a selfish avarice", received a thousand dollar fine and four months in jail.'[4] The Sedition Law was bitterly resented by most Americans as an unwarranted invasion of freedom of speech and of the Press. Its constitutionality was strongly assailed by Thomas Jefferson, who pardoned all persons imprisoned under it when he became President in 1800. Congress eventually ordered all fines to be repaid, and the law itself was permitted to expire in 1801, though, in the words of Mr Justice Story, 'it has continued, down to this very day, to be a theme of reproach'.[5]

More than a century passed before the Congress again attempted to curb sedition by placing statutory restrictions upon freedom of speech and Press. During that time, those rights became firmly ingrained in the American system. Then, in 1917 and 1918, after the entry of the United States into the First World War, Congress, in the so-called Espionage and Sedition Acts, rendered criminal such activities as wilfully making or conveying false statements with intent to interfere with the success of the American war effort or to promote the success of its enemies, wilfully obstructing the recruitment of military personnel or attempting to cause the disloyalty of such personnel, saying or doing anything with intent to

1 Carr, *The House Committee on Un-American Activities* (1952), 8–9.
2 Chafee, *Free Speech in the United States* (1948), 27.
3 See Swisher, *American Constitutional Development* (2nd ed. 1954), 94–7.
4 Schlesinger, *The Vital Center* (1949), 193, quoted in Carr, *op. cit.* 9.
5 Story, *Commentaries on the Constitution of the United States* (1833), §1886.

obstruct the sale of government bonds, uttering or writing any disloyal, profane, scurrilous or abusive language to cause contempt, scorn, contumely, or disrepute in regard to the form of government of the United States, the flag, or the uniform of the army or navy, or urging the curtailment of production of anything necessary to the prosecution of the war.[1]

These laws of 1917 and 1918 constituted the first important legislative restrictions of the right of free discussion in the United States since the Alien and Sedition Laws. 'Never in the history of our country', states the leading American treatise on the subject, 'since the Alien and Sedition Laws of 1798, has the meaning of free speech been the subject of such sharp controversy as during the years since 1917.'[2] It may well be, as a former Attorney-General of the United States has conceded, that 'On its face, the Espionage Act of 1917, under which most of the war cases were tried, does not seem objectionable. *Willfully* false reports with *intent* to interfere with the operation of the war, *willful* attempts to cause insubordination or disloyalty, *willful* obstruction to recruitment or enlistment were punishable.'[3] It should, however, be noted that what was made punishable under it and the Act of 1918 was not only *action* interfering with the war effort, but also speech or writing made with that end in view. Emphasis in the laws was as much on exhortation as upon action. In this respect, they constituted, as had the Alien and Sedition Laws of 1798 before them, a legislative revival of the common-law crime of sedition, which has been thought by most Americans to be incompatible with the rights guaranteed by the Federal Bill of Rights. 'One of the objects of the Revolution', asserts one author, 'was to get rid of the English common law on liberty of speech and of the press.... Liberty of the press as declared in the First Amendment, and the English common-law crime of sedition cannot co-exist.'[4]

A member of Parliament visiting the United States writes, with regard to the Second World War and post-war restrictions on freedom of discussion there, 'Some older American Socialists with whom I discussed this are inclined to be philosophical. They remember the wave of intolerance that swept America for a time after the first war, and believe this too will blow itself out in due course.'[5] One who is familiar with the cases under the Espionage and Sedition Acts of 1917 and 1918 cannot help but feel that the characterization of the movement which produced them as a 'wave of intolerance' is not unduly extreme. About two thousand prosecutions were brought under the 1917 law alone,[6] and many of them seem as

---

1 Chafee, *op. cit.* 3.   2 Carr, *op. cit.* 9–10.
3 Biddle, *The Fear of Freedom* (1951), 58.
4 Schofield, quoted in Chafee, *op. cit.* 20.
5 Callaghan, *New Statesman and Nation*, 4 April 1953, p. 389.
6 Biddle, *op. cit.* 58.

ridiculous today as the standing of a tanner in the pillory during Queen Anne's reign because of his remark that Charles I had been rightly served in having his head cut off.[1] The cases under the American Espionage Act of 1917 have been summarized as follows: 'It became criminal to advocate heavier taxation instead of bond issues, to state that conscription was unconstitutional though the Supreme Court had not yet held it valid, to say that the sinking of merchant vessels was legal, to say that a referendum should have preceded our declaration of war, to say that war was contrary to the teachings of Christ. Men have been punished for criticizing the Red Cross and the Y.M.C.A., while under the Minnesota Espionage Act it has been held a crime to discourage women from knitting by the remark, "No soldier ever sees these socks".'[2]

Certainly, the American experience during and after the First World War was, in many ways, at least as extreme as anything that has occurred since the recent conflict. It can, of course, be argued that the transitory nature of the earlier experience need not necessarily be repeated. 'Whether the current phenomenon is of the same essentially ephemeral sort, no one can know, just as no one at the bottom of an economic cycle knows for sure that prosperity will ever come around the corner.'[3] Those familiar with the United States and the cyclical nature of its political, as of its economic, history are, however, not unwarranted in hoping that the present American atmosphere will give way to a calmer one, in which 'cold war' pressures, passions, and fears will subside. 'Reading what everybody now agrees about the panic-stricken alarmists of 1920,' states an outstanding American advocate of freedom of speech, 'I wonder what will be said thirty years from now about the alarmists of 1952.'[4]

SMITH ACT OF 1940

Some twenty years after the close of the First World War, the threat, and then the reality, of a new conflict led the Federal Congress once more to turn its attention to the danger of seditious and subversive activity. In June 1940, over a year before the United States entered the war, it passed the first peace-time Sedition Act since the Sedition Law of 1798.[5] This was the so-called Alien Registration Act, usually known as the Smith Act, after its sponsor in the House of Representatives. The official title of this law is wholly misleading. 'Its official title', writes Professor Chafee,

1 Chafee, *op. cit.* 498.
2 *Ibid.* 51. See also Note, 32 *Harvard L. Rev.* (1919), 417.
3 Frank, *Cases and Materials on Constitutional Law* (1952), 883.
4 Chafee, *Thirty-five Years with Freedom of Speech* (1952), 6.
5 Carr, *op. cit.* 10.

'would make us expect a statute concerned only with finger-printing foreigners and such administrative matters. Indeed, that was the impression received from the newspapers at the time of its passage. Not until months later did I for one realize that this statute contains the most drastic restrictions on freedom of speech ever enacted in the United States during peace. It is no more limited to the registration of aliens than the Espionage Act of 1917 was limited to spying. Most of the Alien Registration Act is not concerned with registration, and the very first part of it has nothing particular to do with aliens. Just as the 1917 Act gave us a war-time sedition law, so the 1940 Act gives us a peace-time sedition law—for everybody, especially United States citizens.'[1]

The provisions of the Smith Act, which are directed against sedition, are contained in sections 2 and 3. They read:

'Sec. 2. (*a*) It shall be unlawful for any person—

'(1) to knowingly or willfully advocate, abet, advise, or teach the duty, necessity, desirability, or propriety of overthrowing or destroying any government in the United States by force or violence, or by the assassination of any officer of any such government;

'(2) with intent to cause the overthrow or destruction of any government in the United States, to print, publish, edit, issue, circulate, sell, distribute, or publicly display any written or printed matter advocating, advising, or teaching the duty, necessity, desirability, or propriety of overthrowing or destroying any government in the United States by force or violence;

'(3) to organize or help to organize any society, group, or assembly of persons who teach, advocate, or encourage the overthrow or destruction of any government in the United States by force or violence; or to be or become a member of, or affiliate with, any such society, group, or assembly of persons, knowing the purposes thereof. ...

'Sec. 3. It shall be unlawful for any person to attempt to commit, or to conspire to commit, any of the acts prohibited by the provisions of this title.'[2]

The Smith Act provisions just quoted were originally 'adopted in the overwrought atmosphere which followed the German "fifth column" and "Trojan horse" infiltration of countries soon to be invaded'.[3] In practice, however, they have been enforced almost exclusively against the leaders of the American Communist party, as part of the governmental measures aimed at meeting the problems presented by the 'cold war'. It should be noted that, like the Sedition Laws of 1798 and 1918, as well as

1 Chafee, *Free Speech in the United States*, 440.
2 There have thus far been 82 convictions under the Smith Act (*N.Y. Times*, 11 April 1955).   3 Biddle, *op. cit.* 109.

the common-law crime of sedition, the Smith Act seeks to penalize not so much seditious acts, as seditious teaching or advocacy, or, to use the familiar British term, seditious libel. As such, it clearly constitutes a restriction upon the rights of freedom of speech and of the Press guaranteed by the First Amendment. Is such a legislative restriction contrary to the Federal Constitution? This question was answered by the Supreme Court in 1951 in disposing of the appeals of ten Communist leaders who had been convicted for violation of the Smith Act.[1] But before we can deal directly with that case, a word must first be said about the so-called 'clear and present danger' test, which has been developed by the Supreme Court to aid it in determining the validity of legislative interferences with the rights safeguarded by the First Amendment.

'CLEAR AND PRESENT DANGER' TEST

It has been strongly urged that the absolute nature of the language of the First Amendment to the Federal Constitution renders invalid all governmental restrictions upon speech. 'No one who reads with care the text of the First Amendment', asserts the leading recent exponent of this view, 'can fail to be startled by its absoluteness. The phrase, "Congress shall make no law...abridging the freedom of speech", is unqualified. It admits of no exceptions. To say that no laws of a given type shall be made means that no laws of that type shall, under any circumstances, be made. That prohibition holds good in war as in peace, in danger as in security. The men who adopted the Bill of Rights were not ignorant of the necessities of war or of national danger. It would, in fact, be nearer to the truth to say that it was exactly those necessities which they had in mind as they planned to defend freedom of discussion against them. Out of their own bitter experience they knew how terror and hatred, how war and strife, can drive men into acts of unreasoning suppression. They planned, therefore, both for the peace which they desired and for the wars which they feared. And in both cases they established an absolute, unqualified prohibition of the abridgement of the freedom of speech.'[2]

As has already been indicated, this absolutist view of the rights guaranteed by the First Amendment is one which has not been followed by the United States Supreme Court. 'In a series of decisions', Mr Justice Frankfurter informs us, 'which presented most sharply the constitutional extent of freedom of speech, this Court had held that the Constitution did not allow absolute freedom of expression—a freedom unrestricted by the duty to

1 *Dennis* v. *United States*, 341 U.S. 494 (1951).
2 Meiklejohn, *Free Speech* (1948), 17.

respect other needs fulfilment of which makes for the dignity and security of man.'[1]

The decisions referred to by the learned judge arose out of convictions for violating the Espionage and Sedition Acts passed during the First World War, which have been discussed above. The leading case is *Schenck v. United States*,[2] where a unanimous court, speaking through Mr Justice Holmes, 'left no doubt that judicial protection of freedom of utterance is necessarily qualified by the requirements of the Constitution as an entirety for the maintenance of a free society'.[3] In rejecting the absolutist view of the rights safeguarded by the First Amendment, Justice Holmes stated in the *Schenck Case* that 'the character of every act depends upon the circumstances in which it is done.... The most stringent protection of free speech would not protect a man in falsely shouting fire in a theatre and causing a panic.'[4] And then, in one of the most famous passages contained in a Supreme Court opinion, he went on to enunciate the test to determine the validity of restrictions upon speech. 'The question in every case', said he, 'is whether the words used are used in such circumstances and are of such a nature as to create a clear and present danger that they will bring about the substantive evils that Congress has a right to prevent. It is a question of proximity and degree.'[5]

The 'clear and present danger' test, thus articulated by Justice Holmes in the *Schenck Case*, 'served to indicate the importance of freedom of speech to a free society but also to emphasize that its exercise must be compatible with the preservation of other freedoms essential to a democracy and guaranteed by our Constitution. When those other attributes of a democracy are threatened by speech, the Constitution does not deny power to the [government] to curb it.'[6] As characterized by Mr Justice Brandeis in a later case, the Holmesian test 'is a rule of reason. Correctly applied, it will preserve the right of free speech both from suppression by tyrannous, well-meaning majorities and from abuse by irresponsible, fanatical minorities.'[7]

In the 'clear and present danger' test enunciated by him, Justice Holmes drew the boundary line of constitutionality of restrictions upon speech very close to the test of incitement at common law.[8] 'I do not doubt for a moment', he declared, soon after his *Schenck* decision, 'that by the same reasoning that would justify punishing persuasion to murder, the United States constitutionally may punish speech that produces or is intended to

---

1 *Pennekamp v. Florida*, 328 U.S. 331, 351 (1946).   2 249 U.S. 47 (1919).
3 *Pennekamp v. Florida*, 328 U.S. 331, 351 (1946).
4 *Schenck v. United States*, 249 U.S. at 52.   5 *Ibid.*
6 *Pennekamp v. Florida*, 328 U.S. 331, 353 (1946).
7 *Schaefer v. United States*, 251 U.S. 466, 482 (1920).   8 Chafee, *Free Speech*, 82.

produce a clear and imminent danger that it will bring about forthwith certain substantive evils that the United States constitutionally may seek to prevent.'[1]

COMMON-LAW SEDITION COMPARED

'A prosecution for seditious libel', stated Mr Justice Coleridge almost fifty years ago, 'is somewhat of a rarity. It is a weapon that is not often taken down from the armoury in which it hangs, but it is a necessary accompaniment to every civilized government.'[2] It has already been indicated that the framers of the American Bill of Rights rejected the common-law crime of sedition. 'I wholly disagree', declared Mr Justice Holmes in a case which has already been referred to, 'with the argument of the Government that the First Amendment left the common law of seditious libel in force. History seems to me against the notion.'[3] It should be realized, however, that the common-law crime of sedition, to the extent that it still exists in Britain, is not at all like what it was at the time of the founding of the American Republic. It is not helpful, as Professor Wade informs us, to quote the precedents of the eighteenth and early nineteenth centuries for an understanding of the scope of the offence today.[4] And, as it has been interpreted during the present century, common-law sedition can be seen to bear comparison with the 'clear and present danger' test articulated by Mr Justice Holmes.

In *The King* v. *Aldred*,[5] one of the very rare reported cases of sedition during the past half-century,[6] there is to be found in the charge of Coleridge, J., to the jury what is characterized by one commentary as a summary of the law of seditious libel which represents the modern attitude to this offence.[7] According to the learned justice's charge, if the defendant 'makes use of language calculated to advocate or to incite others to public disorders, to wit, rebellions, insurrections, assassinations, outrages, or any physical force or violence of any kind, then whatever his motives, whatever his intentions, there would be evidence on which a jury might, on which I think a jury ought, to decide that he is guilty of a seditious publication'.[8] And what is the test to determine whether or not particular utterances are seditious? 'You are entitled to look at all the circumstances

1 *Abrams* v. *United States*, 250 U.S. 616, 627 (1919).
2 (1909), 22 Cox C.C. 1, quoted in Dicey, *op. cit.* 579.
3 *Abrams* v. *United States*, 250 U.S. 616, 630 (1919).
4 In Dicey, *op. cit.* 580.
5 (1909), 22 Cox C.C. 1, quoted in Dicey, *op. cit.* 579.
6 The only other case appears to be *R.* v. *Caunt*, discussed in Wade, Note, 64 L. Q. Rev. (1948), 203.
7 Wade, in Dicey, *op. cit.* 579.
8 (1909), 22 Cox C.C. 1, quoted in Dicey, *op. cit.* 579.

surrounding the publication with a view to seeing whether the language used is calculated to produce the results imputed.'[1]

This test is not too far removed from that enunciated by Justice Holmes. If there is no 'clear and present danger' in view of the circumstances surrounding the publication, it cannot be said that the language used is actually calculated to produce the results imputed. And whether there is a real threat of such results being brought about depends upon the particular pattern of fact in each case—'that is to say you are entitled to look at the audience addressed, because language which would be innocuous, practically speaking, if used to an assembly of professors or divines might produce a different result if used before an excited audience of young and uneducated men. You are entitled to take into account the state of public feeling. Of course there are times when a spark will explode a magazine.'[2]

It should, of course, be borne in mind that the test enunciated by Coleridge, J., is one to determine whether the common-law crime of sedition has occurred, while that of Justice Holmes is one to determine whether a legislative restriction upon freedom of speech is constitutional. But, this distinction apart, the approach of the two justices to what is, after all, the same question, namely, under what circumstances speech alone is rendered unlawful, is not dissimilar.

That the answer given to that question by both the English and the American courts is a sound one can be seen by the interesting analogy of the law of criminal attempts. Just as a criminal attempt must come sufficiently near completion to be of public concern, so must there be an actual danger that speech will bring about an unlawful act before it can be restrained. And, in both cases, the question how near to the unlawful act itself the attempt or the speech must come is a question of degree to be determined in each case upon the special facts of the case.[3] This relation between the free-speech problem and the problem of criminal attempts is neatly illustrated by Professor Chafee. 'If I gather a few sticks', says he, 'and buy a can of kerosene for the purpose of starting a fire in a house ten miles away and do nothing more, I cannot be punished for attempting to commit arson. However, if I put the sticks beside the wall of the house and pour on some kerosene and I am caught before striking a match, I am guilty of a criminal attempt. The fire is the main thing, but when no fire has occurred, it is a question of the nearness of my behavior to the wished for outbreak of a fire. So under the First Amendment, lawless acts are the

1 (1909) 22 Cox C.C. 1, quoted in Dicey, *op. cit.* 579.
2 *Ibid.* Compare the important Canadian case of *Boucher* v. *The King*, [1950] 1 D.L.R. 657, [1951] 2 D.L.R. 369.
3 Beale, 'Criminal attempts', 16 *Harvard L. Rev.* (1903), 491, 501.

main thing. Speech is not punishable for its own sake, but only because of its connection with those lawless acts whether they occur or not. But more than a remote connection is necessary here, just as in the case of the attempted fire. The fire must be close to the house; the speech must be close to the lawless acts. So long as the speech is far away from action, the Constitution protects it.'[1]

COMMUNIST TRIAL

The 'clear and present danger' test enunciated by Mr Justice Holmes received its most striking application in *Dennis* v. *United States*,[2] which was decided in 1951 by the highest American court. The defendants in that case, ten of the principal leaders of the American Communist party, were indicted for violating section 3 of the Smith Act by wilfully and knowingly conspiring (1) to organize as the Communist party of the United States of America a society, group and assembly of persons who teach and advocate the overthrow and destruction of the Government of the United States by force and violence, and (2) to advocate and teach the duty and necessity of overthrowing the Government of the United States by force and violence. The case was tried at great length. The trial extended over nine months, six of which were devoted to the taking of evidence, resulting in a record of 16,000 pages. The jury brought in a verdict against all the defendants, and they were sentenced in accordance with the criminal penalties provided in the Smith Act.

Upon appeal by defendants to the appropriate court of appeals, that tribunal held that the record of the evidence presented at the trial amply supported the finding of the jury that defendant leaders of the American Communist party were unwilling to work within the framework of the democratic system, but intended to initiate a violent revolution whenever the propitious occasion appeared. The court of appeals found from the record that the policies of the Communist party, in the post-war period covered in the indictment, were changed from peaceful co-operation with the United States and its economic and political structure to a policy which had existed before the United States and the Soviet Union were fighting a common enemy, namely, a policy which worked for the overthrow of the American Government by force and violence; that the Communist party is a highly disciplined organization, adept at infiltration into strategic positions, uses of aliases, and double-meaning language; that the party is rigidly controlled; that Communists, unlike other political parties, tolerate no dissension from the policy laid down by the guiding forces, but that the

1 Chafee, *Thirty-five years with Freedom of Speech*, 7.
2 341 U.S. 494 (1951).

approved programme is slavishly followed by members of the party; that the literature of the party and the statements and activities of its leaders advocated and the general goal of the party was, during the period in question, to achieve a successful overthrow of the existing order by force and violence. And, based upon these findings, the intermediate appellate court upheld the jury's verdict that defendants were guilty of violating the Smith Act.[1]

Under the limited review afforded by the federal Supreme Court in the American system, that tribunal in the *Dennis Case* did not directly consider the question of the sufficiency of the evidence to support the jury's determination that the defendants were guilty of the offence charged. The issue before the Supreme Court was instead the legal issue, whether either section 2 or section 3 of the Smith Act, inherently or as construed and applied in that particular case, violated the First Amendment and other provisions of the Federal Bill of Rights.

The problem presented to the Supreme Court in the *Dennis Case* has been stated as follows by one commentator. 'The Smith Act was aimed to protect the Government against revolution by punishing conspiracy to advocate such revolution. How long, in a democracy which is based on freedom of speech and of association, must the government wait before it can take preventive measures against revolt? As usual the extremes are easy to envisage and judge. The government may resist any actual or attempted revolt but, on the other hand, may not proscribe mere belief in the desirability of overthrowing the government or a prophesy that it may eventuate. What happens in between when beliefs and actions are combined, when there is thus an advocacy of action?'[2] The great difficulty of the *Dennis Case* arises from the fact that it does fall within the extremes of overt incitement to riot and mere expression of belief. 'Nobody doubts', as Judge Learned Hand expressed it in the Court of Appeals, 'that, when the leader of a mob already ripe for riot gives the word to start, his utterance is not protected by the [First] Amendment. It is not difficult to deal with such situations; doubt arises only when the utterance is at once an effort to affect the hearers' beliefs and a call upon them to act when they have been convinced.'[3]

The essential element of the Smith Act, according to Mr Chief Justice Vinson, who delivered the judgment of the Supreme Court in the *Dennis Case*, is to be found in its purpose 'to protect existing Government, not

1 *United States* v. *Dennis*, 183 F. 2d 201 (2d Cir. 1950).

2 Bischoff, 'Constitutional law and civil rights', *Annual Survey of American Law*, (1951), 74, 77.

3 183 F. 2d at 207.

from change by peaceable, lawful and constitutional means, but from change by violence, revolution and terrorism'.[1] The Act aims, however, not to protect the Government directly against changes brought about by revolution: its provisions are not directed against overt acts of terror and violence. Instead, they seek to extend the prophylactic process one step further by suppressing the teaching or advocacy of the overthrow of the Government by force or violence. As such, it seeks to restrict words rather than deeds.

It is clearly within the power of the Congress, as of any legislative body in a sovereign State, to protect the Federal Government from armed rebellion. 'No one could conceive that it is not within the power of Congress to prohibit acts intended to overthrow the Government by force and violence.'[2] Under the 'clear and present danger' rule laid down by Justice Holmes, legislative limitations upon speech must be justified by direct danger from the proscribed speech of a substantive evil which the legislature has the right to prevent. In the case of the Smith Act, under the Holmesian test, restriction of speech teaching or advocating the overthrow of the Government by force is valid only if there is some 'clear and present danger', from the speech proceeded against, of a violent attempt at revolution—in this case, the substantive evil which the Congress clearly has the power to prevent. 'In this case', as the Chief Justice notes in his *Dennis* opinion, 'we are squarely presented with the application of the "clear and present danger" test, and must decide what that phrase imports.'[3]

'The question before us,' stated Judge Hand in the Court of Appeals, 'and the only one, is how long a government, having discovered such a conspiracy, must wait. When does the conspiracy become a "present danger"?'[4] In answering that question, the Supreme Court indicated that the validity of restrictions upon advocacy of violent revolution did not depend upon the immediacy of revolt resulting from such advocacy. 'Obviously, the words cannot mean that before the Government may act, it must wait until the *putsch* is about to be executed, the plans have been laid and the signal is awaited. If Government is aware that a group aiming at its overthrow is attempting to indoctrinate its members and to commit them to a course whereby they will strike when the leaders feel the circumstances permit, action by the Government is required. The argument that there is no need for Government to concern itself, for Government is strong, it possesses ample powers to put down a rebellion, it may defeat the revolution with ease needs no answer. For that is not the question. Certainly an attempt to overthrow the Government by force, even though

1 341 U.S. at 501.   2 *Ibid.*
3 *Ibid.* at 508.   4 183 F. 2d at 213.

doomed from the outset because of inadequate numbers or power of the revolutionists, is a sufficient evil for Congress to prevent.'[1]

In this particular case, the Supreme Court concluded that the activities of defendants in teaching and advocating the overthrow of the Government by force could constitutionally be prohibited by legislation such as the Smith Act. 'In each case [courts] must ask whether the gravity of the "evil", discounted by its improbability, justifies such invasion of free speech as is necessary to avoid the danger.'[2] Here, the finding below that the requisite danger existed was affirmed. 'The mere fact that from the period 1945 to 1948 petitioners' activities did not result in an attempt to overthrow the Government by force and violence is of course no answer to the fact that there was a group that was ready to make the attempt. The formation by petitioners of such a highly organized conspiracy, with rigidly disciplined members subject to call when the leaders, these petitioners, felt that the time had come for action, coupled with the inflammable nature of world conditions, similar uprisings in other countries, and the touch-and-go nature of our relations with countries with whom petitioners were in the very least ideologically attuned, convince us that their convictions were justified on this score.'[3]

Judge Hand, in his opinion in the Court of Appeals, used even stronger language on this point. 'True,' said he, 'we must not forget our own faith; we must be sensitive to the dangers that lurk in any choice; but choose we must, and we shall be silly dupes if we forget that again and again in the past thirty years, just such preparations in other countries have aided to supplant existing governments, when the time was ripe. Nothing short of a revived doctrine of *laissez-faire*, which would have amazed even the Manchester School at its apogee, can fail to realize that such a conspiracy creates a danger of the utmost gravity and of enough probability to justify its suppression. We hold that it is a danger "clear and present".'[4]

CRITIQUE OF DENNIS CASE

Any realistic discussion of the Supreme Court decision in the *Dennis Case* must begin by recognizing the true nature of the contemporary threat of the Communist movement. 'The Communists present a perplexing problem to the American people. Those who gloss over the problem distort reality no less than those who are obsessed by it to the point of seeing no other dangers in the world today.'[5] As it was expressed by Mr Justice

1 *Dennis v. United States*, 341 U.S. at 509.   2 *Ibid*. at 510.
3 *Ibid*.   4 183 F. 2d at 213.
5 Barth, *The Loyalty of Free Men* (1951), 20.

Frankfurter, in a concurring opinion in the *Dennis Case*, 'The Communist Party was not designed by these defendants as an ordinary political party. . . . The Party rejects the basic premise of our political system—that change is to be brought about by nonviolent constitutional process. . . . The Party advocates the theory that there is a duty and necessity to overthrow the Government by force and violence. . . . The Party entertains and promotes this view, not as a prophetic insight or as a bit of unworldly speculation, but as a program for winning adherents and as a policy to be translated into action.'[1]

Perhaps the most striking judicial statement of the actual character of the American Communist party is to be found in a 1950 opinion of Mr Justice Jackson, which has been described by one commentator as 'remarkable for the sweep of its dicta and its judicial notice of data not in evidence before the Court'.[2] 'From information before its several Committees', reads the opinion referred to, 'and from facts of general knowledge, Congress could rationally conclude that, behind its political party façade, the Communist Party is a conspiratorial and revolutionary junta, organized to reach ends and to use methods which are incompatible with our constitutional system. A rough and compressed grouping of this data would permit Congress to draw these important conclusions as to its distinguishing characteristics.

'1. The goal of the Communist Party is to seize powers of government by and for a minority rather than to acquire power through the vote of a free electorate. . . .

'2. The Communist Party alone among American parties past or present is dominated and controlled by a foreign government. . . .

'3. Violent and undemocratic means are the calculated and indispensable methods to attain the Communist Party's goal. It would be incredible naïveté to expect the American branch of this movement to forego the only methods by which a Communist Party has anywhere come into power. . . .

'4. The Communist Party has sought to gain this leverage and hold on the American population by acquiring control of the labor movement. . . .

'5. Every member of the Communist Party is an agent to execute the Communist program.'[3]

Although unsupported by the kind of evidence that would usually be required in a law court, the broad indictment of the Communist party in Justice Jackson's opinion comports with the common sense of the subject.[4]

---

1 341 U.S. at 546.   2 Barth, *op. cit.* 21.
3 *American Communications Assn.* v. *Douds*, 339 U.S. 382, 424–31 (1950) (*emphasis* omitted).   4 Compare Barth, *op. cit.* 22.

Nor is it an answer to Justice Jackson's view merely to point to the political impotence of the Communist party in the United States. The weakness of American communism was, indeed, stated with some emphasis by Mr Justice Douglas as his principal ground for dissenting from the court's decision in the *Dennis Case*. 'Communists in this country', he asserts, 'have never made a respectable or serious showing in any election. I would doubt that there is a village, let alone a city or county or state, which the Communists could carry. Communism in the world scene is no bogeyman; but Communism as a political faction or party in this country plainly is. Communism has been so thoroughly exposed in this country that it has been crippled as a political force. Free speech has destroyed it as an effective political party.... How it can be said that there is a clear and present danger that this advocacy will succeed is, therefore, a mystery.'[1]

The political sterility of the Communist party in the United States does not necessarily mean that it does not constitute a danger to American institutions. On the contrary, the very lack of success in the political market-place may induce resort to the techniques of a secret cabal. 'The Communist program does not presently, nor in foreseeable future elections, commend itself to enough American voters to be a substantial political force. Unless the Communist Party can obtain some powerful leverage on the population, it is doomed to remain a negligible factor in the United States. Hence, conspiracy, violence, intimidation and the *coup d'état* are all that keep hope alive in the Communist breast.'[2]

It is important to bear in mind that the Supreme Court in the *Dennis Case* was not at all concerned with the question of the desirability of legislative restrictions upon speech such as those contained in the Smith Act. The sole issue for the court was that of the existence of the legislative power to enact such a statute. And, in deciding that issue, it was not for the court to overturn the legislative judgment on the need for such a law merely because it might have made a different choice between the competing interests had the initial legislative choice been for it to make. 'It is not for us', declared Mr Justice Frankfurter in his *Dennis* opinion, 'to decide how we would adjust the clash of interests which this case presents were the primary responsibility for reconciling it ours. Congress has determined that the danger created by advocacy of overthrow justifies the ensuing restriction on freedom of speech.... Can we say that the judgment Congress exercised was denied it by the Constitution? Can we establish a constitutional doctrine which forbids the elected representatives of the people to make this choice? Can we hold that the First Amendment

1 341 U.S. at 588.
2 Jackson, J., in *American Communications Assn.* v. *Douds*, 339 U.S. at 430.

deprives Congress of what it deemed necessary for the Government's protection?'[1]

In a democratic system, the primary responsibility for determining when there is danger that speech will induce the substantive evil that the Government has a right to prevent—in this case, violent attempts at revolution—must surely lie with the elected representatives of the people. For the Supreme Court to substitute its own independent judgment in each case on the existence of the danger would be for it to return to the concept of 'government by judiciary', against which so many criticisms were rightly directed prior to 1937. It is only if the legislative judgment in a case like this is unreasonable that it should be set aside. 'Our duty to abstain from confounding policy with constitutionality demands perceptive humility as well as self-restraint in not declaring unconstitutional what in a judge's private judgment is unwise and even dangerous.'[2]

Can a tribunal like the federal Supreme Court affirm with any assurance that the teachings of the Communist party do not constitute a 'clear and present danger' to the American system? Judicial prescience in this respect could turn out to be as unreliable as would a similar judgment with regard to the Bolsheviks in pre-revolutionary Russia or the National Socialists in the early days of the Weimar Republic. 'To make validity of legislation depend on judicial reading of events still in the womb of time—a forecast, that is, of the outcome of forces at best appreciated only with knowledge of the topmost secrets of nations—is to charge the judiciary with duties beyond its equipment. We do not expect courts to pronounce historic verdicts on bygone events. Even historians have conflicting views to this day on the origin and conduct of the French Revolution. . . . It is as absurd to be confident that we can measure the present clash of forces and their outcome as to ask us to read history still enveloped in clouds of controversy.'[3]

LOYALTY PROCEEDINGS

Before 1939, the American people took it for granted that those whom they employed as government servants were loyal to the United States. They set certain standards for appointment to the civil service designed to exclude the criminal and the unfit. They sought to have government jobs, at least those below the policy-making level, awarded on the basis of merit rather than through patronage. But, so far as loyalty was concerned, they asked only that civil servants take an oath to support and defend the Federal Constitution.[4]

1 341 U.S. at 550.   2 *Ibid.* at 552.
3 *Ibid.* at 551.   4 Barth, *op. cit.* 97.

Starting in 1939, however, influenced by the worsening international situation, a new American legislative and executive policy on loyalty was gradually developed. 'At least since 1939, increasing concern has been expressed, in and out of Congress, as to the possible presence in the employ of the Government of persons disloyal to it.'[1] In that year, the Congress made it unlawful for any federal employee 'to have membership in any political party or organization which advocates the overthrow of our constitutional form of government in the United States'. As interpreted by the Civil Service Commission, the agency charged with administering the federal civil service laws, these provisions were applicable to 'the Communist Party, the German Bund, or any other Communist, Nazi, or Fascist organization'. And, beginning in 1941, the Congress began the practice of attaching to all appropriation Acts a provision that no part of the funds appropriated should 'be used to pay the salary or wages of any person who advocates, or who is a member of an association that advocates, the overthrow of the Government of the United States by force or violence'.[2]

The so-called 'loyalty programme' of the federal civil service, though it may have been strongly stimulated by legislative acts of this type, was, in its essentials, developed by the executive branch of the Government itself. In 1942, the Civil Service Commission, with the approval of President Roosevelt, issued regulations which provided that an individual could be barred from government employment where there existed 'a reasonable doubt as to his loyalty to the Government of the United States'. Under this formula the commission dealt with all questions of loyalty with respect to employees entering the federal service in the war years. The loyalty proceedings instituted under the 1942 regulations were, however, somewhat haphazard, for the Civil Service Commission lacked funds and personnel to investigate more than a fraction of the great mass of employees brought into the Government during the war.[3]

It has been in the post-war period, under the stresses of the 'cold war', that comprehensive loyalty measures for the civil service have been instituted by the American executive. On 21 March 1947, President Truman promulgated Executive Order no. 9835,. which established such a full-scale proceeding. That order provided that there 'shall be a loyalty investigation of every person entering the civilian employment of any department or agency of the executive branch of the Federal Government'.

1 *Joint Anti-Fascist Refugee Committee* v. *McGrath*, 341 U.S. 123, 126 (1951).
2 See Emerson and Helfeld, 'Loyalty among government employees', 58 *Yale L. J.* (1948), 1, 14–15.
3 Barth, *op. cit.* 100.

Such investigation was to be made with the aid of 'all available pertinent sources of information'. Whenever derogatory information with respect to the loyalty of an applicant was revealed, or on the request of the employing agency, 'a full field investigation shall be conducted'.

As to individuals already in the federal service, the President's order made the head of each agency 'personally responsible for an effective program to assure that disloyal civilian officers or employees are not retained in employment'. Every agency head was required to submit to the Federal Bureau of Investigation the names and other identifying material of all incumbent employees. The bureau was directed to check those names against its records and to notify the employing agency of any substantial evidence indicating disloyal activity or association.[1]

It should not be assumed, from the many criticisms which have been directed against the loyalty proceedings instituted by Executive Order 9835, that the American civil servant was left without any safeguards, when once a charge of disloyalty was made against him. 'The executive order', as an outstanding critic of the loyalty proceedings has conceded, 'takes cognizance of the danger that men may be mistakenly or maliciously accused of disloyalty. To offset this danger, it provides an elaborate procedure of review.'[2] Under the President's order, there was established in each agency a so-called loyalty board, composed of not less than three representatives of the agency, which was entrusted with the task of making the initial determination, based upon the results of the Federal Bureau of Investigation's report, that a charge of disloyalty was warranted. In such cases the individual concerned was to be afforded an opportunity for a hearing before the board, with the right to be accompanied by counsel or representative of his own choosing and to present evidence on his own behalf, through witnesses or by affidavit. Before such a hearing, if he was an incumbent civil servant, he was to be served with a written notice setting forth the nature of the charges against him 'as specifically and completely as, in the discretion of the employing department or agency, security considerations permit'.

If the agency's loyalty board ruled adversely to the individual, he had a right of appeal to the head of the agency. Nor, under the procedure provided for in President Truman's order, did the latter have the last word. 'To assure uniformity and fairness throughout the Government in the investigation of employees', Mr Justice Reed informs us, 'a Loyalty Review Board was created to review loyalty cases from any department or agency, disseminate information pertinent to employee loyalty programs,

1 See Emerson and Helfeld, *loc. cit.* 30.
2 Barth, *op. cit.* 103.

and advise the heads thereof.'[1] The Loyalty Review Board referred to was a central agency set up in Washington as the ultimate appellate tribunal in loyalty proceedings.[2] Before this board also, the individual was given the right to appear personally with counsel and could present evidence through witnesses and affidavits.

One who analyses the procedural machinery set forth in the presidential order establishing the federal loyalty investigation cannot help but conclude that the American administration, while seeking to counteract criticisms against claimed infiltrations of the civil service by individuals disloyal to the Government, did not lose sight of the need to protect federal employees from unfounded and arbitrary action. 'It was evident', declares a former Attorney-General who has strongly opposed the Federal Government's loyalty proceedings, 'that President Truman was deeply concerned that there should be no "witch hunts". The charges were to be made in sufficient detail to enable the employee to prepare his defence, although "in some unusual situations security considerations" might not "allow full disclosure". The President, realizing "fully...the stigma attached to a removal for disloyalty", directed that hearings should be held.'[3]

Despite the manifest attempt of the federal administration to make its loyalty procedure a fair one, it cannot, however, be said that it has been entirely satisfactory from the point of view of the civil servants affected. An investigation such as that instituted by President Truman's 1947 order is bound to be defective because of the lack of a clear objective standard for determining the 'loyalty' of particular government employees. The loyalty order was designed to secure—though in a degree not capable of precise definition—additional protection to government operations beyond that afforded by existing penal statutes on treason, sedition, espionage and the like, and beyond that afforded by customary rules of civil service discipline.[4] Under the President's order, the 'standard for the refusal of employment or the removal from employment in an executive department or agency on grounds relating to loyalty shall be that, on all the evidence, reasonable grounds exist for belief that the person involved is disloyal to the Government of the United States'.[5] As a leading com-

1 Dissenting, in *Joint Anti-Fascist Refugee Committee* v. *McGrath*, 341 U.S. 123, 190 (1951). In addition, there were established fourteen regional loyalty boards to serve as intermediate appellate tribunals.

2 The board was composed of twenty members who have been characterized, even by a consistent opponent of the loyalty proceedings, as 'well-known citizens, many of them outstanding, about three-quarters of them lawyers'; Biddle, *op. cit.* 207.

3 *Ibid.*　　　　　4 Emerson and Helfeld, *loc. cit.* 35.

5 In 1951, this standard was changed so that removal from civil service or refusal of employment therein was forthcoming if 'on all the evidence there is a reasonable doubt as to the loyalty of the person involved to the Government of the United States.'

mentary has aptly pointed out, 'One of the striking features of the Loyalty Order is that it does not define "disloyalty". Under the Order the right of a person to become or to remain a Federal employee turns upon a legal finding as to whether "reasonable grounds exist for belief that the person involved is disloyal...". Despite the controversy that had raged for the previous ten years over the meaning of "disloyal", draftsmen of the Order preferred to use the word without definition.'[1]

It should be noted that, though the President's 1947 order establishing the loyalty investigation did not define disloyalty, it did undertake to list six kinds of 'activities and associations' of applicants and civil servants which 'may be considered in connection with the determination of disloyalty'. The first four activities listed included sabotage, espionage, treason, sedition, advocacy of force or violence to alter the constitutional form of government, and disclosure of confidential documents or information obtained as a result of government employment. All of these are the usual, overt forms of disloyalty and cause little difficulty. The fifth and sixth types of disloyal activities are, however, less clear-cut. The fifth is 'performing or attempting to perform his duties, or otherwise acting, so as to serve the interests of another government in preference to the interests of the United States'. What constitutes disloyalty under this criterion is far from self-evident. 'Would the transfer of 50 destroyers to Great Britain in 1940 serve the interests of that country in preference to the United States? Many people thought it did. What about military aid to Greece or Turkey?...Does not every issue of foreign policy raise a question as to the interest of the United States in relation to foreign countries, and does not the answer turn upon a complicated political judgment as to which people may differ in good faith? Nothing is said about motive or intent. Is this meant to be the touchstone? If so, just what is the requisite evil intent? And how is it to be shown or proved?'[2]

The sixth category of 'activities and associations' which might be considered in determining disloyalty under President Truman's 1947 order was 'membership in, affiliation with, or sympathetic association with, any foreign or domestic organization, movement, group or combination of persons, designated by the Attorney General as totalitarian, fascist, communist, or subversive'. Under this category, disloyalty depends, not on the acts of the particular civil servant or applicant, but upon his associations. 'The technique', as Mr Justice Douglas characterized it, 'is one of guilt by association—one of the most odious institutions of history. The fact that the technique of guilt by association was used in the prosecutions at Nuremberg does not make it congenial to our constitutional scheme.

1 Emerson and Helfeld, *loc. cit.* 37.   2 *Ibid.* 38.

Guilt under our system of government is personal. When we make guilt vicarious we borrow from systems alien to ours and ape our enemies.'[1]

It may well be that the worst features of such 'guilt by association' were avoided at the Nuremberg trials by clearly specifying the criminal acts which, if proved, would place a Nazi organization on the proscribed list. But the same is not true of organizations listed as 'totalitarian, fascist, communist, or subversive' by the American Attorney-General. Especially is this true of those designated as 'subversive'. How 'can anyone in the context of the Executive Order say what it means? It apparently does not mean "totalitarian", "fascist" or "communist" because they are separately listed....Does it mean an organization that thinks the lot of some peasants has been improved under Soviet auspices? Does it include an organization that is against the action of the United Nations in Korea? Does it embrace a group which on some issues of international policy aligns itself with the Soviet viewpoint? Does it mean a group which has unwittingly become the tool for Soviet propaganda? Does it mean one into whose membership some Communists have infiltrated? Or does it describe only an organization which under the guise of honorable activities serves as a front for Communist activities?'[2]

LOYALTY PROCEDURE

The failure to define disloyalty with any detailed precision appears to constitute an inherent weakness of a proceeding such as that established for the American civil service by President Truman's 1947 order. The federal loyalty investigation has been aimed, not only at those civil servants who have committed positive disloyal acts, but also against those who are 'potentially disloyal'.[3] 'In essence the loyalty program is a comprehensive, continuing and aggressive effort to weed out the "potentially disloyal". Existing legislation and administrative regulations afford adequate protection against *actions* of public employees that are dangerous to the operation of government. The program is designed to purge from government service individuals whose ideas, associations and legal activities give rise to an inference that such persons may in the future engage in conduct injurious to the government.'[4] A proceeding designed with this end in view cannot, by its very nature, be based upon criteria as exact as those contained in laws directed against overt acts, such as those dealing with treason or espionage.

1 Concurring, in *Joint Anti-Fascist Refugee Committee* v. *McGrath*, 341 U.S. 123, 178 (1951).   2 *Ibid.* at 176.
3 The phrase used by President Truman himself. See Biddle, *op. cit.* 208.
4 Emerson and Helfeld, *loc. cit.* 134.

Nor can a loyalty proceeding be carried on with all of the procedural safeguards that are deemed necessary in other fields of American law. Basic in the jurisprudence of the common-law countries is the requirement of notice and an opportunity for a full and fair hearing before administrative action is taken which adversely affects the individual citizen —a requirement which, in the American system, has been elevated to a constitutional position by the provision of the federal organic instrument that no person shall be deprived of life, liberty, or property without 'due process of law'.[1] 'Notice and opportunity to be heard', as Mr Justice Douglas has told us, 'are fundamental to due process of law.'[2] Under the principles of administrative law which have been developed by the American courts, the administration may not act in a manner which adversely affects an individual unless he is afforded a defensive hearing at which he can present his side of the case. At such hearing, he must be permitted to bring forward any oral or documentary evidence that he may have, must be fully apprised of the administration's case against him, and must be allowed to cross-examine the witnesses upon whom the administration's case rests. And the administrative decision, when rendered, must be based solely upon evidence contained in the record of the hearing. These principles are all given express legislative articulation in the Federal Administrative Procedure Act of 1946.[3]

So far as proceedings under the American Government's loyalty investigation have been concerned, it has been almost inevitable that not all of the procedural safeguards just mentioned have been observed. 'It is an ironic and not altogether happy reflection', caustically declares former Attorney-General Biddle, 'that although Congress has written into the law the elementary requirements of fair procedure for the Government to follow in administrative hearings involving property rights, the same safeguards have been denied to its own employees.'[4] And it should be emphasized that the failure of the procedures followed in loyalty proceedings to measure up to those required under the Administrative Procedure Act was not caused by the American administration's disregard of its employee's adjective rights. On the contrary, as we have seen, President Truman's order setting up the loyalty investigation provided for an elaborate procedure of hearing, decision, and review, in order to protect individual civil servants charged with disloyalty.

By its very nature, a proceeding such as that envisaged by the President's

1 Fifth Amendment, U.S. Constitution.
2 Concurring, in *Joint Anti-Fascist Refugee Committee* v. *McGrath*, 341 U.S. 123, 178 (1951).
3 See Schwartz, *American Administrative Law* (1950), chs. V and VI.
4 Biddle, *op. cit.* 209.

order cannot be effectively executed if hearings under it are to comply fully with all of the procedural demands imposed upon the administration in other cases. The right of cross-examination can serve to illustrate this point. Every party to an administrative proceeding, reads the relevant section of the American Administrative Procedure Act, 'shall have the right...to conduct such cross-examination as may be required for a full and true disclosure of the facts'.[1] In cases involving the loyalty of civil servants, however, to allow those charged with disloyalty to confront and cross-examine those who have given the Federal Bureau of Investigation the information upon which the charge is based might impair the functioning of the investigative network which the Bureau has built up. 'In nearly all cases', stated the chairman of the Loyalty Review Board in 1947, in explaining why the right of cross-examination could not be fully protected in loyalty cases, 'the bureau [Federal Bureau of Investigation] secures the facts for inclusion in its reports from confidential sources, many of them closely connected with considerations sounding in national security. We are advised by the bureau, that, in its experienced opinion, practically none of the evidential sources available will continue to be available to the bureau if proper secrecy and confidence cannot at all times be maintained with respect to the original source of information, and that if the source of such information is to be disclosed—save in the exceptional cases—the bureau can be of much less service to the board in making the essential basic investigation.'[2]

The point of view of the Federal Bureau of Investigation in these cases is not difficult to understand. 'The FBI is certainly not going to endanger its undercover operatives by disclosing their identity for the mere purpose of keeping an individual of doubtful loyalty out of a clerical job in the Agriculture Department's Bureau of Entomology and Plant Quarantine. That game, from the FBI's point of view, is plainly not worth the candle.'[3]

At the same time, it must be admitted that the failure to accord the rights of confrontation and cross-examination has often made it most difficult for civil servants in individual cases to defend themselves against charges of disloyalty. What this can mean in practice is shown by the one case on the subject to have thus far reached the United States Supreme Court.[4] In that case, the civil servant in question, who had been in the federal service over fourteen years, was charged with being a Communist and with being active in a Communist 'front organization'. The Loyalty

1 Section 7 (c).

2 Richardson, quoted in Emerson and Helfeld, *loc. cit.* 107.

3 Barth, *op. cit.* 133. That this is, in fact, the view of the Federal Bureau of Investigation is shown by the comment of its head, J. Edgar Hoover, in 58 *Yale L. J.* (1949), 401, 410.   4 *Bailey* v. *Richardson*, 341 U.S. 918 (1951).

Review Board stated that the case against her was based on reports, some of which came from 'informants certified to us by the Federal Bureau of Investigation as experienced and entirely reliable'. A member of the Supreme Court has described the efforts of this civil servant to learn the identity of these informants as follows:

'Counsel for Dorothy Bailey asked that their names be disclosed. That was refused.

'Counsel for Dorothy Bailey asked if these informants had been active in a certain union. The chairman replied, "I haven't the slightest knowledge as to who they were or how active they have been in anything".

'Counsel for Dorothy Bailey asked if those statements of the informants were under oath. The chairman answered, "I don't think so".'[1]

In cases like this, where the individual does not know the identity of his accusers, it may be well-nigh impossible for him adequately to disprove their charges, even if, in fact, they are prejudiced and irresponsible. 'The Loyalty Board', as the justice just quoted has put it, 'convicts on evidence which it cannot even appraise. The critical evidence may be the word of an unknown witness who is "a paragon of veracity, a knave, or the village idiot". His name, his reputation, his prejudices, his animosities, his trustworthiness are unknown both to the judge and to the accused. The accused has no opportunity to show that the witness lied or was prejudiced or venal. Without knowing who her accusers are she has no way of defending.'[2]

THE BAILEY CASE

How, it may be asked, can a loyalty proceeding such as that just outlined be reconciled with the adjective requirements imposed upon the American administration by the Administrative Procedure Act and the 'due process' clause of the Federal Constitution? As far as the Administrative Procedure Act is concerned, the answer is clear. For that statute, by its own terms, does not apply to cases involving 'the selection or tenure of an officer or employee of the United States'.[3] It consequently cannot be claimed that proceedings under the loyalty investigation are invalid because the procedural requirements of the Administrative Procedure Act have not been complied with. As far as the 'due process' question is concerned, the answer is, it is true, a more difficult one. But here, too, the federal courts have held that, under the prevailing principles of American administrative law, the procedural rights of the civil servant have not been violated.

In order to understand the holding of the federal courts upon this point

1 Douglas, J., concurring, in *Joint Anti-Fascist Refugee Committee* v. *McGrath*, 341 U.S. 123, 180 (1951).   2 *Ibid.*   3 Section 5.

one must realize that, though, in the American system, one starts with the proposition that administrative action which adversely affects individual citizens must be preceded by notice and a full and fair hearing as a matter of due process, the courts have held that this is true only in cases involving personal or property 'rights'. If the case is characterized by the American courts as one involving only a so-called 'privilege', there is no requirement that those affected be fully heard, unless the enabling Act expressly imposes such requirement. 'Due process', declares a leading American treatise, 'does not prevent the government from denying bounties or privileges without a hearing.'[1]

The application of this 'privilege-right' distinction in cases arising under the Federal Government's loyalty investigation can be seen in the leading case of *Bailey* v. *Richardson*,[2] which has already been referred to, at least so far as the procedure before the Loyalty Review Board in that case was concerned. After the Board had found the civil servant in question to be 'disloyal to the Government of the United States' and she had been discharged by the agency which employed her, she sought, in the appropriate federal court, a declaratory judgment and an order directing her reinstatement in government employment. Among other things, her complaint alleged that she had not been afforded before the Loyalty Review Board a hearing such as due process required in a case of this type. The Court of Appeals for the District of Columbia upheld the administrative procedure which had been followed. The Supreme Court affirmed, four concurring and four dissenting;[3] and, as is customary in cases where there is an equal division in the highest American tribunal, the court did not deliver any opinion. The opinion of the Court of Appeals thus remains *the* opinion in the case and, because of the significance of the problem involved, it is important to go into its basis.

According to Judge Prettyman, who delivered the opinion of the Court of Appeals, the 'due process' clause does not restrict the President's discretion or the prescriptive power of Congress in respect to executive personnel. The reason why he reached this conclusion can be gathered from the following passage in his opinion:

'In the absence of statute or ancient custom to the contrary, executive offices are held at the will of the appointing authority, not for life or for fixed terms. If the removal be at will, of what purpose would process be?

1 Davis, *Administrative Law* (1951), 246. See Schwartz, 'Procedural due process in federal administrative law', 25 *New York University L. Rev.* (1950), 552.
2 341 U.S. 918 (1951).
3 Justice Clark, who had been the Attorney-General at the time the Loyalty Board had acted, took no part in the consideration or decision of the case. It was his abstention which opened the way to the even split in the court.

To hold office at the will of a superior and to be removable therefrom only by constitutional due process of law are opposite and inherently conflicting ideas. Due process of law is not applicable unless one is being deprived of something to which he has a right.'[1]

The opinion of the federal court thus turns upon the fact that the government employee does not have any 'right' to his employment which the courts will protect. As it was expressed by the New York Court of Appeals, in an opinion dealing with basically the same problem as that presented in the *Bailey Case*, 'A public employee has no vested, proprietary right to his position..., public employment as a teacher is not an uninhibited privilege.'[2]

When once the civil servant is treated as having only a 'privilege' and not a 'right' in his position, under the weight of American authority, he would appear not to be protected by the procedural requirements of the 'due process' clause. The result in the *Bailey Case* thus depends upon the conception of government employment which prevails in the American legal system. American jurists tend to look upon employment by the State as analogous to employment by a private employer. The relationship as between employer and employee is a contractual one, and the employee has only the rights and obligations contained in his employment contract. Civil servants, in the American conception, are thus solely 'employees' of the Government and, as such, have only the status which the law generally accords to employees. 'The situation of the Government employee is not different in this respect from that of private employees.'[3] In the absence of provisions to the contrary in statutes or regulations, the State has the same discretion with regard to the appointment and dismissal of its employees that any private employer has.[4]

The result of this assimilation of the position of the civil servant to that of the ordinary private employee is that the civil servant is not protected, *qua* employee, by the principles of administrative procedure that have been developed by the American courts. American administrative law is a system which governs the relations between the administration and private individuals. Its principles are not applicable where the administration acts only with regard to its employees, in matters relating to their employment. In the American system, the government employee is not treated as one

1 182 F. 2d 46, 58 (App. D.C. 1950).
2 *Thompson* v. *Wallin*, 301 N.Y. 476, 489 (1950).
3 *Bailey* v. *Richardson*, 182 F. 2d 46, 60 (App. D.C. 1950).
4 In this respect, it should be noted, the American system differs drastically from that which prevails in a Continental country like France. See Schwartz, *French Administrative Law and the Common-Law World* (1954), 85–6; *Le Droit administratif américain: notions générales* (1952), ix.

vested with 'rights' which the courts will enforce. 'The petitioner may have a constitutional right to talk politics,' reads a famous statement of Mr Justice Holmes, 'but he has no constitutional right to be a policeman.'[1]

The use of the distinction between so-called property rights and privileges as the basis for determining whether notice and full hearing are constitutionally required in the American system, upon which, as we have seen, the *Bailey Case* turns, has been much criticized in recent years, especially in its application to cases involving civil servants. 'Certain procedures', asserts a former American Attorney-General, 'are recognized in both administrative and judicial trials as being essential prerequisites to fair decisions: confrontation of witnesses with the right of cross-examination, specific charges, findings, a written record. To say that the individual has no right to a job is not to say that he has no right to fair treatment.'[2] The fact that the legislature can, in other words, deny a privilege such as government employment altogether should not mean that it can be denied to particular individuals without notice and full hearing. It should, however, be recognized that the American courts have tended to follow the 'right-privilege' distinction in determining whether a full hearing need be accorded by the administration in particular cases. *Bailey* v. *Richardson* is but the most recent example of this tendency, though it is greatly to be regretted that the equal division in the American Supreme Court in that case prevented that tribunal from articulating its views upon the subject.

EISENHOWER SECURITY ORDER

The loyalty investigation instituted by the Truman Administration, which has been discussed, went substantially beyond any analogous measures considered necessary by other democratic countries.[3] Certainly, there has been nothing in the British system like the comprehensive system of civil service loyalty surveillance instituted in the United States in 1947. In Britain, with the exception of those in positions 'vital to the security of the State', there is still no limitation on the freedom of government workers to join political parties of their choice, provided that there is adherence to the canons of civil service respectability.[4] As Mr Justice Douglas has put it, in referring to the difficulties arising out of the American loyalty measures, 'The British have avoided those difficulties by applying the loyalty procedure only in sensitive areas and in using it to test the qualifications of an employee for a particular post, not to condemn him for all

1 *McAuliffe* v. *Mayor of New Bedford*, 155 Mass. 216, 220 (1892).
2 Biddle, *op. cit.* 216.
3 See Emerson and Helfeld, *loc. cit.* 120–33; Bontecou, *The Federal Loyalty-Security Program* (1953), 255–71, for a comparative analysis.   4 *Ibid.* 125.

public employment.'[1] The suggestion here that the British system is, like the American one, a 'loyalty' proceeding is not, it should be noted, entirely accurate. As originally announced by the Prime Minister in 1948, the investigation is not one aimed at disloyal civil servants, but intended only to ensure that Communists or Fascists will not be 'employed in connection with work, the nature of which is vital to the security of the State'.[2] The purpose of the British proceeding is not to purge the administration of civil servants whose loyalty may be in doubt; it seeks only to guarantee the reliability of those engaged in work which does, in fact, have a significant relation to national security.

Many Americans who have disapproved of the comprehensive loyalty investigation instituted by President Truman have urged that it be confined, like the British examination, to positions which actually affect the security of the State. 'It is a sheer waste of time and effort to investigate the loyalty of employees in the Interior Department's Fish and Wildlife Service or in the Labor Department's Bureau of Veterans' Re-Employment Rights or in any of a hundred other specialized agencies of the government. The inference is inescapable that the inclusion of such employees in the loyalty program was undertaken not to safeguard the government but to punish Communist sympathizers who might have secured such jobs. So far as security is concerned, it would be hard to think of any safer place to sequester them.'[3]

Other Americans, however, have opposed the drastic narrowing of the loyalty investigation which a following of the British approach would involve and have suggested instead what is, to some extent, a combination of the American and British measures. They would achieve this by retaining the comprehensive nature of the civil service surveillance instituted by President Truman, but, at the same time, substituting for the standard of disloyalty, upon which cases under the Truman order turned, a standard of risk to national security. Their view was well expressed in 1950 by the present Vice-President of the United States. 'It is necessary', he asserted in an address in the House of Representatives, 'that we completely overhaul our system of checking the loyalty of federal employees. Mr Hiss[4] would have passed the present loyalty tests with flying colors. The loyalty checks are based primarily on open affiliations with Com-

1 Concurring, in *Joint Anti-Fascist Refugee Committee* v. *McGrath*, 341 U.S. 123, 181 (1951).
2 See 448 H.C. Deb. 5s., col. 1703, 3418. The standards for the British proceedings are set forth in 451 H.C. Deb. 5s., col. 118.
3 Barth, *op. cit.* 134.
4 Alger Hiss, the former civil servant who was convicted of perjury in falsely testifying that he had never been a Communist. His case has become a *cause célèbre* in the United States. See Jowitt, *The Strange Case of Alger Hiss* (1953); Alistair Cooke, *A Generation on Trial* (1950).

munist-front organizations. Underground Communists and espionage agents have no open affiliations and it is therefore almost impossible to apprehend them through a routine loyalty investigation under the President's order. Serious consideration should be given to changing the entire approach under the loyalty order and placing the program on a security risk basis.'[1]

One of the first acts of the administration of President Eisenhower, which took office at the beginning of 1953, was to give effect to this demand. After two and a half months of consideration of the problem by the appropriate executive officers, the President, on 27 April 1953, promulgated Executive Order no. 10450, entitled 'Security Requirements for Government Employment'. The President's order repealed the loyalty order of the Truman administration[2] and instituted in its stead, a security-risk investigation for the federal civil service. The Eisenhower investigation differs from that of his predecessor in two basic respects: (i) in the standards upon which it is based, and (ii) in the procedures under which it is carried out.

The Truman loyalty investigation was designed to eliminate intentionally disloyal civil servants. It did not apply to those who were unintentionally dangerous, for example, those who might be indiscreet in their acts or associations. The latter 'are the persons properly called "security risks" as distinguished from "disloyalty cases". They are much more dangerous, if only because they are much more common, than the deliberately disloyal. Professional spies, operating in obscurity outside the government and the scrutiny of loyalty boards, can use such persons to glean isolated, seemingly trivial bits of information which, pieced together, provide the real substance of foreign intelligence activities.'[3] President Eisenhower's 1953 order did away with the line between loyalty and security-risk cases. Under it, any person may be barred from the federal civil service if his employment is not 'clearly consistent with the interests of the national security'. The President's order sets forth eleven criteria for determining whether a person is ineligible for federal employment—including subversive activities or associations of the types which had been listed in President Truman's

1 Nixon, quoted in Barth, *op. cit.* 136.
2 While the Truman loyalty order was in effect, 4,756,705 loyalty forms on individuals were checked with the files of the F.B.I. and other sources. Detailed investigations were instituted for 26,236 persons whose cases were considered by the appropriate loyalty boards. Of these, 16,503 persons were cleared by favourable decisions on loyalty; 560 persons were removed or denied federal employment on loyalty grounds; proceedings were discontinued in 6,828 cases because these persons left the service or withdrew their applications; and the cases of 569 persons were considered by the Department of the Army solely under security laws. Loyalty proceedings involving the remaining 1,776 persons were incomplete when the 1947 order was repealed.   3 Barth, *op. cit.* 135.

1947 order, acts of indiscretion, or 'any behavior, activities, or associations which tend to show that the individual is not trustworthy'. The standard of security risk enunciated by the Eisenhower order, it should be noted, appears to suffer from all of the lack of precision which has already been noted with regard to the loyalty standard applied by the Truman administration.

From the procedural point of view, the 'most significant thing about the Eisenhower order is the elimination by it of the system of review by a central board, such as that which had characterized the Truman loyalty proceedings. Under the latter, it will be recalled, civil servants aggrieved by loyalty decisions within the agency where they worked could appeal to a Loyalty Review Board. The Eisenhower order abolished that board and placed full responsibility for administering the security investigation instituted by it upon the heads of the different federal agencies. Under it, the initial decision, when a civil servant is charged with being a security risk, is made by so-called security officers within the employing agency. In cases where such decision is adverse, the civil servant is given a hearing before a Security Hearing Board of three appointed by his agency's head from a roster of civil servants maintained for the purpose by the Attorney-General. No employee of a particular agency can serve on its board. The Security Hearing Board then makes its decision and sends it to the agency's head. The latter alone has the power of final decision, though he generally approves the decision of the board.

It is under the Eisenhower order of 1953 that American civil servants are now screened to determine whether they shall be retained in federal employment.[1] So far as affected civil servants are concerned, the investigation established by that order is, if anything, even more pervasive than President Truman's loyalty proceeding. Certainly, the standard for exclusion from the government service under the 1953 order—i.e. that the civil servant's retention is not clearly consistent with the interests of the national security—is wider in scope than that of disloyalty under the Truman order. Today, not only those who are deliberately disloyal, but all federal employees who constitute any danger, though inadvertently, to national security may be removed. In other words, for the subjective standard of the Truman order, there has now been substituted an objective standard. Yet that standard is, in most respects, no more precise than that upon which the Truman proceedings turned. And from the procedural point of view, the Eisenhower order seems to be some-

---

1 According to a report issued on 11 October 1954 by the United States Civil Service Commission, in the first thirteen months after the Eisenhower order was issued, a total of 6,926 'security risks' left the federal civil service.

what less solicitous of the rights of the civil servant than was its predecessor. Though, as far as effective administration was concerned, the Truman procedure of review outside the particular agency by a central board might have appeared too greatly to spread out the responsibility and to involve too many lengthy steps, it cannot be denied that it constituted a substantial safeguard for civil servants charged with disloyalty. The elimination of the central review board under the Eisenhower order removes this safeguard, though some check upon arbitrariness is provided by the independent Security Hearing Boards within each federal agency.

It should not, however, be thought that the deficiencies just noted of the Eisenhower security order in any way affect its legality. The holding of the *Bailey Case*, which has been discussed at length, indicates that such measures, designed to deal with the impact of the 'cold war' upon the American civil service, do not present any legal issues. Since the civil servant has only a 'privilege' and not a 'right' in his position, under the American case law, his position cannot be protected by the courts, at least not as a matter of constitutional law. Unless a statute or regulation imposes procedural safeguards, he is not protected by them. Nor may he have the merits of his case reviewed by the American courts. It may well be that the approach of the American administration to the problem of purging the civil service has not been a wise one, in not affording the procedural guarantees which apply in cases involving the 'rights' of private citizens.[1] 'Able pleas', writes the court of appeals in its *Bailey* opinion, 'are made based upon the American passion for fair play and upon the sincere fears of patriotic men that unqueried and unrestricted power of removal in the President may lead to tyranny.'[2] Pleas of this type, based upon the wisdom of governmental action, are not, however, for the American courts, whose concern is solely with the legality of challenged action. 'Such pleas are to be neither ignored nor belittled, but their forum is the Congress and the President's office.'[3]

TEST OATHS

One of the most significant developments in the American reaction to the pressures of the 'cold war' has been the widespread employment of what are usually called 'loyalty oaths'—which has been acutely characterized by a member of the Federal Supreme Court as a revival of the 'test oath' technique in the American system.[4] Under this technique, as it is at present used in the United States, the legislature imposes upon specified classes, usually civil servants or teachers, the obligation to take an oath attesting

1 Compare Biddle, *op. cit.* 212.   2 182 F. 2d at 65.   3 *Ibid.*
4 Black, J., dissenting, in *American Communications Assn.* v. *Douds*, 339 U.S. 382, 447 (1950).

their loyalty to the American Government. Such oath normally declares that the individual concerned does not advocate, nor is he a member of an organization that advocates, the overthrow of the Government by force or violence.

A loyalty oath of this type as a condition for securing or remaining in public employment is now a common feature of the American scene. The validity of an ordinance of the City of Los Angeles requiring such an oath was dealt with by the United States Supreme Court in *Garner* v. *Board of Public Works*.[1] The ordinance in question required all city employees to take an oath affirming that they did not advocate or teach the forcible over-throw of the Government, nor were they affiliated with an organization that did so, nor had they done so within the period beginning five years prior to the effective date of the ordinance. In addition, an affidavit had to be filed stating whether or not the employee was or ever had been a member of the Communist party.

Whatever may be thought about the desirability of a test oath of this type, it seems clear that the answer to the question of its legality must be the same as that given with regard to the validity of the loyalty investigation instituted for the federal civil service. 'The Constitution', wrote Mr Justice Frankfurter in the *Garner Case*, 'does not guarantee public employment'. City, State and Nation are not confined to making provisions appropriate for securing competent professional discharge of the functions pertaining to diverse governmental jobs. They may also assure themselves of fidelity to the very presuppositions of our scheme of government on the part of those who seek to serve it. No unit of government can be denied the right to keep out of its employ those who seek to overthrow the government by force or violence, or are knowingly members of an organization engaged in such endeavor.'[2]

Nor is the loyalty oath device in the American system confined in its use to government employees, such as civil servants and teachers. Thus, it has been used in connexion with elections, under laws requiring candidates for public office to take loyalty oaths in order to obtain a place on the ballot. And, under an important federal law in the field of labour relations, the benefits of the law which otherwise inhere in labour unions are denied to unions the officers of which have not filed so-called 'non-Communist' affidavits with the appropriate administrative agency. The affidavits re-ferred to have to affirm that the union officers are not members of, or affiliated with, the Communist party and are not members or supporters of any organizations which believe in or teach the overthrow of the

Government by force or illegal methods.[1] In both of these cases, the Supreme Court has upheld the constitutionality of the loyalty oath requirement.[2] The State can exclude from office those who advocate revolutionary methods, and it can also deny to them or organizations which they control the benefits of a labour law enacted by the Congress.

It should not be thought from the above that the legislative authority in regard to the use of the loyalty oath technique is an unrestricted one. That there are, in fact, some limits is shown by a case decided by the highest American court at the end of 1952.[3] It involved an oath prescribed by the Oklahoma legislature of all State employees similar to those which have been discussed. This particular oath went further, however, than the others, in that it required the civil servant or other employee to affirm that he was not affiliated with any organization which had been officially determined by the United States Attorney-General or other authorized federal agency to be a 'communist front or subversive organization'. This portion of the oath, said the Supreme Court, rendered it invalid, for an individual could have joined an organization now designated as subversive by the Attorney-General without having known its true character. 'Membership may be innocent. A state servant may have joined a proscribed organization unaware of its activities and purposes.'[4] Yet, under the Oklahoma law, the *scienter* of the public employee was irrelevant in determining whether he was to be removed. Under the statute, the fact alone of membership in an organization on the Attorney-General's list disqualified.

According to the case just discussed, the loyalty oath device cannot be used to bar individuals from the American civil service solely on the basis of organizational membership, regardless of their knowledge concerning the organization to which they had belonged.[5] Yet, even though it may be important in protecting individual civil servants from being 'asked, on pain of giving up public employment, to swear to something they cannot be expected to know',[6] the 1952 Supreme Court decision clearly does not go so far as to invalidate the loyalty oath technique. Indeed, as

1 Under the recently enacted Communist Control Act of 1954, no union found by the relevant agency to be 'Communist-infiltrated' is now entitled to the benefits of the labour law.

2 *Gerende* v. *Elections Board*, 341 U.S. 56 (1951); *American Communications Assn.* v. *Douds*, 399 U.S. 382 (1950).

3 *Wieman* v. *Updegraff*, 344 U.S. 183 (1952).

4 *Ibid.* at 190.

5 The court's opinion does not tell us why even this limitation applies, in view of the fact that public employment has been held to be a 'privilege' and not a 'right' in the American system.

6 Frankfurter, J., in *Garner* v. *Board of Public Works*, 341 U.S. at 728.

we have seen, the legality of that technique, when properly limited to cases involving *scienter*, is now beyond question in the American system.

The desirability of the use of the loyalty oath device is, however, quite another matter. 'The argument most commonly advanced in favor of a loyalty oath is simply, "Why not?" Why should any loyal American object to swearing that he does not advocate the forcible overthrow of the government and that he is not and will not become a member of any organization so advocating? "But:...a prior and more apposite question is Why?" Why should public employees "be singled out as a special class and be asked to profess their innocence of an attitude which there is no good reason to suspect them of holding?"'[1] The legal answer to this last question, as has been emphasized, is clear. As the Supreme Court has expressed it, the governmental employer is not disabled from inquiring of its employees as to matters that may prove relevant to their fitness and suitability for the public service.[2] But the legal answer of the Supreme Court does not wholly suffice to justify what is essentially a recrudescence of the test oath technique in the United States. It is asserted, declares a dissenting member of the Supreme Court, 'that members of the Communist Party or its "affiliates" can be individually attainted without danger to others because there is some evidence that as a group they act in obedience to the commands of a foreign power. This was the precise reason given in Sixteenth-Century England for attainting all Catholics unless they subscribed to test oaths wholly incompatible with their religion. Yet in the hour of crisis, an overwhelming majority of the English Catholics thus persecuted rallied loyally to defend their homeland against Spain and its Catholic troops.'[3]

RESTRICTIONS UPON ALIENS

One of the features of the American legal system that has attracted much unfavourable attention outside of the United States in recent years has been that portion of the federal statute book dealing with the control of aliens. Americans who comment unfavourably upon the institutions of other countries are often met with counter-criticisms based upon the treatment of aliens in the United States. 'We have no "Ellis Island" in France!' writes a distinguished member of the French Conseil d'État in reply to

1 Byse, 'A report on the Pennsylvania Loyalty Act', 101 *U. of Pennsylvania L. Rev.* (1953), 480, 484.
2 *Garner* v. *Board of Public Works*, 341 U.S. at 720.
3 Black, J., in *American Communications Assn.* v. *Douds*, 339 U.S. 382, 450 (1950).

an American commentary noting the existence of a residue of unrestrained administrative power in France.[1]

The unfavourable attitude of outsiders toward the immigration laws of the United States has undoubtedly grown stronger since the enactment in 1952 of the revision of those laws in the now notorious McCarran Act. 'The 270 French seamen who refused to swear they were not Communists', states an English observer at the beginning of 1953, 'and did not belong to any Communist-dominated organization—including a trade union—ate their Christmas dinners on board the ironically named *Liberté* almost under the shadow of the Statue of Liberty. They were the first aliens to feel the teeth of the McCarran-Walter Immigration Act which went into effect on Christmas Eve.'[2]

Until the First World War, there was relatively little regulation of aliens by the United States, the American policy in this respect reflecting the need for immigration to help populate an undeveloped country that prevailed in the first century after the founding of the Federal Republic. Yet, even before the end of the last century, some controls had been set up. In 1875, a law listed certain grounds upon which aliens might be refused entry into the country, and, in 1888, the policy of deporting undesirable aliens was established. Both of these alien control laws were, however, very limited in scope, applying to obviously undesirable aliens, such as criminals and immoral persons. In 1917, the grounds for exclusion and deportation were both greatly broadened. And, in 1921, a law restricting the entry of aliens upon a quota basis of national origins was passed. The quota system thus established, which has more and more been criticized as discriminatory because it unduly favours immigrants from northern Europe, has continued to remain the basis upon which immigration to the United States is permitted.

It was almost inevitable that the pressures imposed by the Second World War and the deterioration of relations between the Communist and non-Communist countries in the post-war period would be reflected in a further tightening-up of the American laws relating to aliens. For the foreigner has always been looked upon with some suspicion and, in times of tension, his lack of full allegiance to his new residence is felt to make him particularly prone to subversive activities. The past decade has consequently seen the imposition, in the name of internal security, of additional restrictions upon aliens in the United States, and the McCarran Act of 1952 is but the culmination of the movement in that direction.

1 Letter from M. Letourneur, senior *commissaire du gouvernement*, to the author, 21 February 1952.
2 *The Economist*, 3 January 1953, p. 24.

Among the most important restrictions imposed in recent years have been provisions for the exclusion and deportation of aliens who are members of, or affiliated with, the Communist party or any other totalitarian party, who advocate world communism or the establishment of totalitarian dictatorship or who advocate or teach the overthrow of the Government by force or violence, are affiliated with an organization which does so, or who write, publish or circulate matter so doing.[1] It should be noted that the deportation provisions apply to aliens who, at any time after entry, come within the provisions specified, and not only to those who do so at the time of the deportation proceeding.

As far as the exclusion of aliens because they come within these provisions is concerned, it is clear, under the American law, that such exclusion is wholly within the congressional power. The power of exclusion of foreigners, stated the United States Supreme Court as early as 1889, is an incident of sovereignty belonging to the Government, and it has the right to exercise such power whenever, in its judgment, the interests of the country require it.[2] Or, as the Supreme Court put it in 1950, 'an alien who seeks admission to this country may not do so under any claim of right. Admission of aliens to the United States is a privilege granted by the sovereign United States Government. Such privilege is granted to an alien only upon such terms as the United States shall prescribe.'[3] If entry into the United States is a 'privilege', which can be granted on any terms which the Government wishes, there is clearly no constitutional limitation to restrain the Congress from excluding any classes of aliens whom it chooses.

In its impact upon the alien, a deportation proceeding is normally far more drastic than one involving exclusion from the country. For deportation may occur after the alien has severed most of his ties with his homeland and established his roots in his new residence. Deportation, as Mr Justice Brandeis once eloquently declared, 'may result...in loss of both property and life; or of all that makes life worth living'.[4] Even with regard to deportation, however, the American courts have consistently held that it is for the Congress to determine the classes of deportable aliens. 'The Government's power to terminate its hospitality has been asserted and sustained by this Court since the question first arose.... That aliens remain vulnerable to expulsion after long residence is a practice that bristles with severities. But it is a weapon of defense and reprisal confirmed

1 First enacted in 1940, these provisions were greatly extended by the McCarran Act of 1952.
2 *Chinese Exclusion Case*, 130 U.S. 581, 609 (1889).
3 *United States ex rel. Knauff* v. *Shaughnessy*, 338 U.S. 537, 542 (1950).
4 *Ng Fung Ho* v. *White*, 259 U.S. 276, 284 (1922).

by international law as a power inherent in every sovereign state. Such is the traditional power of the Nation over the alien and we leave the law on the subject as we find it.'[1] Nor could it be contended that the exercise of the congressional power against alien Communists was an improper exercise of this traditional power. 'Under the conditions which produced this Act,' asks Mr Justice Jackson, 'can we declare that congressional alarm about a coalition of Communist power without and Communist conspiracy within the United States is either a fantasy or a pretense?... Certainly no responsible American would say that there were then or are now no possible grounds on which Congress might believe that Communists in our midst are inimical to our security.'

It should be emphasized once again that a decision on the legality of legislative action in this field is not necessarily a decision on its desirability. In the case of alien restrictions, as is true of much of the congressional reaction to the 'cold war', it can reasonably be urged that 'for a mouse of security a great deal of resentment is being built up'.[3] But this does not mean that the American laws in question are unconstitutional, which was the sole matter that the federal courts have had to deal with in the cases that have been discussed. 'We, in our private opinions,' stated Mr Justice Jackson in the case upholding the validity of a statute providing for the deportation of Communist aliens, 'need not concur in Congress' policies to hold its enactments constitutional. Judicially we must tolerate what personally we may regard as a legislative mistake.'[4]

CONCLUSION

The above analysis has given a picture of the reaction of American law to the stresses of actual war and the 'cold war'.[5] The problem with which the Federal Congress has sought to deal in the restrictive legislation which has been discussed is one which has not presented itself to the American

1 *Harisiades* v. *Shaughnessy*, 342 U.S. 580, 587 (1952).
2 *Ibid.* at 590. It should, however, be noted that an alien, in a deportation proceeding, still has the right to a full hearing before a deportation order can be issued against him. 3 *The Economist*, 3 January 1953, p. 25.
4 *Harisiades* v. *Shaughnessy*, 342 U.S. 580, 590 (1952).
5 An important statute, which has not been dealt with because of space limitations, is the so-called Internal Security Act of 1950. It provides for the registration of subversive organizations with the Federal Subversive Activities Control Board, and for the emergency detention of Communists and others who might endanger security, but the latter only in the event of invasion, insurrection, or declaration of war. Nor has it been possible to treat of the Communist Control Act of 1954, enacted while this work was being printed. It provides that the Communist Party is not entitled to 'any of the rights, privileges, and immunities attendant upon legal bodies created under the jurisdiction of the laws of the United States or any political subdivision thereof.'

legislature alone. It first became apparent in Europe between the two world wars, especially after the fall of the Weimar Republic, which was brought about by an anti-democratic party, which took full advantage of the rights guaranteed by the German Constitution, in order to attain the power to obliterate those rights. 'Clearly realizing the dangerous situation from mere acquiescence or from the treacherous belief that in the long run, the inherent superiority of democratic values will assert itself over fascist ideology, the democratic states of Europe were prompted, particularly since the successful overthrow of democracy in Germany by Hitler, to protect, by elaborate legislative devices, the democratic form of government and its institutions against subversive activities of both communist and fascist parties.' [1]

And a similar problem has arisen in the Europe that was liberated after the last conflict. 'Influenced by the tragic experience of the democracies between the two wars, modern constitutional thinking has endeavored to resolve this fundamental problem. Can we, in effect, find...a criterion for limiting the Rights of Man when their abusive exercise risks the overthrow of the very system of government which guarantees them?' [2] The problem of reconciling the freedoms safeguarded by a bill of rights with the security of the State is tending more and more to be resolved in favour of the latter by contemporary constitutional theory. 'In all countries... legislation for the defense of the democratic form of government has one feature in common: The customary complacency of traditional liberalism toward the danger from extremism...has largely disappeared. Democratic instrumentalities and constitutional rights, too long held sacrosanct by democratic fundamentalists, are no longer insuperable obstacles to a militant defense. Democracy, fighting fire with fire, tends to become militant. Liberal democracy, style 1900, slowly gives way to "disciplined" or even "authoritarian" democracy of the postwar...pattern.' [3]

The reaction of the American legislature to the problems presented by foreign totalitarian Governments and their domestic agents is thus far from unique, even in the democratic portion of the world. And, from a constitutional point of view, as has been shown, the congressional measures are unassailable. It is not for the American courts to upset legislation designed to deal with the Communist threat merely because they differ from the congressional judgment on the gravity of the threat. 'It would be easy', as the highest American tribunal has declared, 'for

1 Loewenstein, 'Legislative control of political extremism in European democracies. I', 38 *Columbia L. Rev.* (1938), 591, 593.

2 Mirkine-Guetzévitch, *op. cit.* 138.

3 Loewenstein, 'Legislative control of political extremism in European democracies. II', 38 *Columbia L. Rev.* (1938), 725, 774.

those of us who do not have security responsibility to say that those who do are taking Communism too seriously and over-estimating its danger.'[1] If the Supreme Court is not, in effect, to revert to its role as a super-legislature, it must refrain from declaring laws unconstitutional unless, in Mr Justice Brandeis's famous phrase, they transcend the bounds of reason. 'That is, [unless] the provision as applied is so clearly arbitrary or capricious that legislators acting reasonably could not have believed it to be necessary or appropriate for the public welfare.'[2]

At the same time, however, it should be recognized that the decisions by the Supreme Court upon the constitutionality of restrictive laws such as those which we have been discussing are in no way an answer to the broader question of the desirability of such legislation. 'The wisdom of the assumptions underlying the legislation. . . is another matter. In finding that Congress has acted within its power, a judge does not imply that he favors the implications that lie beneath the legal issues. Considerations there enter which go beyond the criteria that are binding upon judges within the narrow confines of their legitimate authority.'[3]

It is the question of the desirability of the widespread anti-Communist measures in the United States that tends to give pause, regardless of how clearly one may be convinced of the constitutionality of the legislative matters concerned under American law. The 'unbounded freedom of discussion' was one of the outstanding features of the American system which impressed Lord Bryce over half a century ago. 'Every view, every line of policy,' he wrote, 'has its fair chance before the people. No one can say that audience has been denied him, and comfort himself with the hope that, when he is heard, the world will come round to him. For the sense of grievance and injustice, which so often feeds the flame of resistance in a persecuted minority, there is less cause in a country like this. . .than anywhere else in the world.'[4]

It cannot be denied that these words are not as true today as they were when they were written. The legislative measures, which have been dealt with, have, in large part, been aimed at speech and political beliefs. It is true that the speech and beliefs in question have been extremely unpopular and even undesirable. But that does not change the fact that it is speech and belief, as such, which have been penalized. The Communist leaders, who were convicted in the *Dennis Case*,[5] were punished not for any overt acts but for teaching and advocating their political philosophy. Their

1 *Harisiades* v. *Shaughnessy*, 342 U.S. 580, 590 (1952).
2 Dissenting, in *Burns Baking Co.* v. *Bryan*, 264 U.S. 504, 534 (1924).
3 Frankfurter, J., concurring, in *Dennis* v. *United States*, 341 U.S. at 553.
4 Bryce, *The American Commonwealth* (1889 ed.), vol. 2, 303.
5 341 U.S. 494 (1951).

views may have been highly repugnant to most Americans, but should they be rendered criminal when expressed in speech alone?

It is not enough to justify the suppression of speech by relying only upon the fear of the danger flowing from such speech. 'Fear of serious injury' reads a noted passage by Justice Brandeis, 'cannot alone justify suppression of free speech and assembly. Men feared witches and burnt women. It is the function of speech to free men from the bondage of irrational fear.'[1] And it is no answer to state that, after all, it is only the Communists, a small and obnoxious minority, who are affected by the legislative restrictions in question. 'Centuries of experience testify that laws aimed at one political or religious group, however rational these laws may be in their beginnings, generate hatreds and spread prejudices which rapidly spread beyond control. Too often it is fear which inspires such passions, and nothing is more reckless or contagious.'[2]

It is one thing drastically to limit speech in time of actual war. 'I think', said Mr Justice Holmes, in a letter sent to Harold J. Laski, in 1919, on the restrictions imposed on speech during the First World War, 'the clauses under consideration not only were constitutional but were proper enough while the war was on. When people are putting out all their energies in battle I don't think it unreasonable to say we won't have obstacles intentionally put in the way...—by persuasion any more than by force.'[3] It is quite another thing to assert the wisdom of restrictions upon speech during peace-time—or even in the quasi-peace of the 'cold war' era. As long as overt acts are not involved, one may well say, with Justice Holmes, 'in the main I am for aeration of all effervescing convictions—there is no way so quick for letting them get flat'.[4]

One point should be borne in mind in considering the wisdom of legislative limitations upon Communist beliefs and speech alone. The Anglo-American system of justice is at present under strong attack from certain quarters. 'Bourgeois theorists', asserts a leading Soviet jurist, 'strive to depict the court as an organ above classes and apart from politics, acting, supposedly, in the interests of all society and guided by commands of law and justice common to all mankind, instead of by the interests of the dominant class. Such a conception of the court's essence and task is, of course, radically false. It has always been an instrument in the hands of the dominant class, assuring the strengthening of its dominance and the protection of its interests.'[5]

---

1 *Whitney* v. *California*, 274 U.S. 357, 376 (1927).
2 Black, J., dissenting, in *American Communications Assn.* v. *Douds*, 339 U.S. 382, 448 (1950). 3 *Holmes-Laski Letters* (1953), 203. 4 *Ibid.* 204.
5 Vyshinsky, *The Law of the Soviet State* (1948 ed.), 500.

It is of the utmost consequence, especially in cases involving exponents of this school of thought, for the courts in the non-Communist world not to appear to lend any credence to such Soviet assertions about our kind of justice. One of the most disturbing aspects of the cases under the anti-Communist legislation in the American courts has been the view asserted outside the United States that they illustrate how the American judiciary, like the other branches of the Federal Government, are willing to deprive those whose beliefs are opposed to the American ideology of their basic civil liberties. The analysis which has been given above of this field of American constitutional law should, it is believed, show the fallacy of this view. Legislative restrictions upon civil liberties in the United States which have been imposed in answer to the problems posed by the 'cold war' have been sustained by the federal courts, as has been shown, in accordance with the ordinary principles of American constitutional law. But, all the same, it is somewhat disquieting that, to some at least, the role of the American judiciary in the anti-Communist cases has appeared less than wholly impartial. 'Vyshinsky wrote in 1938', eloquently states a member of the United States Supreme Court, 'in The Law of the Soviet State, "In our state, naturally, there is and can be no place for freedom of speech, press, and so on for the foes of socialism." Our concern should be that we accept no such standard for the United States. Our faith should be that our people will never give support to these advocates of revolution, so long as we remain loyal to the purposes for which our Nation was founded.'[1]

1 Douglas, J., dissenting, in *Dennis* v. *United States*, 341 U.S. at 591.

Chapter XI

ADMINISTRATIVE LAW

If it were written some fifty years ago, a work like the present one, seeking to explain the essentials of American constitutional law to a British audience, would hardly have included a chapter devoted to administrative law. The British jurist could not be expected to show an interest in developments abroad in a field whose existence he had been accustomed to deny at home. If, however, a half-century ago it required the 'prophetic sense of a Maitland'[1] to realize the great growth of administrative law, today awareness of that growth has become a commonplace. Administrative law, as a leading American judge has recently affirmed, is now recognized as 'the outstanding legal development of the twentieth century, reflecting in the law the hegemony of the executive arm of the government'.[2] Nor, it should be noted, is the realization of this confined to members of the legal profession. Indeed, as significant to the student of administrative law as the tremendous extension of his subject, has been the widespread public interest displayed in it in recent years.

Public concern over trends in this field reflects an increasing awareness of its importance in dealing with the many problems arising out of the expansion of the role of the State. Human existence is inconceivable outside of society.[3] At the same time organized society threatens to overwhelm the individual. 'There is not a moment of his existence where modern man does not find himself in contact with government and its agents.'[4] In the contemporary State, government tends more and more to become the all-dominant factor in society, by taking over or controlling the functions hitherto performed by private institutions. As it does so it comes into ever-increasing contact with the individual life. 'It is in this ceaseless contact of the individual with the State that the danger of arbitrariness has especially arisen.'[5]

The dangers arising out of the expansion of State power were well put a generation ago by Lord Macmillan's Committee on Finance and Industry: 'The most distinctive indication of the change of outlook of the

1 Sieghart, *Government by Decree* (1950), 1.
2 Vanderbilt in Introduction to Schwartz, *French Administrative Law and the Common-Law World* (1954), xiii.
3 Pinto, *Éléments du droit constitutionnel* (1948), 23.
4 Duguit, *Manuel de droit constitutionnel* (1923), 39.
5 *Ibid.* 40.

government of this country in recent years has been its growing preoccupation, irrespective of party, with the management of the life of the people. A study of the Statute Book will show how profoundly the conception of the function of government has altered. Parliament finds itself increasingly engaged in legislation which has for its conscious aim the regulation of the day-to-day affairs of the community, and now intervenes in matters formerly thought to be entirely outside its scope. This new orientation has its dangers as well as its merits. Between liberty and government there is an age-long conflict. It is of vital importance that the new policy, while truly promoting liberty by securing better conditions of life for the people of this country, should not, in its zeal for interference, deprive them of their initiative and independence which are the nation's most valuable assets.' [1]

It is the task of administrative law to avoid at least part of the danger referred to by Lord Macmillan's committee. It does so by ensuring that governmental functions will be exercised 'on proper legal principles' [2]— 'according to the rules of reason and justice' [3]—and not at the mere caprice of the magistrate. It defines the remedies available to the citizen when he has been adversely affected by improper governmental action.

In determining whether a system of administrative law has adequately fulfilled its task, comparison with other systems can often prove most useful. This is especially true when the law compared is based upon common-law traditions and techniques, similar to those upon which the law of England is grounded. It is from this point of view that a survey of recent trends in administrative law in the United States should be of value. An understanding of the more significant American developments can aid the English legal profession in its evaluation of analogous tendencies in Britain.

POWERS OF THE ADMINISTRATION

Anyone contemplating the powers of modern administration cannot fail to note that they fall into two general categories in their effect on private individuals. On the one hand, the administration is vested with authority to promulgate rules and regulations of general applicability. On the other, it has the power to render decisions adversely affecting the person or property of particular citizens.

In this respect the powers exercised by the administration can be compared to those normally possessed by the legislature and the courts. The

1 Quoted in *Report of the Committee on Ministers' Powers* (Cmd. 4060, 1932), 5.
2 *Pioneer Laundry and Dry Cleaners, Ltd.* v. *Minister of National Revenue*, [1940] A.C. 127, 136.
3 *Sharp* v. *Wakefield*, [1891] A.C. 173, 179.

legislature usually acts by determinations of *general* applicability addressed to indicated but unnamed and unspecified persons and situations. A court, on the contrary, acts by decisions that are *specific* in applicability and addressed to particular individuals or situations.[1] Legislation is thus distinguished from adjudication in that 'the former affects the rights of individuals in the abstract and must be applied in a further proceeding before the legal position of any particular individual will be definitely touched by it; while adjudication operates concretely upon individuals in their individual capacity'.[2]

The possession of legislative and judicial powers is perhaps the most striking characteristic of modern administration on both sides of the Atlantic. As the Attorney-General's Committee on Administrative Procedure (the American counterpart of the Committee on Ministers' Powers) has stated, the distinguishing feature of an administrative agency is its possession of the authority to determine, either by rule or by decision, private rights and obligations.[3] The grant to the administration of legislative and judicial powers is essential if it is effectively to perform the regulatory tasks entrusted to it by the legislature. 'If in private life we were to organize a unit for the operation of an industry, it would scarcely follow Montesquieu's lines.'[4] Nor can the regulation of industry be adequately carried out under a rigid separation of powers. The administration has consequently been made the repository of all three types of governmental power. In the administrative process, the various stages of making and applying law, traditionally separate, 'have been telescoped into a single agency'.[5] Delegated legislation and adjudication have become the chief weapons in both the British and American administrative armouries.

POWERS OF DELEGATED LEGISLATION

The extent of delegated legislation in England has become almost a commonplace since Sir Cecil Carr called attention to it in 1921. Yet, in the United States, too, as the Attorney-General's Committee on Administrative Procedure aptly pointed out, 'the promulgation of general regulations by the executive acting under statutory authority, has been a normal feature of Federal administration ever since the Government was established'.[6] The need for delegation of legislative power to the executive was clearly explained in the *Report of the Committee on Ministers' Powers*. 'The

1 See Fuchs, 'Procedure in administrative rule-making', 52 *Harvard L. Rev.* (1938), 259, 265.
2 Dickinson, *Administrative Justice and the Supremacy of Law* (1927), 21.
3 *Report of the Attorney-General's Committee* (1941), 8.
4 Landis, *The Administrative Process* (1938), 10.
5 *Report of the Attorney-General's Committee*, 204.   6 *Ibid.* 97.

truth is', reads the committee's conclusion on the subject, 'that if Parliament were not willing to delegate law-making power, Parliament would be unable to pass the kind and quantity of legislation which modern public opinion requires.'[1]

Objections to delegations of legislative power in America, as in England, have been based upon the doctrine of the separation of powers. 'The legislature cannot transfer the power of making laws to any other hands, reads a well-known passage from Locke, 'for, it being but a delegated power from the people, they who have it cannot pass it over to others.'[2] Yet, as Mr Justice Frankfurter asserted, in referring to the separation of powers, the 'practical demands of government preclude its doctrinaire application', for 'we are dealing with what Madison called a "political maxim" and not a technical rule of law'.[3]

There are many cases, the learned judge pointed out, which show that there are necessary areas of interaction among the departments of government. 'Functions have been allowed to courts, as to which Congress itself might have legislated; matters have been withdrawn from courts and vested in the executive; laws have been sustained which are contingent upon executive judgment on highly complicated facts. By these means Congress has been able to move with freedom in modern fields of legislation, with their great complexity and shifting facts, calling for technical knowledge and skill in administration. Enforcement of a rigid conception of separation of powers would make modern government impossible.'[4]

The American courts today refuse to invalidate legislation merely because it, in form, delegates legislative power to administrative authorities. Their approach to the delegation problem has shifted from one of formal application of an inflexible maxim against delegations of legislative power to one of determining whether the legislative grant of power is in fact inordinate. And, with this, the focus of judicial inquiry has centred upon the adequacy of the standards contained in enabling legislation.

Under present-day American theory, legislative power can be conferred upon the executive branch, provided that the grant of authority is limited by prescribed standards. 'Congress cannot delegate any part of its legislative power except under the limitation of a prescribed standard.'[5] The discretion conferred must not be so wide that it is impossible to discern its limits. There must instead be an ascertainable legislative intent to which the exercise of the delegated power must conform.

---

1 *Report of the Committee on Ministers' Powers*, 23.
2 Locke, *Of Civil Government*, §141.
3 Frankfurter, *The Public and its Government* (1930), 77.   4 *Ibid.* 78.
5 *United States* v. *Chicago, M., St. P. and P. R. R.*, 282 U.S. 311, 324 (1931).

A somewhat similar principle was expressed by the Committee on Ministers' Powers. 'The precise limits of the law-making power which Parliament intends to confer on a minister should always be expressly defined in clear language by the statute which confers it; when discretion is conferred, its limits should be defined with equal clearness.'[1]

The recommendation of the British committee on this point has received 'scant attention'.[2] The requirement of standards imposed by the courts in the United States has, of course, been of much greater importance, so far as American law is concerned. In Britain, excessive delegations of legislative power are political questions; in the United States they are primarily judicial.[3] The consequences of this are shown by *Schechter Poultry Corp.* v. *United States*,[4] where an Act of Congress was held invalid because of its failure to contain any standards to limit the exercise of the power delegated.

It should be noted, however, that recent federal statutes commonly make use of broad, general standards rather than prescriptions of detail. It has been felt that, if the legislature were required to specify with minute particularity the course to be followed by the administration, much of the advantage of delegation would be lost. The attitude of the United States Supreme Court toward this type of statute can be seen from several of its recent decisions. In *Lichter* v. *United States*,[5] petitioners claimed that the Renegotiation Act unlawfully attempted to delegate legislative power. That law provided for the renegotiation of contracts made by the Government during the war and authorized administrative officers to recover profits which they determined to be 'excessive'. But the Act did not define the term 'excessive profits' other than to state that it 'means any amount of a contract or subcontract price which is found as a result of renegotiation to represent excessive profits'—which, as one commentator has pointed out, is to define the term by saying, in effect, that 'excessive' means 'excessive'.[6]

Despite this lack of specificity, the court upheld the Act. 'It is not necessary', said Mr Justice Burton, 'that Congress supply administrative officials with a specific formula for their guidance in a field where flexibility and the adaptation of the congressional policy to infinitely variable conditions constitute the essence of the program.... The statutory term "excessive profits", in its context, was a sufficient expression of legislative policy and standards to render it constitutional.'[7]

1 *Report of the Committee on Ministers' Powers*, 65.
2 Carr, *Concerning English Administrative Law* (1941), 175.
3 Weeks, 'Legislative power versus delegated legislative power', 25 *Georgetown L. J.* 314, 330 (1937). 4 295 U.S. 495 (1935).
5 334 U.S. 742 (1948). 6 Davis, *Administrative Law* (1951), 49.
7 334 U.S. at 785, 783 (*emphasis* omitted).

It may well be that the court was led in this case to sustain what has been termed 'in some respects the greatest delegation upheld by the Supreme Court'[1] by the fact that the law at issue was enacted to deal with the war emergency. Justice Burton was manifestly influenced by the fact that the challenged authority was 'essential to an effective use of its war powers by Congress'.[2] 'In time of crisis', he declared, 'nothing could be more tragic and less expressive of the intent of the people than so to construe their Constitution that by its own terms it would substantially hinder rather than help them in defending their national safety.'[3]

The fact that it may rest primarily upon the war power makes it difficult to assess the true effect of a case like *Lichter* upon the law concerning delegation. Though it implies a relaxation in the requirement of defined standards, it can readily be distinguished from the normal peace-time case, if the Supreme Court chooses to do so. Yet a number of such 'normal' cases appear to show that, even in statutes not related to the war power, the standards regulating delegations of authority to administrative officials need not be any more detailed than those contained in the law upheld in the *Lichter Case*.

Under section 5 (d) of the Home Owners' Loan Act of 1933, the Federal Home Loan Bank Board was empowered to prescribe by regulation the terms and conditions upon which a conservator might be appointed for a federal savings and loan association. The district court had held that this constituted an invalid delegation, in that no criterion was established to guide the Board in its exercise of the authority conferred. The Supreme Court candidly conceded that there was no express legislative standard. But that did not lead it to declare the law at issue invalid. 'It may be', said Mr Justice Jackson, 'that explicit standards in the Home Owners' Loan Act would have been a desirable assurance of responsible administration. But the provisions of the statute under attack are not penal provisions.... The provisions are regulatory.... A discretion to make regulations to guide supervisory action in such matters may be constitutionally permissible while it might not be allowable to authorize creation of new crimes in uncharted fields.'[4]

With the court's explicit recognition that standards are not necessary in a law of this type should be compared its opinions dealing with grants of power under the Communications Act of 1934. Under that Act, the Federal Communications Commission is given wide authority to regulate radio broadcasting. 'The Commission was, however, not left at large in performing this duty. The touchstone provided by Congress was the

---

1 Davis, *op. cit.* 49.   2 334 U.S. at 779.
3 *Ibid.* at 780.   4 *Fahey* v. *Mallonee*, 332 U.S. 245, 250 (1947).

"public interest, convenience, or necessity", a criterion which "is as concrete as the complicated factors for judgment in such a field of delegated authority permit".'[1] In a field where the subject-matter of regulation is as fluid and dynamic as radio, a detailed prescription of standards could have made effective administration impossible. Congress would have frustrated 'the purposes for which the Communications Act of 1934 was brought into being by attempting an itemized catalogue of the specific manifestations of the general problems for the solution of which it was establishing a regulatory agency. That would have stereotyped the powers of the Commission to specific details in regulating a field of enterprise the dominant characteristic of which was the rapid pace of its unfolding.'[2]

But how does this affect the requirement of an ascertained standard in enabling legislation? Plainly, a standard such as that contained in the Communications Act is not mechanical or self-defining; it implies wide areas of judgment and, therefore, of discretion.[3] If such a broad standard is considered adequate, then has not the requirement of a defined standard become a purely formal one and, if that is the case, has not the American law, in practice if not in theory, become similar to that in Britain, where there are no constitutional limitations to restrain Parliament from delegating authority how it will?

The Supreme Court would answer this by asserting that the generality of the phrasing in a statute, such as the Communications Act of 1934, does not mean that the applicable standards are too vague to regulate administrative discretion effectively. The statutory language is not to be read in a vacuum; a general standard may be given specific form and content when looked at in the light of the statutory scheme and its background. Thus the standard of 'public interest' in the Communications Act is not so vague and indefinite as to be unconstitutional. 'It is a mistaken assumption that this is a mere general reference to public welfare without any standard to guide determinations. The purpose of the Act, the requirements it imposes, and the context of the provision in question, show the contrary.'[4]

One wonders, however, whether a standard such as that contained in the Communications Act really furnishes an effective legislative guide. As it has been put by one authority, 'telling the agency to do what is in the public interest is the practical equivalent of instructing it: "Here is the problem. Deal with it."'[5] Certainly a legislative direction to act in the

1 *National Broadcasting Co.* v. *United States*, 319 U.S. 190, 216 (1943).
2 *Ibid.* at 219.
3 Paraphrasing *Secretary of Agriculture* v. *Central Roig Refining Co.*, 338 U.S. 604, 611 (1950).
4 *National Broadcasting Co.* v. *United States*, 319 U.S. 190, 226 (1943).
5 Davis, *op. cit.* 46.

'public interest' appears to add little to an enabling Act. Would the Federal Communications Commission be likely to act any differently in specific cases if the Communications Act did not specifically instruct it to be guided by 'public interest, convenience or necessity'?[1]

It cannot be denied, in the light of the above, that the American law on the subject of permissible delegations of legislative power has been tending to approach that which prevails in Britain. If standards such as those contained in the Renegotiation and Communications Acts, discussed above, are upheld as adequate, it becomes apparent that the requirement of standards in American law has become more a matter of form than substance. Provided that there is no abdication of the congressional function,[2] the enabling law will be upheld, even though the only standard which the federal courts can find is so broad as to be almost illusory.

ADMINISTRATIVE PROCEDURE ACT OF 1946

Background. In 1929, the Lord Chief Justice of England descended from Olympus and launched his now famous attack upon the 'lawlessness' of English government departments.[3] In the United States, there has been nothing as spectacular as Lord Hewart's *New Despotism*. This is not to say, however, that the forces working for the reform of administrative procedure have been less potent there than they have been in Britain. If anything, they have been stronger in America. In Britain, the movement for administrative procedure reform largely begins and ends with the Report of the Committee on Ministers' Powers. In the United States, the Report of the Attorney-General's Committee on Administrative Procedure, the American counterpart of the British committee, marks only a starting-point for efforts to improve the administrative process.

The Attorney-General's Committee issued its Report in 1941. One of the chief points of difference in that committee arose over the proposal of a minority of its members for a Code of Standards of Fair Administrative Procedure. This was intended to serve as a set of procedural principles to govern administrative action—a more detailed legislative formulation of what the United States Supreme Court has termed the 'fundamentals of fair play'.[4] 'An adequate pattern of procedure is imperatively needed to serve as a guide to and check upon administrative officials in the exercise

1 Cf. Davis, *op. cit.* 64.
2 As there was, for example, in *Schechter Poultry Corp.* v. *United States*, 295 U.S. 495 (1935).
3 Willis, *The Parliamentary Powers of English Government Departments* (1933), 3.
4 *Federal Communications Commission* v. *Pottsville Broadcasting Co.*, 309 U.S. 134, 143 (1940).

of their discretionary powers.'¹ The majority among the committee differed from this idea of a complete and rounded code. The great number and variety of administrative agencies, in their view, were seen to preclude the adoption of a code applicable to all.

Both the majority and minority of the committee submitted bills embodying their views, which were introduced in the Congress in 1941. That of the majority sought to give legislative effect to certain basic recommendations which the committee's report had made. That of the minority was more detailed, but certainly fell short of the particularized code which the minority's statement of additional views had advocated. A subcommittee of the Senate Judiciary Committee held exhaustive hearings on the proposed measures, but the gathering storm of national emergency and war dissipated the interest which the Report of the Attorney-General's Committee had aroused, and the problem of administrative procedure reform was put aside for the moment.² As a leading jurist expressed it in surveying American administrative-law developments during 1942, 'Had it not been for the War, 1942 might well have been signalized as a year of great achievement in the movement for reforming federal administrative procedure.... The War, coming to the United States at the close of 1941, blocked any prospect of administrative reform the following year.'³

As the war progressed towards a successful conclusion, and war legislation no longer completely dominated the congressional calendar, efforts to give legislative effect to the proposals of the Attorney-General's Committee were revived. This time, the movement was successful, and the result was the Administrative Procedure Act, whose enactment has been well described by Mr Justice Jackson. 'The McCarran-Sumners bill, which evolved into the present Act, was introduced in 1945. Its consideration and hearing, especially of agency interests, was painstaking. All administrative agencies were invited to submit their views in writing. A tentative revised bill was then prepared and interested parties again were invited to submit criticisms. The Attorney General named representatives of the Department of Justice to canvass the agencies and report their criticisms, and submitted a favorable report on the bill as finally revised. It passed both Houses without opposition and was signed by President Truman June 11, 1946.'⁴

Provisions. The enactment of the Administrative Procedure Act must rank as the most significant American administrative-law development

1 *Report of the Attorney-General's Committee*, 215.
2 See *Wong Yang Sung* v. *McGrath*, 339 U.S. 33, 40 (1950).
3 Vanderbilt, 'Administrative law', *Annual Survey of American Law* (1942), 89.
4 *Wong Yang Sung* v. *McGrath*, 339 U.S. 33, 40 (1950).

during the past generation. That Act, in the words of the federal Supreme Court, 'is a new basic and comprehensive regulation of procedures in many agencies'.[1] Though the Act 'has been aptly described as the most important statute affecting the administration of justice in the federal field since the passage of the Judiciary Act of 1789',[2] its effect is clearly not a revolutionary one. It is a far cry from the complete code demanded by the minority of the Attorney-General's Committee. Instead of being such a detailed code, the Act of 1946 is a statement of the basic procedural principles which are to govern the administrative process. The Act's formulation of these principles is, in large measure, only an adoption of the best existing administrative practice. What is important, however, is that the Act states the essentials of such practice in statutory form and imposes the best existing procedure upon the administration as a whole. 'It is designed', as a prominent American judge informs us, 'to protect the individual citizen from the hazards of uncertain and slipshod administrative procedures resulting in arbitrary action, while at the same time seeking to preserve the flexibility, the resourcefulness and progressiveness of the administrative agency at its best.'[3] It is as the first attempt by the Congress to state the essentials of the procedures to be followed by the administrative process that the Administrative Procedure Act is of moment. Hitherto, the control of American administrative procedure had been largely limited to intervention by the courts, based upon the constitutional concept of procedural due process. With the Act of 1946, the federal legislature has now assumed a cardinal role.

The procedural provisions of the 1946 Act are based primarily upon the distinction between the legislative or rule-making functions of administrative agencies, on the one hand, and their judicial or adjudicative activities on the other. Generally speaking, the procedure prescribed with regard to rule-making (or delegated legislation, to use the term which is more familiar to the British lawyer) is informal in character. The requirements imposed where administrative adjudications are concerned, on the contrary, tend to be more formal in nature, modelled upon the procedure of the judicial process.

As far as delegated legislation is concerned, the Administrative Procedure Act provides for what has been termed a system of antecedent publicity.[4] General notice of proposed rules or regulations is to be published in the

---

1 339 U.S. at 36.

2 Vanderbilt in *The Federal Administrative Procedure Act and the Administrative Agencies* (1947), iv.

3 Vanderbilt, *The Doctrine of the Separation of Powers and its Present-day Significance* (1953), 87.

4 *Report of the Committee on Ministers' Powers*, 44.

Federal Register, the publication in which, in the American system, all delegated legislation promulgated by the federal administration must be published. The agency concerned must then afford interested persons the opportunity to participate in the rule-making process through submission of written data, views, or arguments, with or without opportunity to present the same orally, and all relevant matter so presented is to be considered by the agency. These provisions appear to be modelled upon those contained in the English Rules Publication Act, 1893,[1] and constitute a laudable effort to obtain some democratization of the rule-making process without, at the same time, destroying its flexibility by imposing procedural requirements which are too onerous.

As far as adjudications are concerned, the basic portions of the American Act of 1946 are those establishing a semi-independent corps of hearing officers called examiners, who are to preside over cases which are not heard by the agency's heads themselves.[2] Their appointment and tenure is placed under the control of the Civil Service Commission (an independent agency in the executive branch) with the object of enabling qualified examiners to be chosen and of permitting them to maintain the independence appropriate to a quasi-judge, by freeing them from direct control by the administrative agency in which they work. 'Congress', the American Supreme Court has recently declared, 'intended to make hearing examiners "a special class of semi-independent subordinate hearing officers" by vesting control of their compensation, promotion and tenure in the Civil Service Commission to a much greater extent than in the case of other federal employees.'[3]

These examiners are given substantial powers at the administrative hearing and in the process of decision, and their position is thus far superior to that of the inspectors who preside at the public local inquiries which are common in English administrative law. They are vested with authority to preside over the hearing analogous to that exercised by a trial judge in the American system. They are empowered to issue initial decisions, which become the decision of the agency unless appealed, in cases where the agency does not require (in specific cases or by general rule) the entire record to be certified to it for initial decision. The intent of the Act here is

1 Such provisions for antecedent publicity are not, however, contained in the Statutory Instruments Act, 1946, which repeals the 1893 English Act.

2 It should be noted that, in the American system, the 'due process' clauses of the Fifth and Fourteenth Amendments to the Constitution are held to require a formal hearing prior to administrative adjudications which adversely affect individual rights.

3 *Ramspeck* v. *Federal Trial Examiners' Conference*, 345 U.S. 128, 132 (1953). The congressional purpose here has, however, thus far been in part frustrated by the administration of the Act's provisions on this point. See Schwartz, 'The Administrative Procedure Act in operation', 29 *New York University L. Rev.* (1954), 1173, 1214 *et seq.*

to assimilate the roles of hearing and deciding officers within the agency to those of trial and appellate courts, though this has been defeated in part by the tendency of some federal agencies to provide, by general rule, that they, rather than the examiners, shall make the initial decision.[1]

So far as the conduct of the hearing itself is concerned, the American Act provides that the common-law rules of evidence do not prevail, but no administrative decision is to be rendered except 'as supported by and in accordance with the reliable, probative, and substantial evidence'. The rights of counsel and cross-examination are expressly preserved. The problem presented in cases like *Errington* v. *Minister of Health*[2] is dealt with by provision for the insulation of the hearing examiner. No such officer is to 'consult any person or party upon any fact in issue except upon notice and opportunity for all parties to participate'. Attempts by administrative officials to influence decisions in which they are interested are likewise precluded. And, finally, the administrative decision itself must be a reasoned one. It must include 'findings and conclusions, as well as the reasons or basis therefor, upon all the material issues of fact, law, or discretion presented on the record'.

Value. The above summarizes the essentials of the procedures prescribed by the American Administrative Procedure Act. While the Act may not yet have wholly achieved the intent of its draftsmen in practice, this does not mean that it has not been of great value in regularizing federal administrative law. Certainly, to quote a leading American jurist's recent conclusion on this point, 'Seams have appeared and, as in the case of the Federal Rules of Civil Procedure after a similar trial period, it may sooner or later require a revision, but even with its defects it has gone far to achieve the goal asserted by Mr Justice Brandeis, "In the development of our liberty, insistence upon procedural regularity has been a large factor".'[3]

The value of the federal Act of 1946 has, however, been doubted by some British jurists. 'The introduction of statutory procedures for administrative agencies...', asserts one such writer, 'judged by the experience in the United States with the Administrative Procedure Act, 1946, has little to commend it.'[4] To one familiar with the provisions of the American Act, it is difficult to see the basis for such an extreme criticism. From the point of view of individuals who are adversely affected by administrative action, the 1946 Act would, on the contrary, seem to mark a substantial

---

1 In such cases, it should be noted, the hearing examiner makes a recommended decision.   2 [1935] 1 K.B. 249.

3 Vanderbilt, *The Doctrine of the Separation of Powers*, 94.

4 Northey, 'Curial review of the determinations of administrative tribunals', 28 *New Zealand L. J.* (1952), 135, 136. Cf. Griffith and Street, *Principles of Administrative Law* (1952), 188.

step forward in the direction of ensuring adequate procedural safeguards in their dealings with the administration.

It may well be that the criticism quoted above is based upon the view that the provisions of the American Act, though motivated by a laudable purpose, must, as a practical matter, prove ineffective. This is, indeed, a key point in the consideration of any law. A statute is not self-executing. The legislative *ought* must run the gauntlet of judicial interpretation before it attains the practical status of an *is*. This is so in all legal systems; but it is particularly the case in the United States where the courts of law play so prominent a constitutional role. The Administrative Procedure Act, like other legislation, would lose much of its efficacy if its terms were to be read by the courts in a destructive spirit.

The American courts have, however, clearly indicated that they will give to the Procedure Act the full remedial effect that the legislature intended it to have. The leading case is *Wong Yang Sung* v. *McGrath*,[1] a 1950 decision of the United States Supreme Court. In that case, the court set aside an order for the deportation of an alien, where the alien had not been afforded a hearing before an independent examiner, such as that required under the American Act. A case like this, in which an administrative decision is quashed because of the administration's failure to observe the essentials of fair procedure prescribed by the Administrative Procedure Act, furnishes a pragmatic answer to those who deride the value of that law. Certainly, it would be difficult for Wong Yang Sung, saved from deportation only by the American Act, to agree with the assertion already quoted that an Act like it 'has little to commend it'.

American developments in the field of administrative procedure are, despite such criticisms, particularly pertinent in other countries. The Administrative Procedure Act represents the first legislative attempt in the common-law countries to ameliorate the defects that have arisen in the administrative process. It is not contended, of course, that a detailed code of administrative procedure is desirable or even feasible. One must ever bear in mind the warning of Lord Shaw against the over-crystallization of the principles of natural justice.[2] The recognition of that fact does not, however, deny the need for a rigid insistence upon the 'fundamentals of fair play'[3] in administrative action. 'There are certain fundamentals of just procedure which are the same for every type of tribunal and every type of proceeding.'[4] The American Administrative Procedure Act points the way

1 339 U.S. 33 (1950).
2 *Local Government Board* v. *Arlidge*, [1915] A. C. 120, 138.
3 *Federal Communications Commission* v. *Pottsville Broadcasting Co.*, 309 U.S. 134, 143 (1940).
4 Pound, *Administrative Law* (1942), 75.

to a legislative formulation of these fundamentals. As it has recently been expressed by an acute English observer, 'American administrative law is so much more developed than the British that there is little for the American lawyer to learn from British experience—except to be on guard against a weakening of judicial control. Cannot Marshall Plan Aid include "administrative law"?'[1]

JUDICIAL REVIEW—AVAILABILITY

Legislative silence. Under an adequately developed system of administrative law, the citizen who has been adversely affected by improper governmental action must be given a remedy. If that remedy is to be an effective one, it should be available before some body which is wholly independent of the active administration. In the common-law countries, such remedy has traditionally been afforded before the ordinary courts of law.

The importance of such a judicial remedy was stated in strong language by the Committee on Ministers' Powers. 'We are...unanimously of opinion', read the committee's conclusion on this point, 'that no considerations of administrative convenience, or executive efficiency, should be allowed to weaken the control of the courts, and that no obstacle should be placed by Parliament in the way of the subject's unimpeded access to them.'[2] In Anglo-American theory, the availability of the judicial remedy is intimately connected with the doctrine of the rule of law. 'For just in so far as administrative determinations are subject to court review, a means exists for maintaining the supremacy of law, though at one remove and as a sort of secondary line of defence.'[3]

Whether judicial review is available in a given case depends in the first place upon the provisions which the legislature has seen fit to make in the matter. Thus, it is clear, as stated by Swift, J., in a leading English case, that appeals from administrative decisions cannot be taken in the absence of statutory provisions. 'An appeal is the creature of statute.... If a person desires to appeal from one tribunal to another, be the former a judicial tribunal in the ordinary sense of the term, or a tribunal such as the Minister of Health and his department, for purposes such as I am considering in this case, he can only do so if a statute has given him the right, and only within the limits which the statute giving him the right lays down.'[4]

---

1 Street, Book Review, 59 *Yale L. J.* (1950), 590, 593. Compare Puget, 'Les recours quasi-contentieux en droit comparé', 5 *Revue internationale de droit comparé* (1953), 255, 264.
2 *Report of the Committee on Ministers' Powers*, 45.
3 Dickinson, *op. cit.* 37.　　　　4 *In re Bowman*, [1932] 2 K.B. 621, 633.

The absence of statutory provisions for appeal to the courts does not, however, necessarily mean that all access to the judiciary is barred. Even in the absence of statute, the courts have developed means for controlling administrative officers in their relation to private right.[1] An administrative tribunal, as Farwell, L.J., has affirmed, 'is not an autocrat free to act as it pleases, but is an inferior tribunal subject to the jurisdiction which the Court of King's Bench for centuries, and the High Court since the Judicature Acts, has exercised over such tribunals'.[2]

In the United States, too, the mere fact that one starts in a particular case with a statute that makes no provision for judicial review is not decisive. 'For the silence of Congress as to judicial review is not necessarily to be construed as a denial of the power of the federal courts to grant relief in the exercise of the general jurisdiction which Congress has conferred upon them.'[3]

This basic principle has become firmly established in the jurisprudence of the federal courts. The leading case is *Stark* v. *Wickard*,[4] decided in 1944. The court there held that a review action could be maintained, even though there was no direct judicial review granted by statute. 'Here, there is no forum', reads the opinion of Justice Reed, 'other than the ordinary courts, to hear this complaint.'[5] The silence of Congress is not to be construed as indicating a legislative intent to preclude review. The courts, in such cases, may exercise the inherent review power which they possess through the delegation to them of *the* judicial power under the Constitution. 'When Congress passes an Act empowering administrative agencies to carry on governmental activities, the power of those agencies is circumscribed by the authority granted. This permits the courts to participate in law enforcement entrusted to administrative bodies only to the extent necessary to protect justiciable individual rights against administrative action fairly beyond the granted powers. The responsibility of determining the limits of statutory grants of authority in such cases is a judicial function entrusted to the courts by Congress by the statutes establishing courts and marking their jurisdiction.'[6]

Forms of action. In England, as is well known, access to the courts, in the absence of statutory provisions for review, has been obtained through the prerogative writs and their modern equivalents. As stated by Atkin, L.J., in a famous passage, 'Wherever any body of persons, having legal authority to determine questions affecting the rights of subjects, and having the duty

---

1 *Report of the Attorney-General's Committee*, 80.
2 *Rex* v. *Board of Education*, [1910] 2 K.B. 165, 178.
3 *Estep* v. *United States*, 327 U.S. 114, 120 (1946).
4 321 U.S. 288 (1944).
5 *Ibid.* at 309.   6 *Ibid.*

to act judicially, act in excess of their legal authority, they are subject to the controlling jurisdiction of the King's Bench Division exercised in these writs.'[1]

In the American States, too, judicial review of administrative action in the absence of statute has generally been obtained through the prerogative writs. In the federal courts, however, those writs have not played an important role, thanks in large part to a 1913 Supreme Court decision which held that certiorari, the most commonly used of the prerogative writs in the field of administrative law, could not be employed to obtain review of an administrative order.[2] In its place, the federal courts have relied primarily upon the injunction. In recent years, there has also been a growing use of the procedure by declaratory judgment, and the present tendency is for individuals seeking review to bring an action seeking both a declaration and an injunction. This combined proceeding is, as a recent English treatise points out, much the most important non-statutory method of securing judicial review in the United States federal system.[3]

The injunction, which has thus been of such consequence in American administrative law, has been comparatively unimportant as a method of judicial review of administrative action in England.[4] And the same has been true, though perhaps to a lesser extent, of the action for a declaratory judgment. From the point of view of individuals adversely affected by administrative action, this has been most unfortunate. Certiorari and the other prerogative writs 'have accumulated so vast a cargo of technicalities that the citizen desirous of challenging an administrative power or privilege finds himself frequently engulfed in a procedural bog which bars him from his goal'.[5]

It is to be hoped that the recent decision of the Court of Appeal in *Barnard* v. *National Dock Labour Board*[6] signals the beginning of a *rapprochement* between English and American administrative law on the subject of forms of review action. 'It is axiomatic', stated Denning, L.J., in that case, 'that when a statutory tribunal sits to administer justice, it must act in accordance with the law. Parliament clearly so intended. If the tribunal does not observe the law, what is to be done? The remedy by certiorari is hedged round by limitations and may not be available. Why then should not the court intervene by declaration and injunction? If it cannot so intervene, it would mean that the tribunal could disregard the law, which is a thing no one can do in this country.'[7] If *Barnard's Case* means that the

---

1 *Rex* v. *Electricity Commissioners*, [1924] 1 K.B. 171, 205.
2 *Degge* v. *Hitchcock*, 229 U.S. 162 (1913).
3 Griffith and Street, *op. cit.* 235.   4 *Ibid.*
5 Borchard, *Declaratory Judgments* (2nd ed. 1941), xv.
6 [1953] 2 Q.B. 18.   7 *Ibid.* at 41.

divisional court can normally award a declaration (and, perhaps by implication, an injunction) as an alternative remedy to certiorari, it marks an important step forward in English administrative law and well justifies its characterization by one commentator[1] as having a stronger claim to eminence than any case in administrative law since *Local Government Board* v. *Arlidge*.[2] It is most desirable that actions for declarations and injunctions supersede the prerogative writs as the usual method of obtaining review of administrative action in the English courts, much, as we have seen, as has already occurred in the federal system in the United States.

Legislative preclusion. One of the most controversial issues in English administrative law has arisen from the enactment of statutory provisions for the finality of administrative action. 'It is well known', declares Lord Goddard, C.J., 'that many Acts of Parliament have given the decision of certain matters to tribunals and bodies that are not the King's courts and in many cases have taken away the right of the subject to come to those courts and challenge the decisions of such tribunals or bodies. In such cases all that this court can do is to consider whether or not the legislature has given the right to come to the court or not.'[3]

In the United States, too, statutory provisions for administrative finality have not been uncommon, though they have not been so extreme as the 'conclusive evidence' clause, which has caused such concern to English jurists. An example of the type of provision for finality found in American statutes is contained in the Immigration Act of 1917. That law, authorizing the deportation of aliens who come within its provisions, states that the administrative decision in particular deportation cases 'shall be final'. Interpreted literally, such a provision for administrative finality would place the administrative decision in a conclusive position and bar all recourse to the courts.

The courts in the United States have, however, consistently refused to give literal effect to such provisions for administrative conclusiveness. As a federal court stated in 1948: 'Nevertheless and in spite of such language, it is perfectly clear that it [i.e., the administrative decision] is not final in the sense that courts cannot do anything about it.'[4] It has long been established that an alien against whom a deportation order has been issued could obtain a judicial decision on the legality of that order in a habeas corpus proceeding. Thus, 'while it might look as though judicial review were precluded by the giving to the deportation order the air of finality,

1 De Smith, Note in 16 *Modern L. Rev.* (1953), 506.
2 [1915] A.C. 120.
3 *Rex* v. *Ludlow; ex parte Barnsley Corp.*, [1947] K.B. 634, 638.
4 *United States ex rel. Trinler* v. *Carusi*, 166 F. 2d 457, 460 (3d Cir. 1948).

in practice such finality never existed because of the availability of habeas corpus'.[1]

It may be objected that the American courts, in refusing to interpret literally a provision such as that in the deportation statute, are violating the correct canons of statutory construction. Yet, as Mr Justice Frankfurter has aptly pointed out, 'It is true also of Acts of Congress that "The letter killeth."...In enacting legislation Congress is not engaged in a scientific process which takes account of every contingency. Its laws are not to be read as though every *i* has to be dotted and every *t* crossed.'[2]

Rigid literal construction in these cases would be to free administrative agencies from all judicial control. Such complete preclusion of review, if objectionable anywhere, would seem to be so particularly in deportation proceedings, where the result may be 'loss of both property and life; or of all that makes life worth living',[3] and 'where we frequently meet with a voteless class of litigants who not only lack the influence of citizens, but who are strangers to the laws and customs in which they find themselves involved, and who often do not even understand the tongue in which they are accused'.[4]

'Privilege' cases. It should be noted, however, that the principle in favour of the availability of review, which is the basic principle of American administrative law, even in the face of statutory provisions which seemingly preclude review, has not been applied in an important category of cases. These are the cases involving so-called grants, benefits or 'privileges', in which the State accords to the individual something to which he has no pre-existing legal right. In these 'privilege' cases, a statutory provision for administrative finality is given effect by the American courts in a way to exclude judicial review.

As good an example as any of an American provision for finality in the field of State benefits is the statute applicable to the Veterans' Administration. It provides, in language approaching that of the British 'conclusive evidence' clause, that the decisions of this agency on claims for benefits under the statutory schemes administered by it 'shall be final and conclusive and no other official or any court of the United States shall have power or jurisdiction to review any such decision'. The purpose of this provision appears to have been to remove the possibility of judicial relief

---

1 166 F. 2d at 461. *Heikkila* v. *Barber*, 345 U.S. 229 (1953), is not to the contrary. It held only that review of a deportation order was not available under the Administrative Procedure Act of 1946. The court expressly recognized, however, that the legality of such order could be attacked by habeas corpus.

2 *United States ex rel. Knauff* v. *Shaughnessy*, 338 U.S. 537, 548 (1950).

3 *Ng Fung Ho* v. *White*, 259 U.S. 276, 284 (1922).

4 *Wong Yang Sung* v. *McGrath*, 339 U.S. 33, 46 (1950).

in the cases covered.[1] And, in the words of one federal court, 'the authority of Congress to withhold judicial review here is now beyond question. Veterans' benefits are mere gratuities and "the grant of them creates no vested right".'[2] In these cases, Mr Justice Stone has asserted: 'The United States is not, by the creation of claims against itself, bound to provide a remedy in the courts. It may withhold all remedy or it may provide an administrative remedy and make it 'exclusive, however mistaken its exercise.'[3]

Another important class of 'privilege' cases recently before the Supreme Court is that involving government contractors. In these, too, provisions for administrative finality are so interpreted by the federal courts as completely to bar review.[4] The government contractor, like the applicant for a veterans' benefit, is held to have only the 'privilege' of dealing with the government. He is placed in a different position from that of the private citizen whose property or personal 'rights' are adversely affected by administrative action. Provisions for administrative conclusiveness will be given literal effect by the American courts in the contractor's case.

That administrative finality is explainable legally in these cases because in American law a government contract is considered as a 'privilege', not a 'right', does not, however, mean that the legal result is the desirable one. 'The rule we announce has wide application and a devastating effect', asserted Mr Justice Douglas in dissenting from the Supreme Court's upholding of administrative conclusiveness in the most recent of the government contractor cases. 'It makes a tyrant out of every contracting officer.'[5]

It is unrealistic today to treat the applicant for a pension or a government contract, whose financial well-being may be wholly dependent on the government grant, any differently from one declared to be injured in his personal or property 'rights'. With regard to the availability of judicial review, is there, for example, any adequate reason for differentiating a veteran seeking a pension from an alien being deported, simply because a veteran's benefit is termed a privilege instead of a property right? As far as the effect on the individual is concerned, the veteran's pension case, regardless of the 'tag' used, involves a need for judicial control just as great as that of any other administrative proceeding. And the same is true of

1 *Lynch* v. *United States*, 292 U.S. 571, 587 (1934).
2 *Slocumb* v. *Gray*, 179 F. 2d 31, 34 (App. D.C. 1949).
3 *Dismuke* v. *United States*, 297 U.S. 167, 171 (1936).
4 *United States* v. *Wunderlich*, 342 U.S. 98 (1951); *Moorman* v. *United States*, 338 U.S. 457 (1950). Compare the cases involving civil servants, such as those discussed *supra*, p. 266.
5 *United States* v. *Wunderlich*, 342 U.S. at 101. During May 1954, it should be noted, an Act was passed by the Congress providing expressly for judicial review in Government contract cases despite any provisions for administrative finality in such cases.

other cases involving the grant of so-called privileges or benefits by the State. The power of the State altogether to deny such privileges should not mean that they can be denied by the administration to particular individuals without the latter's being entitled to judicial decisions on the legality of the denials.

JUDICIAL REVIEW—SCOPE

The question of the scope of judicial review of administrative determinations has been a crucial one in American administrative law. Since review tends to be available in most cases in the American system, the extent of review in particular cases may determine whether or not full effect is given to the legislative purpose in creating administrative agencies. 'One of the principal reasons for the creation of such [agencies] is to secure the benefit of special knowledge acquired through continuous experience in a difficult and complicated field.'[1] If the review of administrative determinations is to be very broad, with the reviewing court deciding the case *de novo* upon its own independent judgment, 'administrative tribunals would be turned into little more than media for the transmission of evidence to the courts. It would destroy the values of adjudication of fact by experts or specialists in the field involved. It would destroy the responsibility for administrative adjudications.'[2]

The federal courts in the United States, cognizant of the dangers inherent in over-wide judicial control of the administration, have not joined the ranks of those seeking to broaden the scope of judicial review. 'Even when resort to courts can be had to review a Commission's order', reads an important administrative-law opinion of the American Supreme Court, 'the range of issues open to review is narrow. Only questions affecting constitutional power, statutory authority and the basic prerequisites of proof can be raised. If these legal tests are satisfied, the Commission's order becomes incontestable.'[3]

As the federal courts see it, the judiciary has nothing to do with the wisdom of challenged administrative action. As expressed by Mr Justice Frankfurter, in a case where certain regulations were assailed as arbitrary and capricious: 'If this contention means that the Regulations are unwise, ...we can say only that the appellants have selected the wrong forum for such a plea.... "We certainly have neither technical competence nor legal authority to pronounce upon the wisdom of the course taken by the Com-

1 *Securities and Exchange Commission* v. *Associated Gas & Electric Co.*, 99 F. 2d 795, 798 (2d Cir. 1938).
2 *Report of the Attorney-General's Committee*, 91.
3 *Rochester Telephone Corp.* v. *United States*, 307 U.S. 125, 139 (1939).

mission."·· Our duty is at an end when we find that the action of the Commission was based upon findings supported by evidence, and was made pursuant to authority granted by Congress.'[1]

The American courts' approach to the scope of review has been based upon the well-known distinction between questions of *law* and questions of *fact*. As to the latter, the primary responsibility of decision is with the administrative expert. It is only the former that are to be decided judicially. 'If the action rests upon an administrative determination—an exercise of judgment in an area which Congress has entrusted to the agency—of course it must not be set aside because the reviewing court might have made a different determination were it empowered to do so. But if the action is based upon a determination of law as to which the reviewing authority of the courts does come into play, an order may not stand if the agency has misconceived the law.'[2]

In this respect, the approach of the American courts has been similar to that followed by the British courts. In Britain, too, in the field of judicial review, 'it is generally agreed that the jurisdiction of superior courts should be invoked only on questions of law—a principle which is already familiar in other spheres, such as appeals to the Court of Criminal Appeal,·and cases stated to the High Court by justices, and other authorities of inferior jurisdiction. To reopen all disputed issues of fact might lead to endless litigation, with no very satisfactory conclusion in the end.'[3]

One should, however, note an important difference between American and English administrative law with regard to judicial review of administrative determinations of fact. The American courts will, as an English treatise points out, review administrative findings which are not supported by substantial evidence, that is, by 'such relevant evidence as a reasonable mind might accept as adequate to support a conclusion'.[4] The American theory of review permits at least a limited re-examination of the facts by the reviewing court, and thus seems inconsistent with the oft-expressed English doctrine that administrative findings of fact are not subject to any review. To the British jurist, indeed, the American doctrine of review at first sight appears to be an unwarranted interference by the judiciary in the sphere of administration. 'To my mind', writes Dr Evatt, 'the most surprising feature in the development of administrative law in the United States is the persistence of the notion that the ordinary courts of law should

---

1 *National Broadcasting Co.* v. *United States*, 319 U.S. 190, 224 (1943). Cf. *Associated Provincial Picture Houses* v. *Wednesbury Corp.*, [1948] 1 K.B. 223, 228.

2 *Securities and Exchange Commission* v. *Chenery Corp.*, 318 U.S. 80, 94 (1943).

3 Allen, *Law and Orders* (1945), 159.

4 Griffith and Street, *op. cit.* 219, citing *Consolidated Edison Co.* v. *National Labor Relations Board*, 305 U.S. 197, 229 (1938).

be permitted to review the findings of fact which have been remitted by the legislature to the decision of the administrator.'[1]

According to the English treatise already referred to, one reason why the English courts have not followed the American view on review of findings of fact is that administrative tribunals in England do not usually keep a record. 'If administrative tribunals did keep records it might sometimes be possible to challenge the insufficiency of evidence on the ground that this was an error on the face of the record.'[2] In the federal system in the United States, it should be pointed out, administrative decisions are normally preceded by formal hearings and based upon the record made of such hearings. As a consequence, in the American system, challenges to the insufficiency of the evidence as more or less constituting errors of law on the face of the record have been readily allowed.

It should, however, be emphasized that the inquiry of the American courts into the evidence in these cases is not, as has been erroneously suggested,[3] concerned with the weight of the evidence. An administrative determination of fact, to be upheld by the federal courts, must only be supported by 'substantial' evidence, and evidence in support of a finding may be substantial even though the weight of the evidence be the other way.[4] Looked at in this way, the difference between the American and English rules with regard to review of facts is, as Professor Wade explains, 'of less significance since an English court can fall back on the "no-evidence" rule, i.e. that as a matter of law an inference from the facts does not logically accord with and follow from them, as the late Lord du Parcq once put it'.[5]

Jurisdictional facts. Perhaps the most significant development to note in the recent jurisprudence of the American courts with regard to the scope of review of administrative determinations has been their tendency to abandon the so-called 'jurisdictional fact' doctrine. As has been indicated, the review power of the American courts has been limited primarily to questions of law. Administrative findings of fact are not to be redetermined by the reviewing court.[6] But what if the fact in question is a *jurisdictional* one, in the sense that its existence is a condition precedent to the lawful

1 Evatt, 'The judges and the teachers of public law', 53 *Harvard L. Rev.* (1940), 1145, 1162.

2 Griffith and Street, *op. cit.* 220.   3 See *ibid.*

4 This is true even under *Universal Camera Corp.* v. *National Labor Relations Board*, 340 U.S. 474 (1951), holding that the substantiality of the evidence in support of an administrative finding must be judged in the light of the whole record.

5 Preface to Schwartz, *American Administrative Law* (1950), vi, citing *Bean* v. *Doncaster Amalgamated Collieries, Ltd.*, [1944] 2 All E.R. 279, 284.

6 Though, as has been pointed out, the American courts can see if such findings are supported by substantial evidence.

exercise of the administrative authority? To apply the theory of limited review to such cases would seem to run counter to the general policy of Anglo-American law, against allowing inferior tribunals finally to determine the limits of their own jurisdiction.

The application of the 'jurisdictional fact' doctrine in England is best shown by *White and Collins* v. *Minister of Health.*[1] There, the Court of Appeal reversed a decision of Charles, J., refusing to set aside the confirmation of a compulsory purchase order by the Minister of Health.[2] The enabling legislation limited the administrative power in such a case to the acquisition of land which did not form part of any 'park, garden or pleasure ground'.

Luxmoore, L.J., who delivered the principal opinion, held that the administrative finding that the land in question did not come within the statutory exception was not conclusive upon the reviewing court. 'The first and most important question to bear in mind is that the jurisdiction to make the order is dependent on a finding of fact; for unless the land can be held not to be part of a park...there is no jurisdiction in the borough council to make, or in the Minister to confirm, the order. In such a case it seems almost self-evident that the court, which has to consider whether there is jurisdiction to make or confirm the order, must be entitled to review the vital finding on which the existence of the jurisdiction relied upon depends. If this were not so, the right to apply to the court would be illusory.'[3]

The *White and Collins Case* is basically similar to *Crowell* v. *Benson,*[4] the leading American case applying the 'jurisdictional fact' doctrine. That case arose under the Longshoremen's and Harbor Workers' Compensation Act of 1927, which contains two fundamental limitations upon the right of compensation conferred by it. It deals exclusively with compensation in respect of disability or death resulting 'from an injury occurring upon the navigable waters of the United States', and it applies only when the relation of master and servant exists. The administrative findings of fact upon these two issues, the Supreme Court said, cannot be vested with the same finality as ordinary factual determinations. These 'determinations of fact are fundamental or "jurisdictional", in the sense that their existence is a condition precedent to the operation of the statutory scheme',[5] and the reviewing court may judge the issue of their validity upon its own independent judgment. The reasoning of the court here, it will be noted, is strikingly similar to that of Luxmoore, L.J., in the *White and Collins Case.*

---

1 [1939] 2 K.B. 838.   2 *Re Ripon Housing Order*, [1939] 1 All E.R. 508.
3 [1939] 2 K.B. at 855. See Griffith and Street, *op. cit.* 208–11.
4 285 U.S. 22 (1932).   5 *Ibid.* at 54.

The more recent cases, as has been mentioned, indicate that the federal courts are now wholly out of sympathy with attempts to secure broad review based upon the 'jurisdictional fact' doctrine. That the American Supreme Court has, indeed, come close to abandoning the 'jurisdictional fact' doctrine is shown by a number of recent decisions.[1] Perhaps the best known of these has been *National Labor Relations Board* v. *Hearst Publications*.[2] That case arose under the National Labor Relations Act of 1935, whose operation is limited to cases where there exists an employer-employee relationship. The court held that the determination by the administrative agency concerned, regarding the existence of such relationship in the particular case, was to be given the same degree of conclusiveness as any other administrative finding of fact. This is true although the finding at issue was similar to that involved in *Crowell* v. *Benson*, in that the administrative power to act was dependent upon the existence of the relationship.

The court's view on this point has been well expressed by Frankfurter, J.: 'Analysis is not furthered by speaking of such findings as "jurisdictional" and not even when—to adapt a famous phrase—jurisdictional is softened by a quasi. "Jurisdiction" competes with "right" as one of the most deceptive of legal pitfalls. The opinions in *Crowell* v. *Benson*...and the casuistries to which they have given rise bear unedifying testimony of the morass into which one is led in working out problems of judicial review over administrative decisions by loose talk about jurisdiction.'[3]

It seems clear from the above that the American courts have been tending to narrow the scope of judicial review. At the same time it should be emphasized that, while they may be more friendly toward administrative authority than were their predecessors, they have far from surrendered the field to the administrator. In holding the exercise of administrative functions to the procedural level required by the demands of fair play, and in ensuring against arbitrary action by keeping access to the courts available, even though the scope of review may be somewhat narrower than it was—the federal courts still have a vital role to play.

'How to fit ancient liberties, which have gained a new preciousness, into solution of those exigent and intricate economic problems that have been too long avoided rather than faced, is the special task of Administrative Law', wrote a member of the American Supreme Court in 1941.[4] Few would deny that that task is still, in large measure, with us. For those

1 See Schwartz, *American Administrative Law*, 120–6.
2 322 U.S. 111 (1944).
3 *Yonkers* v. *United States*, 320 U.S. 685, 695 (1944).
4 Frankfurter, Foreword, 41 *Columbia L. Rev.* (1941), 585, 586.

of us in the common-law countries, indeed, the problem has become an even more difficult one. For we have come to realize that abdication of the field to the administrator will not lead to a solution. 'It will not do to say that it must all be left to the skill of experts.'¹ The judiciary, too, has a part to perform. 'Courts no less than administrative bodies', the Supreme Court stated significantly in a leading case, 'are agencies of government. Both are instruments for realizing public purposes.'²

1 *Federal Power Commission* v. *Hope Natural Gas Co.*, 320 U.S. 591, 627 (1944).
2 *Scripps Howard Radio* v. *Federal Communications Commission*, 316 U.S. 4, 15 (1942).

Chapter XII

THE UNITED STATES AND THE
UNITED NATIONS

Most Americans tend to adopt a cavalierly complacent attitude toward the working of their Constitution. The spirit with which they look upon that document recalls with singular fidelity that with which, according to Dicey, Englishmen of a century and a half ago looked upon the institutions of their country. 'The constitution was to them, in the quaint language of George the Third, "the most perfect of human formations"; it was to them not a mere polity to be compared with the government of any other state, but so to speak a sacred mystery of statesmanship....It was in short a thing by itself, which Englishmen and foreigners alike should "venerate, where they are not able presently to comprehend".'[1]

The student of comparative law must of necessity look on the American Constitution in a spirit different from the sentiment of the average inhabitant of the United States. He can hardly be expected to share the fervent self-satisfaction of Americans, who attribute the flourishing of their system almost entirely to their political and economic institutions. The comparative jurist, who seeks impartially to examine the constitutional system of the United States, will wish neither to criticize, nor to venerate, but to understand. And one like the present writer, who attempts to enlighten a British audience on the contemporary working of the American Constitution, must feel that he is called upon to perform the part neither of a critic nor of an apologist, nor of a eulogist, but simply of an expounder; his duty is neither to attack nor defend the federal organic instrument, but simply to explain the system set up by it.[2]

To present such an explanation of the workings of the constitutional system of the United States, especially of the significant changes that have occurred therein in recent years, has been the primary purpose of this book. Under contemporary conditions, however, a constitutional law study devoted solely to the domestic side of the subject would be quite incomplete. For, it has become a commonplace that, in the present century, public law has come to have international as well as municipal aspects. And an instrument like the Federal Constitution is now important not only because it is the charter under which American government operates, but

---

[1] Dicey, *Law of the Constitution* (9th ed. 1939), 2.
[2] Cf. *ibid.* 3.

also, and in many ways even more so, because of its effects upon the relations of the United States with the world community. Especially at the present time, when the United States has assumed a position of leadership in the Western world, is an understanding of the international-law aspects of the American Constitution of great consequence. An explanation of those facets of the federal organic instrument appears, indeed, to be particularly fitting in a comparative study like the present work because they are often pointed to by observers outside the United States as calculated more to hinder, than to help, the effective performance of the international role of the United States.

DIFFUSION OF RESPONSIBILITY FOR FOREIGN AFFAIRS

The portions of the American constitutional system that have evoked the most critical comment from students of comparative law are beyond question those providing for the conduct of foreign affairs. The elaborate system of checks and balances provided for by the framers of the federal organic instrument is looked upon by many foreigners as an outmoded vestige of the eighteenth century, 'said to belong to the age of etiquette, the age of overrefinement, when every practical activity was embarrassed by ceremonial and checks'.[1] To the outsider, the proper performance of a nation's external role presupposes a concentration of power over foreign affairs in the executive branch. It is difficult for him to comprehend how a system like the American one, in which the responsibility for the conduct of foreign affairs appears to be parcelled between the President and the Congress, can function effectively under present-day conditions. Such a system, he feels, may well have been satisfactory enough for the fledgling republic established in 1789, whose external concerns related largely to a desire to be allowed to live in isolation from the rest of the world. But the same is hardly true of the United State of the mid-twentieth century, whose international role has expanded to an extent which could scarcely have been conceived of by the men who drew up the Federal Constitution. 'One of the facts of the world situation', stated Mr Clement Attlee in the House of Commons on 11 May 1953, 'is that the American Constitution was framed for an isolationist state. Americans did not want to have anything to do with Europe. For many years they had practically no foreign policy, but I do not think that that situation is particularly well suited to a time when America has become the strongest state in the world and has to give a lead.'[2]

1 Pound, *Administrative Law* (1942), 45.
2 515 H.C. Deb. 5s., col. 1069.

As is well known, the strictures of Mr Attlee on this score were any-thing but well received in the United States. Yet it cannot be denied that they are most pertinent to anyone seeking critically to appraise the working of the American constitutional system. For the diffusion of responsibility in the field of foreign relations between the President and the Congress has, without any doubt, impeded the execution by the United States of a policy of effective world leadership. It is all very well for those dealing with that country to be informed of the constitutional restrictions which limit the authority of the American executive in its dealings with other govern-ments. Such information can, however, hardly enable them to predict the vagaries of the members of the legislative body who often appear to speak with a voice almost equal to that of the President himself, even in matters affecting external affairs.

Even if all this be conceded, it is erroneous to assume that the deficiencies which have been noted in the conduct of American external relations flow primarily from the provisions of the Federal Constitution dealing directly with that field. In the first place, it should be emphasized that that instru-ment, important though it may otherwise be in restricting the powers of the American Government, contains no limitations of consequence upon its authority so far as foreign affairs are concerned. 'The broad statement', the United States Supreme Court has declared, 'that the federal govern-ment can exercise no powers except those specifically enumerated in the Constitution, and such implied powers as are necessary and proper to carry into effect the enumerated powers, is categorically true only in respect of our internal affairs.'[1] So far as the powers of the American Government in respect of foreign affairs are concerned, there is no limitation to the authority expressly or impliedly granted in the organic instrument. The 'investment of the federal government with the powers of external sovereignty did not depend upon the affirmative grants of the Constitu-tion'.[2] The foreign affairs authority of the United States is instead derived from its position as a sovereign State and, under the settled jurisprudence of the Supreme Court, it can exercise all of the external attributes of sovereignty, unhampered by the lack of affirmative constitutional grant. 'As a member of the family of nations, the right and power of the United States in that field are equal to the right and power of the other members of the international family.'[3]

It may consequently be seen that the American Constitution does not prevent the Federal Government from exercising any of the attributes of sovereignty which are essential to the effective performance of its inter-

1 *United States* v. *Curtiss-Wright Export Corp.*, 299 U.S. 304, 315 (1936).
2 *Ibid.* at 318.   3 *Ibid.*

national role. Nor are the provisions of that instrument for foreign affairs directly responsible for the diffusion of authority in the American Government in that field. In reality, the Constitution, except for its division of the treaty-making power between the President and the Senate, says next to nothing about how American foreign policy is to be conceived and executed. As we have already seen, however, the conduct of external relations in the United States, like that in Britain, is, from the constitutional point of view, vested exclusively in the executive, for the delegation to the President of 'the executive power' is held to vest in him the nation's authority in that field. Thus, the American Supreme Court has referred to the 'plenary and exclusive power of the President as the sole organ of the federal government in the field of international relations—a power which does not require as a basis for its exercise an act of Congress'.[1] And this is true even so far as the treaty-making power is concerned, at least until the stage of ratification is reached. The Constitution may provide for the *making* of treaties by the President, only if two-thirds of the Senate approve; but he alone negotiates. 'Into the field of negotiation the Senate cannot intrude; and Congress itself is powerless to invade it.'[2]

If there often appears to be a diffusion of responsibility for foreign affairs in the United States, that is due less to the provisions of the Federal Constitution concerning that field, even to that provision partitioning the treaty-making power, than to the rigid separation of powers which exists in the American system between the legislative and executive branches. This prevents the American administration from exercising a control over the Congress analogous to that exerted by the Government in Britain, and it is consequently far from surprising that the Congress feels far freer to refuse to follow the executive lead than does the legislature in a parliamentary system. The difference in this respect on both sides of the Atlantic was well pointed out by Mr Attlee in his address which has already been referred to. 'The Prime Minister', said he, 'comes to the House and states his policy. It is the policy of the Government. He can, if he wishes, get a vote in this House in support of it.... That policy is Government policy and will be carried out by Ministers and officials. Look on the other side. President Eisenhower makes a great speech. It is the President's speech. He speaks for the Administration, but in America power is divided between the Administration and Congress.... Therefore, the Government in America are not really master in their own house.'[3]

It was not unnatural for Mr Attlee, accustomed to the British system of unified responsibility in the field of foreign affairs, to go on to assert: 'One of the disadvantages of the American system of democracy is that it is

1 *Ibid.* at 320.   2 *Ibid.* at 319.   3 515 *H.C. Deb.* 5s., col. 1068.

sometimes hard to find where effective power lies.'[1] It may well be, as has already been pointed out, that, under the Federal Constitution, the external attributes of American sovereignty are vested almost exclusively in the executive. But the effective implementation of foreign policy depends upon legislative action in voting the necessary appropriations, changes in laws and the like. And a legislature which is as free of executive control as the American Congress is bound to play a more independent role in determining whether to give the necessary support to the foreign policy of the executive than does the legislature in Britain. That is why the spectre of possible congressional repudiation of the executive always hangs over those who negotiate with agents of the United States, however highly placed they may be. 'It would be possible', as Mr Attlee put it, 'for President Eisenhower to attend a conference and, on his return to the United States, to be thrown over, as President Wilson was after the discussions at Versailles.'[2]

In this respect, it is particularly important to bear in mind that the rejection of Woodrow Wilson's peace measures after the First World War was not by the majority of the American people or even that of the Federal Congress. On the contrary, the Treaty of Versailles failed of ratification in the United States only because it was not approved by the two-thirds vote of the Senate which the Constitution requires, even though a majority of that body voted in favour of such approval. It was thus a mere minority of the American upper chamber which was able to frustrate the effective execution of an instrument of foreign policy which was endorsed by a majority of the Congress and the electorate.

In the case of the Versailles Treaty, just cited, it was not the fact of participation by the legislature in the field of foreign affairs that led to the renunciation of the Wilsonian policy. It was rather the essentially undemocratic nature of the legislative participation provided for in the Federal Constitution which enabled a group of senators who spoke for only a small proportion of the American people effectively to block a measure strongly desired by most of the country. If the legislative approval of treaties in the American system had been by majority vote, either of the Senate or of both Houses, there is little doubt but that, in the case of the Versailles Treaty at least, there would not have resulted the unfortunate consequences which did, in fact, ensue under the treaty-making provision of the Federal Constitution.

It is less the fact of wide legislative participation in the field of foreign affairs, resulting from congressional independence of the executive, that is deplorable under contemporary conditions, than the fact that the constitu-

1 515 *H. C. Deb.* 5s., col. 1069.			2 *Ibid.* col. 1074.

tional organization of the Federal Congress enables such participation to be carried on in a manner which appears inconsistent with the principles of representative democracy. So far as treaty-making is concerned, this seems obvious, for, as pointed out above, the two-thirds vote required in the Senate enables a small minority of that body to prevent ratification. What is not, however, generally realized outside the United States is that the same is true, though not perhaps in the same degree, of congressional control of foreign policy in general. There, too, it is the Senate, rather than the House of Representatives, which has the more effective voice, largely because of its smaller size, greater stability, and the longer tenure of its members. And in the Senate, as we have already seen,[1] representation is by States, rather than by population. Hence, even a majority vote in that chamber may be far from truly representative of the country as a whole. The system of voting by States in the more influential upper House often tends to distort the reflexion which the legislature is supposed to give of the popular sentiment on an issue, particularly if, as has so often been the case where questions of foreign policy have been involved, such sentiment has been divided upon sectional lines.

That the division of power in the field of foreign affairs, which exists in practice, if not in constitutional theory, between the President and the Congress has hampered the effective execution of American foreign policy, especially in recent years, cannot be denied. The lack of co-ordination in that field appears, indeed, to constitute perhaps the primary deficiency of the present-day working of the American constitutional system. But it is not the system of congressional participation in external affairs provided for in the federal organic instrument, as such, that is at fault here. On the contrary, the effective exercise of authority of this kind by the elected representatives of the people appears eminently appropriate. Entirely executive control of foreign affairs, such as that which exists in Britain, involves dangers as great as those which inhere in all exercises of unrestrained power by the executive. Legislative control here appears, in fact, to be even more desirable than it does in other areas of executive authority, for there is no real possibility of effective judicial control in this field. The weakness of the American system in this respect stems from the failure of the Federal Congress, at least so far as its upper chamber is concerned, to mirror accurately popular sentiment on more than a sectional basis. If this deficiency were remedied (though one must with candour admit that such an event is most unlikely) congressional participation in foreign affairs would then be the source of strength it should be, instead of the great infirmity of the American system which it seems, to most observers, at present to constitute.

[1] *Supra*, p. 54

EFFECT OF TREATIES IN AMERICAN LAW

An important question, connected with that just discussed, which has become of great significance during the present century, is that of the relation of American municipal law to international law, especially that establishing and administered by supra-national organs. As is well known, the post-1918 experience, when the desire of the majority of the American people to participate in the League of Nations experiment was defeated by the constitutional provision that requires the consent of two-thirds of the Senate before a treaty can be ratified, was happily not repeated after the recent conflict. This time, an overwhelming majority of the Senate voted in favour of the world organization established by the victorious powers, and the United States was hence able to be among the early adherents to the Charter of the United Nations. By that instrument, the United States, like other signatories, engaged itself formally to assume the duties and responsibilities of membership. What have been the effects of such assumption upon the domestic law of the United States? Since the United Nations Charter was adopted at the San Francisco Conference as a formal international treaty, which was ratified by the United States, as by other member nations, the answer to this question involves an inquiry into the legal effect of a treaty in American law.

Under Article VI of the Federal Constitution, 'The Constitution and the Laws of the United States which shall be made in Pursuance thereof; and all Treaties made, or which shall be made, under the Authority of the United States, shall be the supreme Law of the Land.' As early as 1796, the United States Supreme Court held that, under this provision, a treaty overrode the conflicting law of a State. 'A treaty cannot be the supreme law of the land...', reads the opinion of Mr Justice Chase, 'if any act of a State Legislature can stand in its way.... It is the declared will of the people of the United States that every treaty made, by authority of the United States, shall be superior to the Constitution and laws of any individual State; and their will alone is to decide.'[1] It is by virtue of this decision that aliens resident in the United States have been able to invoke the aid of the American courts for the purpose of securing recognition of privileges claimed under treaties with the United States, and with the full assurance that the supremacy of such agreements over any inconsistent State laws would be recognized.[2]

What has just been said of a State statute which conflicts with a treaty of the United States does not, however, necessarily apply to laws of the

1 *Ware* v. *Hylton*, 3 Dall. 199, 236 (U.S. 1796) (*emphasis* omitted).
2 Hyde, *International Law* (1945), vol. 2, 1459.

Federal Congress. Since the constitutional provision quoted above, which gives to treaties their preferred position in the American system, provides that laws of the United States are, like treaties, to be the supreme law of the land, it has consistently been held that a treaty has only the same status as a federal statute. As it was expressed by Mr Chief Justice Taft in his opinion as sole arbitrator in a case arising between Great Britain and Costa Rica, 'the Constitution of the United States makes the Constitution, laws passed in pursuance thereof, and treaties of the United States the supreme law of the land. Under that provision, a treaty may repeal a statute and a statute may repeal a treaty.'[1] Since a treaty in the American system has the same legal effect as an Act of the Congress, it follows that a treaty is deemed to supersede a prior federal statute, in so far as its terms are inconsistent therewith. But the converse of this is also true. It has frequently been held by the American courts that they are bound to sustain an Act of Congress which is at variance with the terms of an existing treaty. The enactment is regarded as superseding the prior international agreement. 'We are of opinion', stated the Supreme Court in the leading case so holding, 'that, so far as a treaty made by the United States with any foreign country can become the subject of judicial cognizance in the courts of this country, it is subject to such acts as Congress may pass for its enforcement, modification, or repeal.'[2]

As the above discussion indicates, under Article VI of the Federal Constitution, a treaty is placed in the same category as an Act of Congress. Like the latter it overrides conflicting State legislation, but must itself give way to an inconsistent later federal law. It should not, however, be thought from this that all properly made treaties must of necessity immediately bind the American courts in cases coming before them. On the contrary, ever since a decision of the federal Supreme Court in 1829,[3] it has been recognized that not all treaties must be given immediate effect by the federal courts. Certain ones must, on the contrary, be implemented by legislation before they can be enforced judicially. A treaty, said Mr Chief Justice Marshall in the case referred to, 'is...to be regarded in courts of justice as equivalent to an act of the legislature, whenever it operates of itself, without the aid of any legislative provision. But when the terms of the stipulation import a contract—when either of the parties engages to perform a particular act, the treaty addresses itself to the political, not the judicial department; and the legislature must execute the contract, before it can become a rule for the court.'[4]

---

1 Quoted *ibid.* 1464.
2 *Head Money Cases*, 112 U.S. 580, 599 (1884).
3 *Foster* v. *Neilson*, 2 Pet. 253 (U.S. 1829).   4 *Ibid.* at 314.

As it is usually expressed by present-day American jurists, a treaty does not supersede local law inconsistent with it, unless the relevant provisions of the treaty are self-executing. And, in determining whether a particular treaty is self-executing, the American courts look to the intent of the signatory parties, as manifested by the language of that instrument. For the treaty to be construed as self-executing, i.e. for its provisions to have the force and effect of a federal statute, it must appear that the framers of the treaty intended to prescribe a rule that, standing alone, would be enforceable in the courts.[1] 'A treaty, then,' stated the highest American court in an important case, 'is a law of the land as an act of Congress is, whenever its provisions prescribe a rule by which the rights of the private citizen or subject may be determined. And when such rights are of a nature to be enforced in a court of justice, that court resorts to the treaty for a rule of decision for the case before it as it would to a statute.'[2]

It should be borne in mind that even with the limitation just dealt with, under which the provisions of a treaty must prescribe a self-executing rule before they become a part of the municipal law, the American law is, in this respect, more favourable to the effective implementation of international agreements than is that which prevails in Britain. The British courts follow the rule that treaties do not become a judicially enforceable part of the domestic law except by an Act of internal legislation. 'Within the British Empire', declared Lord Atkin in 1937, 'there is a well-established rule that the making of a treaty is an executive act, while the performance of its obligations, if they entail alteration of the existing domestic law, requires legislative action. Unlike some other countries, the stipulations of a treaty duly ratified do not within the Empire, by virtue of the treaty alone, have the force of law.'[3] In the United States, on the other hand, as we have just seen, a treaty is, by virtue of the Constitution, placed on a par with a federal statute, unless it is construed by the courts as one whose provisions are not intended to be self-executing.

DOMESTIC EFFECTS OF THE UNITED NATIONS CHARTER

Under the legal principles which have been considered above, what is the effect of the Charter of the United Nations upon American internal law? The answer to this depends upon the extent to which its provisions are self-executing, i.e. prescribe enforceable rules by which rights may be determined without the need of further implementing legislation. Since

1 *Sei Fujii* v. *State*, 242 P. 2d 617, 620 (Cal. 1952).
2 *Head Money Cases*, 112 U.S. 580, 598 (1884).
3 *Attorney-General for Canada* v. *Attorney-General for Ontario*, [1937] A.C. 326, 347.

the charter is a treaty ratified by the United States, its self-executing provisions become a part of American municipal law exactly as does an Act of the Federal Congress.

That certain provisions of the United Nations Charter are manifestly of this kind appears clear. Thus Article 104, under which the United Nations Organization shall enjoy in the territory of its member nations such privileges and immunities as are necessary for the fulfilment of its purposes, immediately vested the United Nations with legal capacity in the United States, without any need for complemental legislation. Hence, no further action by Congress or the States has been necessary to give the world organization the legal capacity to own land in the United States[1] or to maintain actions in the American courts.[2]

Provisions of this type, directly relating to the functioning of the United Nations Organization itself, do not, however, present any real difficulty. Much harder to deal with are those portions of the United Nations Charter which impose responsibilities on member nations, especially those involving the conduct of their internal affairs. The most important of these are contained in the so-called human rights provisions of the charter. By Article 55, 'the United Nations shall promote... universal respect for, and observance of, human rights and fundamental freedoms for all without distinction as to race, sex, language, or religion'. And, under Article 56, 'All Members pledge themselves to take joint and separate action in cooperation with the Organization for the achievement of the purposes set forth in Article 55.'

In *Sei Fujii* v. *State*,[3] a 1950 decision of the intermediate appellate court of the State of California, it was held that the State's Alien Land Law, which restricted ownership of land by aliens who were ineligible for American citizenship, was invalid because it was contrary to the human rights provisions of the United Nations Charter. In practice, the law in question was directed against Asiatic aliens, and, more particularly, against the large number of Japanese who resided on the American West Coast. 'Clearly such a discrimination against a people of one race', reads the opinion of the California court, 'is contrary both to the letter and to the spirit of the Charter which, as a treaty, is paramount to every law of every state in conflict with it. The Alien Land Law must therefore yield to the treaty as the superior authority.'[4]

Although agreeing that the law at issue was invalid on other grounds, the Supreme Court of California, that State's highest tribunal, upon

1 *Curran* v. *City of New York*, 77 N.Y.S. 2d 206 (Sup. Ct. 1947).
2 *Balfour, Guthrie & Co.* v. *United States*, 90 F. Supp. 831 (N.D. Cal. 1950).
3 217 P. 2d 481 (Cal. App. 1950).   4 *Ibid.* at 488.

appeal, refused to follow the view that the statutory discrimination in question was void because it conflicted with the United Nations Charter. The human rights provisions of the charter did not, according to its decision, supersede the California statute, for they are not, by their own terms, self-executing, and, hence, do not automatically become a part of American municipal law. 'Although the member nations', asserts the highest California court, 'have obligated themselves to cooperate with the international organization in promoting respect for, and observance of, human rights, it is plain that it was contemplated that future legislative action by the several nations would be required to accomplish the declared objectives, and there is nothing to indicate that these provisions were intended to become rules of law for the courts of this country upon the ratification of the charter.'[1]

The view of the California Supreme Court that the human rights provisions of the United Nations Charter lack the mandatory quality and definiteness which would indicate an intent to create justiciable rights in private citizens immediately upon ratification appears justified, especially under the American law regarding the effect of treaties upon municipal law, which has already been gone into. It is true that those provisions of the charter do create binding obligations which must be respected by member nations. 'The Charter of the United Nations', writes Professor Lauterpacht, 'is a legal document; its language is the language of law, of international law. In affirming repeatedly the "fundamental human rights" of the individual, it must of necessity be deemed to refer to legal rights— to legal rights recognized by international law and independent of the law of the State.'[2] It is clear that this view is correct if it is limited to the effects of the charter as a matter of international law. To establish that the United Nations Charter is a binding international obligation between member nations does not, however, necessarily mean that its human rights provisions vest rights in individual citizens of the member States which will be directly enforced in their municipal courts. As Professor Lauterpacht himself recognizes, those provisions of the charter mark only 'a significant step towards the recognition of the individual as a subject of the law of Nations. They are not accompanied by the full conferment of international procedural capacity upon the individual to enable him to enforce, in his own right and in the judicial sphere, the legal benefits of the status thus acquired.'[3]

1 *Sei Fujii* v. *State*, 242 P. 2d 617, 621 (Cal. 1952). See, similarly, *Rice* v. *Sioux City Memorial Park Cemetery*, 60 N.W. 2d 110 (Iowa 1953); *Sipes* v. *McGhee*, 25 N.W. 2d 638 (Mich. 1947).
2 Lauterpacht, 'The subjects of the law of nations', 64 *L. Q. Rev.* (1948), 97, 101.
3 Lauterpacht, *International Law and Human Rights* (1950), 159.

It should not be thought from the above that an international instrument like the United Nations Charter has no effect at all upon American municipal law. 'The humane and enlightened objectives of the United Nations Charter', stated the Supreme Court of California in the *Sei Fujii Case*, 'are, of course, entitled to respectful consideration by the courts and Legislatures of every member nation.... The charter represents a moral commitment of foremost importance, and we must not permit the spirit of our pledge to be compromised or disparaged in either our domestic or foreign affairs.'[1] While, in the case referred to, the highest California court, as we have seen, held that the human rights provisions of the United Nations Charter were not self-executing and, hence, did not, by themselves alone, invalidate the Alien Land Law at issue in the case, there is little doubt but that the court, in holding the law void because it violated the equal protection clause of the Fourteenth Amendment to the Federal Constitution, was influenced by the 'moral commitment' of the charter. The provisions of the charter appear to have helped persuade the court in its refusal to follow earlier decisions upholding the constitutionality of the Alien Land Law. As it was expressed by a member of the United States Supreme Court in a case holding part of the California law in question invalid, 'This nation has recently pledged itself, through the United Nations Charter, to promote respect for, and observance of, human rights and fundamental freedoms for all without distinction as to race, sex, language and religion. The Alien Land Law stands as a barrier to the fulfillment of that national pledge. Its inconsistency with the Charter, which has been duly ratified and adopted by the United States, is but one more reason why the statute must be condemned.'[2]

EXTENT OF TREATY-MAKING POWER

What has been said above with regard to the United Nations Charter and its effect upon American municipal law should serve to show that, though the human rights provisions of that instrument are not, of themselves, enforceable in the American courts at the suit of private individuals, they have not been without influence in cases such as those discussed. And, so far as immediate incorporation into the municipal law of the United States is concerned, as we have seen, it is only because they were not treated as self-executing that these portions of the United Nations Charter have been held to be without such direct domestic effect. For, under the Federal

1 242 P. 2d at 622.
2 *Oyama* v. *California*, 332 U.S. 633, 673 (1948). Compare the now celebrated Canadian case of *Re Drummond Wren*, [1945] 4 D.L.R. 674, discussed in Sayre, 'United Nations law', 25 *Canadian Bar Rev.* (1947), 809.

Constitution, the self-executing provisions of a treaty made by the United States immediately become a part of American law, with the same effect as an Act of the Congress, even though no complementing legislation has been passed by that body.

The question of the domestic effect of American treaties has, in recent years, revolved largely around the possible consequences of several projected multilateral agreements originating under the sponsorship of the United Nations. These are the International Convention on the Prevention and Punishment of the Crime of Genocide, intended to end the calculated extinction of racial and other groups; the proposal of the United Nations International Law Commission for the creation of an international criminal court, for the trial of genocide and other crimes; the draft International Covenant on Human Rights of the United Nations Commission on Human Rights; the Convention on Freedom of Information; and the Convention on International Transmission of News and Right of Correction. Of these, the American executive has approved only the Genocide Convention, and that has been pending before the Senate without confirmation, ever since it was transmitted by the President on 16 June 1949.[1]

American opposition to these projected United Nations treaties has stemmed largely from the fact that, as many of their provisions, especially those of the Covenant on Human Rights, appear to be self-executing, they would immediately become a part of the municipal law and automatically supersede conflicting provisions of State and federal law. And this would be true, even though they were not approved by both Houses of the Federal Legislature, since, as treaties, they would have to be concurred in only by the required two-thirds vote of the Senate. 'The realistic fact remains', writes a leading federal judge, 'that every citizen of the United States, if the proposed Covenant of Human Rights is approved by the Senate, ratified, and goes into force, will have domestic law made for him by treaty submitted to only one legislative body, the Senate, and not enacted by his Congress.'[2]

The situation in the United States, where a treaty such as the proposed Human Rights Covenant would, once ratified, immediately operate to override existing State and federal laws, is complicated by the fact that the exact extent of the treaty-making power itself, in relation to the limitations upon federal governmental power otherwise imposed by the Constitution, is not, even today, entirely clear. That this problem is not one which is peculiar to the constitutional system of the United States is shown by the

[1] See Sutherland, 'Restricting the treaty power', 65 *Harvard L. Rev.* (1952), 1305, 1325.
[2] Allen, *The Treaty as an Instrument of Legislation* (1952), 29.

1937 decision of the Privy Council in *Attorney-General for Canada* v. *Attorney-General for Ontario*.[1] That case involved the validity of three Acts of the Canadian Parliament passed pursuant to conventions adopted by the International Labour Organization and ratified as treaties by the Dominion of Canada. The three statutes, regulating hours, wages, and working conditions, were, under the relevant section of the British North America Act, the Canadian organic instrument, exclusively within the legislative competence of the provincial Parliaments. The only possibility of their being *intra vires* the Dominion Parliament was through an extension of the Dominion powers by force of the International Labour Organization conventions.[2] In holding that the statutes in question were not within the power of the Dominion Parliament, Lord Atkin, who announced the judgment of their Lordships, stated: 'It would be remarkable that while the Dominion could not initiate legislation, however desirable, which affected civil rights in the Province, yet its Government...need only agree with a foreign country to enact such legislation, and its Parliament would be forthwith clothed with authority to affect Provincial rights to the full extent of such agreement. Such a result would appear to undermine the constitutional safeguards of Provincial constitutional autonomy.'[3]

The Privy Council decision in this case had its counterpart in the celebrated decision of the United States Supreme Court in *Missouri* v. *Holland*.[4] In 1913, the Federal Congress passed a statute which sought to regulate the shooting of migratory birds within the States. Two lower federal courts held it unconstitutional on the ground that migratory birds were owned by the States in their sovereign capacity for the benefit of their people and that their control in this field was one that Congress had no power to displace.[5] The United States thereupon entered into a treaty with Great Britain, which provided for specified closed shooting seasons in the United States and Canada, and agreed that the two powers would take or propose to their law-making bodies the necessary measures for carrying out the treaty. Subsequently, in 1918, the Federal Congress passed an Act to give effect to the treaty. This law was challenged as unconstitutional, on the same grounds as those upon which the earlier 1913 regulatory statute had been struck down. It was argued that since, under the two cases referred to which invalidated the 1913 Act, the power at issue was one which the Congress could not exercise unaided, it was one which could not be assumed merely because of the existence of the treaty. This argument was,

1 [1937] A.C. 326. 2 See Sutherland, *loc. cit.* 1316.
3 [1937] A.C. at 352. 4 252 U.S. 416 (1920).
5 *United States* v. *McCullagh*, 221 Fed. 288 (D. Kan. 1915); *United States* v. *Shauver*, 214 Fed. 154 (E. D. Ark. 1914).

however, rejected by the Supreme Court. 'Whether the two cases cited were decided rightly or not,' declared Mr Justice Holmes, speaking for the majority of that tribunal, 'they cannot be accepted as a test of the treaty power. Acts of Congress are the supreme law of the land only when made in pursuance of the Constitution, while treaties are declared to be so when made under the authority of the United States. It is open to question whether the authority of the United States means more than the formal acts prescribed to make the convention'. . . .It is obvious that there may be matters of the sharpest exigency for the national well being that an act of Congress could not deal with but that a treaty followed by such an act could.'[1]

If this pronouncement of the highest American court is compared with the decision of the Privy Council in the Canadian case which has been discussed, it will be seen immediately that the two tribunals have differed fundamentally in their answer to the question of the extent of the treaty-making power. According to the Privy Council, the division of authority between the Dominion and provincial Parliaments prescribed by the Canadian organic instrument could not be affected by the exercise of the treaty-making power. In *Missouri* v. *Holland*, on the other hand, the American court held that a treaty entered into by the United States could, in effect, alter the separation of powers prescribed in the Federal Constitution between the States and the nation. For the court's decision there assumed that, even though the statute at issue could not be enacted unaided by the Congress because it encroached upon powers reserved to the States, it was valid when passed to give effect to a treaty. Or, to put it another way, a treaty of the United States can vest in the Federal Government a regulatory power which is not possessed by it under the Constitution. Truly, as Professor Lauterpacht has aptly expressed it, the American court's decision in *Missouri* v. *Holland* gives to a treaty a status 'dangerously approaching that of a constitutional amendment'.[2]

The Supreme Court's decision in *Missouri* v. *Holland* provoked much discussion in the United States on the possibility of the Federal Government's regulating by treaty a great many subjects in connexion with which the exercise of congressional authority appeared constitutionally to be hampered. It was suggested that labour conditions involving the control of hours, wages, child labour, night work for women, and other matters which seemed to be beyond federal authority under the then prevailing Supreme Court jurisprudence,[3] might be made subject to congressional

1 252 U.S. at 433.
2 Lauterpacht, *An International Bill of Rights of Man* (1945), 179.
3 See *supra*, p. 45.

action through the making of treaties on these matters with other countries.[1] Actual developments of this kind have, however, failed to occur, and thus far there has been no attempt worth noting on the part of the American Government to take advantage of the doctrine of *Missouri* v. *Holland* to enlarge its powers. A prominent American writer states that the failure to utilize that doctrine was due mainly to the breaking down of international co-operation in the period between the two world wars which militated against the broadened use of the treaty power which had been suggested.[2] But, he adds significantly: 'In the event of the return of international co-operation on a large scale, the treaty-making power might yet become the basis for the further extension of the regulatory power of Congress.'[3] With the advent of the United Nations Organization, and the proposals of that body for multilateral legislation like the Covenant on Human Rights, we clearly seem to have reached the era of large-scale international co-operation referred to. And that is why the dangers inherent in the doctrine of *Missouri* v. *Holland* appear to be particularly apparent to many American jurists at the present time.

LIMITATIONS UPON TREATY-MAKING POWER

In view of the doctrine of *Missouri* v. *Holland* and the possibility of its use under present-day international conditions, expecially so far as the many proposals for multilateral treaties sponsored by the United Nations, of the type of the Human Rights Covenant, are concerned, it is not surprising that the question of the legitimate extent of the treaty-making power is one which has been much discussed in the United States. In recent years, the attention of American jurists has focused upon the desirability of limiting the treaty-making power, in order to prevent the making of fundamental changes in American law by the adherence of the United States to international conventions. Certainly, it cannot be denied that, under American law, the treaty-making power is a power of tremendous import. Treaties, as Mr John Foster Dulles put it in an address in 1952, 'make international law and they also make domestic law. Under our Constitution, treaties become the supreme law of the land. They are, indeed, more supreme than ordinary laws, for congressional laws are invalid if they do not conform to the Constitution, whereas treaty law can override the Constitution.'[4]

1 Swisher, *American Constitutional Development* (2nd ed. 1954), 836.
2 *Ibid.*   3 *Ibid.* 837.
4 *Treaties and Executive Agreements, Hearings before a Subcommittee of the Committee on the Judiciary of the United States Senate*, 83rd Cong., 1st Sess. (1953), 862; hereafter cited as *Hearings*.

The objectives of those seeking to limit the treaty-making power of the United States were candidly stated by a member of the Senate who is the author of a constitutional amendment on the subject. 'The American people', said he, 'want to make certain that no treaty or executive agreement will be effective to deny or abridge their fundamental rights. Also, they do not want their basic human rights to be supervised or controlled by international agencies over which they have no control.'[1] There is little doubt but that much of the recent American concern with this subject has been roused by a fear of the effects of international legislation, like the International Covenant on Human Rights, whose enactment is not directly controlled by the elected representatives of the people, upon the domestic law of the United States, particularly that provided for in the Federal Constitution and statutes. 'The root of the difficulty', declares a distinguished federal judge, 'lies in the lack of demarcation between domestic and international legislation. A line must be drawn beyond which the international organizations know they cannot pass.... The United States should draw the line by amendment in the federal constitution.'[2]

The attempt to draw such a line has led to one of the sharpest constitutional controversies that has occurred in the United States—a controversy which culminated, in the early part of 1954, in a bitter debate and vote on the floor of the Federal Senate. The controversy in question arose out of the introduction in the Senate of a proposed amendment to the Federal Constitution usually known as the Bricker Amendment,[3] since its author was the senator of that name. Two of the substantive sections of this proposed amendment, which were voted upon by the Senate during February 1954, bear particularly upon what has been discussed above. Section 1, as amended during the debate in the Senate, provided that 'A provision of a treaty or other international agreement which conflicts with this Constitution shall not be of any force or effect.' Its purpose was to avoid the dangerous possibilities inherent in the doctrine of *Missouri* v. *Holland*, under which, as we have seen, the treaty-making power can be used to override the provisions of the federal organic instrument itself. Treaties, to quote John Foster Dulles again, 'for example, can take powers away from the Congress and give them to the President; they can take powers from the States and give them to the Federal Government or to some international body, and they can cut across the rights given the people by the constitu-

1 Senator Bricker, *Hearings*, 3.
2 Allen, *op. cit.* 104.
3 Under Article V of the Federal Constitution, a resolution proposing an amendment to the organic instrument, if concurred in by two-thirds of both Houses of Congress and ratified by the legislatures of three-quarters of the States, is valid to bring about the desired change.

tional Bill of Rights'.¹ Section 1 of the Bricker Amendment, by virtually doing away with the doctrine of *Missouri* v. *Holland* and expressly placing treaties in the same status as Acts of Congress, so far as conflicts between them and the Constitution were concerned, sought to do away with possibilities such as those mentioned by Mr Dulles.

Opponents of this part of the Bricker Amendment based their attacks largely upon the claim that it was unnecessary. The proposal, declared a memorandum of the Department of State submitted to the Senate, seemed 'unobjectionable at first glance, though unnecessary'.² In the view of the Department, section 1 of the Bricker Amendment was redundant, for the 'treaty-making power is a constitutional power, and as such cannot possibly violate the Constitution'.³ And, in a similar vein, a member of the Senate declared, during the debate on this section, that he was voting against it 'because I do not think it is necessary. It is the present law, and an amendment is not needed.'⁴ This would, however, seem unduly to ignore the possibilities inherent in the doctrine of *Missouri* v. *Holland*. Under it, as has been pointed out, the treaty-making power in the United States is, in fact, a possible basis for federal governmental action unrestrained by existing constitutional limitations.⁵ Americans, who are strongly attached to the stability of their organic instrument, which can be changed only in the formal manner by way of amendment provided for therein, have been strongly disturbed by the possibility of *de facto* amendments to the Constitution being made by use of the treaty-making power. It is true that many jurists have not accepted the view that *Missouri* v. *Holland* permits a treaty invariably to override the Constitution, especially so far as its express prohibitions are concerned. But section 1 of the Bricker Amendment was intended to remove any doubts on this score. As stated by Senator Bricker himself, 'The American people resent the argument that rights which they regard as God-given and inalienable can be alienated by the President and two-thirds of the Senate present and voting.'⁶

Section 1 of the Bricker Amendment, redundant or not, did not, however, meet the opposition of more than a small minority of the Senate. When it was put to a vote in that chamber, it was approved by an overwhelming majority.⁷ Far closer was the vote on section 3 of the proposed amendment. That section, which was in many respects the amendment's most significant provision, sought basically to alter the legal effect of

1 *Hearings*, 862.   2 *Ibid.* 830.   3 *Ibid.*
4 100 *Congressional Record* (Feb. 15, 1954), 1652.
5 Cf. Lauterpacht, *International Law and Human Rights*, 158.   6 *Hearings*, 6.
7 The vote in favour of this section, as amended, was 62 to 20.

treaties in American law. Under it, 'A treaty or other international agreement shall become effective as internal law in the United States only through legislation by the Congress unless in advising and consenting to a treaty the Senate, by a vote of two-thirds of the Senators present and voting, shall provide that such treaty may become effective as internal law without legislation by the Congress.'[1]

At the present time, we have seen, the basic principle of American law on the legal effect of treaties is that such instruments have not only international, but also domestic, effect. Under the Federal Constitution, a treaty entered into by the United States is immediately given effect as a law of the land, just as is a federal statute, unless its provisions are construed as not self-executing. This, as has been pointed out, sharply differentiates the American from the British law on the subject. An American treaty, unlike one entered into by the British Government, can be the source of legal obligations affecting private rights, even though it has not been completed by legislative action. Section 3 of the Bricker Amendment would go far towards doing away with this distinction between American and British law. It would render all American treaties ineffective in domestic law, except where two-thirds of the Senate expressly voted otherwise.

It is erroneous to characterize this portion of the Bricker Amendment as unduly imposing shackles on the treaty-making power.[2] In reality, it would not limit the powers of the executive in negotiating treaties, nor that of the Senate in confirming them. Nor would it prevent such treaties from being valid as binding international obligations of the United States, just as are treaties concluded by the British Government. What it would do is to prevent most treaties from becoming incorporated into American municipal law unless there is separate legislation by the Congress. Or, to put it another way, most treaties entered into by the United States would not attain the domestic status of a federal statute until their provisions were enacted in accordance with the formal procedures prescribed for Acts of the Congress. It should be borne in mind that the present American law, under which the self-executing provisions of a treaty automatically become a part of the domestic law as soon as it is ratified, does not find its counterpart in most other countries. And, as explained by proponents of the Bricker Amendment, 'We want the United States to be in the same position as other countries. There is no reason, if a treaty with Great Britain, so far as the British are concerned, is nothing but an international agree-

---

1 The provision empowering the Senate itself, by a two-thirds vote, to make treaties self-executing internally was added at the last moment on the floor of the Senate in order to secure additional support in that chamber.

2 As it was described in *The Economist*, 25 April 1953, p. 220.

ment and has no domestic effect, why it should have a domestic effect in the United States.'[1]

Though one may sympathize with the desire just expressed to make the American law on this point similar to that of most other countries, it should be recognized that, to an international lawyer concerned with improving the status of law in the relations between nations and increasing the respect accorded to international agreements, section 3 of the Bricker Amendment represents a backward step. It has been the constant concern of students of international law to have treaties and other agreements between States treated as binding instruments of legislation. Much of their effort has been devoted towards ensuring that treaties create binding rights and duties not only on the international plane between the signatory States but also on the national plane, as between individual citizens. As a practical matter, this can be accomplished only if international agreements take effect as a part of domestic law and hence create rights and obligations enforceable at the suit of private individuals in municipal courts. To many, indeed, the practical existence of a true international order is conditioned upon the general acceptance of the primacy of international over municipal law. Their view was well expressed by the remarks of a leading French jurist upon the provisions of the 1946 Constitution of France establishing the superiority of treaties over local law. 'France can be truly proud,' he wrote, 'because she has finally provided for what is in accord with international ethics, the primacy of treaty over statute, i.e., of international law over municipal law.'[2] The American Constitution's provision under which existing domestic laws are superseded by treaties has heretofore been looked to as a model by those expressing this point of view. And the desire to have it remain so appears to have prevailed in the Senate vote on the Bricker Amendment section just discussed. Under its provisions, the United States itself would no longer adhere fully to the doctrine of the primacy of treaty over domestic law. This result was, however, avoided, on 25 February 1954, when a majority of the Senate voted against the inclusion of section 3 in the proposed amendment.[3]

When it became clear to the sponsors of the Bricker Amendment that they could not obtain a favourable senatorial vote on their attempt to alter the self-executing effect of treaties in American law, they directed their efforts towards accomplishing the same result for international agreements other than treaties. In our discussion of presidential power in Chapter IV,[4]

---

1 A. J. Schweppe, in *Hearings*, 56.
2 Niboyet, quoted in Mirkine-Guetzévitch, *Les Constitutions européennes* (1952), 118.
3 The vote against this section was 50 to 42.   4 *Supra*, p. 107.

we saw how increasing reliance has come to be placed by the American executive upon his authority to enter into so-called executive agreements with other governments which are not submitted to the Senate for its approval. Such agreements concluded by the President alone have been held by the Supreme Court to have the same legal effect as a formal treaty approved by the constitutionally required two-thirds of the Senate. 'A treaty', stated the court in 1942, 'is a "Law of the Land" under the supremacy clause...of the Constitution. Such international compacts and agreements as the Litvinov Assignment [i.e. the executive agreement involved in the particular case] have a similar dignity.'[1] Executive agreements, like treaties, have the legal effect of a federal statute, in that their self-executing portions immediately become a part of the municipal law.[2]

Even if one strongly approves of the rule of American law under which a treaty is superior to domestic law, even without the aid of complementary legislation, he need not necessarily feel the same way about the extension of that rule to cover international agreements other than treaties. For the treaty-making power is subject to legislative control which serves as a safeguard against executive excesses. A treaty cannot be ratified unless it is approved by the required two-thirds vote of the Senate. An executive agreement, on the other hand, is concluded by the President alone. It is fully operative, both as international and municipal law, even though it has at no stage been subject to any control by the elected representatives of the people.

It has been seen by many that the power to conclude executive agreements which have the same legal effect as treaties may enable the President to avoid the senatorial control over treaties provided for by the Constitution. He can do this by negotiating, in any particular case, an executive agreement, which he alone can make, rather than a treaty, which must be confirmed by the Senate. There is no hard and fast line between executive agreements and treaties, and they have come to be used interchangeably in the conduct of American foreign relations.[3] That even experts in the field cannot really draw other than a purely formal line between treaties and executive agreements is shown by a request addressed to the State Department by a senator asking them how to distinguish a treaty, which must be approved by the Senate, from an executive agreement, which does not. The State Department unhelpfully defined a treaty as 'some-

---

1 *United States* v. *Pink*, 315 U.S. 203, 230 (1942).
2 Under *United States* v. *Guy W. Capps, Inc.*, 204 F. 2d 655 (4th Cir. 1953), *affirmed on other grounds*, 348 U.S. 296 (1955), however, an executive agreement, which is inconsistent with an existing federal statute in an area subject to regulation by Congress under its commerce power, is invalid. 3 See *supra*, p. 108.

thing they had to send to the Senate in order to get approval by a two-thirds vote. An executive agreement was something they did not have to send to the Senate.'[1] This reply, said the senator, who had sent the request, 'reminded me of the time when I was a boy on the farm, and asked the hired man how to tell the difference between a male and a female pigeon. He said, "You put corn in front of the pigeon. If he picks it up, it is a he; if she picks it up, it is a she."'[2]

It may well be that, under contemporary conditions, a power in the executive to make agreements with other countries which have the same effect in international law as formal treaties is an essential one. What is more debatable, however, is whether such agreements, concluded by the executive alone, should have the same internal legal effect as federal statutes. If they are treated as having such effect, does this not, in practice, vest in the President a means of exercising the legislative power which, under the American Constitution, is delegated to the Congress alone?

As has already been mentioned, when the proponents of the Bricker Amendment realized, after the adverse senatorial vote, that they could not hope to prevail in their attempt to alter the self-executing effect of treaties in American law, they then sought to accomplish that result for international agreements other than treaties. They did this by supporting a substitute for the Bricker Amendment, which contained unaltered its first section, already discussed,[3] voiding treaty and international agreement provisions which conflict with the Constitution, and replaced its third section directed, as we have seen,[4] against the self-executing effect of treaties, by one which read: 'An international agreement other than a treaty shall become effective as internal law in the United States only by an act of the Congress.'[5]

A provision like this, aimed solely against executive agreements, was able to obtain far more support in the American Senate than the original Bricker Amendment provision, directed primarily against treaties. It was felt by many senators that some legislative check upon executive agreements was urgently needed, at least so far as their self-executing effect in municipal law was concerned. Under existing American law, since executive agreements concluded by the President alone may immediately have the same internal effect as a federal statute, the President is, in effect, given what one senator characterized as 'a lawmaking power which completely by-passes the Congress, unless something is done to retain that power and

---

1 100 *Congressional Record* (Feb. 15, 1954), 1656.
2 *Ibid.*
3 *Supra*, p. 324.   4 *Supra*, p. 326.
5 This was section 2 of the proposed substitute amendment.

to give Congress a chance to take a look at it and to determine, as the representatives of the people, what shall be done insofar as the internal law is concerned'.[1]

When the substitute for the Bricker Amendment, which has just been discussed, was put to a vote on the floor of the Senate on 26 February 1954, the vote was 60 to 31 in its favour.[2] But though it was thus approved by a substantial majority of the American upper chamber, it did not receive—by a margin of a single vote—the two-thirds vote required by the Federal Constitution[3] for the proposing of a constitutional amendment by the Congress.

Though the vote of the Senate failed—by the narrowest of margins—to approve the amendment proposed as a substitute for the Bricker Amendment, the controversy has by no means ended in the United States over the scope of the power to make treaties and other international agreements. It appears likely, on the contrary, that the questions raised by the Bricker Amendment will be debated by American jurists for some time to come.[4] Certainly they are among the crucial questions of contemporary American constitutional law and of as much concern to foreigners as they are to jurists in the United States.

It should be recognized, in all frankness, that the movement behind the Bricker Amendment and other proposed changes in this field draws its strength, in large part, from fears about the effect of international agreements, especially those proposed by organs of the United Nations of the type of the Covenant on Human Rights, upon American rights and domestic laws. It is true that it was similar fears that helped to keep the United States out of the League of Nations, and true also that such fears are being used by forces in America as the starting-point for a movement to take the United States out of the United Nations itself.[5] However, it is a mistake to assume that the Bricker Amendment and analogous proposals derive their support only, or even primarily, from those neo-isolationists who

1 100 *Congressional Record* (Feb. 26, 1954), 2234.

2 The vote itself provides an interesting illustration of the looseness of party discipline in the American legislature. Although President Eisenhower was strongly opposed to any constitutional amendment in this field, most of the members of his party in the Senate voted in favour of the proposed amendment. Especially significant in this connexion is the vote for the amendment by the leader of the Senate majority. Before the taking of the vote, he stated that he had 'left the desk of the majority leader' and was voting as an individual senator for the amendment, despite the fact that this was contrary to the expressed views of the President, the leader of his party. He did this, it should be emphasized, only as far as this particular vote was concerned, for, after it was taken, he immediately resumed his post as leader of the President's party in the Senate.   3 *Supra*, p. 324, n. 3.

4 It seems certain, indeed, that the Bricker Amendment will be reintroduced in forthcoming sessions of the Congress.   5 *The Economist*, 25 April 1953, p. 220.

would have the United States repudiate the international obligations which she has assumed since the last war. On the contrary, support for the Bricker Amendment has been widespread in the United States, so much so, indeed, that the Secretary of State, in order to quiet the qualms of its proponents, felt it necessary to assure the Senate that the United States would not become a party to international treaties of the type proposed by the United Nations, which tend to effect internal social changes, and he listed specifically in this respect the Human Rights Covenant and the Convention on the Political Rights of Women.[1]

The support which the Bricker Amendment and like proposals have found among American jurists stems from doubts whether the doctrine of *Missouri v. Holland* and the constitutional rule of the immediate effect of treaties and other international agreements in American municipal law are appropriate under contemporary expanding conceptions of the sphere of international legislation. 'During recent years', the Secretary of State, John Foster Dulles, has stated to the Senate, 'there developed a tendency to consider treaty-making as a way to effectuate reforms, particularly in social matters, and to impose upon our Republic conceptions regarding human rights which many felt were alien to our traditional concepts. This tendency caused widespread concern, a concern which is reflected in the proposed resolutions before you.'[2] Certainly, as Mr Dulles himself conceded that concern has been a legitimate one.[3]

It should be borne in mind that a recognition of the problem and the legitimacy of the concern caused by it does not necessarily involve approval of the Bricker Amendment. There are, as we have seen, dangerous implications in some of its provisions, particularly that altering the rule under which treaties now have immediate effect in American municipal law. That section would do away with the pioneer provision of the Federal Constitution, which has served as a model for international lawyers and for an increasing number of similar constitutional provisions, such as that in the organic instrument adopted by the French people in 1946. And it would do so at a time when it is particularly important that the status and prestige of treaties and other international agreements should be increased rather than diminished. Yet, even with this admitted, it cannot be denied that the sponsors of the Bricker Amendment have, in fact, rendered real service in bringing the issues of the making and effect of treaties and executive agreements before the bar of public opinion. The problems involved are so important, both for American and international law, that, whatever the outcome, it is all to the good that there be a full public discussion of

1 *Hearings*, 825.   2 *Ibid.* 824.
3 *Ibid.*

them. 'There is room for honest difference of opinion', stated John Foster Dulles in 1952, 'as to whether our Constitution needs to be amended as proposed or whether the President and the Senate should retain their present powers for possible emergency use, and at the same time insuring more vigilance to the end that treaties will not undesirably or unnecessarily encroach on constitutional distributions of power. Whatever one's views on this matter, it is surely in the public interest that the whole problem should be thoroughly explored.'[1]

1 *Hearings*, 863.

Appendix

CONSTITUTION OF THE UNITED STATES OF AMERICA[1]

We the People of the United States, in Order to form a more perfect Union, establish Justice, insure domestic Tranquility, provide for the common defence, promote the general Welfare, and secure the Blessings of Liberty to ourselves and our Posterity, do ordain and establish this Constitution for the United States of America.

ARTICLE I

SECTION 1. All legislative Powers herein granted shall be vested in a Congress of the United States, which shall consist of a Senate and House of Representatives.

SECTION 2. The House of Representatives shall be composed of Members chosen every second Year by the People of the several States, and the Electors in each State shall have the Qualifications requisite for Electors of the most numerous Branch of the State Legislature.

No Person shall be a Representative who shall not have attained to the age of twenty five Years, and been seven Years a Citizen of the United States, and who shall not, when elected, be an Inhabitant of that State in which he shall be chosen.

Representatives and direct Taxes shall be apportioned among the several States which may be included within this Union, according to their respective Numbers, which shall be determined by adding to the whole Number of free Persons, including those bound to Service for a Term of Years, and excluding Indians not taxed, three fifths of all other Persons. The actual Enumeration shall be made within three Years after the first Meeting of the Congress of the United States, and within every subsequent Term of ten Years, in such Manner as they shall by Law direct. The Number of Representatives shall not exceed one for every thirty Thousand, but each State shall have at Least one Representative; and until such enumeration shall be made, the State of New Hampshire shall be entitled to chuse three, Massachusetts eight, Rhode-Island and Providence Plantations one, Connecticut five, New-York six, New Jersey four, Pennsylvania eight, Delaware one, Maryland six, Virginia ten, North Carolina five, South Carolina five, and Georgia three.

When vacancies happen in the Representation from any State, the Executive Authority thereof shall issue Writs of Election to fill such Vacancies.

The House of Representatives shall chuse their Speaker and other Officers; and shall have the sole Power of Impeachment.

1 The Constitution was submitted to the States for ratification on 28 September 1787. The ninth State ratified on 21 June 1788, and the Constitution went into effect on 4 March 1789.

SECTION 3. The Senate of the United States shall be composed of two Senators from each State, chosen by the Legislature thereof, for six Years; and each Senator shall have one Vote.

Immediately after they shall be assembled in Consequence of the first Election, they shall be divided as equally as may be into three Classes. The Seats of the Senators of the first Class shall be vacated at the Expiration of the second Year, of the second Class at the Expiration of the fourth Year, and of the third Class at the Expiration of the sixth Year, so that one third may be chosen every second Year; and if Vacancies happen by Resignation, or otherwise, during the Recess of the Legislature of any State, the Executive thereof may make temporary Appointments until the next Meeting of the Legislature, which shall then fill such Vacancies.

No Person shall be a Senator who shall not have attained to the Age of thirty Years, and been nine Years a Citizen of the United States, and who shall not, when elected, be an Inhabitant of that State for which he shall be chosen.

The Vice President of the United States shall be President of the Senate, but shall have no Vote, unless they be equally divided.

The Senate shall chuse their other Officers, and also a President pro tempore, in the Absence of the Vice President, or when he shall exercise the Office of President of the United States.

The Senate shall have the sole Power to try all Impeachments. When sitting for that Purpose, they shall be on Oath or Affirmation. When the President of the United States is tried the Chief Justice shall preside: And no Person shall be convicted without the Concurrence of two thirds of the Members present.

Judgment in Cases of Impeachment shall not extend further than to removal from Office, and disqualification to hold and enjoy any Office of honor, Trust or Profit under the United States: but the Party convicted shall nevertheless be liable and subject to Indictment, Trial, Judgment and Punishment, according to Law.

SECTION 4. The Times, Places and Manner of holding Elections for Senators and Representatives, shall be prescribed in each State by the Legislature thereof; but the Congress may at any time by Law make or alter such Regulations, except as to the Places of chusing Senators.

The Congress shall assemble at least once in every Year, and such Meeting shall be on the the first Monday in December, unless they shall by Law appoint a different Day.

SECTION 5. Each House shall be the Judge of the Elections, Returns and Qualifications of its own Members, and a Majority of each shall constitute a Quorum to do Business; but a smaller Number may adjourn from day to day, and may be authorized to compel the Attendance of absent Members, in such Manner, and under such Penalties as each House may provide.

Each House may determine the Rules of its Proceedings, punish its Members for disorderly Behaviour, and, with the Concurrence of two thirds, expel a Member.

Each House shall keep a Journal of its Proceedings, and from time to time publish the same, excepting such Parts as may in their Judgment require Secrecy; and the Yeas and Nays of the Members of either House on any question shall, at the Desire of one fifth of those Present, be entered on the Journal.

Neither House, during the Session of Congress, shall, without the Consent of the other, adjourn for more than three days, nor to any other Place than that in which the two Houses shall be sitting.

SECTION 6. The Senators and Representatives shall receive a Compensation for their Services, to be ascertained by Law, and paid out of the Treasury of the United States. They shall in all Cases, except Treason, Felony and Breach of the Peace, be privileged from Arrest during their Attendance at the Session of their respective Houses, and in going to and returning from the same; and for any Speech or Debate in either House, they shall not be questioned in any other Place.

No Senator or Representative shall, during the Time for which he was elected, be appointed to any civil Office under the Authority of the United States, which shall have been created, or the Emoluments whereof shall have been encreased during such time; and no Person holding any Office under the United States, shall be a Member of either House during his Continuance in Office.

SECTION 7. All Bills for raising Revenue shall originate in the House of Representatives; but the Senate may propose or concur with Amendments as on other Bills.

Every Bill which shall have passed the House of Representatives and the Senate, shall, before it become a Law, be presented to the President of the United States; If he approves he shall sign it, but if not he shall return it, with his Objections to that House in which it shall have originated, who shall enter the Objections at large on their Journal, and proceed to reconsider it. If after such Reconsideration two thirds of that House shall agree to pass the Bill, it shall be sent, together with the Objections, to the other House, by which it shall likewise be reconsidered, and if approved by two thirds of that House, it shall become a Law. But in all such Cases the Votes of both Houses shall be determined by yeas and Nays, and the Names of the Persons voting for and against the Bill shall be entered on the Journal of each House respectively. If any Bill shall not be returned by the President within ten Days (Sundays excepted) after it shall have been presented to him, the Same shall be a Law, in like Manner as if he had signed it, unless the Congress by their Adjournment prevent its Return, in which Case it shall not be a Law.

Every Order, Resolution, or Vote to which the Concurrence of the Senate and House of Representatives may be necessary (except on a question of Adjournment) shall be presented to the President of the United States; and before the Same shall take Effect, shall be approved by him, or being disapproved by him, shall be repassed by two thirds of the Senate and House of Representatives, according to the Rules and Limitations prescribed in the Case of a Bill.

SECTION 8. The Congress shall have Power To lay and collect Taxes, Duties, Imposts and Excises, to pay the Debts and provide for the common Defence and general Welfare of the United States; but all Duties, Imposts and Excises shall be uniform throughout the United States;

To borrow Money on the credit of the United States;

To regulate Commerce with foreign Nations, and among the several States, and with the Indian Tribes;

To establish an uniform Rule of Naturalization, and uniform Laws on the subject of Bankruptcies throughout the United States;

To coin Money, regulate the Value thereof, and of foreign Coin, and fix the Standard of Weights and Measures;

To provide for the Punishment of counterfeiting the Securities and current Coin of the United States;

To establish Post Offices and post Roads;

To promote the Progress of Science and useful Arts, by securing for limited Times to Authors and Inventors the exclusive Right to their respective Writings and Discoveries;

To constitute Tribunals inferior to the supreme Court;

To define and punish Piracies and Felonies committed on the high Seas, and Offences against the Law of Nations;

To declare War, grant Letters of Marque and Reprisal, and make Rules concerning Captures on Land and Water;

To raise and support Armies, but no Appropriation of Money to that Use shall be for a longer Term than two Years;

To provide and maintain a Navy;

To make Rules for the Government and Regulation of the land and naval Forces;

To provide for calling forth the Militia to execute the Laws of the Union, suppress Insurrections and repel Invasions;

To provide for organizing, arming, and disciplining, the Militia, and for governing such Part of them as may be employed in the Service of the United States, reserving to the States respectively, the Appointment of the Officers, and the Authority of training the Militia according to the discipline prescribed by Congress;

To exercise exclusive Legislation in all Cases whatsoever, over such District (not exceeding ten Miles square) as may, by Cession of Particular States, and the Acceptance of Congress, become the Seat of the Government of the United States, and to exercise like Authority over all Places purchased by the Consent of the Legislature of the State in which the Same shall be, for the Erection of Forts, Magazines, Arsenals, dock-Yards, and other needful Buildings;—And

To make all Laws which shall be necessary and proper for carrying into Execution the foregoing Powers, and all other Powers vested by this Constitution in the Government of the United States, or in any Department or Officer thereof.

SECTION 9. The Migration or Importation of such Persons as any of the States now existing shall think proper to admit, shall not be prohibited by the Congress prior to the Year one thousand eight hundred and eight, but a Tax or duty may be imposed on such Importation, not exceeding ten dollars for each Person.

The Privilege of the Writ of Habeas Corpus shall not be suspended, unless when in Cases of Rebellion or Invasion the public Safety may require it.

No Bill of Attainder or ex post facto Law shall be passed.

No Capitation, or other direct, Tax shall be laid, unless in Proportion to the Census or Enumeration herein before directed to be taken.

No Tax or Duty shall be laid on Articles exported from any State.

No Preference shall be given by any Regulation of Commerce or Revenue to the Ports of one State over those of another; nor shall Vessels bound to, or from, one State, be obliged to enter, clear, or pay Duties in another.

No Money shall be drawn from the Treasury, but in Consequence of Appropriations made by Law; and a regular Statement and Account of the Receipts and Expenditures of all public Money shall be published from time to time.

No Title of Nobility shall be granted by the United States: And no Person holding any Office of Profit or Trust under them, shall, without the Consent of the Congress, accept of any present, Emolument, Office, or Title, of any kind whatever, from any King, Prince, or foreign State.

SECTION 10. No State shall enter into any Treaty, Alliance, or Confederation; grant Letters of Marque and Reprisal; coin Money; emit Bills of Credit; make any Thing but gold and silver Coin a Tender in Payment of Debts; pass any Bill of Attainder, ex post facto Law, or Law impairing the Obligation of Contracts; or grant any Title of Nobility.

No State shall, without the Consent of the Congress, lay any Imposts or Duties on Imports or Exports, except what may be absolutely necessary for executing its inspection Laws: and the net Produce of all Duties and Imposts, laid by any State on Imports or Exports, shall be for the Use of the Treasury of the United States; and all such Laws shall be subject to the Revision and Controul of the Congress.

No State shall, without the Consent of Congress, lay any Duty of Tonnage, keep Troops, or Ships of War in time of Peace, enter into any Agreement or Compact with another State, or with a foreign Power, or engage in War, unless actually invaded, or in such imminent Danger as will not admit of delay.

ARTICLE II

SECTION 1. The executive Power shall be vested in a President of the United States of America. He shall hold his Office during the Term of four Years, and, together with the Vice President, chosen for the same Term, be elected, as follows

Each State shall appoint, in such Manner as the Legislature thereof may direct, a Number of Electors, equal to the whole Number of Senators and Representatives to which the State may be entitled in the Congress: but no Senator or Representative, or Person holding an Office of Trust or Profit under the United States, shall be appointed an Elector.

The Electors shall meet in their respective States, and vote by Ballot for two Persons, of whom one at least shall not be an Inhabitant of the same State with themselves. And they shall make a List of all the Persons voted for, and of the Number of Votes for each; which List they shall sign and certify, and transmit sealed to the Seat of the Government of the United States, directed to the President of the Senate. The President of the Senate shall, in the Presence of the Senate and House of Representatives, open all the Certificates, and the Votes shall then be counted. The Person having the greatest Number of Votes shall be the President, if such Number be a Majority of the whole Number of Electors appointed; and if there be more than one who have such Majority, and have an equal Number of Votes, then the House of Representatives shall immediately chuse by Ballot one of them for President; and if no Person have a Majority, then from the five highest on the List the said House shall in like Manner chuse the President. But in chusing the President, the Votes shall be taken by States, the Representation from each State having one Vote; a quorum for this Purpose shall consist of a Member or Members from two thirds of the States, and a Majority of all the States shall be necessary to a Choice. In every Case, after the Choice of the President, the Person having the greatest Number of Votes of the Electors shall be the Vice President. But if there should remain two or more who have equal Votes, the Senate shall chuse from them by Ballot the Vice President.

The Congress may determine the Time of chusing the Electors, and the Day on which they shall give their Votes; which Day shall be the same throughout the United States.

No Person except a natural born Citizen, or a Citizen of the United States, at the time of the Adoption of this Constitution, shall be eligible to the Office of President; neither shall any person be eligible to that Office who shall not have attained to the Age of thirty five Years, and been fourteen Years a Resident within the United States.

In Case of the Removal of the President from Office, or of his Death, Resignation, or Inability to discharge the Powers and Duties of the said Office, the Same shall devolve on the Vice President, and the Congress may by Law provide for the Case of Removal, Death, Resignation or Inability, both of the President and Vice President, declaring what Officer shall then act as President, and such Officer shall act accordingly, until the Disability be removed, or a President shall be elected.

The President shall, at stated Times, receive for his Services, a Compensation, which shall neither be encreased nor diminished during the Period for which he shall have been elected, and he shall not receive within that Period any other Emolument from the United States, or any of them.

Before he enter on the Execution of his Office, he shall take the following Oath or Affirmation:—"I do solemnly swear (or affirm) that I will faithfully execute the Office of President of the United States, and will to the best of my Ability, preserve, protect and defend the Constitution of the United States."

SECTION 2. The President shall be Commander in Chief of the Army and Navy of the United States, and of the Militia of the several States, when called into the actual Service of the United States; he may require the Opinion, in writing, of the principal Officer in each of the executive Departments, upon any Subject relating to the Duties of their respective Offices, and he shall have Power to grant Reprieves and Pardons for Offences against the United States, except in Cases of Impeachment.

He shall have Power, by and with the Advice and Consent of the Senate, to make Treaties, provided two thirds of the Senators present concur; and he shall nominate, and by and with the Advice and Consent of the Senate, shall appoint Ambassadors, other public Ministers and Consuls, Judges of the supreme Court, and all other Officers of the United States, whose Appointments are not herein otherwise provided for, and which shall be established by Law: but the Congress may by Law vest the Appointment of such inferior Officers, as they think proper, in the President alone, in the Courts of Law, or in the Heads of Departments.

The President shall have Power to fill up all Vacancies that may happen during the Recess of the Senate, by granting Commissions which shall expire at the End of their next Session.

SECTION 3. He shall from time to time give to the Congress Information of the State of the Union, and recommend to their Consideration such Measures as he shall judge necessary and expedient; he may, on extraordinary Occasions, convene both Houses, or either of them, and in Case of Disagreement between them, with Respect to the Time of Adjournment, he may adjourn them to such Time as he shall think proper; he shall receive Ambassadors and other public Ministers; he shall take Care that the Laws be faithfully executed, and shall Commission all the Officers of the United States.

SECTION 4. The President, Vice President and all civil Officers of the United States, shall be removed from Office on Impeachment for, and Conviction of, Treason, Bribery, or other high Crimes and Misdemeanors.

ARTICLE III

SECTION 1. The judicial Power of the United States, shall be vested in one supreme Court, and in such inferior Courts as the Congress may from time to time ordain and establish. The Judges, both of the supreme and inferior Courts, shall hold their Offices during good Behaviour, and shall, at stated Times, receive for their Services, a Compensation, which shall not be diminished during their Continuance in Office.

SECTION 2. The judicial Power shall extend to all Cases, in Law and Equity, arising under this Constitution, the Laws of the United States, and Treaties made, or which shall be made, under their Authority;—to all Cases affecting Ambassadors, other public Ministers and Consuls;—to all Cases of admiralty and maritime Jurisdiction;—to Controversies to which the United States shall be a Party;—to Controversies between two or more States;—between a State and Citizens of another State;—between Citizens of different States;—between Citizens of the same State claiming Lands under Grants of different States, and between a State, or the Citizens thereof, and foreign States, Citizens or Subjects.

In all Cases affecting Ambassadors, other public Ministers and Consuls, and those in which a State shall be Party, the supreme Court shall have original Jurisdiction. In all the other Cases before mentioned, the supreme Court shall have appellate Jurisdiction, both as to Law and Fact, with such Exceptions, and under such Regulations as the Congress shall make.

The Trial of all Crimes, except in Cases of Impeachment, shall be by Jury; and such Trial shall be held in the State where the said Crimes shall have been committed; but when not committed within any State, the Trial shall be at such Place or Places as the Congress may by Law have directed.

SECTION 3. Treason against the United States, shall consist only in levying War against them, or in adhering to their Enemies, giving them Aid and Comfort. No Person shall be convicted of Treason unless on the Testimony of two Witnesses to the same overt Act, or on Confession in open Court.

The Congress shall have Power to declare the Punishment of Treason, but no Attainder of Treason shall work Corruption of Blood, or Forfeiture except during the Life of the Person attainted.

ARTICLE IV

SECTION I. Full Faith and Credit shall be given in each State to the public Acts, Records, and judicial Proceedings of every other State. And the Congress may by general Laws prescribe the Manner in which such Acts, Records and Proceedings shall be proved, and the Effect thereof.

SECTION 2. The Citizens of each State shall be entitled to all Privileges and Immunities of Citizens in the several States.

A Person charged in any State with Treason, Felony, or other Crime, who shall flee from Justice, and be found in another State, shall on Demand of the executive Authority of the State from which he fled, be delivered up, to be removed to the State having Jurisdiction of the Crime.

No Person held to Service or Labour in one State, under the Laws thereof, escaping into another, shall, in Consequence of any Law or Regulation therein, be discharged from such Service or Labour, but shall be delivered up on Claim of the Party to whom such Service or Labour may be due.

SECTION 3. New States may be admitted by the Congress into this Union; but no new State shall be formed or erected within the Jurisdiction of any other State; nor any State be formed by the Junction of two or more States, or Parts of States, without the Consent of the Legislatures of the States concerned as well as of the Congress.

The Congress shall have Power to dispose of and make all needful Rules and Regulations respecting the Territory or other Property belonging to the United States; and nothing in this Constitution shall be so construed as to Prejudice any Claims of the United States, or of any particular State.

SECTION 4. The United States shall guarantee to every State in this Union a Republican Form of Government, and shall protect each of them against Invasion; and on Application of the Legislature, or of the Executive (when the Legislature cannot be convened) against domestic Violence.

ARTICLE V

The Congress, whenever two thirds of both Houses shall deem it necessary, shall propose Amendments to this Constitution, or, on the Application of the Legislatures of two thirds of the several States, shall call a Convention for proposing Amendments, which, in either Case, shall be valid to all Intents and Purposes, as Part of this Constitution, when ratified by the Legislatures of three fourths of the several States, or by Conventions in three fourths thereof, as the one or the other Mode of Ratification may be proposed by the Congress; Provided that no Amendment which may be made prior to the Year One thousand eight hundred and eight shall in any Manner affect the first and fourth Clauses in the Ninth Section of the first Article; and that no State, without its Consent, shall be deprived of its equal Suffrage in the Senate.

ARTICLE VI

All Debts contracted and Engagements entered into, before the Adoption of this Constitution, shall be as valid against the United States under this Constitution, as under the Confederation.

This Constitution, and the Laws of the United States which shall be made in Pursuance thereof; and all Treaties made, or which shall be made, under the Authority of the United States, shall be the supreme Law of the Land; and the Judges in every State shall be bound thereby, any Thing in the Constitution or Laws of any State to the Contrary notwithstanding.

The Senators and Representatives before mentioned, and the Members of the several State Legislatures, and all executive and judicial Officers, both of the United States and of the several States, shall be bound by Oath or Affirmation, to support this Constitution; but no religious Test shall ever be required as a Qualification to any Office or public Trust under the United States.

ARTICLE VII

The Ratification of the Conventions of nine States, shall be sufficient for the Establishment of this Constitution between the States so ratifying the Same.

ARTICLES IN ADDITION TO, AND AMENDMENT OF, THE
CONSTITUTION OF THE UNITED STATES OF AMERICA,
PROPOSED BY CONGRESS, AND RATIFIED BY THE SEVERAL
STATES, PURSUANT TO THE FIFTH ARTICLE OF THE
ORIGINAL CONSTITUTION.

ARTICLE [I][1]

Congress shall make no law respecting an establishment of religion, or prohibiting the free exercise thereof; or abridging the freedom of speech, or of the press; or the right of the people peaceably to assemble, and to petition the Government for a redress of grievances.

ARTICLE [II]

A well regulated Militia, being necessary to the security of a free State, the right of the people to keep and bear Arms, shall not be infringed.

ARTICLE [III]

No Soldier shall, in time of peace be quartered in any house, without the consent of the Owner, nor in time of war, but in a manner to be prescribed by law.

ARTICLE [IV]

The right of the people to be secure in their persons, houses, papers, and effects, against unreasonable searches and seizures, shall not be violated, and no Warrants shall issue, but upon probable cause, supported by Oath or affirmation, and particularly describing the place to be searched, and the persons or things to be seized.

1 The first ten amendments were proposed by Congress on 25 September 1789, and ratified by sufficient States by 15 December 1791.

ARTICLE [V]

No person shall be held to answer for a capital, or otherwise infamous crime, unless on a presentment or indictment of a Grand Jury, except in cases arising in the land or naval forces, or in the Militia, when in actual service in time of War or public danger; nor shall any person be subject for the same offence to be twice put in jeopardy of life or limb; nor shall be compelled in any criminal case to be a witness against himself, nor be deprived of life, liberty, or property, without due process of law; nor shall private property be taken for public use, without just compensation.

ARTICLE [VI]

In all criminal prosecutions, the accused shall enjoy the right to a speedy and public trial, by an impartial jury of the State and district wherein the crime shall have been committed, which district shall have been previously ascertained by law, and to be informed of the nature and cause of the accusation; to be confronted with the witnesses against him; to have compulsory process for obtaining witnesses in his favor, and to have the Assistance of Counsel for his defence.

ARTICLE [VII]

In Suits at common law, where the value in controversy shall exceed twenty dollars, the right of trial by jury shall be preserved, and no fact tried by a jury, shall be otherwise re-examined in any Court of the United States, than according to the rules of the common law.

ARTICLE [VIII]

Excessive bail shall not be required, nor excessive fines imposed, nor cruel and unusual punishments inflicted.

ARTICLE [IX]

The enumeration in the Constitution, of certain rights, shall not be construed to deny or disparage others retained by the people.

ARTICLE [X]

The powers not delegated to the United States by the Constitution, nor prohibited by it to the States, are reserved to the States respectively, or to the people.

ARTICLE [XI][1]

The Judicial power of the United States shall not be construed to extend to any suit in law or equity, commenced or prosecuted against one of the United States by Citizens of another State, or by Citizens or Subjects of any Foreign State.

ARTICLE [XII][2]

The Electors shall meet in their respective states, and vote by ballot for President and Vice-President, one of whom, at least, shall not be an inhabitant of the same

1 Proposed 4 March 1794, and declared ratified 8 January 1798.
2 Proposed 12 December 1803, and declared ratified 25 September 1804.

state with themselves; they shall name in their ballots the person voted for as President, and in distinct ballots the person voted for as Vice-President, and they shall make distinct lists of all persons voted for as President, and of all persons voted for as Vice-President, and of the number of votes for each, which lists they shall sign and certify, and transmit sealed to the seat of the government of the United States, directed to the President of the Senate;—The President of the Senate shall, in the presence of the Senate and House of Representatives, open all the certificates and the votes shall then be counted;—The person having the greatest number of votes for President, shall be the President, if such number be a majority of the whole number of Electors appointed; and if no person have such majority, then from the persons having the highest numbers not exceeding three on the list of those voted for as President, the House of Representatives shall choose immediately, by ballot, the President. But in choosing the President, the votes shall be taken by states, the representation from each state having one vote; a quorum for this purpose shall consist of a member or members from two-thirds of the states, and a majority of all the states shall be necessary to a choice. And if the House of Representatives shall not choose a President whenever the right of choice shall devolve upon them, before the fourth day of March next following, then the Vice-President shall act as President, as in the case of the death or other constitutional disability of the President—The person having the greatest number of votes as Vice-President, shall be the Vice-President, if such number be a majority of the whole number of Electors appointed, and if no person have a majority, then from the two highest numbers on the list, the Senate shall choose the Vice-President; a quorum for the purpose shall consist of two-thirds of the whole number of Senators, and a majority of the whole number shall be necessary to a choice. But no person constitutionally ineligible to the office of President shall be eligible to that of Vice-President of the United States.

ARTICLE XIII[1]

SECTION 1. Neither slavery nor involuntary servitude, except as a punishment for crime whereof the party shall have been duly convicted, shall exist within the United States, or any place subject to their jurisdiction.

SECTION 2. Congress shall have power to enforce this article by appropriate legislation.

ARTICLE XIV[2]

SECTION 1. All persons born or naturalized in the United States, and subject to the jurisdiction thereof, are citizens of the United States and of the State wherein they reside. No State shall make or enforce any law which shall abridge the privileges or immunities of citizens of the United States; nor shall any State deprive any person of life, liberty, or property, without due process of law; nor deny to any person within its jurisdiction the equal protection of the laws.

SECTION 2. Representatives shall be apportioned among the several States according to their respective numbers, counting the whole number of persons in

---

1 Proposed 1 February 1865, and declared ratified 18 December 1865.
2 Proposed 16 June 1866, and declared ratified 21 July 1868.

each State, excluding Indians not taxed. But when the right to vote at any election for the choice of electors for President and Vice President of the United States, Representatives in Congress, the Executive and Judicial officers of a State, or the members of the Legislature thereof, is denied to any of the male inhabitants of such State, being twenty-one years of age, and citizens of the United States, or in any way abridged, except for participation in rebellion, or other crime, the basis of representation therein shall be reduced in the proportion which the number of such male citizens shall bear to the whole number of male citizens twenty-one years of age in such State.

SECTION 3. No person shall be a Senator or Representative in Congress, or elector of President and Vice President, or hold any office, civil or military, under the United States, or under any State, who, having previously taken an oath, as a member of Congress, or as an officer of the United States, or as a member of any State legislature, or as an executive or judicial officer of any State, to support the Constitution of the United States, shall have engaged in insurrection or rebellion against the same, or given aid or comfort to the enemies thereof. But Congress may by a vote of two-thirds of each House, remove such disability.

SECTION 4. The validity of the public debt of the United States, authorized by law, including debts incurred for payment of pensions and bounties for services in suppressing insurrection or rebellion, shall not be questioned. But neither the United States nor any State shall assume or pay any debt or obligation incurred in aid of insurrection or rebellion against the United States, or any claim for the loss or emancipation of any slave; but all such debts, obligations and claims shall be held illegal and void.

SECTION 5. The Congress shall have power to enforce, by appropriate legislation, the provisions of this article.

ARTICLE XV[1]

SECTION 1. The right of citizens of the United States to vote shall not be denied or abridged by the United States or by any State on account of race, color, or previous condition of servitude.

SECTION 2. The Congress shall have power to enforce this article by appropriate legislation.

ARTICLE XVI[2]

The Congress shall have power to lay and collect taxes on incomes, from whatever source derived, without apportionment among the several States, and without regard to any census or enumeration.

ARTICLE [XVII][3]

The Senate of the United States shall be composed of two Senators from each State, elected by the people thereof, for six years; and each Senator shall have one

---

1 Proposed 27 February 1869, and declared ratified 30 March 1870.
2 Proposed 12 July 1909, and declared ratified 25 February 1913.
3 Proposed 13 May 1912, and declared ratified 31 May 1913.

vote. The electors in each State shall have the qualifications requisite for electors of the most numerous branch of the State legislatures.

When vacancies happen in the representation of any State in the Senate, the executive authority of such State shall issue writs of election to fill such vacancies: *Provided,* That the legislature of any State may empower the executive thereof to make temporary appointments until the people fill the vacancies by election as the legislature may direct.

This amendment shall not be so construed as to affect the election or term of any Senator chosen before it becomes valid as part of the Constitution.

ARTICLE [XVIII][1]

SECTION 1. After one year from the ratification of this article the manufacture, sale, or transportation of intoxicating liquors within, the importation thereof into, or the exportation thereof from the United States and all territory subject to the jurisdiction thereof for beverage purposes is hereby prohibited.

SECTION 2. The Congress and the several States shall have concurrent power to enforce this article by appropriate legislation.

SECTION 3. This article shall be inoperative unless it shall have been ratified as an amendment to the Constitution by the legislatures of the several States, as provided in the Constitution, within seven years from the date of the submission hereof to the States by the Congress.

ARTICLE [XIX][2]

The right of citizens of the United States to vote shall not be denied or abridged by the United States or by any State on account of sex.

Congress shall have power to enforce this article by appropriate legislation.

ARTICLE [XX][3]

SECTION 1. The terms of the President and Vice President shall end at noon on the 20th day of January, and the terms of Senators and Representatives at noon on the 3d day of January, of the years in which such terms would have ended if this article had not been ratified; and the terms of their successors shall then begin.

SECTION 2. The Congress shall assemble at least once in every year, and such meeting shall begin at noon on the 3d day of January, unless they shall by law appoint a different day.

SECTION 3. If, at the time fixed for the beginning of the term of the President, the President elect shall have died, the Vice President elect shall become President. If a President shall not have been chosen before the time fixed for the beginning of his term, or if the President elect shall have failed to qualify, then the Vice President elect shall act as President until a President shall have qualified; and the Congress may by law provide for the case wherein neither a President elect nor a Vice

1 Proposed 18 December 1917, and declared ratified 29 January 1919.
2 Proposed 4 June 1919, and declared ratified 26 August 1920.
3 Proposed 2 March 1932, and declared ratified 6 February 1933.

President elect shall have qualified, declaring who shall then act as President, or the manner in which one who is to act shall be selected, and such person shall act accordingly until a President or Vice President shall have qualified.

SECTION 4. The Congress may by law provide for the case of the death of any of the persons from whom the House of Representatives may choose a President whenever the right of choice shall have devolved upon them, and for the case of the death of any of the persons from whom the Senate may choose a Vice President whenever the right of choice shall have devolved upon them.

SECTION 5. Sections 1 and 2 shall take effect on the 15th day of October following the ratification of this article.

SECTION 6. This article shall be inoperative unless it shall have been ratified as an amendment to the Constitution by the legislatures of three-fourths of the several States within seven years from the date of its submission.

ARTICLE [XXI][1]

SECTION 1. The eighteenth article of amendment to the Constitution of the United States is hereby repealed.

SECTION 2. The transportation or importation into any State, Territory, or possession of the United States for delivery or use therein of intoxicating liquors, in violation of the laws thereof, is hereby prohibited.

SECTION 3. This article shall be inoperative unless it shall have been ratified as an amendment to the Constitution by conventions in the several States, as provided in the Constitution, within seven years from the date of the submission hereof to the States by the Congress.

ARTICLE [XXII][2]

SECTION 1. No person shall be elected to the office of the President more than twice, and no person who has held the office of President, or acted as President, for more than two years of a term to which some other person was elected President shall be elected to the office of the President more than once. But this Article shall not apply to any person holding the office of President when this Article was proposed by the Congress, and shall not prevent any person who may be holding the office of President, or acting as President, during the term within which this Article becomes operative from holding the office of President or acting as President during the remainder of such term.

SECTION 2. This article shall be inoperative unless it shall have been ratified as an amendment to the Constitution by the legislatures of three-fourths of the several States within seven years from the date of its submission to the States by the Congress.

1 Proposed 20 February 1933, and declared ratified 5 December 1933.
2 Proposed 24 March 1947, and declared ratified 1 March, 1951.

INDEX OF CASES

[FIGURES IN HEAVY TYPE REFER TO PAGES IN THE TEXT]

GENERAL INDEX

Absolute prerogative, *see* President, U.S.
Acheson, D., 122
Actio popularis, see Courts
Acts of State, 154, 155
Adams, J., 243
Administration of Justice (Appeals) Act, 1934, 138
Administration overseer of, *see* Congress, U.S.
Administrative head, *see* President, U.S.
Administrative law
 administrative power, 14, 116–17, 284–5
 Administrative Procedure Act, 263, 264, 265, 290–6, 300
 antecedent publicity, 292–3
 Attorney-General's Committee on Administrative Procedure, 117, 190, 285, 286, 290–1, 297, 302
 certiorari, 203, 298
 Communications Act, 288–9, 290
 'conclusive evidence' clause, 299
 cross-examination, right of, 264, 268, 294
 declaratory judgment, 298–9
 delegation of judicial power, 22
 delegation of legislative power, 8, 17–18, 49, 52, 116, 190, 285–90
 deportation, 277, 295, 299–300, 301
 due process, 263, 265, 266, 267, 293
 examiners, 293–4
 forms of action, 297–9
 'fundamentals of fair play', 290, 295
 government contractors, 301
 Home Owners' Loan Act, 288
 Immigration Act, 299–300
 importance of, 283
 injunction, 202, 298–9
 judicial review, availability of, 296–302, 306; non-statutory, 202–3, 298–9; preclusion of, 156–7, 205, 299–302; scope, 302–6
 jurisdictional facts, 304–6
 law-fact distinction, 303
 legislative silence, 296–7
 Ministers' Powers, Committee on, 284, 285, 286, 287, 290, 292, 296
 'privilege' cases, 266–8, 272, 274, 277, 300–3

 procedural safeguards, 263, 292–4, 306
 prohibition, 203
 Renegotiation Act, 287, 290
 substantial evidence, rule of, 303–4
 veterans' benefits, 300–1
 See also Courts
Administrative Management, President's Committee on, U.S., 110, 118, 120, 122, 123, 124
Administrative power, *see* Administrative law
Administrative Procedure Act, 1946, U.S., *see* Administrative law
Advisory opinions, *see* Courts
Advocacy of revolution, *see* Civil liberties
Agricultural Adjustment Acts, 1933 and 1938, U.S., *see* New federalism
Alibert, R., 151
Alien and Sedition Laws, 1798, U.S., *see* Civil liberties
Alien Registration Act, 1940, U.S., *see* Civil liberties
Aliens, restrictions upon, *see* Civil liberties
Allen, Sir C. K., 6, 190, 303
Allen, J., 320, 324
Amendment of Constitution, *see* Constitution, U.S.
Amos, Sir M., 23
Anne, Queen, 245
Antecedent publicity, *see* Administrative law
Anti-sedition laws, *see* Civil liberties
Anti-trust laws, 118, 128
Appeals, courts of, U.S., *see* Courts
Appointment, power of, *see* Courts; President, U.S.; Senate, U.S.
Armstrong, W. P., 72
Arrest, freedom from, *see* Congress, U.S.
Atkin, Lord, 205, 297, 316, 321
Atkinson, Lord, 202
Attlee, C., 309, 310, 311–12
Atomic Energy Commission, U.S., 72
Attempts, law of, *see* Civil liberties.
Attorney-General's Committee on Administrative Procedure, U.S., *see* Administrative law